Everyman's
Companion to the Brontës

Everyman's Companion to the Brontës

Barbara and Gareth Lloyd Evans

J. M. Dent & Sons Ltd
London, Melbourne and Toronto

First published 1982
© Barbara and Gareth Lloyd Evans, 1982

Printed in Great Britain by
Biddles Ltd, Guildford, Surrey
for J. M. Dent & Sons Ltd
Aldine House, 33 Welbeck Street, London W1M 8LX
This book is set in 11/12½ point Linotron 202 Bembo
by Tradespools Ltd, Frome, Somerset

British Library Cataloguing in Publication Data

Lloyd Evans, Barbara
  Everyman's companion to the Brontës.
  1. Brontë (Family) 2. English fiction—
  19th century—History and criticism
  I. Title   II. Lloyd Evans, Gareth
  823'.8'09   PR4169

ISBN 0-460-04455-9

Contents

III *The Published Works*

IV The Places

List of Illustrations

The Red House *(Photo by Robert Lowthian)*
Ponden Hall *(Photo by Robert Lowthian)*
Oakwell Hall *(Photo by Robert Lowthian)*
Haworth parsonage *(Photo by Robert Lowthian)*
Haworth church and Sunday school *(Photo by Robert Lowthian)*

Preface

The Brontës hold a special place in the minds and hearts of their readers. The mixture of reality and myth in our knowledge of their lives, the haunting atmosphere of their home village and the moors beyond, the apposition of their strange remoteness as people and their almost tangible nearness in their novels – all have left their mark, and the closer we get to grasping hold of them the quicker they slip away. Even the contradictions in their characters are a source of constant puzzlement, of a whole variety of emphases and interpretations: Charlotte, at once both shyly sensitive and very, almost selfishly, determined; Emily, both stubbornly alone and yet demanding compassion and understanding; Anne, perhaps the surest of all in her beliefs, yet always 'poor little Anne'; Branwell, the only boy in a predominantly female household, braggart and drunkard, wild with great expectations; even the Rev. Patrick Brontë, whose easy care for his young family is offset by his stern sense of duty and place, and Aunt Branwell, with her untiring yet undoubtedly demanding involvement in family affairs. This Companion seeks to reflect all this – to catch, wherever possible, and to hold to realities, but not to ignore or dismiss the mirage that lies about them; to see the Brontës, in fact, as naturally as possible, without minimizing either their achievement or the aura that surrounds them.

The book consists of four sections, The Family, The Juvenilia, The Published Works and The Places. The first, **The Family**, is concerned with the lives of the members of the Brontë family – more particularly after the move to Haworth (1820) and Mrs Brontë's death (September 1821), which left in her husband's and sister's charge the six children, of whom the youngest, Anne, was only twenty-one months old. The family, for the purposes of this book, consists of the Rev. Patrick Brontë, Maria Brontë, Aunt Branwell, Charlotte, Emily, Branwell and Anne, and the servants, particularly Tabby (Aykroyd) and Martha (Brown). The events recorded go up to June 1861, the time of Patrick Brontë's death.

The *Calendar of Events* is divided into two parts – one deals with daily affairs, the other with the writings of members of the family. As far as daily affairs are concerned, most of the records are to be found in letters, mainly Charlotte's, although there are some written by other members of the family – with the exception of Emily, who has left only the briefest of terse notes, and Aunt Branwell, none of whose correspondence has survived. Whether Emily wrote other letters, and at greater length, we do not know. If she did, they have not survived.

Charlotte's main correspondent in the early years was her lifetime friend Ellen Nussey, who, despite the Rev. A.B. Nicholls's request, after his marriage to Charlotte, that Ellen should destroy all his wife's letters, kept them and allowed Mrs Gaskell to make use of them (suitably censored by Ellen herself) for her biography of Charlotte. In later years Charlotte wrote many more letters, corresponding with her publishers, particularly W.S. Williams, a reader for Smith, Elder and Co., and also with some of those she met on her infrequent visits to London – W.M. Thackeray, G.H. Lewes, Harriet Martineau, and of course, Mrs Gaskell. What survives of her correspondence with M. Heger, the head of the Pensionnat and her teacher in Brussels, which was used so judiciously by Mrs Gaskell, lest any hint of scandal should arise from crude misinterpretations of the letters, is now in the British Museum. It seems to have been very much a one-sided correspondence for M. Heger, after a time, stopped writing, reluctant presumably to reply to letters which glow with such a barely concealed expression of deep feeling. We know nothing of the tone of his letters to her, for none have survived. In each of Charlotte's sequences of letters to W.S. Williams, George Smith, James Taylor and M. Heger there is, indeed, a marked pattern – first commitment, openly and feelingly expressed, then withdrawal, often resigned and reluctant. The words of a postscript to a letter from Mathilde, a pupil in the Pensionnat, to Charlotte, written in the summer after Charlotte had left Brussels, convey the tone of Charlotte's correspondence with these men very well:

> ... when I write to you it seems to me the door of my heart opens wide and only the want of time and letter paper forces me to close it again.

In these later letters Charlotte often expresses her opinions and attitudes – on her own writing, on the writings of others, on the society she experienced. Some of the more interesting of these comments are referred to in the Calendar, but for reasons of space, no attempt has been made to list them all separately. For the same reason, details of the Rev. Brontë's parish life (meetings with the church trustees, for example) and of his home life (repairs to furniture, the setting up of washing lines etc. that Mr Wood, the local carpenter and coffin-maker, carried out) have had to be omitted.

Much of the activity in the lives of the young Brontës seems to have been concerned as much with the world of their imagination as with daily affairs. The record of this is the concern of the second part of the Calendar. Details about this world and how it came into being is given in the section on the juvenilia. Few of the MSS Charlotte and Branwell wrote have been transcribed, fewer still published, so that precise dating has not been easy, but the very number recorded here suggests that this is a large iceberg, whose tip only has been so far explored.

The *Family Portraits*, on the other hand, are not detailed accounts of the lives of the members of the family. Rather they are essays that attempt to evoke their personalities from what is known and what may reasonably – even provokingly – be conjectured. In this, they and the Calendar complement each other.

Finally in this section, the *Glossary of Friends and Relatives* is a list of the people the Brontës knew, and is intended as a reference source for both the Calendar and the rest of the book. In it, where a real person or place has had some part in the creation of a fictional one, the fictional name is given in brackets.

The second section, **The Juvenilia**, is concerned with the Brontës' juvenile writings which, in their case, continued into their early twenties. What has survived of Emily's and Anne's writings about their imaginary kingdom – Gondal (all poetry except for an occasional prose reference) – has been commented on and used in biographies over the years, all benefiting from reliable published texts' being available. The great mass, however, of Branwell's and Charlotte's writing about Glasstown and Angria has attracted far less attention, mostly, one suspects, because of both the large amount of material involved and its unavailability. The writing in this section, although – like the listing and dating of MSS in the Calendar of Events – beset with difficulties, will, we believe, throw new light on the Brontë family relationships and on the later novels of the three sisters. No other writer with the reputation of Charlotte Brontë, having such juvenilia extant, has had it treated so dismissively. There is a great need for more of the MSS to be transcribed and published, and so made more available to the general reader. The quality of the writing itself which, although uneven and unpolished, is nearly always vivid and amusing, hardly comes into it, for as a literate body of material reflecting the growth and development of childhood imagination it has a claim on our attention. As it reflects the growing imaginations of the Brontës, particularly Charlotte, that claim is all the more clamorous.

One thing should be noted however. Most, if not all, of this childhood writing is to do with the countries and characters the children invented, and taken out of context both prose passages and poems can give a distorted reflection of the authors' own (real) life and attitudes. Moreover, to separate the poems from the prose narratives that contain them is equally dangerous, for the poems are often written in the voice of a particular character and reflect his or her views – not those of the author. Most of the poetry Charlotte wrote was an integral part of either a prose narrative or the presentation of a character, and not a personal statement. Often the dividing line between the two worlds, the real and the imaginary, is unclear. Perhaps it is clearest in Anne's poetry; in Emily's it can be a critical death-trap.

The story of Charlotte's discovery of Emily's poetry and her decision to try to find a publisher for a selection of their poems is told by her in her Notice to the second edition of *Wuthering Heights and Agnes Grey*, published by Smith, Elder and Co. Certainly the *Poems* set their publishing venture going, for no sooner had the details of their printing been settled than Charlotte was inquiring about the possibility of getting published a volume of stories – one by each of the Bell brothers (they had cunningly chosen pseudonyms, Currer (Charlotte), Ellis (Emily) and Acton (Anne) Bell, that left it not at all clear whether the authors were male or female). As it seemed likely that none of the sisters would ever marry, and the only income they had was from the interest on investments of money left them by Aunt Branwell, they seem to have turned to publishing as the one occupation (unlike teaching or 'governessing') that would allow them to stay at home, looking after Papa and working together. This section, **The Published Works**, opens with a critical commentary on the *Poems* (published 1846) and some assessment of the three sisters as poets. Whether, when the *Poems* were published, the novels were already completed or merely in the finishing stages, we do not know, although the date written by Charlotte at the end of *The Professor*, her contribution to the three novels, was 27 June 1846. However, whatever the ins and outs of their motives and methods, a year later they at last found a publisher who agreed to accept *Wuthering Heights* and *Agnes Grey*, but he was adamant that he would not take *The Professor*, which was sent off again on its rounds. Finally one publisher – Smith, Elder and Co. – although rejecting *The Professor* itself (the ninth publisher to do so) was sufficiently interested to say that if the author prepared a three-volume novel they would be ready to see it. Currer Bell, it seems, was already busy on one, for in a few weeks the MS of *Jane Eyre* was on its way by rail to London. Two months later (October) it was published, followed in December by a second edition, and the publication, by T.C. Newby, of *Wuthering Heights and Agnes Grey*.

Each novel in this section is considered separately, with a critical commentary, followed by a brief synopsis, and a list of characters and places that are mentioned in the story. Where, in these lists, the fictional meets the real, the name of the real person or place has been added in brackets.

All three Brontë sisters used unusual words – sometimes local or dialect ones, sometimes ones no longer in current usage – and their books are rich with comparisons and references that testify to the scope of their reading: the Bible, the writings of Shakespeare, Milton and Byron, were all familiar to them. Sometimes the words are self-explanatory, although dialect words seldom are, and certainly with the reduced knowledge today of such books as the Bible, references no longer readily call up the effects the author wishes for in using them. So this part, concerned more particularly with the novels, has a *Glossary* of such words and references.

If the publication of the *Poems* hardly caused a ripple in the literary world, the publication of *Jane Eyre, Wuthering Heights* and *Agnes Grey* set it by its ears. Review followed review – particularly of *Jane Eyre* – and all recognized that the Bell brothers were rough diamonds, the emphasis on the 'rough' or the 'diamond' quality varying from one review to another. All Charlotte's subsequent novels received similar acclamation, each on publication becoming the talk of the town. No Companion to the Brontës would be complete without some reference to this, and in *Contemporary Comments* we have tried to give some idea of the reactions to the novels and the poems – from the formal literary review to the private *cri de coeur* in letters.

The final section deals with **The Places** connected with the Brontës. Like Stratford upon Avon, Haworth is a place of pilgrimage. The atmosphere there – of the moors above the village, of the tall chimneyed factories and mills straddling the local streams, of the grey, weathering-black stone – appeals as much to the visitor perhaps as the actual parsonage and its relics. Somehow the Brontës, as no other English novelists except perhaps Thomas Hardy, belong to a particular landscape. To appreciate *Wuthering Heights* fully, one needs to experience the brown loneliness of the moors in autumn, their fresh clarity in spring, the cries of the curlew and the cackle of the moor grouse. The parsonage is a still-growing museum, with new exhibits of relics or MSS continuing to find their way there. The map, simplified for clarity, has the places associated with the family marked on it, many of which are still almost inaccessible as they were in the days of the Brontës, and a car is needed to replace the gig, horse or donkey of earlier times. But even that will only take you to the edge of the moors and from there, as the Brontës themselves did, you must walk.

1982   Barbara and Gareth Lloyd Evans

Reading List

A selective guide to the Brontës' lives and works. Critical books, articles and commentaries, all of which abound, are not included.

The Family

The Shakespeare Head Brontë, ed. T.J. Wise and J.A. Symington, 19 vols., 1931–8; reprinted Basil Blackwell, 1980. (This edition contains the novels, letters, poems and miscellaneous and unpublished writing. While a primary source, it is not always accurate.)

Juvenilia

Charlotte Brontë

The Twelve Adventurers and Other Stories, ed. C.W. Hatfield, Hodder and Stoughton, 1925.
The Spell: An Extravaganza, ed. G.E. Maclean, Oxford University Press, 1931.
Five Novelettes, transcribed and ed. Winifred Gérin, Folio Press, 1971.
The Secret: Lily Hart. Two Tales, transcribed and ed. William Holtz, University of Missouri Press, 1978.
Legends of Angria, compiled from early writings by Fannie Ratchford, with W.C. DeVane, Kennikat Press, 1933.

Branwell Brontë

And the Weary Are at Rest, ed. J.A. Symington and C.W. Hatfield, private edition, 1924.

The Published Works

Poetry

Poems by Currer, Ellis and Acton Bell, reissued with introd. by M.R.D. Seaward, E.P. Publishing Ltd, 1978.
Charlotte Brontë: Complete Poems, ed. C.K. Shorter, with bibliography and notes by C.W. Hatfield, 1923.
Emily Brontë: Complete Poems, ed. C.W. Hatfield, 1941.
The Poems of Anne Brontë, ed. Edward Chitham, Macmillan, 1979.

Novels

Several volumes of an authoritative edition under the general editorship of Ian Jack have been published by the Oxford University Press, but the full collection is not yet complete. The novels are also available in a number of editions, including paperback.

Biography

A Man of Sorrow: The Life, Letters and Times of the Reverend Patrick Brontë, 1776–1861, J. Lock and W.T. Dixon, 1965. (The most comprehensive study, but to be treated with caution.)

The Life of Charlotte Brontë, Elizabeth Gaskell, 1857. (Revised and reprinted many times and still perhaps the best life, written by one who knew her well.)

Unquiet Soul, Margot Peters, Hodder and Stoughton, 1975. (Very readable and on the whole reliable biography of Charlotte. Available also in Futura Paperback.)

Charlotte Brontë: The Evolution of a Genius, Oxford University Press, 1967; *Emily Brontë: A Biography*, Oxford University Press, 1971; *Anne Brontë: A Biography*, Edinburgh, 1959; *Branwell Brontë: A Biography*, Thomas Nelson and Sons, 1961. (All by Winifred Gérin and characterized by detailed research, but often over-speculative and occasionally imprecise.)

The Infernal World of Branwell Brontë, Daphne du Maurier, Gollancz, 1960. (A highly evocative and imaginative book by the famous novelist. Available also in Penguin.)

Transactions of the Brontë Society, the Keighley Printers, 1895–. (Publishes annually up-to-date criticism and information concerning the Brontës.)

Abbreviations

List of abbreviations used in Calendar and Glossaries

Family and Friends

P.	Rev. Patrick Brontë
M.B.	Maria Branwell/Brontë
Aunt B.	Miss Elizabeth (Aunt) Branwell
C.	Charlotte Brontë
B.	Branwell Brontë
E.	Emily Brontë
Ae.	Anne Brontë

E.N.	Ellen Nussey
Mr N.	Rev. A.B. Nicholls
W.S.W.	W.S. Williams
S/E	Smith, Elder and Co., publishers

Novels

J.E.	*Jane Eyre*
SH.	*Shirley*
V.	*Villette*
W.H.	*Wuthering Heights*
A.G.	*Agnes Grey*
T. of W.H.	*The Tenant of Wildfell Hall*

Acknowledgments

We wish to thank Mrs Sally Stonehouse, Librarian of the Brontë Society, for all her helpfulness in dealing with many queries; and Mrs Judi Payne for her customary patience and expertise in the typing of our manuscript.

I The Family

Calendar of Events 1812–1861

Problems have arisen in the precise dating of events for two reasons: (1) the references in the letters themselves are not always precise, and (2) – more importantly – the only complete edition of the letters, long accepted as authoritative, has many errors. Letters are misdated, some mistranscribed. Some have passages missing, sometimes a quite arbitrary date is given for an undated letter, and sometimes extracts from two letters are printed as one. Perhaps the best example of the kind of problem met with is Charlotte's letter about Emily teaching at Law Hill School. The date at the beginning of the letter in Charlotte's hand is 2 October 1836, on the outside of the letter (Ellen Nussey's hand?) is 6 October 1836, and the postmark on the letter itself is 6 October 1838.

As to the list of early writings, there are at present only two sources, other than inspecting the MSS themselves, for dating them: C.W. Hatfield's *The Early Manuscripts of Charlotte Brontë* in the *Transactions of the Brontë Society*, nos. 32, 33 and 34 (1922–4), and Mildred Christian's *A Census of Brontë Manuscripts in the United States of America* (*The Trollopian*, 1, 2 and 3, 1947–8) and both of these are limited in their value – the Hatfield is out of date and not always accurate, the Christian only refers to MSS in the U.S.A. (As this book goes to press it has just been announced that a new bibliography by Dr Christine Alexander of the University of New South Wales is in preparation, which may perhaps throw fresh light on the matter.) Wherever possible we have traced MSS to their source, to check dates of composition, but we are very conscious that this is a new area of critical exploration, at present only somewhat tentatively mapped out. However, with the growing awareness of the value of this material for any true assessment of, in particular, Charlotte's achievements as a novelist, there may well come to light new MSS and more precise up-datings of the old.

Charlotte often collected pieces she had written over a period of time into one MS with a portmanteau title – *The Scrap Book or a Mingling of Many Things*, for example. In such cases the dates of only the first and last pieces (where known) have been entered in the Calendar. Where Branwell is concerned, most of his MSS are still unpublished, many not even transcribed. They all deal with the developing history of Glasstown/Angria, so those with no specific title of their own are referred to as Glasstown or Angrian MS.

Where an asterisk ★ precedes a date it denotes that the event recorded is known to have occurred by the time indicated.

Main Events		Writings
1812 ——	P. meets M.B. at her uncle's – Rev. John Fennell of Woodhouse Grove, near Bradford.	
Dec. 29	M.B. marries P. at Guiseley Church (near Leeds): brings a £50 annuity.	
1813 ——		P. *The Rural Minstrel: A Miscellany of Descriptive Poems.*
Jan. —	P. and M.B. set up house in Clough Lane, Hightown, Hartshead.	
1814 Apr. 15		P. *Lines Addressed to a Lady on Her Birthday* (for M.B.).
Apr. 23	Maria christened by William Morgan.	
1815 ——		P. *The Cottage in the Wood or The Art of Becoming Rich and Happy* P. 'Conversion' (article in *The Pastoral Visitor* issued by William Morgan).
Feb. 8	Elizabeth born.	
May 19	P. goes to St James's Church, Thornton.	
★June 12	Aunt B. joins the household.	
Aug. 26	Elizabeth christened. During the five years at Thornton the Brontës and their growing family become very friendly with the Firths, with tea-takings, dinners, expeditions together.	
1816 ——	P. employs Nancy Garrs to help his wife.	
Apr. 21	CHARLOTTE born.	

	June 29	C. christened by William Morgan.
	July 28	Aunt B. leaves for Cornwall.
1817	Apr. 22	E.N. born.
	June 26	BRANWELL PATRICK (according to Elizabeth Firth's diary) born.
	July 23	B. christened by Rev. John Fennell.

1818 —— P. employs Nancy Garrs' younger sister, Sarah, to help in the house; Nancy becomes cook.

      P. *The Maid of Killarney or Albion and Marina: A Modern Tale.*
      P. *The Cottage in the Wood* (2nd edition).

	Feb. 12	M.B. poorly.
	July 30	EMILY JANE born.
	Aug. 20	E. christened by William Morgan.
1819	Jan. 8	Maria, Elizabeth and C. go to the Firths' for tea.
	June 2	P. offered the Perpetual Curacy of Haworth by Vicar of Bradford: Trustees object.
	Oct. 4	The 'little Brontës' call at the Firths'.
	Oct. 10	P. takes the duty at Haworth.
	Oct. 21	P. resigns the curacy as the trustees still refuse to accept him as the Archbishop's nominee.
	Nov. 19	P. again takes the duties at Haworth on the Archbishop's orders.
1820	Jan. 17	ANNE born. The others spend the day with the Firths.
	Feb. 8	P. accepts the appointment to Haworth Church now offered by the Trustees.
	Feb. 25	P. licensed to the Perpetual Curacy of Haworth: stipend £180 plus surplice fees £14.
	Mar. 25	Ae. christened by William Morgan.

Apr. —	The Brontë family move to the parsonage, Haworth.
1821 Jan. —	Some time after Jan. 29 and some months before M.B.'s death Aunt B. comes to the parsonage to look after her sister and the children.
Feb. 9	M.B. very poorly: visited by Elizabeth Firth.
May 26	(to June 22) Maria and Elizabeth stay with the Firths.
Sept. 15	M.B. dies of cancer.
Sept. 22	M.B. buried, William Morgan officiating. Aunt B. takes charge of household affairs, paying for her own board.
Dec. 8	P. visits Elizabeth Firth till Dec. 10: possibly to ask her to marry him.
1822 ——	P. proposes to Isabella D(r)ury of Keighley, who was 'not so stupid' as to accept.
July 25	C. completes a sampler.
1823 Apr. 21	P. to Mrs Burder saying he may visit in the summer.
July 28	P. proposes to Miss Burder; reminds her she was the first he ever proposed to – in 1806/ 1807.
Aug. 8	Miss Burder tartly refuses P.
Oct. —	Ae. given a Bible by her godmother, Elizabeth Firth.
Dec. —	Maria and Elizabeth have measles and whooping cough.
1824 ——	Sarah and Nancy Garrs leave. Tabitha Aykroyd engaged. Possibly this year, under cover of a mask, P. questions the children. (P. to Mrs Gaskell, July 1855. *See* Family Portraits: Patrick Brontë.)

1824? (1826?). C. A story – 'There once was a little girl and her name was Ane [sic]'.

Jan. 1	P. to Miss Burder: he loves her still, may he call on her?
Jan. 30	The Clergy Daughters' School, Cowan Bridge, opens.
June —	P. buys B. a set of toy wooden soldiers from Bradford; another set bought from Keighley; B. buys set of Turkish musicians.
July 21	Maria and Elizabeth go to Cowan Bridge School.
Aug. 10	C. registered at Cowan Bridge.
Sept. 2	The bog eruption on the moors at Crow Hill. B., E. and Ae. involved.
Sept. 12	P.'s sermon on the bog eruption.

P. *The Phenomenon: An Account in verse of the Extraordinary Disruption of a Bog which took place in the Moors of Haworth*, pub. London, price 2d.
P. *A Sermon preached in the Church of Haworth on September 12th in reference to the Earthquake*, price 6d.

Sept. 21	Elizabeth Firth marries Rev. James Franks. On their honeymoon they visit Maria, Elizabeth and C. at school, giving them 2s. 6d. each.
Nov. 25	E. registered at Cowan Bridge.
1825 ——	Mechanics Institute, Keighley, founded. P. joins soon after.
Feb. 14	Maria sent home from school ill.
May 6	Maria dies.
May 12	Maria buried, William Morgan officiating.
May 31	Elizabeth brought home 'in decline' by Mrs Hardacre.
June 1	C. and E. come home.
June 15	Elizabeth dies.

1826 June 5	B. acquires a new set of soldiers from Leeds – the Twelves; and a set of ninepins.	
June —		C. and B. *Young Men's Plays* established.
June 26	C. completes a sampler.	
July —	C. given her mother's copy of John Wesley's translation of Thomas à Kempis' *The Imitation of Christ*.	
July 21	(to May 1836). Book of music, with markings by E. and Ae.	
Sept. 4	C. sketch: thatched cottage – inscribed 'A copy for Anne'.	
1827 ——	B. buys another set of Turkish musicians from Halifax.	
Feb. 13	Ae. given Book of Common Prayer by her godmother, Miss Outhwaite.	
Feb. —	Bible given to E. by 'her affectionate Father'.	
Mar. 12		B. *The Battel [sic] of W(ashington)*.
July —		C. and B. 'Our Fellows Play' established.
Dec. —		C. and E.'s 'bed plays' (ie 'secret plays') begun. C. and B. *Plays of the Islanders* established.
1828 ——	B. buys a box of Indians at Haworth (last box of toy figures he bought). B. sketch: sleeping cat.	B. (*c.*1827-8). *History of the Rebellion in* (title incomplete).
Jan. 1	Aunt B. gives the children Scott's *Tales of a Grandfather*.	
Mar. —		C. and E. Other 'bed plays' established.
Apr. —	C. and E. complete samplers.	
May 17	B. sketch: tower and castle, 'For Anne Brontë'.	
July 28	B. sketch: farmyard scene from Bewick.	

Aug. 29	Ae. sketch: a tower with pine trees.	
Sept. 2	C. sketch: ruined tower and gate, 'for Anne – a copy'.	
Sept. 4	C. sketch: thatched cottage, 'A copy for Anne'.	
Nov. 17	B. sketch: round tower and castle, 'for Anne Brontë'.	
Nov. 28	Ae. completes a sampler.	
Dec. 19		B. Glasstown MS (*see* Juvenilia).
1829 ——	C. drawing: a red grouse	C. 'A List of Painters whose works I wish to see' (on the reverse – a page of Ae.'s copywriting).
Jan. —		B. *Magazine*, no. 1.
Jan. 7?	E. sketch: three mullioned window panes.	
Jan. 14?	C. sketch: stone house and girl in Grecian dress.	
Jan. 15	P. writes to *Leeds Intelligencer* on Catholic Emancipation.	
Jan. 24	C. sketch: bird on a rock in the sea.	
Jan. 29	C. sketch: seascape with cormorant.	
Feb. 21		B. Glasstown MS.
Feb. 23	B. sketch: ruined tower and church – 'Copy for Anne Brontë'.	B. Glasstown MS.
Mar. 1	E. completes a sampler.	
Mar. 12		C. *History of the Year*; (reverse) *The True Origin of the O'Deays*.
Apr. 1	E. drawing: 'The Whinchat'.	
Apr. 2	E. sketch: woman, birds and farm building.	C. (to Apr. 15). *A Romantic Tale*.
Apr. 7	Ae. sketch: cottage and trees.	
Apr. 23	Ae. sketch: bird and toad.	
Apr. 28		C. *An Adventure in Ireland*.
May 13	C. sketch: girl with large dog.	
May 22:	C. 'Fancy Piece': sketch of trees and three girls.	
May 22	E. sketch: ring ouzel.	
May 26	C. sketch: 'Revenante Castle'.	

June —		B. *Blackwood's Magazine,* no. 2.
June 30		C. *Tales of the Islanders,* vol. 1.
July —		B. *Blackwood's Magazine,* no. 3 (by the end of July C. took over the *Magazine*).
July 6		C. Leisure Hours.
July 8		C. (to Oct. 2). *Anecdotes of the Duke of Wellington,* ch. 3.
July 13	C. sketch: 'The Keep of the Bridge'.	C. *The Enfant.*
July 14		C.(?) 'Sir, it is well known that the Genii . . .' (on the reverse – copywriting by Ae.)
July 17		C.(?)/B.(?) Doggerel re Napoleon. Signed 'Young Soult July 17 1829, C. Bronte'.
July 20	C. sketch: The Ruins of Gambia's(?) Palace.	
Aug. —		C. *Young Men's Magazine,* no. 1.
Aug. 7		C. (to Aug. 8). 'One cold night in the month of December . . .'
Aug. 8		C. 'On the third day I came to a wide plain . . .'
Aug. 17		C. *The Search after Happiness.*
Sept. 1		B. *The Ammon Cutter.*
Sept. 23	Aunt B., C., E. and Ae. all staying at Uncle Fennell's, learning their lessons and sketching.	
Sept. 25	Family return to Haworth.	C. 'On Sept 25 1829, I put into the Life of the Duke of Wellington . . .'
Sept. 28		U.T. *Found at an Inn Belonging to E.*
Sept. 30		C. *Anecdotes of the Duke of Wellington,* ch. 4.
		B. *A Collection of Poems by Young Soult, the Ryhmer* (sic), vols. 1 and 2.
Sept. —		C. *Anecdotes of the Duke of Wellington,* ch. 4.

Oct. —		C. *Young Men's Magazine,* no. 3.
Oct. 2		C. *Anecdotes of the Duke of Wellington,* ch. 1.
Oct. 7		C. *Lines addressed to the Tower of All Nations.*
Oct. 8		C. *Sunset.* 'Beneath a shady tree . . .'
Oct. 9		C. *Sunrise.* 'Behold that silvery stream . . .'
Oct. 23	Ae. sketch: man fishing.	
Nov. —		C. *Young Men's Magazine,* no. 4.
Nov. 2		U.T. *On the Great Bay (Day?) of Glasstown.*
Nov. 13	B. A New Testament in Latin for B. to study from.	
Nov. 20		C. *The Swiss Artist.* W.T. *Lines spoken by a Lawyer . . .*
Nov. 27		U.T. *Lines by one who was tired . . .*
Dec. —		C. *Young Men's Magazine,* nos. 5 and 6.
Dec. 1		B. (to Dec. 23). *Laussane, a Dramatic Poem.*
Dec. 2		C. *Tales of the Islanders,* vol. 2.
Dec. 12		C. (to Dec. 17). *Characters of Celebrated Men.*
Dec. 17		C. *Book of Rhymes.*
Dec. 24		C. *The Churchyard.*
1830 ——	C. several watercolours.	B. *The Liar Unmasked.*
Jan 9		C. *Poem written upon the Occasion of the Dinner given to the Literati of Glasstown.*
Jan. 12		C. *Written on the Sumit [sic] of a High Mountain.*
Jan. 16		C. *Discription [sic] of the Duke of Wellington's Small Palace.*
Jan. 23	Ae. completes a sampler.	
Feb. 1		C. *A Wretch in Prison by Murray.* 'Oh for the song . . .'
Feb. 3		C. *Winter.* 'Autumn has vanished . . .'

Feb. 8		C. *Pleasure*. 'True pleasure breathes . . .'
Feb. 22		C. (to May 25). *The Adventures of Mon Edouard de Crack.*
Feb. —		C. *Home-sickness*. 'Of College I am tired . . .'
Mar. 11	C. watercolour: 'The Mountain Sparrow'.	
Apr. 13		C. *The Vision*. 'The gentle showery spring . . .'
Apr. 30	B. watercolour: 'The Hermit'.	
May 6	P. writes to the *Leeds Intelligencer* about the criminal code. B. watercolour: man with turban reading.	
May 8		C. *Tales of the Islanders*, vol. 3.
May 11	B. sketch: 'Terror' (a mail-clad warrior).	
May 25		C. *The Adventures of Ernest Alembert.*
May 31		C. *Miscellaneous Poems.* C. *Poem*. 'How sweetly shines . . .'
Summer	(1830?) P. ill – unable to perform his duties for 6 months.	
June 18		C. *An Interesting Passage in the Lives of Some of the Most Eminent Persons of the Age.*
June 22		C. 'The following strange occurrence . . .'
June 26		B. (to June 28). *Caractacus, a two-act dramatic poem.*
June 28		C. *The Evening Walk.*
June 29		C. *Miss Hume's Dream.* C. *Leisure Hours.*
July 6		C. (to July 8). *The Poetaster, a drama in 2 vols.*
July 15	C. watercolour: girl and flowers.	
July 30		C. *Tales of the Islanders*, vol. 4.

Aug. 3		C. *Catalogue of my books . . . up to Aug. 3rd 1830.*
Aug. 11		C. *Voltaire's Henriade* (trans. into verse).
Aug. 12		C. (to Sept. 9). *Young Men's Magazine*, 2nd series for Aug. to Dec. (6 written, 4 extant).
Sept. 6		B. (to Aug. 1832). *Letters from an Englishman to his Relative in London*, 1st series, vol. 1.
Oct. —	C. copies her mother's portrait to give to Aunt B.	
Oct. 12		C. *Albion and Marina.*
Oct. 14		C. *Young Man Naughty's Adventures.*
Nov. 10		C. (to Nov. 14). *The Violet, a Poem, with several small pieces.*
Nov. 23		B. (to Dec. 18). *The Revenge, a Tradgedy* [sic].
Nov. 28		C. *Lament befitting these Times of Night.*
Dec. —	B. watercolour: copy of Martin's 'Queen Esther'.	
Dec. 7		C. (to Dec. 11). *Visits in Verreopolis*, vol. 1.
Dec. 15	C. watercolour: Bessy Bell and Mary Gray.	B. (to May 7, 1831). *History of the Young Men*, vol. 1, chs. 1 and 2.
Dec. 18		C. *Visits in Verreopolis*, vol. 2.
1831 ——	C. sketch: Haddington.	
Jan. 17	C. to Miss Wooler's at Roe Head.	
Jan. 25	E.N. arrives at Roe Head.	B. *History of the Young Men*, vol. 1, ch. 3.
Apr. —	P.'s taxes include payment for dog (8s.) hairpowder (£1.3s.6d.), house (£3.8s.3d.).	
Apr. 29		B. *History of the Young Men*, ch. 4.
May 7		B. completes vol. 1 of the *History of the Young Men*.
May —	B. possibly visits C. at Roe Head. Mrs Franks gives C. a dress and muslin, Miss Outhwaite gives her a shawl.	

June —	C. sketch: 'Gawald Tower, Huntdingdon [sic]'.	
June 8		B. *Letters from an Englishman,* 2nd series, vol. 2.
June 11		B. *Letters from an Englishman,* 2nd series, vol. 3.
July —	C. home for holidays, with 3 prizes and a silver medal for the fulfilment of her duties.	
July 11		C. 'And music all on earth unknown,' followed by prose MS.
Nov. 1	B. Book of flute music.	
Dec. —	Drive against cholera in Haworth.	
Dec. 11		C. 'The trumpet hath sounded . . .'
Dec. 14	C. wins French prize.	
Dec. 15	C. sketch: Muccross [sic] Abbey, Lake of Killarney.	
Dec. 25		C. 'O! there is a land . . .'
1832 ——	C. appointed first superintendent of Haworth National Sunday School.	
Apr. 19		B. *Letters from an Englishman,* vol. 4.
May 11	C.'s first letter (?) to E.N. declining invitation to a lecture on Galvanism.	B. *The Fate of Regina.*
May —	C. leaves Roe Head.	
June 13	C. begins her correspondence with E.N. and Mary Taylor, which was to continue for the rest of her life.	
June 18		B. *Letters from an Englishman,* vol. 5.
June 26		B. *Ode on the Celebrations of the Great African Games.* B. *Ode on the Polar Star.*
July 14		C. (to Aug. 20). *The Bridal.*
Aug. 2		B. *Letters from an Englishman,* vol. 6.
Sept. —	(End of month). C. visits E.N. at Rydings, escorted there by B.	

Oct. 3	(to Aug. 8, 1837). Music Book with markings by E. and Ae.	
Oct. 10	C. wash drawing: Kirkstall Abbey.	
Oct. —	C. drawing: Derwentwater.	
Nov. 27		C. *Lines on Bewick.*
1833 ——	C. agrees to correspond with E.N. once a month.	C. *The Vision – a story.*
Feb. 8		B. *The Pirate.*
Feb. 12		C. MS of prose and verse incl. *The African Queen's Lament.*
Mar. 3		B. *The Pass of Thermopylae.*
Mar. 4	E. sketch: bearded man on stone column.	
Mar. 26		C. *Death of Lord Rowan.* 'Fair forms of glistening marble . . .'
Mar. 27		B. (to Apr. 26). *The Monthly Intelligencer.*
Apr. 8	P. joins Keighley Mechanics Institute – use of library, reading room, lectures etc.	
Apr. 17	C. drawing: of Ae.	
Apr. 30	Aunt B. makes her will – various gifts to the family, the residue of her estate to be divided between C., E., Ae. and a Cornish cousin.	
May 1		C. *Something about Arthur by C.A.F. Wellesley.*
May 31		C. (to June 27). *The Foundling.*
July 1	B. sketch: moorland cottage.	
July 10	E.N. comes to stay at Haworth.	C. (to Sept. 10). *The Green Dwarf.*
July 21:	B. sketch: hilltop house and trees.	
Aug. 14	C. watercolour: a French Brunette.	
Sept. —	E. very ill with erysipelas and bilious attacks. C., B., E. and Ae. visit Bolton Abbey with the Nusseys.	

Sept. 27		C. (to Nov. 20). *Arthuriana or Odds and Ends.*
Sept. —		B. MS re the death of Mary, Northangerland's wife.
Nov. 7		C. *The Secret; Lily Hart.*
Nov. 15		B. *The Politics of Verdopolis.*
Nov. 18		B. (to Dec. 17). *An Historical Narrative of the War of Encroachment.*
Nov. 20		C. *Captain Flower's Last.*
Dec. —	C. sketch: 'Harbour Scene'.	
Dec. 3		B. *The Vision of Velino, composed by W.H. Warner.*
Dec. 27		C. *Richard Coeur de Lion and Blondel.*
1834 ——?	B. portrait of himself and his three sisters – later he painted himself out.	
Jan. —	E. drawing: Gasper, the dog.	
Jan. 5		C. *The Last Will and Testament of Florence Marian Wellesley.*
Jan. 17		C. *Leaf from an Unopened Volume.*
Jan. —		B. (to Jan. 1835). Angrian MS.
Feb. 18		B. Angrian MS re setting up of Angria.
Feb. 20		C. (to Mar. 20). *High Life in Verdopolis.*
Spring		B. *Augusta by Alexander Percy in 1812.*
May 1		C. 'The day is closed . . .' C. 'For the green and lonely den . . .'
May 2		C. *The Death of Darius Codomannus, a poem.*
May 28		C. (to June 15/16). *Corner Dishes – a Collection of Unsubstantial Trifles.*
May —		B. *The Rover.*
June —	Work by J.B. Leyland shown at an exhibition of the Northern Society.	
June 17	C. watercolour: of Ae.	
June 21		C. (to July 21). *The Spell, an Extravaganza.*

June 26		B. *The Wool Is Rising* completed.
July 17		C. *A National Ode for the Angrians.*
Aug. 9		B. *Thermopylae.* 'Now the morning rises . . .'
Aug. 23	C. drawing: 'Geneva'.	•
Sept. 12		B. *Northangerland's Letter to the Angrians.*
Sept. 15		C. (to Mar. 17, 1835). *A Scrap Book – a Mingling of Many Things.*
Sept. —		B. (to Oct.). MS re the opening of the Angrian Parliament.
Oct. 7		C. *Saul.*
Oct. 14		C. *My Angria and the Angrians.*
Oct. 15	C. sketch: 'English Lady'.	
Nov. 10		B. (to Nov. 16). *An Hour's Musings.*
Nov. 24		E. and Ae. 'Diary papers' recording events on that day and in the past year.
Dec. 6		B. *Morning, written at Gazemba.*
Dec. 26	B. signs membership cards for the Haworth Temperance Society.	
Dec. —		B. (to Jan. 1835). *The Massacre of Dongola.*
1835 ——	William Robinson, artist of Leeds, engaged to teach B.	P. *The Signs of the Times . . . on Some Political Indications in the Year,* pub. 6d. B. *The Spirit of Poetry.* 'List to that sound . . .' C. (to 1839). Fragments written at Roe Head (so-called 'Roe Head Diary').
Jan. 19		B. 'Thermopylae's tremendous height . . .'
Feb. —	C. visits E.N. at Rydings.	
*Mar. 13	C. home again, having lost her umbrella.	
May —	Organ installed at Haworth Church through efforts of	

committee, including B.
P. involves himself in
electioneering, aided by B.

May 10		B. (to Oct.). *A Story in Six Chapters.*
May 30	B. purchases Byron's *Childe Harold's Pilgrimage* in Liverpool.	
June 3		B. (to Nov. 17). *Life of Alexander Percy.*
June 15		B. (to July 25). *Angrian MS.*
June 19		B. *A Poster for the elections in Angria.*
July —?	B. draft of letter to the Royal Academy of Arts asking where and when to present his drawings.	
July 2	C. tells E.N. of the plans for B. to go to the Royal Academy, C. to Roe Head as a teacher, E. with her as a pupil.	
July 25		B. Angrian MS. *The Reform of the Navy.*
July 29	C. and E. to Roe Head.	
Aug. 2		C. *Memory.*
Sept. 11	By now B. completes his lessons with W. Robinson.	
Sept. —		C. *Lord Rowan.* B. *Fate of Coomassie.*
Oct. —	By mid-month Ae. replaces E. at Roe Head.	
Oct. 20		B. *Song written by Percy in 1813.* P. *On Halley's Comet.*
Oct. 23	E. sketch: cows.	
Oct. 27	Ae. sketch: oak tree.	
Nov. 13	Ae. drawing: elm trees.	
Nov. 17		B. *Song written by Percy in 1814* (1). B. *Song written by Percy in 1814* (2). B. *The Doubter's Hymn.*
Nov. —		
Dec. 7	B. asks the editor of *Blackwood's Magazine* for James Hogg's position.	

Dec. 14	C. drawing: 'A Lady's Head'.	
Dec. 17		B. *Lines by Percy on his departure from Africa*.
		B. *Elegant Extracts*.
Dec. 18		B. *Misery I*. 'How fast that courser . . .'
Dec. 19		C. 'We wove a web in childhood . . .'
1836 ———		P. *A Brief Treatise on the Best Time and Mode of Baptism*, pub. 3d.
		C. 'Well, here I am in Roe Head . . .'
		B. *A Narrative of the First War*.
Jan. 6		B. *Elegant Extracts II*.
Jan. 7		B. (to Aug. 31). *A New Year Story*.
★Jan. 19		C. *The Wounded Stag and other poems* (MS missing).
Feb. 1	B. proposed as a Mason, attends meetings throughout year.	
Feb. 4		C. 'Friday afternoon . . . Now as I have a little bit of time . . .' (Feb. 4 was a Thursday.)
Feb. 10	Ae. drawing: ruined church.	B. Angrian MS. 'The subject whose consideration . . .'
Mar. 2		B. *Misery II*. 'Wide I hear the wild winds . . .'
Mar. 6	P. joins committee of Mechanics Institute.	
★Apr. 8	B. writes again to the editor of *Blackwood's Magazine*, enclosing *Misery I* and *II*.	
Apr. 21		C. *Passing Events I*.
Apr. 25	B. installed as full member of Masons.	
Apr. 29		C. *Passing Events II*.
May 4		B. Angrian MS.
		B. *Ashworth's Hymn*.
		B. *A New Year's Story*, chs. 2 and 3.
May 10	C. writes to E.N. about her fiery imagination.	
May 17		B. 'The sunshine of a summer sun . . .'

May 28		B. *Charles Wentworth's Visit to Verdopolis.*
May —	(End of month). C. goes to stay with E.N.	
May 30	Ae. drawing: landscape and house.	
June 17	C. and Ae. stay with Mrs Franks for about a week, after breaking up from Roe Head.	
June 21	C. and Ae. spend the day at Lascelles Hall, with Amelia Walker and her family.	
June 22		B. *Lucifer, composed by Charles Wentworth.*
		B. *Northangerland's Address to the Angrians.*
		B. *Percy's Musings upon the Battle of Edwardston.*
		B. (to June 24). *Further events preceding the Angrian Revolution.*
June —		B. *Lines Composed at Daybreak.* 'Now heavily . . .'
July —	E.N. visits Haworth.	
July 9		B. *The Battle Eve, composed by Lord Richton.*
July 12	E. writes her first (extant) poem.	E. 'Will the day be bright . . .'
July 19		C. *Zamorna's Exile.* 'And when you left me . . .'
July 22		B. (or June 23). *Angrian Adventures,* chs. 1, 2 and 3.
July —		B. 'Hours and days my heart . . .'
		B. 'My Ancient Ship upon my Ancient Sea . . .'
		B. *Memory.* 'Memory! how thy magic fingers . . .'
Aug. 8		B. (to Aug. 13). 'Still and bright in twilight . . .'
Aug. 11		C. (to Aug. 31) 'All this day I have been in a dream . . .'
Aug. 20		B. (to Sept. 19). *A New Year Story,* chs. 4, 5 and 6.
Sept. 3		B. *Angrian Adventures,* chs. 4 and 5.

Sept. 19	B. acts as secretary at Masonic meeting.	
Oct. 2	C. writes to E.N. about E.'s departure for a teaching post at Law Hill, which is 'sheer slavery'. (Postmark 1838, letter dated in C.'s and E.N.'s hands as 1836.)	
Oct. 4		B. 'Behold a waste of waving sea . . .'
Nov. 11		B. (to Dec. 10). 'This then has departed from among us . . .'
Nov. 19		B. 'I have detained both myself and my readers . . .'
Nov. 29		B. 'By the end of the first week in November . . .'
Dec. —	C. in a depressed state of mind. Ae. writes her first poem.	Ae. *Verses by Lady Geralda.* 'Why when I hear . . .'
Dec. 13		E. 'High waving heather . . .'
Dec. 15	Ae. drawing: landscape.	
Dec. 16		B. 'From the interview between Greville . . .'
Dec. 17		B. 'The forces under the command of his Grace . . .'
Dec. 20	B. first acts as Junior Warden at Masonic meetings.	
Dec. 29	C. sends some of her writing to Southey, asking for his advice.	
Dec. —		C. (to Jan. 1837). 'Reader, I'll tell you what . . .' B. (to 1837). MS re the Angrian Revolution.
1837 ——		C. 'Gods of the old mythology . . .' B. *On Caroline.* 'The light of thy ancestral hall . . .' B. *Caroline.* 'Calm and clear the day . . .' B. Angrian MS about the battle of Leyden.
Jan 4.	B. demands an interview from the editor of *Blackwood's Magazine.*	

Jan. 9		C. 'Well, the day's toils . . .'
Jan. 13		B. 'Sleep, Mourner, sleep . . .'
Jan. 19	B. sends some of his writing to Wordsworth asking for his opinion (no reply).	
Jan. 23		B. Angrian MS – events after the Revolution.
Jan. 27	B. chairs meeting of Haworth Operative Conservative Society.	
Feb. 9		B. 'Well I will lift my eyes . . .'
*Feb. 20	C. is very unhappy at Roe Head.	
Feb. —		E. 'Redbreasts early in the morning . . .'
Mar. —	Southey advises C. not to embark on a literary career.	
Mar. 1		B. 'Alone she paced . . .'
Mar. 6		E. *A.G.A.* 'There shines the moon . . .'
Mar. 9		B. starts revising and transcribing his poems from 1833 onwards.
Mar. 11		B. *Lines by Percy*, adapted to music. 'We leave our bodies . . .'
Mar. 16	C. replies to Southey, thanking him for his advice; he asks her to visit him.	
Apr. 14		B. Angrian MS.
May 4		B. (to June 15). 'One sweet afternoon . . .'
May 5		C. *The Teacher's Monologue I.* 'The room is quiet . . .'
May 12		C. *The Teacher's Monologue II.* ''Tis not the air . . .'
May 29		C. *The Apostasy.* 'This last denial . . .'
		C. (or May 30). *Regret.* 'Long ago I wished . . .'
May —		C. *Presentiment.* 'Sister, you've sat there . . .'
June —	B. acts as secretary to the Masons. C. tired of doing nothing but 'teach–teach–teach'.	

Date	Activity	Poem
June 4		C. 'Is this my tomb . . .'
June 10		E. 'The night of storms . . .'
June 16		B. *Mary's Prayer*. 'Remember me when death's . . .'
June 26		E. and Ae. write their 'diary paper' describing the household affairs and their writing. Includes a drawing of 'Lady Juliet's hair'.
June 29		C. 'There is, reader, a sort of pleasure . . .' C. 'Why should we ever mourn . . .'
June —		C. 'Deep the Cirhala flows . . .' C. *The Letter*. 'What is she writing . . .'
July —	B. acts as secretary at Masonic meetings.	
July 1		Ae. *Alexander and Zenobia*. 'Fair was the evening . . .'
July 12		B. Angrian MS. 'This will never do . . .' includes poem, 'At dead of midnight drearily . . .' (later known as *Harriet II*).
July 21		C. 'A day or two ago . . .'
July 27		C. *On the Death of a Christian*. 'Calm on the bosom . . .'
July 28		P. *Poem to Miss Sarah Smith*. 'Dear Madam, trust not . . .'
July —		E. 'I saw thee child . . .'
Aug. 7		E. 'O God of Heaven . . .'
Aug. 19		E. *A.G.A. to A.E.* 'Lord of Elbe . . .'
Aug. 27		B. (to Nov. 9). 'How like Eden seem . . .' (*Harriet I*).
Aug. 31	Ae. drawing: child's head.	
Aug. —		E. 'Alone I sat . . .' and fragments.
Sept. 30		E. 'The organ swells . . .'
Oct. 14		E. 'A sudden chasm of ghastly light . . .'
Oct. 20		B. (to Nov./Dec.). Angrian MS. 'I have lately remarked . . .'

Oct. 31		B. Angrian MS. 'Of her who almost forty years . . .'
Oct. —		E. 'The old church tower . . .'
		E. 'Far away is the land of rest . . .'
		Ae. *A Voice from a Dungeon, Marina Sabia*. 'I'm buried now . . .'
Nov. 9		B. 'So that stately minstrel sang . . .'
		B. *Song by Percy*. 'Should Life's first feelings . . .' (printed *Halifax Guardian*, 7 May 1842).
Nov. 15	Ae. drawing: child's head.	
Nov. 17		C. 'A single word . . .'
Nov. 27		B. Angrian MS. 'The season has advanced . . .'
Nov. —		E. 'Now trust a heart . . .'
		E. *A.G.A.* 'Sleep brings no joy . . .'
		E. 'Strong I stand . . .'
		E. 'The night is darken- ing . . .'
		E. 'I'll come when thou art saddest . . .'
		E. 'I would have touched . . .'
Dec. 11		B. *Song. The Present Day's Sorrow by Henry Percy.*
Dec. 13		B. *Sonnet by Northangerland.* 'Why hold young eyes . . .'
Dec. 14		E. 'O mother I am not regretting . . .'
Dec. 15		B. 'Upon that dreary winter's night . . .'
Dec. 18		B. 'It is long since . . .'
Dec. 25	B. acts as organist at the Masonic Christmas Day service.	
*Dec. 29	Tabby breaks her leg, so all have to help out at home. (E.N.'s dating; cf. Dec. 21, 1839.)	
Dec. 30		B. Angrian MS. 'Among all the descriptions . . .'

Dec. —	C. disagrees with Miss Wooler over Ae.'s illness and both return home abruptly from Roe Head.	E. *To a Wreath of Snow by A.G. Almeda*. 'O transient voyager . . .' E. *Song by Julius Angora*. 'Awake! how loud . . .' E. 'I die, but when the grave . . .'
1838 Jan. 17		C. *A Story*. 'The last scene in my last book . . . (*Mina Laury II*).
*Jan. 17		C. Prose MS. Includes *The Death of Lord Hartford*. 'Oh, let me be alone . . .'
Jan. 23		B. 'There's many a grief . . .'
Jan. 24		Ae. *The Captive's Dream, Alexandrina Zenobia*. 'Methought I saw him . . .'
Jan. 26		Ae. *The North Wind, Alexandrina Zenobia*. 'That wind is from the north . . .'
Jan. 29		C. *Parting*. 'There's no use in weeping . . .'
Feb. 7		B. 'It seemed as to one bleeding heart . . .'
Feb. 10		B. 'The subject whose consideration . . .'
Feb. —		E. *H.G.* 'Weaned from life . . .' E. 'I'm happiest when most away . . .' B. *The Life of W.H. Warner, by the Rt. Hon. John, Earl of Richton*.
Mar. —		E. 'The wide cathedral aisles . . .' and fragments.
Apr. 24	E. drawing: Keeper, her dog.	
Apr. 30		B. *Azrael or The Eve of Destruction*.
May —	About this time B. sets up as a portrait painter in Bradford, lodging with Mr and Mrs Kirkby until May 1839.	
May 1		B. ''Twas when the traitorous shepherd . . .'
May 9		E. *A.G.A.* 'Why do I hate . . .'

May 20		E. *A.G.A. to A.S.* 'O wander not . . .'
May 21		E. *Gleneden's Dream.* 'Tell me, watcher . . .'
May 23	C. leaves Miss Wooler's school suffering from nervous depression – 'hypochondria', according to her later letters.	
May 29		C. 'This last denial of my faith . . .'
May —		E. *Song to A.A.A.* 'This shall be thy lullaby . . .'
		E. 'Darkness was over-traced . . .'
		B. *Death Triumphant.* 'Oh! on the first bright . . .'
★June 6	Mary and Martha Taylor come to stay at Haworth.	
June 28		C. Untitled story 'Amen! such was the sound . . .'
June —		E. ''Twas one of those dark . . .'
		E. 'None of my kindred . . .'
July 7		C. *Siesta.* ''Tis the siesta's . . .'
		C. *Review at Gazemba.* 'All the summer plains . . .'
July 9		Ae. *The Parting.* 'The chestnut steed . . .'
July 10		Ae. *The Lady of Alzerno's Hall, Alexandrina Zenobia.*
July 11		E. *Douglas's Ride.* 'Well, narrower draw . . .'
July 21		C. Untitled MS in form of letters from Sir W. Percy.
July 31	E. possibly visiting B. at Bradford (with C.?).	B. *The Wanderer,* copied out and dated 'Bradford, July 31' by E.
Aug. 21		Ae. *Verses to a Child, Alexandrina Zenobia.* 'Oh raise those eyes . . .'
Aug. 30		E. *A.G.A.* 'For him she struck . . .'
Sept. 23		E. 'The evening sun . . .' and fragments.
Oct. 17		E. *Songs by Julius Brenzaida to G.S.* – 'Geraldine the moon . . .' and 'I knew not . . .'

Nov. 1		E. *F. de Samara to A.G.A.* 'Light up thy halls . . .'
Nov. 5		E. 'O dream, where art . . .'
Nov. 11		E. 'Loud without the wind . . .'
Nov. —		E. 'The starry night . . .'
Dec. —	C. visits E.N. at Brookroyd.	
Dec. 4		E. 'A little while . . .'
Dec. 7		E. 'How still, how happy . . .'
Dec. 15		B. 'Five years have now elapsed . . .'
Dec. 18		E. 'The bluebell is . . .'
Dec. 22	B. painting: Thomas Parker of Haworth.	
1839 ——	C. watercolour: 'Flowers'. C. drawing: child and dog.	C. (*c.* 1839–42). *Caroline Vernon*, unsigned, undated.
Jan. 12		E. 'The night was dark . . .'
Jan. 21	C. visits the Walkers at Lascelles Hall.	
Jan. —		B. Angrian MS. 'My Lord, circumstances . . .'
Feb. 4		B. Angrian MS. 'To begin in the received manner . . .'
Feb. 21		B. Angrian MS. 'Matilda, I said to the Countess . . .'
★Feb. 22		C. (to ★Mar. 26). Untitled MS concerning Capt. Henry Hasting (Feb. 22, Mar. 26 are dates in MS).
Feb. 26	Henry Nussey proposes to C.	
Feb/Mar.	Martha and Mary Taylor visit.	
Mar. 5	C. gives Henry N.'s offer 'a decided negative'.	
Mar. 27		E. *A.G.A.* 'What winter floods . . .'
Apr. 8	Ae. goes as governess to the Inghams, Blake Hall, Mirfield.	
Apr. 17		E. *By R. Gleneden.* 'From our evening fireside . . .'
Apr. 20		E. *Song.* 'King Julius left the South Country . . .'
Apr. 28		E. *Song.* 'The soft unclouded blue . . .'
Apr. —		B. Fragment. 'Upon one of the small plantations . . .'

May —	By mid–May B. gives up his studio in Bradford, returning home; possibly begins taking opium.	
May 9		E. *A.G.A.* 'To the bluebell'.
May 24	C. drawing: 'The Remains of the Temple of Venus at Rome'.	
May 25		E. 'May flowers are open-ing . . .'
May 28		E. *Lines by Claudia.* 'I did not sleep . . .'
May 30	William Weightman nominated as curate by P.	
June —	P. plans to study the classics with B.	
★June 8	C. governess to the Sidgwicks at Stonegappe, near Skipton. Goes with the Sidgwicks to Swarlcliffe for 3–4 weeks.	E. 'I know not how . . .'
June 14		E. *Written on returning to the P. of I. on Jan. 10 1827.* 'The busy day . . .'
June 18		E. 'Month after month . . .'
July —	C. unhappy as governess – longing to be home.	
July 12		E. 'And now the house dog . . .' E. *Farewell to Alexandria.*
★July 19	C. leaves the Sidgwicks'.	E. 'Come hither child . . .'
July 26	By now proposals afoot for P. and Aunt B. to take all the family to Liverpool.	E. 'Shed no tears . . .'
July 27		E. 'Mild mist upon the hill . . .'
Aug. —	B. visits Liverpool alone. William Weightman comes as curate.	
★Aug. 4	C. receives a proposal of marriage from Rev. Bryce when he visits the parsonage.	
Aug. 12		E. *The Midnight Hour.* 'How long will . . .'
Aug. —	By mid-month C. goes with E.N. to stay 3 weeks at Easton; one week by the sea at Burlington. C. watercolour: Easton House.	

*Aug. 24	B. is getting into debt.	
Aug. 30		E. 'Fair sinks the summer . . .'
Sept. 6		E. 'Alcona, in its changing mood . . .'
Oct. 15		E. *Song*. 'O between distress and pleasure . . .'
*Oct. 24	C. back home, well and 'very fat'.	
Oct. 29		E. 'The wind I hear it . . .'
Oct. —		E. 'There was a time . . .'
Nov. 13	Ae. sketch: girl looking out to sea.	
Nov. 14		E. 'Well some may hate . . .'
Nov. 23		E. 'The wind was rough . . .'
Nov. 28		E. 'The wind, I used to hear . . .'
Dec. —	Ae.'s position with the Inghams terminated; the children were wearing her out.	
Dec. 14		E. 'I've been wandering . . .'
Dec. 19		E. 'Heaven's glory shone . . .'
Dec. 21	Tabby ill: E. and C. doing all the work (cf. Dec. 29, 1837).	
*Dec. 28	B. has become tutor to the Postlethwaites of Ulverston.	
Dec. 31	B. leaves for Ulverston, spending a riotous night at Kendal on the way.	
1840 ——		C. (to 1843). MS fragment about Mr Ashworth and his son. B. Untitled MS about Alexander Percy.
Jan. 1		Ae. *Self-congratulation*, *Olivia Vernon*. 'Maiden thou wert . . .'
Jan. 6		E. *F. de Samara*. *Written in the Gaaldine Prison Caves to A.G.A.* 'Thy sun is near . . .'
Feb. —	E.N. visits Haworth for 3 weeks when E. becomes known as 'The Major' (for protecting E.N. from the attentions of William Weightman?)	

Feb. 14	William Weightman sends them all valentines.	C. *A Valentine*. 'A Roland for your Oliver . . .'
Mar. —	William Morgan visits P.	
Mar. 2	B. drawing: Broughton Castle.	
Mar. —		E. 'Far away is mirth . . .'
Apr. —	William Weightman persuades P. to lecture at the Mechanics Institute, Keighley; spoken 'highly of' in the newspaper. B. sends verse to Hartley Coleridge, asking for his opinion as to whether B. should go on writing.	
Apr. 15		B. *Sir Henry Tunstall (The Wanderer)*. '''Tis only afternoon . . .'
Apr. —		E. 'It is too late . . .'
May —	(Early?) Ae. goes to the Robinsons, Thorp Green, as governess.	
May 1	B. visits Hartley Coleridge at Ambleside.	
May 4		E. 'I'll not weep . . .'
May 6	Some time between now and Dec. 10, C. writes to Hartley Coleridge sending examples of her prose writing.	E. (to July 28, 1843). *A.G.A. to A.S.* 'At such a time . . .'
May 15	C. advises E.N. on the kind of man to marry – a man 'you respect' then 'moderate love' will follow; 'intense passion' undesirable.	
May 18		E. 'If grief for grief . . .'
May 19		E. ''Tis moonlight, summer moonlight . . .'
June —	B. dismissed by the Postlethwaites; returns home. C. probably visits the Taylors. Mary and Martha Taylor at some time visit Haworth.	
June 27	B. sends Hartley Coleridge his translation of Horace's *Odes*, Bk I.	B. by now completed his translation of Horace's *Odes*, Bk I.

July 28	Ae. drawing: 'What you please' – girl in a wood.	
Aug. —	C. answering advertisements for a position as governess. The Taylor household breaks up; C. receives more than 40 books from them.	
*Aug. 8	Ae. governess at the Robinsons'.	
Aug. 13	(to Aug. 14). Relatives from Cornwall visit.	
Aug. 22		Ae. *The Bluebell*. 'A fine and subtle spirit . . .'
Aug. 28		Ae. *Lines Written at Thorp Green*. 'O! I am very weary . . .' (pub. as *Appeal*).
Aug. 31	B. appointed Assistant Clerk in Charge at Sowerby Bridge Railway Station, at £75 p.a.	
Sept. —	C.'s expected position with Mrs Brook falls through.	
Sept. 11		E. *The Nightwind*. 'In summer's mellow midnight . . .'
Sept. 17		E. *R. Gleneden*. 'Companions, all day long . . .'
Nov. —	Mrs Collins visits P. – tells him the story of her drunken husband and is advised to leave him.	
Nov. 30	(or Dec. 1). Hartley Coleridge drafts letter (never sent) to B. about his poetry.	
Dec. 10	C. writes to Hartley Coleridge about the MS she sent him and the sea-water stained *Lady's Magazines* she read in her youth which her father burnt.	
Dec. 13		Ae. *Retirement*. 'O let me be alone . . .'
1841 Jan. —		E. (to May 1844). *The Death of A.G.A.* 'Were they shepherds . . .'
Jan. 1		Ae. *An Orphan's Lament*. 'She's gone and twice . . .'

Jan. 11	C. in a letter to Henry Nussey denies she is now writing poetry.	
Feb. —	P. concerns himself with the apprenticeship of local orphans.	
Feb. 14	William Weightman again sends valentines.	
Feb. 27		E. 'And like myself lone . . .'
Mar. 1		E. 'Riches I hold in light esteem . . .'
★Mar. 3	C. has governess position with the Whites of Rawdon, near Bradford: £20 p.a. less £4 for laundry.	
Apr. 1	B. moves to Luddenden Foot as Clerk in Charge of the station at £130 p.a.	B. *The Luddenden Foot Notebook* (1841–2), includes drafts of poems with sketches and notes about his railway work.
★Apr. 25	C. goes to E.N.'s for a day, escorted back by George Nussey.	
May 16		E. 'Shall earth no more . . .'
June —	Ae. at home for the holidays.	
June 30	C. returns home, just missing Ae. who returns to Thorp Green.	
July —	C., E. and Ae. plan to start a school of their own, possibly at Burlington.	
July 6		E. 'Aye there it is . . .'
July 17		E. 'I see around me . . .' E. ''Twas night; her comrades . . .'
July —	(Last week). C. returns to Rawdon.	
July 30	Ae. at Scarborough with the Robinsons.	E. and Ae. write their diary papers – separate ones as Ae. is away from home; record the year's activities and their writing ventures.
Aug. —	C. longing to get away – possibly abroad.	
Aug. 8		B. *At Brearley Hill*. 'Oh thou whose beams . . .' (later called *The Triumph of Mind over Body*).

		B. (to Sept. 3). *Lord Nelson*. 'Man thinks too often . . .'
Aug. 17		E. *Geraldine*. ' 'Twas night; her comrades . . .'
Aug. 19		Ae. *Lines Written at Thorp Green*. 'That summer sun . . .'
Sept. —	Miss Wooler suggests C. take over her school, now at Dewsbury Moor.	
Sept. 1		E. *Rosina*. 'Weeks of wild delirium . . .'
Sept. 3		B. *Sonnet*. 'Man thinks too often . . .'
Sept. 11		B. 'Amid the world's wide . . .'
Sept. 29	C. asks Aunt B. for financial help for a 6-month visit to Brussels.	
Oct. 6	E. sketch: curly-haired girl.	
Oct. 17	C. decides against going to Dewsbury Moor.	
Oct 25?	B. attends concert, 'The Creation', at Halifax.	
Oct. 27	E. drawing: Merlin hawk.	
Nov. 10	P. corresponds with Master of Ordnance about adaptations to muskets.	
Nov. 29	P. a second letter to Master of Ordnance.	
Dec. 12		C. *Passion*. 'Some have won . . .'
Dec. 15		B. 'The desolate earth . . .'
Dec. 19		B. *At Luddenden Church*. 'O God while I . . .' E. *A.S. to G.S.* 'I do not weep . . .'
Dec. 20		Ae. *Despondency*. 'I have gone backward . . .'
Dec. 24	C. arrives home.	
Dec. 25	Ae. home for the holidays.	
1842 ——	Martha Brown comes to live in the parsonage.	P. notebook of French phrases, notes on French money. C. copybook of French extracts, and French exercise book. B. *The Epicurean's Song*. 'The visits of sorrow . . .'

*Jan. 20	C. preparing to go to Brussels. William Weightman 'sighing softly' and watching Ae. out 'of the corner of his eye' in church.	
Feb. —		Ae. (to Nov. 10). *In Memory of a Happy Day in February*. 'Blessed be thou . . .'
Feb. 1	C. gives E. a prayerbook.	
Feb. 2	Master of Ordnance rejects P.'s suggested musket adaptations.	
Feb. 8	P., C. and E. leave with Mary and Joe Taylor for Brussels, staying in London en route.	
Feb. 13		B. *The Afghan War* (draft of). 'Winds within our chimney . . .'
Feb. 15	P., C. and E. arrive at the Pensionnat Heger, P. visiting Waterloo while there, then returning home.	
Mar. 26	C. visits Mary Taylor.	
Mar. 31	B. dismissed from Luddenden Foot – the result of a discrepancy in the accounts. Returns home 'ill'.	
Apr. —	Appeals to have B. reinstated, rejected.	Ae. (to Oct. 1843). *The Captive Dove*. 'Poor restless dove . . .'
Apr. 17		C. *Sacrifice d'une Veuve Indienne*. Essay.
Apr. 18		C. *La Jeune Fille Malade*.
Apr. 25		B. 'When side by side . . .'
Apr. 30		C. *Le Nid*.
May —	B. tries to get another position on the railway without success. C. writing to E.N. describes M. Heger as 'a little black ugly being', 'an insane tom-cat', 'a delirious hyena'.	

May 7		B. *The Afghan War* pub. in the *Leeds Intelligencer*.
		B. *On the Callousness Produced by Care*. 'Why hold young eyes . . .' (Undated MS, pub. *Halifax Guardian*.)
May 14		B. *Peaceful Death and Painful Life*. 'Why dost thou sorrow . . .' (Undated MS: pub. *Halifax Guardian*.)
May 15		E. *Le Chat*.
May 17		E. *H.A. and A.S.* 'In the same place . . .'
May 31		C. (1843?). *La Mort de Napoléon*.
June 24	Ae. drawing – 'A very bad picture'.	
June —		E. *Le Roi Harold avant la Bataille de Hastings*.
July 21		C. *Lettre d'Invitation à un Ecclesiastique*.
July 26		E. *Lettre*. 'Ma Chère Maman . . .'
July 27		C. (no year). *La Mort de Moise*.
July 30		C. *Portrait de Pierre l'Hermite*.
Aug. 4	C. a sketch.	
Aug. —	C. gives a sketch to M. Heger, a 'token of affection and respect'.	
Aug 5		E. *L'Amour Filial*.
		E. *Lettre d'un frère à un frère*.
Aug. 11		E. *Le Papillon*.
		C. *La Chenille*.
Aug. 15	The Pensionnat closes for the holidays; C. and E. stay on with the Wheelwright girls and the domestic staff.	
Aug. 20		E. (and 6 Feb. 1843). *Written in Aspin Castle*. 'How I do love . . .'
Sept. 6?	B. sends *The Wanderer* to editor of *Blackwood's Magazine*.	
Sept. 6	William Weightman dies of cholera.	

Sept. 10	Weightman's funeral taken by P.	
Sept. 24	Mary Taylor reports that both C. and E. (in Brussels) are well 'not only in health but in mind and hope'.	
Oct. 2	P. preaches at Weightman's memorial service.	P. Sermon preached for Weightman pub., 6d.
Oct. 6		C. (no year). *Human Justice*.
Oct. 12	Martha Taylor dies of cholera in Brussels.	
Oct. 13	C. visits Martha – too late.	
Oct. 18		E. *Le Palais de la Mort*.
Oct. 23		E. (and 6 Feb. 1843). 'The evening passes . . .'
Oct. 29	Aunt B. dies (internal obstruction).	
Oct. 30	C. and E. visit Martha Taylor's grave at the Protestant Cemetery, spending the evening with Mary Taylor's uncle – 'the one not speaking at all, the other once or twice'.	
Nov. —	Ae. returns to Haworth.	
Nov. 2	C. and E. hear of Aunt B.'s illness.	
Nov. 3	Aunt B.'s funeral. C. and E. hear of her death.	
Nov. 8	C. and E. arrive home.	
Nov. 10		Ae. *To Cowper*. 'Sweet are thy strains . . .'
Nov. 29	C. goes to stay with E.N. Ae. returns to Thorp Green.	
Dec. —		Ae. *To* ———. 'I will not mourn thee . . .'
Dec. 5	C. returns home; gives Mercy Nussey a copy of Felicia Hemans' *Song of the Affections*.	
*Dec. 25	Ae. comes home for the Christmas holidays.	
Dec. 26	B. attends his last Masonic meeting.	
Dec. 28	Aunt B.'s will proved. Total effects under £1500.	
Dec. 30		Ae. 'My soul is awakened . . .'

Dec. —	(or Jan. 1843). Tabby returns to the parsonage.	
1843 ——	P.'s eyesight deteriorates rapidly. E. takes over the management of her and her sister's legacies, invested in the York and Midland Railway.	C. *Master and Pupil*. C. 'The autumn day . . .' C. 'Early wrapt in slumbers . . .'
Jan. —	E.N. visits C. Ae. returns to Thorp Green with B. who is to be tutor to Edmund Robinson.	
Jan. 27	C. leaves for Brussels as a teacher, at £16 p.a., but has to pay for her German lessons and her laundry.	
Jan. 28	C. arrives at the Pensionnat at 7 p.m.	
Feb. —		C. Translation of Louis Belmontet's *The Orphans*.
Feb. 24		E. *On the Fall of Zalona*. 'All blue and bright . . .'
Mar. —	C. gives English lessons to M. Heger.	C. Translation of Auguste Barbier's *Napoléon*.
Mar. 30		C. *La Chute des Feuilles*. B. (Thorp Green). 'I sit this evening . . .'
Apr. —	P. visits Ae. and B. at Thorp Green. C. unhappy in Brussels.	
Apr. 13		E. 'How clear she shines . . .'
Apr. 24	Ae. acquires *Sacred Harmony*, an anthology of Christian writers.	
May —	C. increasingly unhappy at the Pensionnat.	
May 1	C. writes to B. of her continuing interest in the 'world below' (Angria).	E. *To A.S. 1830*. 'Where beams the sun . . .'
May 4		E. *E.G. to M.R.* 'Thy Guardians are asleep . . .'
May 28		Ae. *A Word to the Calvinists*. 'You may rejoice . . .'
May 29	C. writes to E. asking for extra money; C. unhappy at	

	the quarrelling and spying at the Pensionnat.	
May 31		C. *Sur la Mort de Napoléon*. C. Scheme for a magazine tale (or for a May tale).
June —	Ae. home for the holidays, bringing Flossie, her dog, with her.	
July 26		E. 'Had there been false-hood . . .'
Aug. —	C. has to stay at the Pensionnat over the holidays; very homesick.	
Aug. 15	The Hegers go on holiday; M. Heger gives C. a book, a speech of his, a momento of Napoleon.	
Sept. 1	C. visits the Protestant Cemetery, and the fields beyond; then so unhappy she goes to confession at Ste Gudule Church.	
Sept. 6		E. 'In the earth, in the earth . . .'
Sept. 10		Ae. *A Hymn*. 'Eternal power of earth and air . . .'
Sept. 18	C. sees Queen Victoria 'for an instant flashing through the Rue Royale'.	
Oct. —	C. longing to be at home: gives in her notice, but is persuaded by M. Heger not to leave.	
Oct. 6		C. *Athènes Sauvée par la Poésie*.
Oct. 16		C. (no year). *Le Palais de la Mort*.
Oct. 19	Ae. drawing: man and dog.	
Nov. —	Ae. acquires Volpy's *Delectus Sententiarum*.	
Nov. 7		Ae. *The Consolation*. 'Though bleak these woods . . .'
Nov. 20	P. writes to his brother Hugh, asking how he is in these turbulent times in Ireland.	
Nov. 21		Ae. ''Tis strange to think . . .'
Dec. 16	Ae. drawing: pastoral scene.	

*Dec. 16	C. decides to leave the Pensionnat.	
Dec. 17	Mlle Sophie gives C. a parting gift, a little box.	
Dec. 18		E. 'Hope was but . . .' E. *Roderic Lesley 1830*. 'Lie down and rest . . .'
Dec. 19		E. *M.G. for the U.S.* ''Twas yesterday . . .'
Dec 31	C. leaves for home, with book of poems from M. Heger.	
1844 ——		*Ae. *The Prisoner*. 'A prisoner in a dungeon . . .' Ae. *Home*. 'How brightly glistening . . .'
Jan. 2	C. arrives home to find P. ill, in danger of losing his sight. Ae. and B. home on holiday.	
Jan. 23	By now C. thinking of trying to start a school at home as impossible to leave P.	
Jan. 26		Ae. 'Yes, I will take . . .'
Jan. ——	Ae. and B. return to Thorp Green.	C. 'Early wrapt . . .'
Feb. ——		Ae. *The Student's Serenade*. 'I have slept . . .' E. begins copying out her poems into two books, one entitled *Gondal Poems. Emily Jane Brontë*; the other *E.J.B.*
Feb. 2		E. *Castle Wood*. 'The day is done . . .'
Feb. 10		E. *My Comforter*. 'Well hast thou spoken . . .'
Feb. 29	By now P.'s eyes so bad he cannot get out while 'snow is on the ground'.	
Feb. ——		Ae. (/Mar.). *Views of Life*. 'When sinks my heart . . .' (completed June 1845).
Mar. 2		E. *A.G.A. to A.S.* 'This summer wind . . .'
Mar. 5		E. *A Day Dream*. 'On a sunny brae . . .'
*Mar. 7	(to *Mar. 24). C. visits E.N.	

Mar. 7	Ae. acquires *Deutsches Lesenbuch*.	
Mar. 11		E. *E.W. to A.G.A.* 'How few of all the hearts . . .'
Mar. 16	P. writes to the *Leeds Mercury* about the best material to wear to prevent fire accidents.	
Mar. —	B. suffers from 'incessant attacks of illness'.	
Apr. —		Ae. *Reminiscence*. 'Yes, thou art gone . . .'
May —	C., E.N. and Mary Taylor all meet at Hunsworth.	
May 1		E. 'The linnet in the rocky dells . . .'
May 29		Ae. *Memory*. 'Brightly the sun . . .'
June —	Ae. and B. home for a short holiday; B. irritable.	
July —	E.N. comes to stay. C. trying to get pupils for a school at the parsonage. C. corresponds with M. Heger; tells him of her need to see him again.	
Aug. 2		Ae. 'What though the sun . . .'
Aug. 7	(to Dec. 1844). E. and Ae. music book.	
Sept. 16	C. acknowledges they have achieved little as far as setting up a school at the parsonage goes.	
Sept. 3		E. *To Imagination*. 'When weary with . . .'
Oct. —	C. gives up all hope of starting a school. B. is 'always ill'.	
Oct. 2		E. *D.G.C. to J.A.* 'Come, the wind . . .'
Oct. 13		Ae. *A Prayer*. 'My God! O let me . . .'
Oct. 14		E. 'O thy bright eyes . . .'
Oct. 24	C. writes again to M. Heger asking if he received her letters of May and Aug.	

Nov. 6		E. *I.M. to I.G.* 'The winter wind . . .'
Nov. 11	C. realizes Haworth is too remote for a school.	E. *J.B. September 1825. From a Dungeon Wall in the Southern College.* 'Listen when your hair . . .'
Nov. 21		E. *M. Douglas to E.R. Gleneden.* 'The moon is full . . .'
Dec. 2		E. *A.G.A. Sept. 1826. From a D———— W—— in the N———— C————.* 'O Day! he cannot die . . .'
Dec. 16		Ae. *Lines Inscribed on a Wall of a Dungeon in the Southern Palace of Instruction.* 'Though not a breath . . .'
Dec. —	Ae. and B. home for Christmas.	
1845 ————		Ae. *Night.* 'I love the silent . . .' B. (*c.* 1845–7). 'Poor mourner sleep . . .' Ae. (spring). *Dreams.* 'While on my lonely couch . . .' Ae. (1844–5). 'I mourn with thee . . .' Ae. (by autumn) possibly writing *Agnes Grey.* B. (?by autumn). *And the Weary Are at Rest.*
Jan. 4	Mary Taylor visits Haworth.	
Jan. 9	(post date). C. again writes to M. Heger telling him of her misery at not hearing from him.	
Jan. 18	Ae. and B. leave for Thorp Green.	
Jan. 24		Ae. 'Call me away . . .'
Feb. —	C. spends a week with Mary Taylor; ill with headaches, sickness and flatness of spirit.	
Feb. 3		E. 'Enough of Thought, Philosopher . . .'
Mar. 3		E. *R. Alcona to J. Brenzaida.* 'Cold in the earth . . .'

*Mar. 24	C. admits to feeling buried in Haworth.	
Apr. 10		E. 'Death that struck . . .'
Apr. 14		E. 'Ah why because . . .'
Apr. 22		E. 'A thousand sounds . . .'
May —	Rev. A.B. Nicholls appointed curate at Haworth, at £100 p.a.	
May 20		Ae. 'O God, if this indeed . . .'
May 28		B. *The Emigrant I*. 'When sinks from sight . . .'
		B. *The Emigrant II*. 'After the long day . . .' (undated).
June 1		Ae. *Confidence*. 'Oppressed with sin and woe . . .'
June 2		E. 'How beautiful the earth . . .'
June 11	Ae. and B. home on holiday; Ae. decides not to return to Thorp Green.	
*June 18	B. returns to Thorp Green.	
June 30	E. and Ae. go to York, staying overnight, playing at 'Gondals' on the way.	
July 2	E. and Ae. return home.	
July 3	C. goes to stay with E.N. at Hathersage.	
July 17	B. hears the Robinsons have dismissed him and when C. returns she finds him 'ill', very 'often owing to his own fault'.	
July 29	B. sent away to Wales, with John Brown to look after him.	
*July —		B. *Penmaenmawr*.
July 31	E. and Ae. open their 1841 diary papers – a day late.	E. and Ae. write their diary papers giving news of the year and the state of their writing.
Aug. —	C. sketch: Ashburton Church.	
Aug. 3	B. returns from Wales; becomes, by 18th, according to C., hopeless, 'never fit for much'; only when forced to abstain are his health and	

	temper better: by the end of the month, 'forced to abstain'.	
Aug. —		E. *M.A. Written on a Dungeon Wall – N——— C———*. 'I know that tonight . . .'
Sept. 3		Ae. *Song.* 'We know where . . .'
Sept. 4		Ae. *Vanitas Vanitatem.* 'In all we do . . .'
		Ae. *Song.* 'Come to the banquet . . .'
★Sept. 10	B. states he is writing a 3 volume novel, of 'human feelings' 'veiled with deceit'.	
Sept. —	C. discovers and reads E.'s poetry.	Ae. *The Penitent.* 'I mourn with thee . . .' (undated).
Oct. 1		Ae. *Parting Address from Z.Z. to A.E.* 'Oh weep not . . .'
Oct. 9		E. *Julian M. and A.G. Rochelle.* 'Silent is the house . . .'
Oct. 23	B. writes about a secretarial post on the railway: unsuccessful.	
Nov. —	C. writes to M. Heger – she desperately needs to hear from him.	
Nov. 25	B. sends *Penmaenmawr* to the *Halifax Guardian* for publication under his pseudonym, 'North- angerland', which Mrs Robinson will recognize.	
1846 ——		B. (1845–6). *Real Rest.* 'I see a corpse . . .'
Jan. 2		E. 'No coward soul is mine . . .'
Jan. 28	C. makes inquiries about the possibility of publishing a book of poems.	
Feb. 6	C. sends MS of poems to the publishers, Aylott and Jones, as the work of three relatives, the Bell brothers.	

Feb. 15	(to Feb. 21). C. corresponds with Aylott and Jones over the kind of paper, printing and costing of the poems.	
Feb. 18	C. goes to stay with E.N. until Mar. 2.	
Mar. 3	(to Mar. 28). C. sends Aylott and Jones £31.10s. payment for printing the poems; C., E. and Ae. correct the proof sheets from memory and return them.	
★Mar. 31	B. in a 'stupified' condition, changing only for the worse.	
Apr. 3		B. *Epistle from a Father to a Child in her Grave*. 'From earth whose life-reviving . . .'
Apr. 6	C. offers Aylott and Jones three stories the Bell brothers have in preparation, which they reject, but offer C. advice.	
Apr. 20	C. ask for 3 copies of the poems and inquires about advertising them.	
Apr. —	B. goes to Halifax for three days on 'business'.	B. begins *Morley Hall*, a poem about an ancestor of J.B. Leyland.
Apr. 28	In a letter to J.B. Leyland, B. states that he has enough material for a respectable-sized volume, but finds the prospect of trying to get it published disheartening.	B. *Sonnet*. 'When all our cheerful hours . . .'
May 2	B. tells F. H. Grundy of his life of the last few months – of the 'cold debauchery, the determination to see how far mind could carry body without both being chucked into hell'.	
★May 11	The price of the *Poems* is set at 4s. or 5s.	Ae. *Monday Night, May 11*. 'Why should such gloomy silence . . .'
May 25	An additional £5 is sent to Aylott and Jones to defray	

	expenses; C. asks for reviews to be sent.	
May —		(End of month). *POEMS* by Currer, Ellis and Acton Bell published.
June —	B. further upset, after hearing of Mr Robinson's death, that Mrs Robinson may not see him nor may he contact her, though she has given him all her love and he will always care for her.	
June 27		C. date at the end of the MS of *The Professor*.
July —	C. sends the 3 tales to Henry Colburn for consideration. P. now blind, according to B.	
July 4	First review of the *Poems* in *The Athenaeum* and *The Critic*.	
*July 10	C. is denying there is any thought of her marrying her father's curate, Mr N.	
July —	Further copies of the *Poems* sent out for review.	
July 15		Ae. *Mirth and Mourning.* 'O, cast away . . .'
July 24	C. is suffering from toothache.	
July 28		Ae. 'Weep not too much . . .'
*Aug. 2	C. and E. go to Manchester to consult about P.'s eyes.	
Aug. 13		Ae. *The Power of Love.* 'Love, indeed . . .'
Aug. 19	C. goes with P. to Manchester for an operation on the cataract in his left eye; remain there until Sept. 24/5.	
*Aug. 24	C. has *The Professor* returned to her.	
Sept. 14		Ae. *Z———'s Dream.* 'I dreamt last night . . .' E. 'Why ask to know . . .'
Oct. 6	C. writes to thank the editor of the *Dublin University Magazine* for his notice of the *Poems*.	Ae. 'Gloomily the clouds . . .'

*Oct. 14	C. decides there would not be enough profit in a school kept by E.N. and herself.	
Nov. —	P. continues to improve; is now reading prayers in church.	
*Dec. 13	A sheriff's officer arrives demanding payment of B.'s debts or he must go to prison.	
Dec. —	All the family have colds – Ae. asthma.	
1846–7		B. *Morley Hall* completed.
1847 ——	The well at the parsonage is cleared out – eight tin cans in various stages of decomposition found.	Ae. 'Farewell to thee . . .'
Jan. —	C. fears she is falling into 'self-weariness'.	
*Jan. 24	B. in despair; his thoughts of marrying Mrs Robinson and living with her in leisure, gone; has become a 'thoroughly old man – mentally and bodily.'	
Feb. 14	C. still suffering from the cold weather, though her toothache has abated.	
*Mar. 1	Ae. receives frequent letters from the Misses Robinson, her former pupils.	
Apr. 3	Mrs Collins revisits the parsonage; tells them of her life since she left her drunken husband.	
Apr. 4	All have colds again.	
Apr. 21	C. forgets her and E.N.'s birthdays.	
Apr. —		Ae. 'Severed and gone . . .'
May 12	C. invites E.N. to stay but by 20th E.N. has rejected the offer, much to C.'s chagrin and annoyance.	
June 16	C. sends unsold copies of the *Poems* to De Quincey, Hartley Coleridge and G. Lockhart.	

July —	T.C. Newby agrees to publish *W.H.* and *A.G.*, but not *The Professor*.	B. *Percy Hall*. 'The westering sunbeams . . .'
July 15	C. sends *The Professor* to S/E for consideration.	
★July 16	B. restless and ill; cannot sleep or write.	
July 19?	J.B. Leyland visits B.	
July —	(or Aug.) E.N. visits C.	
Aug. —	S/E reject *The Professor*, but are interested in a 3-volume novel.	
Aug. 7	C. has a 3-volume narrative in progress which she hopes to finish in about a month.	
Aug. 11		Ae. *The Three Guardians*. 'Spirit of Earth . . .'
★Aug. 24	C. sends the MS of *J.E.* to S/E by rail.	
Aug. —	The proof sheets of *W.H.* and *A.G.* are in the press.	
Sept. —	C. visits E.N. where according to E.N. she corrects the proofs of *J.E.*; learns S/E think well of the first part.	
Sept. 24	C. returns home, with gifts from the Nusseys – a screen for P., a cap for Tabby, apples and a collar for E. and a jar of 'crab-cheese' for Ae.	
Oct. 2	C. decides there will be no preface to *J.E.*	
★Oct. 7	Mr N. is away; according to C. many parishioners wish he would not trouble to return.	
Oct. 15	B. is getting more difficult, leading P. a wretched life. Mr N. returns — C. comments that it is his narrowness of mind that 'strikes me most'.	
Oct. 16		C. *JANE EYRE* published.
Oct. —	*J.E.* receives good reviews; Thackeray unable to put it down.	

Oct. 28	C. assures her publishers the picture of Helen Burns is true to life.	
★Nov. 10	Surmise starts as to the identity of the Bell brothers.	
★Nov. 17	Last proof sheets of *W.H.* and *A.G.* arrive.	
Nov. —		Ae. (to Apr. 17, 1848). *Self-Communion.* 'The mist is resting . . .' C. Fragment – *The Moores.*
Dec. —		E. and Ae. *WUTHERING HEIGHTS and AGNES GREY* published by T.C. Newby.
Dec. 1	C. informs S/E that they must put 'Miss Brontë' on their communications as Currer Bell 'is not known here'.	
★Dec. 13	C. decides, if there is a 2nd edition of *J.E.*, she will add a preface dedicating it to Thackeray.	
★Dec. 14	C. has made three beginnings to her next novel, but discarded them all.	
★Dec. 14	E. and Ae. receive 6 copies of *W.H. and A.G.* which abound in errors.	
Dec. 21	Date C. puts to her revised preface of the 2nd edition of *J.E.*	
★Dec. 31	C. is denying that Currer Bell is the author of all three novels.	
Dec. —		C. 2nd edition of *J.E.*
1848 ——		
★Jan. 4	*J.E.* reached Haworth area; a local parson recognizes Cowan Bridge School in Lowood School.	
★Jan. 11	B. is always sick and has 'fallen down in two or three fits'; C. comments – 'What will be the ultimate end God knows.'	

*Jan. 22	Newby is using the confusion over the identity of the Bell brothers to his own advantage.	
Jan. 28	C. learns of the unfortunateness of her dedication of the 2nd edition of *J.E.* to Thackeray, whose private circumstances akin to those of Rochester.	
Feb. 15	Newby writes to E. (Ae.?) telling 'him' to take time over the next novel.	
Mar. 3	C. comments on the unfairness of the *Christian Remembrancer* review – merely 'smart and sarcastic'.	
Mar. 11	C. regrets she has not the ability to illustrate *J.E.* herself.	
Mar. 13	C. adds a note to the 3rd edition of *J.E.* making it clear that Currer, Ellis and Acton Bell are 3 separate persons.	
*Mar. 31	C., E. and Ae. have flu'.	
Apr. —		C. 3rd edition of *J.E.*
Apr. 17		Ae. *Self-Communion* completed.
Apr. 24		Ae. *The Narrow Way*. 'Believe not those . . .'
Apr. 20	C. starts receiving parcels of books from S/E; asks if she may be allowed to pay for them.	
May 3	C. authorizes E.N. to deny she is publishing – such affirmations 'humbug'.	
*May 12	C. writes to W.S.W. about the position of women in society, particularly as teachers or governesses.	
May 13		E. (unfinished). 'Why ask to know . . .'
June —		Ae. THE TENANT OF WILDFELL HALL published.

June 26	C. tells E.N. she cannot comment on the new book that is all the rage in London (i.e. *J.E.*) – as she has not been able to get hold of a copy to read.	
July 1	Mary Taylor writes C. her comments on *J.E.* (C. sent her a copy); says she has burnt all C.'s letters to her in a 'fit of caution'.	
July 4	P. sends the Marquis of Anglesey an idea for a horizontal firing device.	
July 7	C. and Ae. go to London to prove their separate existence to S/E.	
July 8	C. and Ae. go to the opera with George Smith and his sisters; visit the Great Exhibition.	
July 10	C. and Ae. go to the Royal Academy Exhibition and the National Gallery.	
July 11	C. and Ae. return home, pleased to have ended the mystery of the authorship of the novels.	
July 22	B. receives a court summons for non-payment of his debts.	Ae. Preface to 2nd edition of *The T. of W.H.*
July 28	According to C., B.'s 'constitution is shattered'; he sleeps all day' and is 'awake all night'.	
July 31	C. warns S/E never to refer to E. except by her pseudonym – Ellis.	
Aug. —	B.'s deterioration continues, as the fame of the Bells grows.	
Aug. 14	C. writes to W.S.W. about the duties of an author, first 'allegiance to Truth and Nature', second, to the study of Art – to enable him to interpret these eloquently.	

*Sept. 7	S/E seems likely to take over the unsold copies of the *Poems*; very few sold.
Sept. 22	B. goes to the village for the last time; according to C. a new calm fills his mind.
Sept. 23	B. confined to bed.
Sept. 24	B. dies ('chronic bronchitis; marasmus').
Sept. 28	B. buried. William Morgan officiates.
Sept. 28/9	C. becomes ill.
Oct. 1	B.'s memorial service. Mr N. officiates.
Oct. 2	C. declares B. knew nothing of their publishing ventures.
Oct. 9	C. ill with headaches and sickness; E. a cough and cold.
Oct. 18	C.'s next novel laid aside because of her illness.
Oct. —	*Poems* re-issued by S/E with new binding and title page.
*Nov. 2	C. better, but E. and Tabby still ill; E. refuses all help.
*Nov. 7	E. too ill to write but able still to read.
*Nov. 23	E. very ill, refuses to see a doctor; scarcely allows her condition to be referred to.
Dec. —	The Misses Robinson visit Ae.; 'overjoyed' to see her.
Dec. 7	E. has read Dr Curie's work on homeopathy, but does not regard it as efficacious.
Dec. 9	C. sends a description of E.'s illness to Dr Epps, via S/E, to see if he can prescribe treatment.
Dec. 10	E. worse, but determined 'no poisoning doctor' shall come near her.
Dec. 18	E. falls when going to feed the dogs, but refuses any help; she dresses with great difficulty and does not recognize the sprig of heather C. brings her from the moors.

Dec. 19	E. dies in the early afternoon, after agreeing too late to see a doctor (consumption – 2 months).	
Dec. 22	E. buried – her coffin 5ft 7ins by 16ins; Mr N. officiates.	
Dec. 24		C. 'My darling thou . . .' *For Emily Brontë.*
Dec. 25	P. and Ae. far from well.	
1849 Jan. —	E.N. visits C.	Ae. (to Jan. 28). 'A dreadful darkness . . .'
Jan. 10	Ae. being given blisters and one dose of codliver oil – 'tastes like train oil'.	
Jan. 15	Ae. no better; C. also ill, being treated with 'pitch plasters and bran tea'.	
Jan. 18	The doctors report Ae. unlikely to live; she herself guesses this from her father's reaction: she is forbidden to travel.	
Jan. 22	Ae. a little better; asks E.N. to get her a respirator.	
★Feb. 1	C. sends the first volume of her new novel to S/E.	
Feb. 5	The administration of E.'s estate – died intestate, estate under £450.	
Feb. 16	C. says it is self delusion to think Ae. any better.	
Mar. 2	C. believes Ae. slightly better; assures W.S.W. the curates (*SH.*) were 'photographed from life'.	
Mar. 24	C. tells M. Wooler that Ae. is resigned and looking beyond this life.	
Mar. 29	Plans afoot to take Ae. to the seaside.	
Apr. 5	Ae. asks E.N. to go on holiday with her in May; there is no time to be lost, but Ae. has no horror of death – 'God's will be done'.	

Apr. 16	C. comments on the treatments used on Ae. – Mr Teale's remedies, hydropathy, and Gobold's Vegetable Balsam.
May —	C. has to delay writing her new novel because of Ae.'s illness.
*May 8	Ae. is left £200 in Miss Outhwaite's will and decides to use it to go to Scarborough to 'if not restore' her health, at 'least prolong her existence'.
May 24	C., Ae. and E.N. leave for Scarborough, via York where they buy bonnets, visit the Minster and spend the night.
May 25	They arrive at Scarborough.
May 26	Ae. drives on the sands for an hour in a donkey cart, worrying about the wellbeing of the donkey.
*May 27	Ae.'s 'slow ebb' continues.
May 28	Ae. rises early; about 11a.m. she feels a change in herself; the doctor is sent for and tells her she has not long to live; she dies in the early afternoon.
May 30	Ae. is buried in St Mary's Churchyard, Scarborough.
June 7	C. and E.N. go up the east coast; then on to Bridlington.
June 21	C. returns to Haworth.
July 4	C. records her unhappy loneliness 'with the clock ticking loud through the house'.
July 26	C. rejects the idea of getting a companion – it would be too hard on the companion.
July 27	C. sends E.N. £4. 10s. for a 'bath-shower', a fur boa – preferably grey – and some cuffs, and 10s. commission for E.N.
Aug. 3	C. asks E.N. to visit.
Aug. 21	C. tells her publishers she prefers *Shirley* as a title for her

C. 'There is little joy . . .' *For Anne Brontë.*

	next novel, rather than *Hollow's Mill* or *Fieldhead*.	
★Aug. 29	*SH*. completed. C. not sure it is equal to *J.E.*	
Aug. 31	C. refuses to alter the preface she has written for *SH*. in which she answers the criticism of her made in the *Quarterly*.	
Sept. 6	Ae.'s estate administered – died intestate; her estate under £600.	
Sept. 8	The MS of *SH*. is collected from the parsonage by James Taylor.	
Sept. 10	C. ill – bilious attack, the first since she returned from the sea; she had them every month before.	
Sept. 10	(to Sept. 29). C. corresponds with her publishers about *SH*., offering to substitute something in English for the French chapter – 'Le Cheval Dompté'; she is glad to hear there is no falling-off in her writing.	
★Sept. 24	Martha and Tabby ill; C. in a poor state.	
★Sept. 28	The 'bath–shower' arrives – C. promises E.N. a 'thorough drenching' in it when she comes to visit.	
★Oct. 4	C. fears that although she may lose her income from the fall in value of her railway investments, many may lose their livelihood.	
Oct. 23/ 24	C. visits E.N. until Oct. 31.	
Oct. 26		C. *SHIRLEY* published.
★Nov. 1	Trouble arises over the presentation of the curates in ch. 1 of *SH*.	
Nov. 5	C. receives her copies of *SH*., delayed at Bradford for 2 weeks.	
Nov. 15	C. comments to W.S.W. on the reactions to *SH*. – those who do not like *J.E.* like *SH*. and vice versa.	

*Nov. 20	C. receives a letter from Mrs Gaskell; sends a copy of *SH*. to Harriet Martineau.	
Nov. 29	C. goes to London, staying with the Smiths.	
Dec. 3	C. dines with Thackeray.	
*Dec. 5/ 6	C. sees and dislikes Macready's performances in *Othello* and *Macbeth*.	
Dec. 9	C. goes to see the new Houses of Parliament.	
Dec. 10	C. meets Harriet Martineau.	
Dec. 14	C. dines with the literary critics of *The Times*, *Athenaeum*, *Spectator*, *Examiner* and *Atlas*.	
Dec. 15	C. returns home, stopping at Derby en route, tired out from over-excitement of the evening before.	
Dec. 21	Joe Taylor visits the parsonage.	
Dec. 27	E.N. comes to stay.	
1850 ——	Rooms in the parsonage repainted.	C. One-volume edition of *J.E.* published.
Jan. 19	Mr N. finishes *J.E.* and is crying out for 'the other book' (*SH*.).	
Jan. 28	Mr N. finishes *SH*., is delighted with it, reading all the scenes about the curates aloud to P., and triumphing in his own character.	
*Feb. 4	*J.E.* is ordered for the Keighley Mechanics Institute.	
Feb. 14	C. tartly informs M. Wooler *J.E.* 'is only coarse' to the 'coarse-minded'.	
*Feb. 16	P. gives C. her mother's letters to read which affect her greatly.	
Mar. 1	Sir Kay Shuttleworth and his wife visit C.	
Mar. 6	(to Mar. 9). C., at her father's insistence, goes to stay with the Shuttleworths, where she takes to the German governess.	
Mar. 19	C. tells W.S.W of the marvellous reception of *SH*. in the 'North' (i.e Haworth) – even by the curates.	

Apr. 4	P. instigates inquiries into the Haworth water supply.
Apr. 12	C. comments on Jane Austen's style, its 'Chinese fidelity' and 'miniature delicacy', dealing with 'surface' of 'lives of the genteel'.
Apr. 18	C. goes to see E.N. who is ill.
Apr. 22	C. writes to W.S.W. about E.'s love of the moors.
Apr. 23	Joe Taylor calls to talk to C. about his love for Amelia Ringrose.
Apr. 29	P. ill, Martha ill, C. cold and sore throat – visit to London with the Shuttleworths cancelled.
May 18	C.'s visit to London again cancelled – Sir Kay ill.
May 30	(to June 25). C. in London, stays with the Smiths. Visits the Royal Academy, the Zoo and goes to the opera; sees the Duke of Wellington – 'a real grand old man'; has her portrait drawn by George Richmond. While she is away the parsonage is re-roofed.
June 25	C. visits E.N.
July 3	C. goes to Edinburgh, meeting George Smith and his sisters there – 'a glorious city'.
July 6	C. returns to E.N.'s where she is ill.
*July 15	C. returns home. Finds P. in a state of nervous alarm – he thought she was either very ill or might have got married.
*Aug. 1	C.'s portrait arrives, with one of the Duke of Wellington, which Tabby thinks is of P.
Aug. 14	(or Aug. 15). Mrs Ferrand, Lord John Manners and Mr Smythe call with some grouse for P.
Aug. 18	C. goes to Windermere to stay with the Shuttleworths;

	the German governess is pleased to see her.
Aug. 19	C. meets Mrs Gaskell for the first time; the weather prevents them from driving to Coniston to meet the Tennysons.
Aug. 25	C. returns home, glad the visit is over.
Sept. 5	C. approves of the idea of S/E reprinting *W.H.* and *A.G.* in one volume; does not find it desirable to preserve *T. of W.H.* C. is to write a 'notice' about her sisters for it; she gives George Smith details of Newby's arrangements for the first publication.
Sept. 28	C. sends Mrs Gaskell a copy of the *Poems*.
Sept. 29	C. busy revising and transcribing *W.H.* – modifying the orthography of Joseph's speech; she becomes 'laden down' by memory.
Oct. 25	C. tells E.N. of her agony in reading over her sisters' papers.
Dec. 10	E. and Ae. *W.H. and A.G.* – new edition with 'Notice' about her sisters by C. to give 'a just idea of their identity'.
Dec. 18	C. goes to stay at Ambleside with Harriet Martineau whom she both 'admires and wonders at'; Harriet tries to mesmerize her but has to stop because C. is so susceptible.
Dec. 23	C. goes to stay at E.N.'s.
Dec. 26	C. returns home.
1851 Jan. 8	C. records she is trying the 'wet sheet' treatment (for colds, fevers etc) which she likes and thinks does her good.
Feb. 5	C. tells George Smith how *The Professor* was rejected by nine publishers, including S/E.
Mar. —	E.N. comes to stay with C.
Mar. 30	A census is taken in which C.

is listed as having no profession.

*Apr. 5   James Taylor calls to say goodbye before he leaves for India. C. reports to E.N. things are 'just as they were'; that it would be impossible to marry Mr Taylor as 'every time he came near' her 'veins ran ice' and anyway he is 'thoroughly second rate'.

Apr. 12   C. asks E.N. to get her a lace cloak, in black or white, and some chemisettes of a small size – 'full woman's size don't fit me'.

Apr. 19   Plans for C. and the Smiths to go on a tour down the Rhine are cancelled.

May 5   C. is suffering from a 'fiery tic'.

*May 10   C. buys a pink-lined bonnet in Leeds – which she fears is too gay.

May 21   P. threatens that if C. marries and leaves him, he will go into lodgings.

May 28   (to June 27). C. goes to London where she attends Thackeray's lectures; sees the Great Exhibition three times; hears D'Aubigny preach; attends Cardinal Wiseman's confirmation service – 'impiously theatrical'; meets the Earl of Carlyle; breakfasts with Mr Rogers, the 'patriarch' poet, and sees Rachel act twice; she also visits Dr Brown, a phrenologist, where she and George Smith (as Mr and Miss Fraser) have their characters read.

June 27   C. stays with Mrs Gaskell for two days, where she loses a 'part of her heart' to Julia, Mrs Gaskell's daughter.

June 30   C. returns home.

July —   E.N. comes to stay.

July 27   Mr N. takes tea with C. on

	the eve of his departure for Ireland.
Sept. —	William Morgan comes to stay – 'fat, well and hearty'.
Sept. 29	M. Wooler comes to stay – P. gets on well with her.
Sept. —	By the end of the month C. is not well – finds the 6 months before the equinox – 'the weird' – very trying.
Nov. —	C. still waiting, 'Quaker-like', on the spirit to get her new book started.
*Nov. 20	C. has begun her new book – hopes to get it finished by next autumn.
Dec. 1	Keeper, E.'s dog, dies.
*Dec. 10	C. suffering from influenza, headaches and toothache, with no appetite; the doctor will not let her take the codliver oil which she has.
*Dec. 20	E.N. comes to stay.
*Dec. 31	Doctor diagnoses C.'s illness as a sensitive and irritable condition of the liver.
1852 *Jan. 1	C. unable to stoop over her desk to write without great pain in her chest.
Jan. 5	C. is 'very, very' sick; is given a mixture of mercury which makes her condition worse – unable to talk and only able to take spoonfuls of liquid, no solid food.
Jan. 16	C. is mending slightly.
Jan. 22	She is progressing well but is very thin; hoping to visit E.N.
Jan. 27	C. goes to E.N.'s; asks for only the plainest of fare – no butter, no tea, just milk and water with a little sugar, dry bread and an occasional mutton chop.
Feb. 10	C. returns home; starts taking hop tea, which she thinks does her good.

Feb. 24	C. now 'well enough' but still has headaches and indigestion.
Mar. 5	C. still has frequent headaches, a swollen face and a 'tic' in her cheekbone.
★Mar. 7	P. ill with his spring attack of bronchitis, so impossible for C. to accompany E.N. to Sussex.
★Mar. 11	C. now revising *SH.* for a possible reprint.
★Apr. 22	C. still thin, with a little pain.
★May 23	C. goes to stay at Filey, East Riding of Yorkshire, to recuperate.
★June 6	C. has bathed once – 'it seemed to do me good'; still has headaches and a pain in her side; visits Ae.'s grave, to find errors on the gravestone.
★July 1	C. home again, feeling better – very sunburnt.
July 26	P. ill – thrombosis of the eye, possible apoplexy, partially paralysed for 2 days.
Aug. 25	Tabby ill with 'English cholera', prevalent in the area.
Sept. —	C. asks M. Wooler as she is near Scarborough to check the new inscriptions on Ae.'s grave.
Sept. 24	C. feeling 'lonely' and 'fettered'.
Oct. 15	E.N. comes to stay for a week.
Oct. 26	C. is busily writing – must get on while the mood is right.
Oct. 30	C. asks George Smith what he thinks of the first part of *V.*
Nov. —	C. discusses with S/E various aspects of *V.*
Nov. 10	C. writes that she will probably have the 3rd volume of *V.* ready in 3 weeks.
Nov. 20	C. sends off the 3rd volume of *V.*
Nov. 23	C. busy proof-reading.
Nov. 24	C. stays with E.N.
Dec. —	C. receives £500 for *V.* – hoped she would get £700.
Dec. 8	C. returns home.

Dec. 13	Mr N., after spending his usual time with P., comes into the parlour and proposes to C.; P. so furious when C. tells him that he seems likely to have another thrombosis, so C. agrees to refuse Mr N.'s offer.
Dec. 14	C. writes to Mr N. rejecting him; P. shows nothing but 'hardness' and 'contempt' for Mr N., considers that the match would be degrading to C.
Dec. —	Mr N. offers P. his resignation, but is allowed to withdraw it provided he never broaches the subject of marriage to C. or P. again. P. wishes C. to go to London – presumably to get her 'out of the way'.
1853 Jan. 5	C. goes to London; corrects the proofs of *V.* while there; also visits Bethlehem Hospital, Newgate and Pentonville prisons, the Exchange and the Foundling Hospital.
Jan. 12	Publication of *V.* delayed so as to give Mrs Gaskell's *Ruth* a clear run.
Jan. 24	C. *VILLETTE* published.
Feb. 2	C. returns home, accompanied by E.N.
Feb. 3	Harriet Martineau's review of *V.* in the *Daily News*.
*Feb. 15	E.N. goes home; C. comments that the reviews of *V.* are pleasing, except for Harriet Martineau's.
*Feb. 24	C. going on 'long walks' on the 'cracking snow'.
*Mar. 4	The Bishop of Ripon visits the parsonage; Mr N. does not behave too well.
*Mar 10	C. writes to E.N. that the reviews of *V.* are either 'sugar candy' or 'wormwood' flavoured.

*Apr. 6	Mr N. has got a curacy elsewhere – he and P. never speak; C. 'pities him inexpressibly'.	
Apr. 18	C.'s bitter feelings over Harriet Martineau's opinion of *V.* leads her to end their friendship.	
Apr. 22	C. goes to stay with Mrs Gaskell.	
Apr. 28	C. visits E.N.	
*May 2	C. returns home.	
May 26	Mr N. takes his last service at Haworth; calls at the parsonage to say goodbye; C. discovers him sobbing his heart out at the garden gate.	
May —		C. (or June). *Willie Ellin* (fragment) begun.
June —	P. ill – seizure with temporary blindness.	
July ?	(or Aug.?). C. sets out for a week in Scotland with Joe Taylor and his wife and baby; the baby becomes ill, so all have to return.	
Sept. 13	C. goes to Ilkley to stay with M. Wooler.	
Sept. 19	(to Sept. 23). Mrs Gaskell stays with C., who finds, when she leaves, the silence depressing.	
Sept. —	C. visits E.N., then goes to stay with M. Wooler at Hornsea.	
Oct. 6	C. returns home with purchases – mops, carpets, rugs and crockery.	
Nov. 27		C. *Emma* (fragment with date on p. 1 of MS).
1854 Jan. —	Mr N. in Haworth but not happily received at the parsonage.	
Jan. 27	P. receives the 'ice apparatus'	

	(for his shoes?) which fits him admirably.
Feb. 21	P. declares he is too old to meet a deputation from the Church Pastoral Aid Society.
Feb. 24	Mary Taylor writes to E.N. disagreeing with her disapproval of C. marrying – why shouldn't she if she wants to?
Mar. 28	P. has bronchitis; C. leaves, by mistake, a note for Mr N. in her letter to E.N.
Apr. 8	Mr N. comes to Haworth; he and C., with P.'s permission, have been corresponding and C. has seen a lot of him since January.
*Apr. 11	C. and Mr N. are engaged; C. sees 'some germs of real happiness' in the future, though P.'s 'convenience and seclusion' are to be 'scrupulously respected'.
Apr. 18	C. writes to tell Mrs Gaskell of her engagement – 'my destiny will not be brilliant' but she is 'very grateful' to Mr N.
May 1	C. visits Mrs Gaskell.
May 4	C. goes to Hunsworth.
May 8	C. goes to E.N.'s; home by the 14th.
May 23	Mr N. comes to Haworth – wedding cards are ordered.
June 16	C. informs E.N. and M. Wooler of the wedding arrangements.
June 29	C. marries Mr N., Rev. Sutcliff Sowden officiating; only E.N., M. Wooler and Mr Sowden are at the ceremony; M. Wooler gives her away as P. at the last moment refuses to attend. C. and Mr N. leave for Wales,

	arriving at Conway in the evening.
July 4	C. and Mr N. cross to Ireland, meeting cousins of Mr N.'s in Dublin.
July 7	They go on to Banagher, stay with Mr N.'s uncle and aunt who brought him up.
July 14	They go on to the West End Hotel at Kilkee on the S.W. coast of Ireland.
*July 27	At Cork, C. is thrown from her horse and nearly trampled on.
Aug. 1	C. and Mr N. return to Haworth, to live at the parsonage, looking after P.
*Aug. 9	C. is finding her new life very busy, constantly 'called for and occupied', 'time no longer my own'.
Aug. 29	C. asks E.N. to visit, but E.N. unable to – C. bitterly disappointed.
Sept. 19	C. tells M. Wooler of her busy parish life and that she no longer expects to be of 'general interest'.
Sept. 21	E.N. comes to stay.
Oct. 10	C. and Mr N. attend a party, which leaves Mr N. 'out of patience'. E.N. is told Mr N. wants a pledge from her that she will burn C.'s letters, or there can be no more.
Oct. 31	E.N. is told Mr N. insists she must either burn C.'s letters or allow him to censor them: she must write out a promise to that effect.
Nov. 8	E.N. agrees to burn C.'s letters if he in turn will pledge to 'have no Authorship in the matters communicated'; Mr N. agrees. (E.N. did not destroy them.)

Nov. 6	Mr Sowden and his brother George stay the night.
*Nov. 14	C. hopes to visit E.N. for the first time in a long while; all goes well with her – she is free from headaches, sickness and indigestion in the last 3 months.
Nov. 29	C. and Mr N. walk to the waterfall on the moors, are caught in the rain; C. gets a cold.
*Dec. 6	Mr N. will not let her visit E.N. as there is typhus in the area; C. hopes to come before Christmas.
Dec. 7	C. tells E.N. she cannot 'get leave' to come before Christmas.
Dec. 26	C. hopes to visit E.N. in 3 or 4 weeks – a quiet visit 'in the circumstances'.
1855 *Jan. 9	C. becomes ill – nausea and vomiting.
Jan. 19	C. tells E.N. she must not conjecture, 'too soon yet, though I certainly never before felt as I have done recently'.
Jan. 21	C. unwell – sickness and loss of appetite.
Jan. 23	Mr N. writes to tell E.N. that C. is ill and cannot visit her before the 31st and then only if she improves.
*Jan. 25	C. so ill she has to stay in bed.
Jan. 29	Mr N. tells E.N. she cannot come to see C. while she is unwell.
*Feb. 14	C. prostrated with weakness, sickness and fever; unable to write; P. has bronchitis.
Feb. 17	Tabby dies. C. makes her will, leaving everything to Mr N. unless

	there should be any surviving children.
★Feb. 21	C. sends a pencil note to E.N. – 'Arthur is the tenderest nurse'.
Feb. —	C. becomes very emaciated, cannot talk, constantly sick until she vomits blood.
Mar. 8	C. seems a little better.
Mar. 15	C. not so well again.
Mar. 20	P. writes to tell E.N. that C. is on the verge of death; the doctors give no hope.
★Mar. 27	C. conscious but speaks very little.
Mar. 31	C. dies (phthisis; exhaustion from sickness during the early stages of pregnancy).
Apr. 4	C. buried in Haworth Church, Rev. Sutcliff Sowden officiating.
June —	P. invites Mrs Gaskell to write C.'s biography.
1861 June 7	P. dies (chronic bronchitis; dyspepsia; convulsions, duration 9 hours).
June 12	P. interred at Haworth Church, Rev. Dr Burnet, Vicar of Bradford, officiating.

Family Portraits

Patrick Brontë (1777–1861) and Maria Brontë (1783–1821)

The Rev. Patrick Brontë was a survivor. He outlived all of his direct family, having lived through the deaths of his wife, five daughters, a son, and a sister-in-law who, after his wife's demise, became in effect his housekeeper. There is something almost absurd in the spectacle of a man thought to be frail and physically vulnerable, and treated as such, living through one premature death after another. But there is nothing absurd in the surviving photograph of a face of strong texture with elegantly carved contours of nose and cheek and chin – it is the face of a man who could weather and contain catastrophe. He wears his famous stock – the wrap-around scarf-like protection which could be raised over his mouth – like a surgeon's mask. With it he combated consumption, bronchitis, ubiquitous chills and colds, and the lurking menace of cholera that hung around Haworth. He was a survivor and he looks like one.

He had not always been Brontë, for he was the son of a Hugh Brunty. His mother was Eleanor McClory. She was married to Brunty in 1776 at a Protestant church in Ireland, after she had renounced her Catholic faith. Her husband was not particularly religious, and had no regular work. Eventually he took his bride to a thatched cabin at Loughbrickland, in the parish of Drumballyroney-cum-Drumgooland, County Down. He built a corn-kiln and made a scanty living from it. Patrick, the first of ten children, was born on St Patrick's Day, 17 March 1777.

In 1778 the family moved to a small house in Lisnacrevy where Brunty helped as a farm-labourer and fence and road repairer. From there-on he maintained a very modest but not perilously low standard of living.

Hugh Brunty never discouraged Patrick's obvious attraction to books and men of words. He read *Pilgrim's Progress* and heard John Wesley preach when quite young. From 1789 he satisfied his thirst to read by borrowing books and buying a few out of the very small remittances from his apprenticeships, first to a blacksmith, then to a manufacturer of linen web, then as assistant to a linen draper. Virgil, Homer and Herodotus, Shakespeare and Spenser were added to his repertoire of study.

His first steps in the direction that was to lead him eventually to Haworth were taken when he was appointed as teacher to Glascard Hill Presbyterian church school, where he also assisted as music conductor. He was a good and successful teacher. The steps became more decisive when he became teacher to the church school at Drumballyroney and tutor to the sons of Thomas Tighe, Rector of Drumgooland, friend of Wesley. The Rector's influence and his library were at his elbow.

Patrick saved money, and nurtured his patrons. He was regarded as a rising young star and in 1802 it was arranged that he should go to St John's College, Cambridge. He arrived there with the status of Sizar (entitled, thereby, to receive an allowance from the College) on 1 October. He left in 1806 with a respectable BA. Of his intermediate life little is known, but obviously nothing had happened to deflect him from what seems to have been an early ambition to enter the Church. Later in 1806 he was ordained Deacon at Fulham chapel, and was subsequently licensed to his first curacy at Weathersfield in Essex.

His landlady there was Miss Mildred Davy whose niece was Mary Mildred Davy Burder who lived but three miles away. The susceptible young Irishman was much attracted to her and she to him. Ordination as a priest of the established Church on 21 December 1807 does not seem to have turned his mind towards marriage – a goal of most young curates of the time – and the affair with Mary Burder, of whatever intensity it was, appears just to have ended. Whether its end was bittersweet or sad or acrimonious we do not know, but Mary Burder was brought back into his life some fourteen years later, with results that only too clearly suggest the acid taste.

In January 1809 Patrick became assistant curate at Wellington in Shropshire (there was an insistent northerly bias to his career), where he was hard-working and much liked. There he met a fellow-curate – the Rev. William Morgan BA, a rotund, cheerful, rosy-cheeked Welshman. They became firm and lifelong friends, and Morgan's name figures large in the subsequent Brontë family history as a frequent witness and sympathetic participant in the actualities and official recordings of marriage and death. But in this green time of Patrick Brontë's life Morgan's influence was crucial. He was in close touch with many Wesleyans and Evangelicals in Yorkshire, and was almost certainly instrumental in forwarding the process which eventually saw Patrick's removal further north to Dewsbury, Hartshead, Thornton and eventually to Haworth – in the very heart of Wesley country.

At the end of the first decade of the new century Patrick was not only furthering his career but increasing the amount of his writing of poetry. He had something of the conventional physical image of 'poet'

– a tall, erect figure with almost classical features, auburn hair, a determined expression with pale blue eyes that looked weakened by much study. In the spring of 1810 he published a poem, 'Winter-Evening Thoughts', which was printed in Wakefield. A volume, *Cottage Poems*, appeared in 1811 and, in this, his name was published for the first time as Brontë.

John Fennell, the headmaster of the new Wesleyan academy at Woodhouse Grove, near Guiseley, wanted Patrick as school examiner in 1812. The requirements were to examine the boys especially in Latin and the scriptures. Patrick accepted the appointment, which was for one year. There he met Maria Branwell.

She was born in 1783 at Penzance, fifth daughter of Thomas and Anne Branwell. She came to Woodhouse Grove as companion to her cousin, Jane Fennell, and on 26 August 1812 she wrote what was probably her first letter to the Rev. Patrick Bronte (sic), A.B., Hartshead. What had preceded the letter is suggested in her reference to walks in 'our accustomed rounds' – the process which led to marriage had begun – but for us the most interesting aspect is what it reveals of this woman:

> To Rev. Patrick Bronte, A.B., Hartshead.
> Wood House Grove, September 18th, 1812.
>
> How readily do I comply with my dear Mr. B.'s request! You see, you have only to express your wishes, and as far as my power extends I hesitate not to fulfil them. My heart tells me that it will always be my pride and pleasure to contribute to your happiness, nor do I fear that this will ever be inconsistent with my duty as a Christian. My esteem for you and my confidence in you is so great, that I firmly believe you will never exact anything from me which I could not conscientiously perform. I shall in future look to you for assistance and instruction whenever I may need them, and hope you will never withhold from me any advice or caution you may see necessary.
>
> For some years I have been perfectly my own mistress, subject to no control whatever – so far from it, that my sisters who are many years older than myself, and even my dear mother, used to consult me in every case of importance, and scarcely ever doubted the propriety of my opinions and actions. Perhaps you will be ready to accuse me of vanity in mentioning this, but you must consider that I do not boast of it, I have many times felt it a disadvantage; and although, I thank God, it never led me into error, yet, in circumstances of perplexity and doubt, I have deeply felt the want of a guide and instructor.

On Tuesday, 29 December 1812 Patrick and Maria were married by William Morgan at St Oswald's Church, Guiseley, not far from

Woodhouse Grove. It is not without possibility, on the evidence of Patrick's subsequent attempts to find a second wife after Maria's death, that his notions of a love-match were not unmixed with his requirements for a housekeeper and mother-to-be. But in marrying Maria he was joining himself to a woman of more than usual sensibility.

Nine of Maria's letters to Patrick survive, and they provide more than sufficient evidence that she had remarkable mental and emotional qualities, that her writing was unusually fluent, graceful and incisive and that Patrick Brontë was a very fortunate man to have met a woman of such fidelity, delicacy of feeling and subtle humour:

> My Dearest Friend, Having spent the day yesterday at Miry Shay, a place near Bradford, I had not got your letter till my return in the evening, and consequently have only a short time this morning to write if I send it by this post. You surely do not think you *trouble* me by writing? No, I think I may venture to say if such were your opinion you would *trouble* me no more. Be assured, your letters are and I hope always will be received with extreme pleasure and read with delight. May our Gracious Father mercifully grant the fulfillment of your prayers! Whilst we depend entirely on Him for happiness, and receive each other and all our blessings as from His hands, what can harm us or make us miserable? Nothing temporal or spiritual.
>
> Jane had a note from Mr Morgan last evening, and she desires me to tell you that the Methodists' service in church hours is to commence next Sunday week. You may expect frowns and hard words from her when you make your appearance here again, for, if you recollect, she gave you a note to carry to the Doctor, and he has never received it. What have you done with it? If you can give a good account of it you may come to see us as soon as you please and be sure of a hearty welcome from all parties. Next Wednesday we have some thoughts, if the weather be fine, of going to Kirkstall Abbey once more, and I suppose your presence will not make the walk less agreeable to any of us.

Maria's letters also show her to have been very direct in address and, while preserving the proprieties and priorities, never to have allowed either to obscure the truth:

> Oh, what sacred pleasure there is in the idea of spending an eternity together in perfect and uninterrupted bliss! This should encourage us to the utmost exertion and fortitude. But whilst I write, my own words condemn me – I am ashamed of my own indolence and backwardness to duty. May I be more careful, watchful, and active than I have ever yet been!

My uncle, aunt, and Jane request me to send their kind regards, and they will be happy to see you any time next week whenever you can conveniently come down from Bradford. Let me hear from you soon – I shall expect a letter on Monday. Farewell, my dearest friend. That you may be happy in yourself and very useful to all around you is the daily earnest prayer of yours truly,

Maria Branwell.

She was not afraid of berating him if she felt it necessary – and it would appear that he had a forgetful nature which often created difficulties and embarrassments:

Sat. morn. – I do not know whether you dare show your face here again or not after the blunder you have committed. When we got to the house on Thursday evening, even before we were within the doors, we found that Mr and Mrs Bedford had been there, and that they had requested you to mention their intention of coming – a single hint of which you never gave! Poor I too came in for a share in the hard words which were bestowed upon you, for they all agreed that I was the cause of it. Mr Fennell said you were certainly *mazed*, and talked of sending you to York [asylum], etc. And even I begin to think that *this*, together with the *note*, bears some marks of *insanity!* However, I shall suspend my judgement until I hear what excuse you can make for yourself. I suppose you will be quite ready to make one of some kind or another.

And sometimes his forgetfulness hurt:

How could my dear friend so cruelly disappoint me? Had he known how much I had set my heart on having a letter this afternoon, and how greatly I felt the disappointment when the bag arrived and I found there was nothing for me, I am sure he would not have permitted a little matter to hinder him. But whatever was the reason of your not writing, I cannot believe it to have been neglect or unkindness, therefore I do not in the least blame you, I only beg that in future you will judge of my feelings by your own, and if possible never let me expect a letter without receiving one.

Maria's expression of her innermost feelings has all the controlled passion, honesty of purpose and spiritual certitude that (the comparison is inescapable) we find in Charlotte's novels:

My Dear Saucy Pat, Now don't you think you deserve this epithet far more than I do that which you have given me? I really know not what to make of the beginning of your last; the winds, waves, and rocks almost stunned me. I thought you were giving me the account of some terrible dream, or that you had had a presentiment of the fate of my poor box, having no idea that your lively imagination could make so much of the slight reproof conveyed in my last. What will you say when you get a *real, downright scolding?* Since you show such a readiness to atone for your offences after receiving a mild rebuke, I am inclined to hope you will seldom deserve a severe one. I accept with pleasure your atonement, and send you a free and full forgiveness. But I cannot allow that your affection is more deeply rooted than mine. However, we will dispute no more about this, but rather embrace every opportunity to prove its sincerity and strength by acting in every respect as friends and fellow-pilgrims travelling the same road, actuated by the same motives, and having in view the same end. I think if our lives are spared twenty years hence I shall then pray for you with the same, if not greater, fervour and delight that I do now. I am pleased that you are so fully convinced of my candour, for to know that you suspected me of a deficiency in this virtue would grieve and mortify me beyond expression.

What Charlotte's deepest emotions must have been when, late in life, her father showed her her mother's letters we can now only imagine. Perhaps she recognized a kindred spirit breathing through their lines and possibly had some realization of the source of her own art and craft of setting the soul's story down on paper.

Little else is known of Maria Brontë, other than bare biographical details of birth and death, and a brief glimpse in Charlotte's memory of her playing in the rectory garden with the infant Branwell.

We may infer that the happiest times of her married life were spent at Thornton, a village in the Bradford diocese where Patrick officiated. They seem to have had a busy social life, for all the village's smallness; her children were born there; they all made lifelong friends there, and Patrick was well loved.

He must, however, have been aware that over the moors at some ten miles' distance was the larger village and more important parish of Haworth, important for its relative size and for the resonances of its recent religious history. A certain William Grimshaw had been appointed Haworth's perpetual curate in May 1742, and Haworth had gained much fame during his time there.

Grimshaw was powerful, physically and spiritually. He dealt with his parishioners with a blunt directness, even coarseness, but with inner compassion and practical kindness. He was a mixture of evangelist and worker-priest. He would walk scores of miles to help the needy. He rampaged into public houses and whipped astounded drinkers to church; if he met anyone on the moors he would stop them and make them pray. It was said that if a dying person refused to see him he would pray very loudly outside the window so that, 'At least he will die with the word of God in his lugs.'

At his invitation John and Charles Wesley frequently preached at Haworth where the latter 'never saw a church better filled'. Other famous evangelists clamoured to preach there, and Grimshaw invited them, one after another. Selina, Countess of Huntingdon, related how during the sermon by one such evangelist – George Whitefield – a man cried out and fell dead. Grimshaw could not miss such an opportunity, and shouted, 'Brother Whitefield, you stand amongst the dead and the dying – an immortal soul has been called into eternity – the destroying angel is passing over the congregation, cry aloud, and spare not.' At which injunction, the Countess records, a person next to her obliged by also falling dead.

By 1760 Grimshaw ranked third in the Methodist hierarchy, after John and Charles Wesley: indeed John decided that if he and his brother died first Grimshaw should become trustee for all the Methodist circuits.

Through Grimshaw, therefore, Haworth had acquired some (if different) fame before the Brontës perpetuated it. His name and reputation still resonated when Patrick Brontë arrived in Yorkshire.

On 25 May 1819 the Rev. James Charnock, incumbent at Haworth, died. He had been there since 1791. The Rev. Samuel Redhead, who had looked after the parish during Charnock's last illness, was asked to continue the curacy until a successor was appointed. In June the Vicar of Bradford, Henry Heap, announced Patrick as the successor. But by a deed of 1559 the Trustees of Haworth had the right to reject the Vicar of Bradford's nominee; they could refuse to pay him. Heap had not consulted them and when they heard of Patrick's appointment they were considerably affronted. Patrick decided to visit Haworth and talk to the Trustees. In fact he seems to have spoken to only one – an influential one – Stephen Taylor, who suggested he should send his resignation to the Vicar of Bradford, wait a month or two for tempers to subside, then apply to the trustees for the living.

Patrick wrote as Taylor suggested, but the reaction from Heap and other influential ecclesiastics was that he should not resign – it would highly displease the Archbishop (of York). So Patrick withdrew his resignation and told Taylor so, but a week later reversed his decision, and told Taylor so again.

This salved the trustees' pride and they agreed to appoint Brontë, but first they wanted to hear him preach. His reaction, considering how much he presumably wanted the job, was remarkable. His Irish spirit rose and on 21 July 1819 he wrote to the Trustees a letter in whose lines burned an evangelical, protesting fire. The gist of it was that he resented their demand that he should preach a sermon at Haworth before them, so that they could assess his competence and worthiness for the post. But the Trustees' response was adamant – if Patrick would not preach to order at Haworth, they would not travel to order to hear him preach elsewhere!

Henry Heap, who handled the whole affair with what seems consummate absence of tact, decreed that Samuel Redhead should continue. He and two colleagues administered at Haworth while Patrick remained at Thornton.

By September matters were brought to a head when Patrick was commanded by the Archbishop to preach in Haworth Church – this cut right across his pride, but on 15 October 1819 he went to preach at St Michael's, Haworth. Patrick made it clear that he accepted the Trustees' right to their share in his appointment; they, in turn, informed the Vicar of Bradford and the blundering Heap, that they could not accept him as the Vicar's nominee alone, but only as a jointly agreed nominee. Heap made no attempt at reconciliation and decided to give the living to someone else. He then appointed the hapless Redhead as perpetual curate.

The first Sunday of Redhead's incumbency saw a crowded church. During the second lesson, however, the entire congregation rose to its feet and marched out noisily leaving Redhead and his clerk as sole occupants. The following Sunday proceedings were more violently disrupted. During the second lesson a man rode into the church on an ass, facing the tail, with a pile of hats on his head, and urged the beast round the aisles to hoots of laughter.

Redhead made one further attempt to conduct a normal service, but the third Sunday, 14 November 1819, brought disaster. He rode up Haworth village hill accompanied by several Bradford gentlemen. They left their horses at the Black Bull inn and went into the church. There awaiting him was an inebriated soot-covered chimney-sweep. He stood below the pulpit and grimaced a great deal while Redhead preached. Eventually he tried to climb the pulpit's three-decker steps in order to kiss the minister. Chaos erupted; sweep, Bradford gents and minister were swept out of the church and into a pile of soot in the churchyard. They found refuge from a wild chasing mob in the Black Bull. Sugden, the kindly landlord, ensured their escape from the rear of the Bull and they disappeared out of town. Redhead went back to his former incumbency at Horton, near Bradford, an unfortunate victim of botched bureaucracy and angry pride. He had incited nothing, being a kind, considerate man.

The incredible Henry Heap, after accepting Redhead's resignation from Haworth, now nominated two or three other clergymen. Only after a further flurry of letters, including one to his Grace, the Archbishop of York, was the matter settled and Patrick, having performed his last ceremony – a baptism – at Thornton in February 1820, proceeded to get ready to go to Haworth where he was now established as perpetual curate.

One waggon and seven carts took Mrs Brontë, the Rev. Brontë, Elizabeth, Maria, Charlotte, Emily, Branwell and the baby, Anne, to Haworth on Thursday, 20 April 1820. They were accompanied by Nancy and Sarah Garrs, nurses to the children and general cooks and bottle-washers. They were presumably met at least by the sexton, William Brown, and possibly his teenage son, John, who was to figure large in Branwell's life in years to come. But of that and of her daughters' fortunes Maria Brontë was to know nothing. In seventeen months she was to die.

Cancer approached her suddenly, not with stealth, but it held its final stab for several agonizing months. She died on 15 September 1821 and her burial service at Haworth was performed by William Morgan. Her death was a terrible harbinger of domestic tragedy for Patrick, but even in his grief that curious reserve, almost verging upon detachment, is apparent. Two months after his wife's death he wrote to his friend, the Rev. John Duckworth, at Dewsbury:

And when my dear wife was dead, and buried, and gone, and when I missed her at every corner, and when her memory was hourly revived by the innocent, yet distressing prattle, of my children, I do assure you, my dear Sir, from what I felt, I was happy at the recollection, that to sorrow, not as those without hope, was no sin; that our Lord Himself had wept over His departed friend; and that He had promised us grace and strength sufficient for such a day. Indeed, throughout all my troubles, He stood by me and strengthened me, and kindly remembered mercy in judgement; and when the scene of death was over, and I had incurred considerable debts, from causes which I could neither foresee, nor prevent, He raised me up friends to whom I had never mentioned my straitened circumstances, who dispensed their bounty to me in a way truly wonderful, and evidently in answer to prayer. I received on one day, quite unexpectedly, from a few wealthy friends in Bradford, not less than *one hundred and fifty pounds!* I received also several pounds from my old and very kind friend at Bradford (William Morgan, bless his heart), *fifty pounds* as a donation from the Society in London; and what is, perhaps, not less wonderful than all, a few days ago, I got a letter, containing a bank post bill, of the value of *fifty pounds*, which was sent to me by a benevolent individual, a wealthy lady, in the West Riding of Yorkshire.

Patrick spent the rest of his life in Haworth, making but few excursions, some of them abroad. He did not by any means hide himself from the world but, in the parsonage, he spent long hours alone. His introspection, intermittent though it might be, was real. Patrick was a decided mixture of loner and gregariously spirited man. He would not have been so successful a person had he always shrunk from the contact of his fellow men.

His introspection was in sharp contrast to his lust for activity and action. He never ceased, despite his faithful adherence to the Anglican calling, to be an evangelical with leanings to the passion and fire of Wesleyan Methodism. Moreover his political persuasion, which was Tory, was not one of passive acceptance but of a frequently indignant disposition to protest and to demand reform. He loved the physical effort of walking and riding, he seemed to excel in the drama of the sermon, and his obsession with military matters and the activities of war seems often to have produced behaviour (like shooting off his pistol in the early morning) which terrified his flock.

He wrote to the Master General of the Ordnance making a case that British army muskets should be three inches longer than they were, and suggesting a number of improvements in design. In Haworth parsonage there is extant a plan-drawing of his for what seems like a particularly devilish bomb. All the children were excited and inspired by men of action and by soldiers in particular. Small wonder that they were.

But behind the action, the talk of it, and the controlled drama of his writing, was the introspective man. His poems, the progeny of his silent hours, are, frankly, of little value – jog-trot iambics, mawkish sentiments, conventional themes – they are all exemplified in almost any section of five or ten lines one chooses:

Ye feathered songsters of the grove,
Sweet Philomel and cooing dove,
Goldfinch and linnet gray,
And mellow thrush, and blackbird loud,
And lark, shrill warbler of the cloud,
Where do ye pensive stray?
The milk white thorn, the leafy spray,
The fragrant grove, and summer's day,
Are seen by you no more;
Ah! May you light on friendly sheds,
To hide your drooping pensive heads,
From winter's chilling roar.

('Winter')

He seems, however, to have been a very fine preacher and just as capable of high-sounding dramatics as he was of quiet, graceful simplicities. When he preached a sermon on the meaning of the minor earthquake which occurred near Haworth in September 1824, he must have held the congregation's attention by his directness.

> As the day was exceedingly fine, I had sent my little children, who were indisposed, accompanied by servants, to take an airing on the common, and as they stayed rather longer than I expected, I went to an upper chamber to look for their return. The heavens over the moors were blackening fast. I heard the muttering of distant thunder, and saw the frequent flashing of lightning. Though ten minutes before, there was scarcely a breath of air stirring, the gale freshened rapidly, and carried along with it clouds of dust and stubble; by this time, some large drops of rain, clearly announced an approaching heavy shower. My little family has escaped to a place of shelter, but I did not know it.

But when, in September 1842, he preached the funeral sermon of his curate, the Rev. William Weightman, dead at twenty-eight of cholera and beloved of Anne Brontë, he surely wrung their hearts:

> As he was himself a friend to many, and an enemy to none, so by a kind of reaction, he had, I think I might say, no enemies and many friends. He was a conscientious Churchman, and true Protestant – but tolerant to all his differing brethren; where he could not cordially unite, he determined that separation should be no ground of hostility... Thus, our reverend friend lived – but, it may be asked, how did he die? During his illness, I generally visited him twice a day, joined with him in prayer, heard his request for the prayers of this congregation ... heard of his pious admonitions to his attendants, and saw him in tranquility close his eyes on this bustling, vain, selfish world; so that I may truly say, his end was peace, and his hope glory...

Perhaps it was his quite marked diversity of character which gave Patrick a blessed access of a liberal spirit which distinguishes him from some of his Methodist Wesleyan friends and colleagues. His mind did not always contemplate piety or the immortal soul or right behaviour; at times his imagination took him to war's ramparts, to the utmost frontiers of the explored world, to the despatch box of Westminster. He could never have been a Wesley or a Grimshaw simply because he had an instinct towards curiosity. They travelled on tracks laid for them; so did he, but his had points and junctions unknown to them.

He made his small but varied library accessible to his children, and they obviously made great use of it. It included a book on anatomy, an historical grammar, a biography of Scott, his *The Lay of the Last Minstrel*, Dryden's *Virgil*, Byron's works, and the like. He was an avid reader of newspapers and informative/critical periodicals like *Blackwood's*, and his children had a like enthusiasm – the day some new number was due seems to have put them en fête for its arrival. He taught them English, geography and history, and the classics – the evidence of his good teaching is the knowledge which became embedded in their imagination and is present everywhere in their writings. He seems to have been fond of discussion and debate with his children, and Maria, in particular, was revealed as outstanding in these encounters.

Myths and legends are no less prevalent about the Brontës than about other notabilities. It is these which the majority of people best know and accept for fact. A well-authenticated episode (the source is a letter from Patrick Brontë to Mrs Gaskell) throws bright illumination both on the children and the father:

> When my children were very young, when as far as I can remember the oldest was about ten years of age, and the youngest about four – thinking that they knew more than I had yet discover'd, in order to make them speak with less timidity, I deem'd that if they were put under a sort of cover, I might gain my end – and happening to have a mask in the house, I told them all to stand and speak boldly from under cover of the mask. I began with the youngest [Anne]. I asked what a child like her most wanted. She answered, age and experience. I asked the next [Emily] what I had best do with her brother Branwell, who was sometimes a naughty boy. She answered, reason with him, and when he won't listen to reason, whip him. I asked Branwell what was the best way of knowing the difference between the intellects of men and women. He answer'd, by considering the difference between them as to their bodies. I then asked Charlotte what was the best book in the world. She answer'd, the Bible. And what was the next best? She answer'd, the Book of Nature. I then asked the next [Elizabeth] what was the best mode of education for a woman. She answer'd, that which would make her rule her house well. Lastly, I asked the oldest, what was the best mode of spending time. She answer'd, by laying it out in preparation for a happy eternity. I may not have given you precisely their words, but I have nearly done so, as they made a deep and lasting impression on my memory. The substance, however, was what I have stated . . .

Aged memory may have tidied the answers somewhat, but it is important that this is what an old man remembered of his dead children. Intrigued by what it tells us of those children we may be inclined to ignore what it says of the father. This was an act of imagination born of affectionate curiosity about his children. It surely supports the strong impressions of his intellectual and emotional liberalism.

Did he have his favourite among his children? When Charlotte wrote to Ellen Nussey on the death of Branwell she said, 'My poor father naturally thought more of his *only* son than of his daughters, and, much and long as he had suffered on his account, he cried out for his loss like David for that of Absalom – My son! my son! – and refused at first to be comforted. . .' When Emily died he is said by some to have lost the one he felt nearest to. When Anne died, Charlotte spared him the anguish of attending her funeral, and he seems to have concurred with the general opinion that in a sense Anne's passing, in its astonishing resignation, patience and strength of courage, was more to be accepted as an example than grieved over for its sadness. When Charlotte died he wrote a number of letters to those who knew her, and subsequently to Mrs Gaskell. These contain formal expressions of his grief, but here and there he shows the extent to which he had relied upon her and admired her, perhaps even more than he loved her. 'I never knew one less selfish than she was, or more disposed to suffer herself, to save others from suffering' (to Mrs Gaskell, 20 June 1855). 'Sometimes, Charlotte walk'd out alone, and when she return'd home her countenance seem'd lighted up with delighted contemplation. She was an ardent admirer of the sublime and beautiful – it often seem'd to me, however, that the sublime was the greater favourite. . . At the different schools she was at, she always distinguished herself – and generally got the highest award. . .' (to Mrs Gaskell, 24 July 1855).

It was probably Branwell's death that seared him most. He was the only son, he showed high promise as a child, and in youth he flattered many times by his apparent talents, only to deceive. We have an impression that, perhaps, Anne was least close to him: her absolute piety may have pleased his soul, but its accompanying diffidence may well have irritated his volatile spirit. Emily who, if the story be true, is the one he taught to shoot, shared deeply his love of dogs and of physical activity and is perhaps the one with whom he felt most kinship.

He seems to have concerned himself little with their literary work – 'when my daughters were at home they read their mss to each other and gave their candid opinions of what was written. I never interfered with them at such times – I judged it best to throw them upon their own responsibility. . . I never saw their works till they appeared in print' (to Mrs Gaskell, 20 June 1855). When he saw *Jane Eyre* in print he produced one of those memorable *mots* that have the force of aphorism: he pronounced it as 'better than likely'.

But when he left them to their own judgement he did it consciously, for this man seems to have had an instinct that his group of progeny was to be left free, for it was extraordinary. As he later wrote to Mrs Gaskell:

> When mere children, as soon as they could read and write, Charlotte and her brother and sisters used to invent and act little plays of their own, in which the Duke of Wellington, my daughter Charlotte's hero, was sure to come off the conquering hero – when a dispute would not infrequently arise amongst them regarding the comparative merits of him, Bonaparte, Hannibal and Caesar. When the argument got warm and rose to its height, as their mother was then dead, I had sometimes to come in as arbitrator and settle the dispute according to the best of my judgement. Generally, in the management of these concerns, I frequently thought I discovered signs of rising talent which I had seldom, or never before, seen in any of their age. As they had few opportunities of being in learned and polished society, in their retired country situation, they formed a little society amongst themselves – with which they seem'd contented and happy. After they got older, and had been at different good schools, the same habits and ways of proceeding were carried out by them, during the vacations and at other opportunities, only then, their compositions and plots were more matur'd and had less of romance and more of taste and judgement. They often walked out together, in company with a favourite dog, and express'd themselves greatly pleas'd with the beautiful irregularity of uncultivated nature.

Whatever else he may have been, Patrick Brontë was a shrewd and wise father.

But what a different idea of the man we get when we contemplate his relationships with women. Perhaps, indeed, Maria Brontë is even the more to be admired for having tackled him and handled him apparently so well. If the now missing letters which he wrote to her about love and marriage were of the same type as those he wrote to another woman, after Maria's death, then his wife's magnificent replies, which we have noted, acquire an even greater resonance.

His eventual relationship (not, of course, a 'romantic' one) with Elizabeth Gaskell, was stormy, though she was not entirely blameless. But in general he seems to have had an unfailing ability to get hold of the wrong end of the female stick. He was completely tactless. At the end of 1821, soon after Maria's death, he proposed marriage to Elizabeth Firth, a family friend from Thornton days. Any unfavourable feelings which may be generated by this haste can tolerate some mitigation – after all, he was left with four young children, a large house and, moreover, Elizabeth was no stranger to him. But what did he write, and what was its manner, that prompted her to respond so swiftly, and so positively negatively? It was all over in a flurry of four days.

But this was a mere dummy run for what happened in the period beginning 21 April 1823 when, incredibly, and after having been subject to a great many rumours in the Haworth area about who was to be the next 'victim' of his marital intentions, he wrote to Mrs Burder, the mother of that Mary Burder with whom he had had no contact whatsoever for fourteen years. This letter contains no direct proposal to marry Mary – but its very indirectness is so studied as to blazon forth what he is really after. It is an attempt at tactics which founders on the reefs of tactlessness.

He reminds Mrs Burder that it is fourteen years since he had any contact with her, then he gives a brief account of his activities, emphasizing his perpetual curacy at Haworth and adding, 'it is mine for life, no one can take it from me' – as if it were a recommendation. His avoidance of explicit mention of marriage is undercut by his studied emphasis on widowhood and by his evasion of the fact that he has four young children, although he does say that the church has a large congregation – another recommendation?

He eventually comes to some kind of point: the letter now inquires about the marital status and welfare (in that order) of all her children. He encloses a post-paid envelope for her reply!

It took Mrs Burder a long time to reply – and her letter is not extant – but, nothing daunted, he directed his next letter to Mary Burder. He says, 'I experienced a very agreeable sensation in my heart, at this moment, in reflecting that you are *still* single, and so selfish as to wish you to remain so, even if you would never allow me to see you.' His next sentence is a masterpiece of inept strategy – '*You* were the *first* whose hand I solicited, and, no doubt, I was the *first* to whom *you* promised to give that hand.' He says he still loves her after fifteen years and hopes he is wiser and better than he was. He has a '*small*', but '*sweet*' little family, who have 'endearing little ways' and who soothe his heart. He sets the seal on this consummate exercise in self-destruction by saying that, 'I want but *one* addition to my comforts, and then I think I should wish for no more on this side eternity.' In other words – one more card (Mary Burder) and he has a nap hand! As a back-up he actually gives the name of the Vicar of Dewsbury as a reference. Then he asks if he may come down to see Mary in Essex.

That letter asks for trouble but the coruscating reply sent on 8 August 1823 makes it clear that Mary Burder had no cause to recall his behaviour of fifteen years before with any joy whatsoever, quite apart from her contempt for his sudden announcement of his rediscovered love for her.

She begins with ruffled coolness, addressing him as 'Reverend Sir' and immediately declaring that his letter produced 'sensations of surprise and agitation'. She finds it difficult to define his motives for writing, saying that after his long silence she cannot understand why he should write again. But she has been reviewing that long-past time – 'This review, Sir, excites in my bosom increased gratitude and thankfulness to that wise, that indulgent Providence which then watched over me for good and withheld me from forming in the very early life an indissoluble engagement with one whom I cannot think was clear of duplicity.'

What disturbed her so profoundly years ago and still rankles so gratingly we will never know but if, as appears, she did not speak up then, she does not flinch now – 'Many communications were received from you in humble silence which ought rather to have met with contempt and indignation considering the sacredness of a promise . . . indeed I must give a decided negative to the desired visit.' That sounds very like an accusation of breach of promise. She says she shares his sorrow for she has lost a brother as he has lost a wife and been left with poor 'little innocents', but even this access of remorse is streaked with most penetrating sarcasm – 'The Lord can supply all your and their needs. It gives me pleasure always to hear the work of the Lord prospering. May he enable you to be as faithful, as zealous, and as successful a labourer in his vineyard as was one of your predecessors, the good old Mr Grimshaw who occupied the pulpit at Haworth more than half a century ago, then will your consolations be neither few nor small.'

Patrick's singular inability to stop when the going was getting too rough now became inextricably mixed up with pride and perhaps a suspicion of false report. He waited, however, until 1 February 1824 (an unconscionable time for one who says he is so much in love) before replying. His opening is superbly inappropriate: 'Dear Madam, In the first place, I wish you the compliments of the season.' Then follow tendentious-sounding remarks about the love of the Lord. He says that many things in her letter surprised and grieved him, that she might have spared him 'many keen sarcasms'. He confesses he has done things for which he is sorry but these were committed in very difficult circumstances which 'were produced chiefly by yourself' – which remark is a wild scattering of grapeshot. He adds that even if she hates him now, he is sure that she once loved him, but he is at a loss, he says, to know what it was he said those many years ago that has so displeased her. He apologizes if what he said was 'unbecoming and improper' but he claims not to know – this suggests some actions or words in addition to the probable breach of promise which Mary has hugged to her vengeful and hurt bosom. He recalls their walks, and says that if she married him she would be happier than she now is or ever can be. He again asks if she has any objection to his visiting her, if only that they might meet as friends.

The letter remained unanswered. Later in 1824 Mary Burder married the Dissenting Minister of the Wethersfield Meeting House. In his old age Patrick sent her a photograph of himself!

There is something which it has become customary to call 'Irish' in this episode between Patrick and Mary Burder. The strange mixture of comic and pathetic, the outrageous, unexpected responses, the indefatigable determination to press on in the face of impossible odds, the venom mixed with sentiment. In short, the sad endearing lunacy of it all. Two very notable episodes of Patrick's life fall into this category – one wished upon him, the other (this one) wished upon himself. The story of his acquisition of Haworth perpetual curacy has many of the ingredients of the Mary Burder saga. One side of Patrick's character seemed very vulnerable both to creating and being magnetized by events which seem to become high fable even as they happen.

The dichotomy in Patrick's character is very well, although unconsciously, implied in Ellen Nussey's reminiscences of her first visit to the parsonage in 1833. It is a vivid portrait of the Brontë environment and of its volatile pater familias:

> There was not much carpet anywhere except in the sitting-room and on the study floor. The hall floor and stairs were done with sandstone, always beautifully clean, as everything was about the house; the walls were not papered, but stained in a pretty dove-coloured tint; hair-seated chairs and mahogany tables, book shelves in the study, but not many of these elsewhere. Scant and bare indeed, many will say, yet it was not a scantness that made itself felt. Mind and thought, I had almost said elegance, but certainly refinement, diffused themselves over all, and made nothing really wanting.
>
> A little later on, there was the addition of a piano [in Patrick's study]. Emily, after some application, played with precision and brilliancy. Anne played also, but she preferred soft harmonies and vocal music. She sang a little; her voice was weak, but very sweet in tone. [Branwell also played the piano – and the organ.]
>
> Mr Brontë's health caused him to retire early. He assembled his household for family worship at eight o'clock; at nine he locked and barred the front door, always giving as he passed the sitting-room door a kindly admonition to the 'children' not to be late; half-way up the stairs he stayed his steps to wind up the clock, the clock that in after days seemed to click like a dirge in the refrain of Longfellow's poem, 'The Old Clock on the Stairs': 'Forever-never! Never-

forever!' Every morning was heard the firing of a pistol from Mr Brontë's room window.

On Monday, 13 December 1852, Arthur Bell Nicholls asked Charlotte to marry him. He was Patrick's curate, thirty-four years old, and of Scottish descent, though with strong connections in Ireland. He had been at Haworth since 1845. For the few weeks before his declaration of love to Charlotte his mood had been nervous, his appetite bad, his attention to his duties scattered – and Patrick had noted this. Charlotte reports that he had commented on Nicholls's symptoms with 'little sympathy and much indirect sarcasm'. His reaction to the proposal is expressed also by Charlotte – 'The veins on his temples started up like whipcord, and his eyes became suddenly bloodshot. I made haste to promise that Mr Nicholls should, on the morrow, have a distinct refusal. . .' Charlotte adds that her own 'blood boiled with a sense of injustice, but Papa worked himself into a state not to be trifled with. . .'

The atmosphere generated in the parsonage by Nicholls's own state of mind and Patrick's ill-disguised animosity must have been electric. Charlotte, to judge from her letters, was the coolest of them all – a remarkable achievement in circumstances so near to flash-point as this letter to Ellen Nussey suggests;

> You ask how papa demeans himself to Mr Nicholls. I only wish you were here to see papa in his present mood; you would know something of him. He just treats him with a hardness not to be bent, and a contempt not to be propitiated. The two have had no interview as yet: all has been done by letter. Papa wrote, I must say, a most cruel note to Mr Nicholls on Wednesday. . .

Why did Patrick react so strongly against Nicholls? Perhaps it was because Nicholls was a Puseyite, inclining to the belief that in doctrine and discipline the Church of England should move back to that conjectured time when there was no ground for separation between itself and the Church of Rome; this would have been to Patrick as a red rag to a bull. Perhaps it was because he was a mere curate, and not a particularly well-liked one, earning only £100 a year. But Patrick had also voiced the belief that Charlotte was not strong enough for marriage. When later, as Mrs Nicholls, she suffered her fatal illness and the specialist pronounced no hope, he is supposed to have said to their servant, Martha Brown – 'I told you, Martha, that there was no sense in Charlotte marrying at all, for she was not strong enough for marriage.'

But once again a touch of the near-incredible enters into the life of Patrick Brontë. Charlotte says, in the same letter quoted above, that her father believed that Mr Nicholls behaved disingenuously in hiding his intentions towards Charlotte for so long and that he 'forged an Irish fiction' – that is, alleging that the Nicholls family had considerable property in Ireland. In fact they had!

In the midst of all this Nicholls went seriously off his food and his work, and his stock in Haworth did not improve – Martha Brown did not like him and John Brown said he would like to shoot him (Charlotte, letter to Ellen, 5 January 1853). Those were strong enough words, but even their finality seems somehow to lack the menace of a letter Patrick wrote to Charlotte when she was staying in London in the same month:

> You may wish to know how we have all been getting on here, especially in respect to master and man; on yesterday I preached twice, but my man, was every way very quiet – He shun'd me as if I had been a Cobra de Capello – turning his head from the quarter where I was, and hustling away amongst the crowd to avoid contact – it required no Levater to see that his countenance was strongly indicative of mortified pride and malevolent resentment – people have begun to notice these things, and various conjectures are afloat – You thought me too severe – but I was not candid enough – this conduct might have been excus'd by the world in a confirmed rake – or unprincipled Army officer, but in a clergyman, it is justly chargeable with base design and inconsistency – I earnestly wish that he had another and better situation – as I can never trust him any more in things of importance – I wish him no ill – but rather good, and wish that every woman may avoid him forever, unless she should be determined on her own misery.

These sentiments are the more distasteful since the first part of the letter is mawkishly written as if it had been the work of the Brontë dog, Flossie!

Not surprisingly Nicholls made the classic response to the situation – the early nineteenth-century version of flight into the arms of the French Foreign Legion was a speedy retreat into the welcoming bosom of a missionary society. He applied to go to Australia as a missionary. The Assistant Secretary of the Society for the Propagation of the Gospel wrote to Patrick for a testimonial for Nicholls. Again, not surprisingly, Patrick made the classic response – a helpful kick into oblivion, by the aid of transparent hypocrisy. On 1 April 1853, Nicholls withdrew this application, on the grounds of rheumatism!

Throughout all this, there is no indication in Charlotte's extant letters that she felt any love for Nicholls. She stood up for him but without undue firmness, she felt sorry for him, but she exhibits nothing of warm emotion towards him:

I cannot help feeling a certain satisfaction in finding that the people here are getting up a subscription to offer a testimonial of respect to Mr Nicholls on his leaving the place. [A gold watch, engraved with this inscription: 'Presented to the Revd A. B. Nicholls, B.A., by the teachers, scholars, and congregation of St Michael's, Haworth, Yorkshire, May 25th, 1853.'] Many are expressing both their commiseration and esteem for him. The Churchwardens recently put the question to him plainly. Why was he going? Was it Mr Brontë's fault or his own? 'His own,' he answered. Did he blame Mr Brontë? 'No! He did not: if anybody was wrong it was himself.' Was he willing to go? 'No! it gave him great pain.' . . . Papa addressed him at the school tea-drinking, with *constrained* civility, but still with *civility*. He did not reply civilly; he cut short further words. This sort of treatment offered in public is what papa never will forget or forgive; it inspires him with a silent bitterness not to be expressed. . .

Nicholls's testimonial was presented to him on his leaving Haworth. What events led up to this we do not clearly know, and at first even Charlotte did not know Nicholls's destination. In fact it was a curacy at Kirk Smeaton, near Pontefract.

By October 1853 correspondence between Charlotte and Nicholls had begun and in November they decided on marriage. On 28 March 1854 Nicholls returned to Haworth to take up the curacy he had vacated. Some reconciliation, lacking in substance, texture and spirit though it may have been, must have taken place between Patrick and his curate. Two months before her marriage Charlotte wrote to Mrs Gaskell to announce her engagement:

There was much reluctance, and many difficulties to be overcome. . .
Be this as it may, in January last papa gave his sanction for a renewal
of acquaintance. Things have progressed I don't know how. It is no
use going into detail.

On Thursday, 29 June 1854 Charlotte Brontë married Arthur Bell Nicholls at Haworth Church. Sutcliffe Sowden officiated. Ellen Nussey was a bridesmaid and Margaret Wooler (Charlotte's friend and former employer) gave Charlotte away – the latter became thus involved at the very last minute since Patrick refused to attend his daughter to or at the church. Was he trying to avoid hypocrisy, or was he being very 'Irish' about it? – he did not miss the subsequent wedding breakfast!

Patrick Brontë never accommodated himself to Nicholls. After Charlotte's death they lived under the same roof in uneasy truce. As John Brown, the old friend of Branwell said – 'Mister Brontë and Mister Nicholls lived together still *ever* near, but still *ever* separate.'

Patrick's last years must have been in every way twilight ones. Tabitha Aykroyd, one of the last servant links with the old days, died only a few months before the final blow, the death of Charlotte, of whom he was so proud, so severely caring, and perhaps so apprehensive. He had to contend, too, with her posthumous presence in the literary world. The cogs and wheels of the Brontë industry began to turn, if only slowly, before he died. Mrs Gaskell's visits and letters in quest of information for her biography of Charlotte were essential for posterity as it turned out, but probably bothersome to the old man.

Mrs Gaskell was a civilized and kindly woman, but even she seems not to have realized how wounding some of her revelations about Patrick were to him. Their authenticity has become a matter of debate, and in subsequent editions of her book she expunged some of them.

But even at the end there is again a touch of that zany spirit which possessed him. When we look at what he most objected to (though he declared himself to be well satisfied with Mrs Gaskell's book in general) we can easily understand that certain things were not flattering to his character; but they are less defamatory than redolent of a kind of quirky blarney of the personality.

Probably relying on local hearsay, Mrs Gaskell related how he fired his pistol in anger each morning (he fired it, but not in anger); how he stuffed a hearthrug up a chimney and watched it burn (but he was terrified of fire); how he burned some red boots – a present to the children from William Morgan – because they were too flashy (but no one ever reported missing shoes on such a large scale); how he did not allow his children to eat meat (but Emily records in her diary a menu for 'Boiled Beef, Turnips, Potatoes, and apple pudding'); how he destroyed a silk dress of his wife's because it lacked propriety (but this appears to be a distortion of a practical joke).

It is a kind of justice that these matters should be refuted or explained, but it does not alter the fact that they were related of him and, at the least, suggest that he was thought to be a fey man. He denied them all, with great dignity.

And so the pendulum swings again. For if his last years bring examples of that side of him that was vulnerable to the eccentric, the ambiguous, the ridiculous, the preposterous, they also show the other Patrick Brontë – dignified (sometimes to the edge of pomposity), well-meaning, thoughtful and not without shrewdness. In November 1856 he wrote Mrs Gaskell a letter which shows that he knew himself well:

> But the truth of the matter is – that I am, in some respects, a kindred likeness to the father of Margaret, in 'North and South' – peaceable, feeling, sometimes thoughtful – and generally well-meaning. Yet

unlike him in one thing – by occasionally getting into a satirical vein – when I am disposed to dissect and analyze human character and human nature, studying closely its simples and compounds, like a curious surgeon. And, being in early life, thrown on my own resources – and consequently obliged, under Providence, to depend on my own judgement and exertions, I may not be so ready as some are, to be a follower of any man, or a worshipper of conventionalities or forms, which may possibly, to superficial observers, acquire me the character of a little eccentricity. Thus freely have I spoken to you – in order that, in your work, you may insert such facts as may counteract any false statements that have been made, or might be made, respecting me or mine.

And in July 1857, to the same lady, he wrote another which is as good a summing-up of this wracked survivor as could ever be penned:

Had I been numbered amongst the calm, sedate, concentric men of the world, I should not have been as I now am, and I should in all probability never have had such children as mine have been. I have no objection whatever to your representing me as a little eccentrick, since you and other learned friends will have it so – only don't set me on in my fury to burning hearthrugs, sawing the backs of chairs, and tearing my wife's silk gowns – With respect to tearing my wife's silk gown, my dear little daughter must have been misinform'd – This you will be convinced of when I assure you that it was my repeated advice to my wife and children, to wear gowns and outward garments made *only of silk or wool*, as these were less inflammable than cotton or linen – on account of my wife and children all being near-sighted I had an eccentrick dread of accidents by fire.

. . . I have faults – I have many – and, being a Daughter of Eve, I doubt not that you also have some. Let us both try to be wiser and better as Time recedes and Eternity advances.

Charlotte Brontë (1816–1855)

For the majority of those interested in the Brontë family their first reaction to the surname is to prefix the word 'Charlotte'. She is the usual entrée into the family's strange, brooding, rich world of sighs, sorrows and fitful sunshine. It is natural that this should be so. She survived all, except, incredibly, her disease-fearing father; she wrote much more than any of the others; her activities and her character are, quantitatively, very much more on record than those of the rest of her family; she is the subject of one of literature's greatest, most detailed biographical works. It is in Mrs Gaskell's *Life* that we have the most precise description of her appearance:

In 1831, she was a quiet, thoughtful girl of nearly fifteen years of age, very small in figure – 'stunted' was the word she applied to herself, – but as her limbs and head were in just proportion to the slight, fragile body, no word in ever so slight a degree suggestive of deformity could properly be applied to her; with soft, thick, brown hair, and peculiar eyes, of which I find it difficult to give a description, as they appeared to me in her later life. They were large, and well shaped; their colour a reddish brown; but if the iris was closely examined, it appeared to be composed of a great variety of tints. The usual expression was of quiet, listening intelligence; but now and then, on some just occasion for vivid interest or wholesome indignation, a light would shine out, as if some spiritual lamp had been kindled, which glowed behind those expressive orbs. I never saw the like in any other human creature. As for the rest of her features, they were plain, large, and ill set; but, unless you began to catalogue them, you were hardly aware of the fact, for the eyes and power of the countenance over-balanced every physical defect; the crooked mouth and the large nose were forgotten, and the whole face arrested the attention, and presently attracted all those whom she herself would have cared to attract. Her hands and feet were the smallest I ever saw: when one of the former was placed in mine, it was like the soft touch of a bird in the middle of my palm. The delicate long fingers had a peculiar fineness of sensation, which was one reason why all her handiwork, of whatever kind – writing, sewing, knitting – was so clear in its minuteness. She was remarkably neat in her whole personal attire; but she was dainty as to the fit of her shoes and gloves.

So far as posterity was concerned Charlotte therefore had every-thing going for her, and, indeed, it is not an overindulgence to test the validity of her dominant historical status by imagining what, if anything, the status of the Brontë family would now have been had she never lived. The conclusion is inescapable that we would very probably have heard nothing of any of them, and Mrs Gaskell herself might have been allocated to a minor place in the history of the novel instead of a major place in the history of biography. Charlotte was a catalyst as well as being a potent element in her own right. Perhaps without Charlotte's existence and persistence her sisters' work, including, of course, the greatest poems and novel produced by any of them, might never have been published, perhaps never written. Those who believe that Charlotte has received too much of the limelight might well ponder on this.

Nevertheless some might be prepared to sacrifice a portion of the voluminous documentation of and about Charlotte if more could have remained about her artistically greater sister, Emily. Biographers can rest easier with Charlotte after grappling with Branwell and Emily, the complexities of whose personalities are qualitatively taxing. Charlotte's character, by comparison, is taxing more in the width of its activities than in its depth – she was not an unsophisticated woman but she was neither complex nor profound.

In certain ways she directed her family, though that does not mean that Patrick Brontë ever seriously abrogated his responsibilities. Charlotte naturally took the lead in matters connected with the world of publishing, and her own temperament and age relative to her sisters and brother assured her place in the forefront of influence on most of their activities – their Angrian and Gondal worlds, their trips and excursions, and, eventually (where the girls were concerned), their careers as governesses/teachers. In the most important matter of all – their writing – there seems to have been an additional force behind Charlotte's assumption of leadership. She, of them all, seemed to grasp more quickly, easily and firmly the possibility of being a professional writer. For Branwell writing was only one of a number of prestigious alternatives to be dallied with; for Anne, certainly at first, probably a way for the youngest to keep up with the family; and for Emily, simply, but profoundly, a necessity, unaccompanied at first with thoughts of her writing having currency in the world.

Charlotte's part in the Angrian saga was crucial. Her juvenilia, which are still unavailable to the vast majority of readers, testify to her creative, wilful and energetic part in the whole process of their imaginative young lives. Years later her friend and biographer, Mrs Gaskell, was astonished when she held in her hand the tiny hand-stitched books for which the children's imaginations had provided the material and in whose preparation Charlotte had played a major part. Mrs Gaskell wrote, 'They gave one the idea of creative power carried to the verge of insanity.'

Angria became the centre of interest for Charlotte, as for her brother and sisters – as Branwell's overheated prose confirms:

> ... the air suddenly darkened, the hall shook and streams of fire continually flashed through the room, followed by long and loud peals of thunder. While all were standing pale and affrighted at the unusual phenomenon, a dreadful Monster ... entered the room ... and said in a loud voice 'I am the chief Genius Brannii, with me there are 3 others; she, Wellesley, who protects you is named Tallii; she who protects Parry is named Emmii; she who protects Ross is called Annii. Those lesser ones whom ye saw are Genii and Fairies, our slaves and minions ... we are the guardians of you all.

As the complications of illness and responsibilities gradually descended on the Brontë family Charlotte became more and more regarded as the one to turn to – though not exclusively, for Emily, for a time, was there, and Emily never quailed from offering aid and was much loved. But Charlotte's letters show so many preoccupations with her family – her father's money, his health, Anne's health, Branwell's behaviour – that we may wonder if, at times, she did not feel a sense of being some kind of sacrificial victim. In letters written over a period of years the strain of coping shows – at times in something not much short of vehemence:

> The death of Mr Robinson, which took place about three weeks or a month ago, served Branwell for a pretext to throw all about him into hubbub and confusion with his emotions, etc., etc. Shortly after, came news from all hands that Mr Robinson had altered his will before he died and effectually prevented all chance of a marriage between his widow and Branwell, by stipulating that she should not have a shilling if she ever ventured to reopen any communication with him. Of course, he then became intolerable. To papa he allows rest neither day nor night, and he is continually screwing money out of him, sometimes threatening that he will kill himself if it is withheld from him. He says Mrs Robinson is now insane; that her mind is a complete wreck owing to remorse for her conduct towards Mr Robinson (whose end it appears was hastened by distress of mind) and grief for having lost him. I do not know how much to believe of what he says, but I fear she is very ill. Branwell declares that he neither can nor will do anything for himself; good situations have been offered him more than once, for which, by a fortnight's work, he might have qualified himself, but he will do nothing, except drink and make us all wretched.

But more often there is a stoicism that tangs a little of self-pity, as in this letter to W.S. Williams after the death of Emily:

> . . . as to me, God has hitherto most graciously sustained me – so far I have felt adequate to bear my own burden and even to offer a little help to others – I am not ill, – I can get through daily duties – and do something toward keeping hope and energy alive in our mourning household. My father says to me almost hourly, 'Charlotte, you must bear up – I shall sink if you fail me.' These words – you can conceive are a stimulus to nature. The sight too of my sister Anne's very still but deep sorrow wakens in me such fear for her that I dare not falter. Somebody *must* cheer the rest.

But anyone who had to undergo the blows of misfortune so repeatedly as Charlotte might well be excused an indulgence which was not typical of her.

Stoicism rather than self-indulgence was Charlotte's habitual state, and its depth and tenacity was tested hard not only by external circumstance but by her own physical and mental condition. Apart from Anne, who suffered from chronic asthma, Charlotte was probably the unhealthiest of the Brontës. She was frail and perhaps seemed more so to herself, for she gives evidence of being a prey to psychosomatic states, when the left hand of the imagination is in constant and unwanted attention on the right hand of the body's chemistry. Because of this it is not easy fully to grasp the implications of Charlotte's many symptoms. She had frequent bilious attacks, she was badly myopic, she was susceptible to colds, she had at least one severe liver ailment – part of the treatment for which included the administration of mercury which caused, as the least of its results, a terribly ulcerated mouth and loss of voice. She suffered, too, from the fashionable-sounding but unpleasant-looking tic douloureux (a twitching squint) – but she missed the cholera which carried off so many of Haworth's population in the first half of the nineteenth century.

In all probability Charlotte's frail physical presence – she would undoubtedly have become an exquisitely dainty old lady – misled those who met her without knowing her. This small package secreted the most potent contents – the little lady was a formidable reality. But she also nurtured a grief, as Mrs Gaskell reports:

> Much of this nervous dread of encountering strangers I ascribed to the idea of her personal ugliness, which had been strongly impressed upon her imagination early in life, and which she exaggerated to herself in a remarkable manner. 'I notice,' said she, 'that after a stranger has once looked at my face he is careful not to let his eyes wander to that part of the room again!'

We will never know how much emphasis to ascribe to this, but it is not easy to reject its implications. None of her heroines (who have so much of herself in them) are anything but plain; the greatest beauty is often associated in her work either with moral turpitude or with empty-headedness.

But Charlotte's relentless self-knowledge turns our sympathy into a kind of admiration. She may have felt the fates had done badly by her, but she never announced it – on the contrary she often overrode her feelings with fine aplomb:

> We had by no means understood that it was settled we were to go to the Opera, and were not ready. Moreover, we had no fine, elegant dresses with us, or in the world. However, on brief rumination I thought it would be wise to make no objections – I put my headache in my pocket, we attired ourselves in the plain, high-made country garments we possessed, and went with them to their carriage, where we found Mr Williams. They must have thought us queer, quizzical-

looking beings, especially me with my spectacles. I smiled inwardly at the contrast, which must have been apparent, between me and Mr Smith as I walked with him up the crimson-carpeted staircase of the Opera House and stood amongst a brilliant throng at the box door, which was not yet open. Fine ladies and gentlemen glanced at us with a slight, graceful superciliousness quite warranted by the circumstances. Still, I felt pleasantly excited in spite of headache and sickness and conscious clownishness, and I saw Anne was calm and gentle, which she always is.

Charlotte was always embarrassed when she was out of the company of those she knew and could trust. Perhaps she thought that everyone shared her possession of powers of severe observation and appraisal and would, therefore, make her run the gauntlet of their silent, but detailed, disapproval. Perhaps, to use modern vernacular, she wanted to feel normal – the phrase used by all those who are as much conscious of their own deficiencies as they are of others'. No one who has read the first chapter of *Shirley* can have any illusion that Charlotte was a mild commentator on the world and its works. Over even the most affectionate observations (as, writing here to Ellen Nussey of her sister Anne, and Anne's beloved young curate, William Weightman) irony hovers:

> Your darling 'his young reverence' as you tenderly call him – is looking delicate and pale – poor thing don't you pity him? I do from my heart – when he is well and fat and jovial I never think of him – but when anything ails him I am always sorry – He sits opposite to Anne at Church sighing softly and looking out of the corners of his eyes to win her attention – and Anne is so quiet, her looks so downcast – they are a picture – He would be the better of a comfortable wife like you to settle him, you would settle him I believe – nobody else would. – Yours affectionately.
>
> (C.B.)

Charlotte seems to have believed that everyone's judgement of her was in standing water between acceptance and rejection. She might have been happier in the society of the early decades of the eighteenth century, when irony, cynicism and satire gave wit a bad yet gloriously piquant name.

Insufficient attention has been paid to Charlotte's possession of a satirical spirit which had a wide gamut of association and powerful moral propulsion. All her novels, to a degree, contain paragraphs of description, sentences, phrases and, in the case of *Shirley*, one whole chapter (the first) where we become conscious that the novelist's eye has a mocking look, that the lips have that smile which is the prerogative of anyone who enjoys the act of judgement by the

Haworth parsonage and church: drawing by Elizabeth Gaskell

Mrs Maria Brontë

Reverend Patrick Brontë in old age

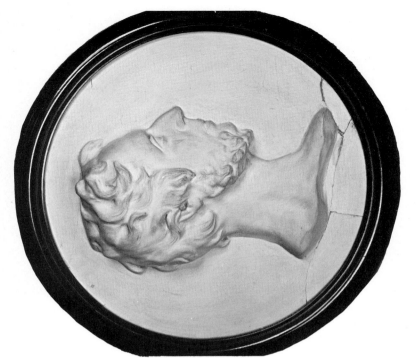

Medallion of Branwell by J. B. Leyland

The three sisters: (*l. to r.*) Anne, Emily and Charlotte: oil
painting by Branwell

Anne: watercolour by Charlotte   Emily (Anne?): oil painting by Branwell

Keeper: watercolour by Emily

application of mockery. But she satirizes only people, and she does it as frequently in her letters as in her novels.

We can only speculate how far this satirical spirit extended in the Brontë family – the father, certainly on the evidence of his letters, took himself very seriously; Branwell was not averse, when in a state of relative intellectual balance, to letting forth a shaft or two of cunning, wounding fun; Anne perhaps took everything seriously, but one guesses that deep inside Emily was a kindred disposition to Charlotte's. The evidence is scant but, in one case, plain enough. This is the first chapter of *Wuthering Heights* where, from time to time, Emily sends out sly scouts of ridicule, occasionally wearing the garb of absurdity:

> Joseph was an elderly, nay, an old man, very old, perhaps, though hale and sinewy.
> 'The Lord help us!' he soliloquized in an undertone of peevish displeasure, while relieving me of my horse: looking, meantime, in my face so sourly that I charitably conjectured he must have need of divine aid to digest his dinner, and his pious ejaculation had no reference to my unexpected advent.
> Wuthering Heights is the name of Mr Heathcliff's dwelling. 'Wuthering' being a significant provincial adjective, descriptive of the atmospheric tumult to which its station is exposed in stormy weather. Pure, bracing ventilation they must have up there, at all times, indeed.

And, for what the stories told of her are worth, they are at least related of no one but Emily; she had a marked liking for pranks in her childhood – it is but a few steps from permissive prankishness to the planned, directed, humour of satire.

There is nothing gentle about Charlotte's satirical gaze, but however much we may speculate on the source of her satirical spirit – and we must not forget her Irish blood – its relentlessness was born out of her never-wavering closeness of observation of the human scene. For one so myopic her awareness of the minutest visual detail is often astonishing, and she also had a fine ear for voices.

Charlotte placed a great deal of weight on the importance of detailed observation of people. Mrs Gaskell and others commented on her watchfulness in company and on the unnerving effect it had on those subjected to it. But she had the great artist's gift of not only applying herself to observation but of being able to store and recall what, to others, would be the unconsidered trifles of life. There is no more telling evidence as to the constancy and consciousness of her observation than in the matter of Anne's illnesses. She comments in her letters on how others do not seem to have observed the changes in

Anne's appearance as she herself has done, and she tacitly reprimands them for it.

Although the affairs of mankind were her abiding subject, her observation (like Emily's) of natural phenomena was exact. In her descriptions, for example, of the weather, a single phrase will frequently give individuality to a cloud, a rainstorm, a shaft of sunlight, which to anyone else would present no singularity:

> The keen, still cold of the morning was succeeded, later in the day,
> by a sharp breathing from Russian wastes: the cold zone sighed over
> the temperate zone, and froze it fast. A heavy firmament, dull, and
> thick with snow, sailed up from the north, and settled over expectant
> Europe. Towards afternoon began the descent. I feared no carriage
> would come, the white tempest raged so dense and wild.

There was a close connection between Charlotte's satirical inclination and her moral principles. When she disapproved of a person, or of a fictional character, it was always on moral grounds and often accompanied by satirical enfilading – as in her portrait of Mrs Yorke in *Shirley*.

But likewise Charlotte also only finally approved on moral grounds; when she did, she put aside her satirical armoury. She could never cement a relationship purely on emotional terms: she did not lack feeling, but, for her, feeling was not enough. Her letters to Ellen Nussey constantly testify to this; time and time again she will seem to be advancing in emotional terms only to call a halt and replace them with sternly moralistic ones, sometimes so severe as to seem aphoristic. Thus the relationships between Caroline and Richard Moore and, particularly, between Jane and Rochester, are in the end bound fast only when all the moral tests have been passed – only then can the emotional receive its licence.

It is worth reflecting that Emily's apparent popularity both as a child and as an adult (though her 'oddness' was also clearly recognized) was in some contrast with the reserve which so many people experienced and expressed about Charlotte. It is dangerous to assume the existence of a line where fiction and actuality are supposed to meet but it is tempting to do so. If one were to follow up this generalization – that Emily was relatively popular and Charlotte was not because the former, odd as she might be, was not averse to showing her emotions occasionally whereas the other never did – into their created work, there is alluring confirmation.

Nowhere in *Wuthering Heights* is moral approval or disapproval allowed to subsume emotional surrender or withdrawal. The relationship of Cathy and Heathcliff might well have morally appalled

Charlotte and, indeed, one reason why her sister's novel seems freer, wider, larger, perhaps more liberal in spirit, is because its deepest human relationships are not at the final mercy of moral dictates. Jane's surrender to Rochester has much in it of love hedged by codicil, but Cathy's absorption by Heathcliff is a triumph of ferocious emotional fusion.

There is nothing whatsoever in accounts of Charlotte's life by her contemporaries, nor in her letters, to suggest that this generalization should be rejected out of hand. On the contrary her life, particularly in the latter part, is to an extent a record of tentative advances followed by decisive withdrawals, both on her part and on the part of others towards her. George Smith perhaps more than anyone had reason to know the stratagems which Charlotte's reserve and moral principles used to prevent access to her natural instincts and desires. He declared that, 'She had an almost exaggerated sense of duty.'

And yet this picture is manifestly incomplete. The letters and the novels equally amply demonstrate her possession of another quality that creates a kind of paradox in her personality. Charlotte had a certain tenderness in her. This reveals itself in her caring. She had no thoughts that she might be putting herself out when she visited, sometimes as representative of her father, but just as frequently from her own volition, the sick, the aged and the dying. Her concern for those in trouble and difficulty is expressed with that softness of expression and uncomplicated sweetness of tone which is the signature of tenderness.

In her fiction this tenderness, equally direct and honest, fulfils a more subtle role. It reveals itself almost exclusively in depictions of relationships which begin with friendship and take it up to and beyond the frontier where love takes over. Jane and Rochester, Caroline and Richard Moore, Caroline and her mother, Jane and Helen Burns – in these and other couples the point where friendship is replaced by love is accompanied by a moment of intensely poignant sweetness which is pure and innocent. Its real name is tenderness. It becomes poignant as the reader is made aware of the fragility of what is happening. Love is about to be born and its coming is accompanied with the softest of the emotions – though this will soon have to give place to the testing of that love by the mechanics of morality. We might well declare, as we feel the moment then see it slip away, that if philosophy may clip an angel's wings morality can paralyse cupid's:

> Till the very close of the evening, he did not indeed, address me at all, yet I felt, somehow, that he was full of friendliness. Silence is of different kinds, and breathes different meanings; no words could inspire a pleasanter content than did M. Paul's wordless presence. When the tray came in, and the bustle of supper commenced, he just

said, as he retired, that he wished me a goodnight and sweet dreams; and a goodnight and sweet dreams I had. (*Villette*.)

There are few other novelists who can arouse quite so intensely in the reader that precise moment when love is recognized, accepted and uninhibitedly celebrated without let or hindrance. There is nothing emotionally vapid about its expression for, yet again, Charlotte's observing eye has seized upon its exact nature. She embodies, in fact, a truth to experience – our own. This evokes and gives a specific shape and delicacy to something we perhaps had forgotten. Charlotte's writing (both fiction and non-fiction) was not immune to the romantic movement. She was not by any means so imbued with it as Emily but her antennae had received some of its signals. Indeed, it is tempting to express the 'romanticism' of Charlotte's depiction of that instant of love's birth with words that Wordsworth, Shelley and Keats would recognize – she depicts the reality of the heart's affection.

But one of the most tenacious aspects of Charlotte's personality was her relentlessly expressed and complete commitment to the unmarried woman without money in society. Adherents of twentieth-century women's 'movements' might be quick to claim Charlotte for their own particular persuasions, but it is doubtful whether Charlotte would find any patience for, or logic in, the confused militancy of so much modern vociferation about the liberation of women. Charlotte's approach was eminently practical, and she was most concerned with the terrible vulnerability to exploitation of all kinds of young women, like herself and her sisters, who were forced by the exigencies of birth, of social situation, to seek employment of the kind described in *Jane Eyre* and *Villette*. These two books are justly acclaimed for many reasons, but it is rare to find, among those reasons, any reference to the fact that they are major examples of a kind of propaganda on behalf of a very large, virtually silent and powerless minority. Earlier, minor and more strident novels like Lady Blessington's *The Governess* (1839) and Elizabeth Sewell's *Amy Herbert* (1844) had spoken out for governesses, and they, with Mary Shelley, can be safely left to be enfolded in the embraces of modern female liberation movements. Charlotte, however, is as much, perhaps more, concerned with the details of particular exploitations as with rhetorical militancy. She recognized the importance of stating the problem before yelling for a solution.

Her attitude was in marked contrast to that of Harriet Taylor Mill, wife of the famous John Stuart Mill who, in an article in *The Westminster Review*, wrote:

The literary class of women are ostentatious in disclaiming their desire for equality or citizenship, and proclaiming their complete satisfaction with the place which society assigns to them, exercising in this, as in many other respects, a most noxious influence over the feelings and opinions of men, who unsuspectingly accept the servilities of toadyism as concessions to the force of truth, not considering that it is the personal interest of these women to profess whatever opinions they expect will be agreeable to men... They depend on men's opinion for their literary as well as for their feminine successes; and such is their bad opinion of men, that they believe there is not more than one in ten thousand who does not dislike and fear strength, sincerity or high spirits in a woman. They are therefore anxious to earn pardon and toleration for whatever of these qualities their writings may exhibit on other subjects, by a display of studied submission on this: that they may give no occasion for vulgar men to say (what nothing will prevent vulgar men from saying), that learning makes women unfeminine, and that literary ladies are likely to be bad wives.

Charlotte's reaction sums up the difference between them:

... well argued it is – clear, logical – but vast is the hiatus of omission, harsh the consequent jar on every finer chord of the soul. What is this hiatus? I think I know; and knowing I will venture to say. I think the writer forgets there is such a thing as self-sacrificing love and disinterested devotion.

But this does not mean that Charlotte was prepared to accept her lot – Charlotte's revenge was to savage some of the employers of governesses that we find in her novels, and to acquire a fame that would make any thought that she needed liberation seem ridiculously superfluous. And one feels on very safe ground indeed in assuming that Emily would have agreed with what she wrote in this letter, which exposes, with an intimacy that mere propaganda can never achieve, the trap of what was called 'service':

I see now more clearly than I have ever done before that a private governess has no existence, is not considered as a living and rational being except as connected with the wearisome duties she has to fulfil.

Some modern sociologists might smile forbearingly if they read Charlotte's words to Emily – 'I would like to work in a mill. I would like to feel mental liberty. I would like this weight of restraint to be taken off.' Surely, even the meanest, dreariest, cruellest employer and environment suffered by a governess could not compare to the horrors of factory life? The facts are that in early Victorian England, governesses were often treated with callous cruelty, were without any personal freedom, often had no one with whom to share their miseries, and were employed for longer hours and poorer wages than many mill-hands.

When we examine and reflect upon what might seem to us to be the longueurs, the ambiguities, the hedging, the emotional to-ing and fro-ing, the moral wrangling, the prevarications, which attend the preliminaries to a declaration of love or an acceptance of love by, for example, Lucy Snowe and Jane Eyre we should not attribute them exclusively to Charlotte's stern moral codes and attention to the fine points of proper behaviour. Rather, we should remember that for a governess it was absolutely essential for her to be sure that her acceptance of a proposal was not only morally sound but, so to speak, cast-iron. Marriage might well offer an escape from the serfdom of service, but a bad one would only produce a worse servitude with no hope of escape.

When Jane rejects Rivers's proposal that she should marry him and join him as a missionary she does so on the grounds that the marriage is being proposed in strict business terms – no love is involved. Moreover, the proposal is made in terms which suggest that Jane is naturally Rivers's inferior. A grim analogy between the state of governess and that of wife begins to emerge. Jane's refusal is made on emotional and logical grounds, both of them strongly buttressed by her inflexible morality.

But there was another factor which shaped Charlotte's morality – her religion. One simple fact should be immediately acknowledged and given due weight – Charlotte was a daughter of the manse. Her religious education was both intensive and comprehensive. Moreover, regular and committed observance of religion was required as a constant and natural element in everyday life. Only Emily seems to have been exempted by her father from the full rigours; she does not seem to have been required to teach at Sunday School. There is no reason to believe that Charlotte had any reservations about acceding to her father's will, vocation, persuasion or, indeed, her own convictions.

Charlotte was probably what we might expect from one of Patrick Brontë's cut of the cloth. He was a minister of the established Church, but the established Church itself was considerably under the influence, and particularly in this area of the West Riding of Yorkshire, of Wesleyan Methodism. He had been one of a group of what we would now call establishment pastors who had the strongest leanings towards the tones and tenets of Charles Wesley.

Like her father Charlotte took her religion and its everyday implications seriously. There was nothing remote about Patrick's relation to his flock and he had more than a touch of evangelical zeal in his make-up. Charlotte, probably in company with her sisters, helped him to aid the needy, sick and aged and, like him, had a strong sense of the need for justice to be done in society on earth as it would be in heaven. Perhaps, in her innermost heart, she did not believe (as Anne seems to have done) that this life was best spent as a preparation for a better after-life and, therefore, she does not seem to have thought it necessary to ignore creature comfort here either for herself or others. Above all, like her father, she believed that everyone was capable of achieving salvation – Calvinism, with its emphasis on pre-ordained and selective redemption she both abhorred and feared:

> I am uncertain that I have ever felt true contrition . . . smitten at times to the heart with the conviction that – ghastly Calvinistic doctrines are true, darkened in short, by the very shadow of Spiritual Death! If Christian perfections be necessary to Salvation, I shall never be saved . . . I feel in a strange state of mind still; gloomy but not despairing. I keep trying to do right . . . I abhor myself, I despise myself – if the Doctrine of Calvin be true I am already an outcast. . .

Nevertheless, salvation had to be worked for, and throughout her life Charlotte was conscious of the need to guard against wrong action and its possible consequence – Sin. Intermittently, especially during her youth, she was haunted by the spectre of Calvinistic damnation. Her fears saturated some of her letters and percolated into her novels, and her pressing fear of a Calvinist eternity had subtle relationships with her duties as a governess/teacher at Roe Head and with the alluring world of Angria.

Her days at Roe Head were filled with the raucous irony of children requiring to be taught and inimical to teaching. She retired at the end of each day exhausted in body and mind, the more so because each moment spent in such a profitless occupation increased the sense of time lost from the joy of creative writing.

Frustration jangled her nerves and left a void in her mind and spirit ready to be filled with whatever potent visitation would be most likely to find habitation. In fact there were two, and they were mutually reactive. The first was by way of being a blessed antidote to the tedium of her work at the school. All it required from Charlotte was a willing surrender to the overwhelming pleasures of the imaginative world of Angria. She would sit in her ordinary bedroom at the end of a day at Roe Head and give herself, or be given to, the extraordinary visionary life that she and her brother and sisters had helped to create:

> Remembrance yields up many a fragment of past twilight hours spent in that little unfurnished room. There have I sat on the low bed – with my eyes fixed on the window, through which appeared no other landscape than a monotonous street – of moorland, a grey church tower, rising from the centre of a church-yard so filled with

graves that the rank weed and coarse grass scarce had room to shoot up between the monuments... Such was the picture that threw its reflection upon my eye but communicated no impression to my heart. The mind knew but did not feel its existence. It was away. It had launched on a distant voyage – haply it was nearing the shores of some far and unknown Island under whose cliffs no bark had ever cast anchor. In other words – in other words a long tale was perhaps evolving itself in my mind...

The void is filled with pictures and narratives of astounding vividness, invention and colour; Charlotte was aware of the contrast between the world of so-called reality which surrounded her, and the world being born inside her head. She writes of how 'the toil of the day succeeded by this moment of divine leisure had acted on me like opium and was coiling about me a disturbed but fascinating spell such as I never felt before' and she describes how, through her window at Roe Head, 'Huddersfield and the hills beyond it were all veiled in blue mist, the woods of Hopton and Heaton Lodge were clouding the water-edge and the Calder silent. I shut the window and went back to my seat. Then came on me rushing impetuously all the mighty phantasm that we had conjured from nothing to a system strong as some religious creed.'

But the second invader of the void was unwanted and feared. Her anguished letters to Ellen Nussey echo with fear, apprehension and guilt, for when the imaginary world of Angria is absent, Calvin enters and she is 'smitten at times to the heart with the conviction that _____'s ghastly Calvinistic doctrines are true, darkened, in short by the very shadows of spiritual Death. If Christian perfection be necessary to Salvation, I shall never be saved...'

Why was Charlotte so fearful? Often when a close friend like Ellen Nussey, in a spirit of help and caring and love, takes up the posture of advising confessor to one in a state of perturbation, the comfort given, the advice tendered, is counterproductive. This was never truer than of religious matters and, moreover, never more dangerous than when the friend is innocent, naive and guileless, and the recipient subtle and sensitive. For a short period in their youth Ellen Nussey probably established what we would now call psychological ascendancy over Charlotte, which seems to date from the days when Charlotte's mind became fraught by boredom and frustration and torn between her teaching duties and the anxious desire to write. When she wrote to Ellen Nussey about her own utter worthlessness, and when she compared her coarseness and commonplaceness with Ellen's simple purity, she seems to have got straightforward unexceptionable responses – examine your conscience and trust in God implicitly.

Unfortunately, when complicated minds and fiery imaginations begin to examine the conscience they rarely emerge with a simple solution, and for Ellen to invoke blind trust in God was to ask too much of a mind and soul that were subtle as well as troubled. Ellen Nussey's well-meaning naivety does not seem to have done more than offer temporary periods of relative calm to Charlotte. There is a chilling image in one of her letters which suggests that she saw Ellen's offering as forbidding, unattractive and grim; in the letter Charlotte describes Ellen in these words:

> ... It is a stormy evening, and the wind is uttering a continual moaning sound that makes me very melancholy. At such times, in such moods as these, Ellen, it is my nature to seek repose in some calm, tranquil idea (formerly the idea would have been of Verdopolis or Angria) and I have now summoned up your image to give me rest. There you sit upright and still in your black dress and white scarf, your pale, marble-like face looking so serene and kind – just like reality.

Despite its references to serenity and kindness the total effect is that of one looking into the face of a barely benign Death. Charlotte seems to have attached Ellen's rigid insistence on acceptance to the worst fears of Calvinistic predestination.

But there was another guilt and fear lurking in Charlotte's imagination because of the very existence of Angria. We may recall the telling sentence in what she wrote at Roe Head (sometimes called the Roe Head Journal) on 11 August 1836 – 'Then came on me rushing impetuously all the mighty phantasm that we had conjured from nothing to a system strong as some religious creed.'

Angria's 'possession' of Charlotte had the force of a religious creed and in her mind, therefore, particularly in a disturbed state, may well have had the status of an alternative allurement to her Christian faith. This could have increased her guilt, the more so when we recall that many of the ingredients of Angria were more than dipped in the forbidden liquors of crime, violent death, lust, infidelity and intrigue – perpetrated or enjoyed by personages, some of whom were demonic in both spirit and flesh:

> O Zamorna! what eyes those are glancing under the deep shadow of that raven crest! They bode no good. Man nor woman could ever gather more than a troubled, fitful happiness from their kindest light. Satan gave them their glory to deepen the midnight gloom that always follows where their lustre has fallen most lovingly. . . All here is passion and fire unquenchable. Impetuous sin, stormy pride,

diving and soaring enthusiasm, war and poetry, are kindling their fires in all his veins, and his wild blood boils from his heart and back again like a torrent of new-sprung lava.

This tension between God and the Devil may well have important implications for and in Charlotte's novels, and also in defining one of the differences between her and Emily's spiritual experience. In *Jane Eyre* and *Villette* there are points where the heroines seem to be sucked into a kind of hell of the imagination which induces in them a sense both of momentary demonic possession, of persecution and – sometimes – of being punished for some deed that they have committed or contemplated.

The young Jane Eyre is locked in the red-room, old Mr Reed's death-chamber, for a misdemeanour she did not commit. As they thrust her into it, Miss Abbot cries, 'God will punish her: he might strike her dead in the midst of her tantrums, and then where would she go?' Jane then experiences a kind of hell. Eventually, gibbering with fear, she is released and, though she has a sense of injustice, Jane cries, 'Oh aunt, have pity! Forgive me! I cannot endure it – let me be punished some other way! I shall be killed if —.'

Lucy Snowe does not know whether the ghostly figure of the nun who so disturbs the night is an agent of hell or not, but it so possesses her imagination that she loses contact with reality. The fact that the nun has a rational (not to say absurd) explanation is neither here nor there – while Lucy experiences it she feels possessed by something menacing. She does not have Jane's fear of guilt but she is very near it.

The moral system of Charlotte's novels where there is a weighing of right and wrong action, of good against evil, to such an extent that the process towards a balanced resolution can seem tedious, is a reflection of her constant awareness of God on one side and the Devil on the other. The choice the individual is faced with is complicated because one false move can force him to slip one way or the other very quickly.

With Emily (and it is embodied very clearly in *Wuthering Heights*) there is no sense that any choice is required – certainly of the 'hero' or 'heroine'. They subsume Heaven and Hell, Right and Wrong, Virtue and Vice with the curious effect that when one is, as it were, alone with them, one is looking at two people who are both guilty yet not guilty; who are passionately, primitively naive in their love and therefore neither good nor bad; who are, by the moral codes of the world, guilty, but who do not feel it, of cruelty, hatred, violence, tacit infidelity. For them, 'that's all one'.

There is no more telling demonstration of this than in the character of Heathcliff. The reader cannot condemn him outright as despicable and yet, of course, one cannot embrace him as virtuous – he is neither, and both.

At the end of the novel we are given a description of Heathcliff as a corpse – he arouses both a terrible revulsion and a harrowing pity; he is both culpable and vulnerable, guilty yet not guilty. Emily's characters do not have to choose because Emily did not have Charlotte's acute sense of the gulf between right and wrong.

The idea of the Brontës as entirely a family of shy, retiring people, with the females falling naturally into the status of wallflowers, possessed of some dark force, imprisoned in an isolated Yorkshire village, is inaccurate, even absurd. They had many contacts with the larger world outside Haworth, and with divers kinds of people. Even Emily, who sought solitariness when she could, knew many people and, what is more, journeyed to London and to the Continent. Charlotte went to Brussels twice, visited London (accompanied by Anne) a number of times, and helped to entertain a large company of people at the parsonage – their father's parishioners, casual acquaintances and close friends.

More than this, the suggestion that they were isolated from such normal human procedures as falling in love, from being attracted to members of the other sex, from excitedly gossiping about the qualities, or lack of them, of their male and female friends, is very wide of the mark. In the case of Branwell, his falling in love was done with quite sensational bravura and intensity; Anne, on the other hand, came to love with all the shy excitement of many a young girl.

But the case of Charlotte is overwhelming proof that the common traffic of human activities involved this family as it does any other. At any point from her adolescence onwards, if the absolutely right man had been available Charlotte would have used all her endeavours to try and marry him. In fact she married late-ish in life, and although we may have the feeling that Arthur Bell Nicholls was not entirely suitable the fact remains that her marriage to him bespeaks Charlotte's wish to take to herself a mate. She wanted to get married not just because it was the customary destiny of young ladies of her class at the time, but because she desired it. There was nothing in her personality which would cause her to shun either the non-physical or the physical commitments of marriage – she was pregnant, or had been pregnant, when she died.

It comes as a very great shock to those who see or prefer to see Charlotte and her brother and sisters with some kind of mystic, *nole me tangere* halo about them to realize that Charlotte had very close relationships with at least six men in her life. For some of them she entertained, in varying degrees, thoughts of a more permanent and intimate relationship than actually existed. With one of them (W.S. Williams, the kindly publisher's editor) the result could only have been disastrous, for he was already married. But this did not prevent her from pursuing as close a relationship as was feasible in the circumstances.

Six is a goodly number even in these days of social permissiveness. Henry Nussey, a clergyman, and brother of Ellen Nussey; James Taylor, who worked for a publisher; George Smith, an up-and-coming publisher; W.S. Williams; M. Heger, Belgian director of a school; Arthur Bell Nicholls, her father's curate – these were the men.

Charlotte did not, so to speak, proceed from one to another – strong attachments to Smith were being forged while she was, at the same time, in close correspondence with Taylor; her deep friendship with Williams persisted during the time she knew Taylor and Smith; her deep love for Heger (for that is what it was) probably persisted, if secretly, to the end of her life. Interestingly, it is only of the two men of the cloth – Nussey and Nicholls – that we can entertain doubts about the depth of her committal. Nussey, from whom she received a proposal, was rejected almost peremptorily, even slightly ironically:

> I have no personal repugnance to the idea of a union with you, but I feel convinced that mine is not the sort of disposition calculated to form the happiness of a man like you.

Nicholls, one feels, was *faute de mieux*, the last chance, convenient, and although it seems that she grew into an affection for him, there is nothing whatsoever in her letters, as in this one to Mrs Gaskell, to suggest the warmth of feeling that was generated between her and her other male friends:

> I cannot deny that I had a battle to fight with myself; I am not sure that I have even yet conquered certain inward combatants... After various visits and as the result of perseverance in one quarter and a gradual change of feeling in others, I find myself what people call 'engaged'.

So, she rejected one curate, and married another, but one suspects her experience of true love lay elsewhere.

Again contrary to popular notions, there was animated address, romantic speculation and fancy, emotional excitement, involved in Charlotte's relationship with her other men. As her letters to Ellen Nussey amply show, Charlotte was very much the normal young lady in her physical and romantic desires. The idea of a man being interested in her excited and intrigued her.

But each of her men, including Nussey and Nicholls, shared one common characteristic which tells us much about Charlotte and, indeed, helps to crystallize her attitude towards men. To a degree they were all father figures, and, certainly, to a degree she regarded them as such. They seem, all of them, to have had a paternal attitude towards her. *Jane Eyre, Villette, The Professor* depict the experience of a girl/ governess whose desire for love is inextricably linked with a desire to have a protector – someone to be respected, looked up to, someone to whom she can indulge her yearning to be subservient without losing respect, love, or, what is most important, freedom of action. The basic paradox of Charlotte's character, as of her fictional characters, was the co-existence of a quest for immolation and an assertion of personal independence.

It is perhaps inevitable that we should ask the question – which of these men was most suited to Charlotte Brontë? Putting aside their shared characteristic, they were surprisingly different from one another – different enough, in fact, to have provided, eventually, splendid copy to enable Charlotte to present them to us in fictional form. Heger, obviously, has to be considered first. He is the one who seems most to have attracted her, most to have agitated her, most, indeed, to have caused her that particular grief which is the emblem of unrequited love.

He taught French and mathematics at the Athenée Royal, a boys' school adjacent to his own wife's school where Charlotte taught. Zoë Heger was his second wife. They seem to have been deeply attached and both equally devout and committed to their profession of teaching. He, in particular, was a superb teacher, but a hard disciplinarian. He was a fair man, a generous man, but given to explosions of temper and to unexpected moods which were dark and dismissive. The moods reversed with equal unexpectedness. He was charming, he expected and received respect, he commanded obedience. He was, in fact, in some things very like Paul Emmanuel in *Villette*, and Charlotte found him irresistible.

Heger found her preferable to Emily whom, he said, should have been a man. He thought Charlotte had great potential as a teacher and an iron will to succeed. He spent much time teaching her French and, indeed, how to teach, and in one letter to Ellen, describing her life at the school, Charlotte wrote, 'I am happier submitting to authority than exercising it' – though she sometimes burst into tears when Heger remonstrated with her. Perhaps she learned to do this, too, for Heger had the trick of offering sweets to any unfortunate whose tears he had caused to flow.

At some point in her second visit to Brussels (having been invited back by Madame Heger) Charlotte realized, Madame Heger realized and, unless he was blind and deaf, Heger himself realized that Charlotte was deeply in love with the man she came to call her 'master'.

Madame Heger seems to have reacted with efficiency and diplomacy. Nothing appeared to ruffle the surface of the school's life, but Heger was carefully insulated from Charlotte and, eventually, stopped giving her French lessons and taking English lessons from her. The extent of Charlotte's isolation from Heger appears in poignant phrases in a letter to Branwell:

> Mr Heger has just been in and given me a little German Testament as a present. I was surprised, for since a good many days he has hardly spoken to me . . .

– and, on its flyleaf, she wrote in a fashion which typifies the way depth of feeling is often expressed by a kind of playful offhandedness:

> Herr Heger hat mir dieses Buch gegeben,
> Brüssel, Mai 1843. C.B.

In a letter to Ellen, almost desperate in tone, she uses the word 'homesickness' to describe what was, surely, heartsickness.

During this second stay at Brussels the pressures on Charlotte to leave were very strong, but it is a testimony to the strength of her love for Heger that she resisted for a long time. When she did offer her resignation there was no hesitation from Madame Heger in accepting it. Neither was there any hesitation in the same lady's immediate return to her former mood of cordiality towards Charlotte. Heger himself attempted to prevent her going and, for a time, his efforts succeeded. But Charlotte could stand no more, and in December 1843 she returned to Haworth.

The deepest record of Charlotte's despair appears in a number of letters she wrote to Heger in subsequent months – to none of which is there a reply extant. Indeed we owe the preservation of some of them to the fact that after Heger had torn them up upon receiving them, his wife painstakingly glued the pieces together – and her motives for this can only be guessed at.

The tenor of the letters is plain. They are as dignified as the passion of love can be when it encounters cold silence in response; they are as candid as pride can be when it is a part of love; they are as beseeching as only anguish can be when it realizes that its cause is hopeless. Nowhere else did Charlotte bare her soul so completely. In the letters she is all woman and terribly vulnerable because she does not care what the world thinks. This, indeed, is Charlotte Brontë the woman, not the novelist, nor the champion of woman's freedom, the chronicler of the fate of governesses, the parson's careful daughter:

Day and night I find neither rest nor peace. If I sleep I am disturbed by tormenting dreams in which I see you, always severe, always grave, always incensed against me.

Forgive me then, monsieur, if I adopt the course of writing to you again. How can I endure life if I make no effort to ease its sufferings?

In the present absence of Heger's replies to any of her letters – Charlotte complained several times that she had received none – it is impossible to come to any conclusion about how Heger felt for her. It is worth remembering that he spoke warmly of Charlotte to Mrs Gaskell and, significantly, asked her if she had seen any of the letters he (Heger) had sent in reply to Charlotte's.

Speculation can take us a long way, particularly if we are prepared to see something dramatic in the repaired letters, in Madame Heger's suspicion, in the little gifts that Heger gave Charlotte, in his successful attempt to postpone Charlotte's departure from Brussels.

Heger was a susceptible man, probably vain, certainly kind, doubtless a little insensitive, but, in the long run, probably more concerned with preserving the marriage he had than embarking on a liaison with a sweet mouse of virtue. The only cogent conclusion possible, perhaps, is that if Charlotte was not necessary to him, he was necessary to her – and the proof is *Villette*.

Of her other men friends the nearest she came to feelings of even approximate similarity to those she had for Heger was with George Smith and, to a lesser extent, James Taylor.

Smith was a bustling young publisher-in-a-hurry, ambitious, good-looking, intelligent, easy of speech and manner, a good judge of literature. In many respects he squared with his fictive self – John Graham Bretton in *Villette* – even to the extent of having an acquisitive and domineering mother. There can be little doubt that Charlotte was flattered by Smith's obvious attentions, but she may well have totally misinterpreted their significance. He wined and dined her in London, took her to the theatre and art galleries, involved her in the literary social round, invited her to stay with himself (and his mother) in London and when he (with his mother) took holidays. Through Smith she came to recognize and accept herself as a literary figure.

But, as her letters show, she also seems to have manoeuvred herself into the position of assuming a closer relationship than is implied by any of the activities and rounds that Smith so eagerly involved her in. At times she doth protest reluctance too much; she cannot hide the depth of her feelings;

... I am content to have him as a friend – and pray God to continue to me the common-sense to look on one so young, so rising and so hopeful in no other light.

But Smith did not love her, although she seems to have encouraged herself to believe that he did. He excited that part of her which responded so easily to what was young, intelligent, frank, kindly and with a touch of derring-do. To her, perhaps, Smith might well have been one of the cleaner-cut heroes of Angria. And, as with Heger, the best he could do for her was to be a source for *Villette*.

The first time Charlotte saw James Taylor she took an instant dislike to him, although, with his red hair and nervous habits, he reminded her of her brother Branwell. He was several rungs below Smith in the ladder of publishing, but this did not prevent him from pressing a kind of suit, or her from speculating on her feelings for him. He sent her books, newspapers, long letters. His approach had an ardour about it that Smith lacked, and Charlotte was both attracted and repelled:

... each moment he came near me – and that I could see his eyes fastened on me – my veins ran ice. Now that he is away I feel far more gently towards him...

But there can be no question that she seriously considered him as a candidate for marriage. After he departed, she wrote to Ellen:

... I do assure you – dear Nell – not to deceive either you or myself, a more entire crumbling away of a seeming foundation and prospect of hope – can scarcely be realised.

This strange, intense little man left England for India. Charlotte was taken aback at the apparent suddenness of his departure. He wrote to her from Bombay, and she wrote to Ellen about her feelings. What we learn from her letters is that distance lent a little enchantment to Taylor; she more than hints that, despite the physical effect his presence had on her, she might have consented to marriage – but this was at a time when she had realized that George Smith was not for her. Poor James Taylor is a somewhat pathetic figure in the Brontë history. We shall never know his true feelings for Charlotte – all we do know is that, for her, he was not much more than a possibility in the marriage stakes.

There is an irony in the fact that the one man (other than Heger) who might have best suited her was disqualified from marriage to her by his existing and happy marriage to someone else. This was W.S. Williams.

When she knew him far less closely than she knew George Smith, Charlotte compared him slightly unfavourably with the younger man:

> Mr Smith made himself very pleasant. He is a *practical* man. I wish Mr Williams were more so, but he is altogether of the contemplative, theorising order. Mr Williams has too many abstractions.

But she learned, particularly during Emily's final illness, that Williams was a staunch and kindly friend. He never was less or more than warmly respectful in his addresses to her, his letters always cheered her, his advice and comfort in her anxiety for Emily was direct, good and unsentimental. Charlotte referred to one of his letters as 'eloquent in its sincerity', and later compared him most favourably with James Taylor, who:

> has a determined, dreadful nose in the middle of his face which when poked into my countenance cuts into my soul like iron. Still he is horribly intelligent, quick, searching, sagacious, and with a memory of relentless tenacity. To turn to Williams after him, or to Smith himself, is to turn from granite to easy down or warm fur.

Charlotte was very fortunate in her dealings with the Smith, Elder publishing company in having as an advisor a member of that firm who was more interested in art, artists and the processes of the literary imagination than he was in making money out of authors. Williams was an intelligent and shrewd man, who encouraged her in the long disappointment of *The Professor* and gave her tremendous moral support when a good deal of adverse criticism broke about her after the publication of *Shirley*. He seems to have written both voluminously and wisely to her when she was in Haworth – particularly during the period of anguish when Branwell, Emily and Anne died. He sent her parcels of books and, on her visits to London, graciously accompanied her to literary affairs and on sight-seeing tours.

There is no suggestion that Williams ever felt more for Charlotte than a kind of protective affection and wise admiration. Neither does Charlotte express for him in her letters anything of the sense of emotional disturbance we find in her references to Taylor and Smith. Probably Williams was simply the best friend, other than Ellen Nussey, that she ever had – he was also the one who perhaps understood her best.

So, had other things been equal, Williams might well have been the best kind of husband for Charlotte. He was sympathetic and sensitive to her profession, shrewd in his judgements, kindly, protective, yet not proprietary. But she married Arthur Bell Nicholls.

Nicholls became the Rev. Brontë's curate at Haworth in 1845, but they never hit it off with each other, despite their shared nationality. Nicholls came from an Irish family which Patrick explicitly believed to be far less distinguished than his own. Moreover, Nicholls was a Puseyite – the pejorative name given to the supporters of Dr Pusey's Tractarian movement which proposed the reintroduction of Catholic observance into the Church of England. No doubt Patrick baulked at this, but perhaps he just could not find much to enthuse at anyway in this large man with thick hair, bushy eyebrows, tiny eyes, podgy hands, sepulchral voice, strained stance, whose intelligence seemed (and was) limited, and whose religious convictions barely stopped this side of bigotry. But, although she found him dull and narrow and uninteresting at first, Charlotte thought him kindly and considerate, and he was an assiduous worker.

So, gradually, through what process we shall never know beyond the fact that, perforce, they were thrown together in close company over a long period of time, their relationship grew. In December 1852, as Charlotte reported in a letter to Ellen Nussey, this happened:

> After tea I withdrew to the dining-room as usual. As usual, Mr Nicholls sat with papa till between eight and nine o'clock, I then heard him open the parlour door as if going. I expected the clash of the front-door. He stopped in the passage: he tapped: like lightning it flashed on me what was coming. He entered – he stood before me. What his words were you can guess; his manner – you can hardly realise – never can I forget it. Shaking from head to foot, looking deadly pale, speaking low, vehemently yet with difficulty – he made me for the first time feel what it costs a man to declare affection where he doubts response.
>
> The spectacle of one ordinarily so statue-like, thus trembling, stirred, and overcome, gave me a kind of strange shock. He spoke of sufferings he had borne for months, of sufferings he could endure no longer, and craved leave for some hope. I could only entreat him to leave me then and promise a reply on the morrow. I asked him if he had spoken to papa. He said, he dared not. I think I half led, half put him out of the room. When he was gone I immediately went to papa, and told him what had taken place. Agitation and anger disproportionate to the occasion ensued; if I had *loved* Mr Nicholls and had heard such epithets applied to him as were used, it would have transported me past my patience; as it was, my blood boiled with a sense of injustice, but papa worked himself into a state not to be trifled with, the veins on his temples started up like whipcord, and

his eyes became suddenly bloodshot. I made haste to promise that Mr Nicholls should on the morrow have a distinct refusal.

The story of their courtship and marriage is not without its comedy, pathos and, indeed, theatricality, and a great part of this mixture was the result of Patrick Brontë's intractable attitude towards Nicholls. The latter must have undergone a good deal of mental and spiritual anguish and frustration – enough, at one point, to make him determined to emigrate as a missionary to Australia (shades of St John Rivers!). Although he left Haworth and took a curacy elsewhere, his successor was so unsatisfactory that Patrick Brontë was glad to have Nicholls back!

When, in June 1854, Charlotte and the beleaguered curate were married, Patrick refused to attend the marriage service, but presided with 'grandiloquent manner' at the wedding breakfast. Subsequently, he appears to have withdrawn much of his obvious antipathy to Nicholls, and for the six years from his daughter's death in 1855 to his own in 1861 he lived in uncertain amicability with Nicholls at the parsonage – the old survivor ironically at the mercy (which was a kindly one) of the man he did not want as his daughter's husband.

If the simplistic question, 'Did Charlotte love Arthur Bell Nicholls?' is asked, the answer is almost certainly 'No'. Her letters to Ellen Nussey have in them absolutely nothing to indicate more than a mild affection which grew somewhat in the face of his solicitude for her. What she felt is best summed up in a letter written to Ellen in April 1854:

> I am still very calm, very inexpectant. What I taste of happiness is of the soberist order. I trust to love my husband – I am grateful for his tender love to me. I believe him to be an affectionate, a conscientious, a high-principled man, and if, with all this, I should yield to regrets, that fine talents, congenial tastes and thoughts are not added, it seems to me I should be most presumptuous and thankless.

What is significant is not so much her use of the word 'love' but the circumscription of its meaning. She had written a year earlier to Harriet Martineau, the champion of woman's liberation, about her adverse comments on *Villette*, particularly on the love-elements in the book. In the letter Charlotte declares:

> I know what *love* is as I understand it; and if man or woman should be ashamed of feeling such love, then is there nothing right, noble, faithful, truthful, unselfish in this earth, as I comprehend rectitude, nobleness, fidelity, truth, and disinterestedness.

It is unlikely that she could have applied that statement to her relationship with Nicholls. Indeed, perhaps any human love she would have been likely to experience with Taylor or Smith or Heger or Nicholls, or anybody, would have fallen far short of what she *knew* love could be – and one suspects that it could only be found somewhere deep in those chambers of her heart and soul in which the country and citizens of Angria had their being.

Emily Jane Brontë (1818–1848)

Remarkably little is known about the life and activities of Emily Brontë, compared with those of her father, and of Charlotte and Branwell. This is the more remarkable when realized in the light of the fact that the Brontë family gives every evidence of having both indulged in and enjoyed copious correspondence with friends and acquaintances, quite apart from their early and mature literary outpourings.

One of the most tenable explanations is that Emily was disposed to cover her tracks and that others also took it upon themselves to have them covered. No one who has read her so-called 'diary-papers' (brief notes on the year's events written in 1834, 1837, 1841 and 1845, by Emily and Anne) could easily conclude that she was uninterested in the bits and pieces of the workaday world; no one who knows *Wuthering Heights* could safely assume that Emily was uninterested in the babbling gossip of the air of Haworth and its surroundings.

But equally she seems to have been assiduous in not wanting her casual recordings of the world's traffic and tattle to be known to anyone except herself and her very nearest – of whom the closest was probably Anne. Her very strong reaction to Charlotte's discovery and proposal to print her poems should alert us to the probability that Emily was, above all, very sensitively antagonistic to being exposed – Ellen Nussey commented on Emily's reluctance to 'reveal' herself. Perhaps she was less shy than determinedly bent on protecting her inner integrity. Shyness seems too soft a quality to attribute to Emily, but embattled secretiveness might well have been one of her strongest characteristics:

> O for the time when I shall sleep
> Without identity,
> And never care how rain may steep
> Or snow may cover me! . . .
> O let me die, that power and will
> Their cruel strife may close,
> And vanquished Good, victorious Ill
> Be lost in one repose.

We shall never know exactly what occurred between the two sisters after Charlotte discovered and read the poems of Emily's most secret heart:

> One day, in the autumn of 1845, I accidentally lighted on a MS volume of verse in my sister Emily's handwriting. Of course, I was not surprised, knowing that she could and did write verse; I looked it over, and something more than surprise seized me – a deep conviction that these were not common effusions, nor at all like the poetry women generally write. I thought them condensed and terse, vigorous and genuine. To my ear, they had also a peculiar music – wild, melancholy, and elevating.
>
> My sister Emily was not a person of demonstrative character, nor one on the recesses of whose mind and feelings even those nearest and dearest to her could, with impunity, intrude unlicensed; it took hours to reconcile her to the discovery I had made, and days to persuade her that such poems merited publication. I knew, however, that a mind like hers could not be without some latent spark of honourable ambition, and refused to be discouraged in my attempts to fan that spark to flame.

But it is a fair guess that Charlotte was left in no uncertainty about the depth of her incursion into what Emily not only regarded as her own, but as hers alone:

> I was sternly rated at first for having taken an unwarrantable liberty. This I expected . . . But by dint of entreaty and reason I at last wrung out a reluctant consent to have the 'rhymes' as they were contemptuously called, published. The author never alludes to them, or, when she does, it is with scorn. But I know no woman that ever lived that ever wrote such poetry before.

So little remains of Emily's correspondence, of correspondence to her and of her diary-papers – so nearly clean was the slate wiped – that it would seem that Charlotte eventually overreacted to Emily's feelings and perhaps to her own conscience, so that after her sister's death when, ironically, it mattered little, with typical efficiency she destroyed all she could lay her hands on – perhaps through overanxiety to protect Emily's privacy. We do not know that this act happened, only that it is feasible. If Charlotte did this she deprived posterity of at least some insights into, and about, the one member of the family who as well as being the most mysterious was also undeniably entitled to the accolade of greatness.

Seen from this distance Emily Brontë is a paradoxical being, and that impression remains even after allowance is made for the paucity of information about her. The sum total of descriptions and accounts of her activities is made up of apparently irreconcilable details. This irreconcilability can be given a general description – Emily's personality was at one and the same time both intensely physical and intensely spiritual, both down-to-earth and other-worldly. This image is wonderfully embodied in Ellen Nussey's description:

> She chose a white stuff patterned with lilac thunder and lightning, to the scarcely-concealed horror of her more sober companions. And she looked well in it; a tall, lithe creature, with a grace half-queenly, half-untamed in her sudden supple movements, wearing with picturesque negligence her ample purple-splashed skirts; her face clear and pale; her very dark and plenteous brown hair fastened up behind with a Spanish comb; her large grey-hazel eyes, now full of indolent indulgent humour, now glimmering with hidden meanings, now quickened into flame by a flash of indignation, 'a red ray piercing the dew'.

So much emphasis has been placed on Emily's spirituality that some prominence must be given in any assessment of her personality to the evidence that exists about the scope and nature of her physicality, commonsense, down-to-earthness.

It is paradoxical, after one has read the accounts of her suffering before death, to have to realize that up to the beginning of her last illness she was, apart from Patrick Brontë, almost certainly the healthiest of all the Brontës. Her figure was long, lissom and sturdy, she had great resources of energy, constantly employed in walking on the moors, in household chores and mental work, though her chief delight was 'to roam on the moors, followed by her dogs, to whom she would whistle in masculine fashion'. There might well have been more than a touch of the tomboy about her when she was a child, but from all accounts she grew into a presentable young woman – 'Her hair, which was naturally as beautiful as Charlotte's, was in the same unbecoming tight curl and frizz, and there was the same want of complexion. She had very beautiful eyes... Their colour might be said to be dark grey, at other times dark blue, they varied so.' Indeed, for her figure and her eyes she was perhaps the most physically attractive of the surviving Brontë females.

Yet, the sense of a kind of hard ruggedness and of a strain of the 'masculine', lingers. Here is one example:

> Mr Brontë formerly took very great pleasure in shooting – not in the way generally understood by the term, but shooting at a mark, merely for recreation. He had such unbounded confidence in his daughter Emily, knowing, as he did, her unparalleled intrepidity and firmness, that he resolved to learn her to shoot too. They used to

practice with pistols. Let her be ever so busy in her domestic duties, whether in the kitchen baking bread at which she had such a dainty hand, or at her ironing, or at her studies, raped [sic] in a world of her own creating – it mattered not; if he called upon her to take a lesson, she would put all down; his tender and affectionate 'Now my dear girl, let me see how well you can shoot to-day' was irristable [sic] to her filial nature, and her most winning and musical voice would be heard to ring through the house in response, 'Yes, papa'.

But a more sensational, even repelling example occurs in the same source – the diary of John Greenwood, the Haworth stationer:

On one occasion a person went to tell them that Keeper and another great powerful dog out of the village were fighting down the lane. She was in the garden at the time, and the servant went to tell her, as a matter of course, what was up. She never spoke a word, nor appeared the least at a loss what to do, but rushed at once into the kitchen, took the pepper box, and away into the lane where she found the two savage brutes each holding the other by the throat, in deadly grip, while several other animals, who thought themselves men, were standing looking on like cowards as they were, afraid to tuch [sic] them – there they stood gaping, watching this fragile creature spring upon the beasts – seizing Keeper round the neck with one arm, while with the other hand she dredges well their noses with pepper, and separating them by force of her great will, driving Keeper, that great powerful dog, before her into the house, never once noticing the men, so called, standing there thunderstruck at the deed.

In assessing the significance of this episode, whose author is to be trusted, we ought to remember that the nineteenth century was free from our modern anthropomorphic attitude and that Emily, in common with her contemporaries, had no compunction about showing the animal world who was the master, although she exhibited solicitous mercy once that authority, however brutally applied, was established.

But it is her addiction to the power of the moors that proves the extent to which physical, sensual activity and experience was vital to her life and imagination. Ellen Nussey recalls:

Emily, Anne and Branwell used to ford the streams, and sometimes placed stepping-stones for the other two; there was always a lingering delight in these spots – every moss, every flower, every tint and form, were noted and enjoyed. Emily especially had a gleesome delight in these nooks of beauty – her reserve for the time vanished. One long ramble made in these early days was far away over the moors to a spot familiar to Emily and Anne, which they called 'The

Meeting of the Waters'. It was a small oasis of emerald green turf, broken here and there by small clear springs: a few large stones serving as resting-places; seated here, we were hidden from all the world, nothing appearing in view but miles and miles of heather, a glorious blue sky, and brightening sun. A fresh breeze wafted on us its exhilarating influence; we laughed and made mirth of each other, and settled we would call ourselves the quartette. Emily, half reclining on a slab of stone, played like a young child with the tadpoles in the water, making them swim about, and then fell to moralizing on the strong and the weak, the brave and the cowardly, as she chased them with her hand.

Curiously, though, in this very description there is more than a hint of a different kind of person. One can almost feel the smooth sliver of the tadpoles as they glance Emily's fingers, but our minds cannot help pondering that it is an unusual personality which moralizes as it feels – for Emily, as for Hamlet, 'there is a special providence in the fall of a sparrow'.

As she grew older this conjunction came more and more to occupy Emily's imagination – so much so that some commentators have claimed that she was a mystic. Others have denied this, finding it difficult to believe that, for example, *Wuthering Heights* could possibly have been written by one who was experiencing the special rigours and unshakable aspirations of religious mysticism. A comparison of Emily's poems with those of recognized mystical writers yields a number of similarities, but there is much reason to doubt whether they are sufficient to be conclusive.

For one thing it is still not, and probably never will be, certain how many of her poems are 'Gondal' in origin (i.e. poems which relate incidents and depict characters derived from Emily's childhood equivalent to Charlotte's and Branwell's 'Angrian' world). Every Gondal poem obviously had a special place in Emily's imaginative world and cannot safely be regarded as an embodiment or record of a unique religious experience; in fact the existence of Gondal weakens the argument for mysticism.

Moreover, Emily's poems, though they undoubtedly record profound metaphysical experiences do not, regarded as a whole, seem to be a record of a journey towards the final union with God – the mystic's destination. Apart from this, they lack two characteristics of the mystical experience as it habitually expresses itself in words. The first is a certain kind of simplicity which amounts to a distillation (though it can never be an explanation) of a profound and complex experience: in a sense this simplicity is a kind of shorthand thrust upon the mystic as a makeshift to give some notation to the inexpressible.

Emily's simplicity seems less a sparse substitute for an experience beyond words than a tense, often poignant essence of a powerful vision demanding to be communicated:

> And am I wrong to worship where
> Faith cannot doubt nor Hope despair
> Since my own soul can grant my prayer?
> Speak, God of visions, plead for me
> And tell why I have chosen thee!

Indeed the meaning and tone of the last line of that stanza from one of her first poems, 'God of Visions', might be regarded as the very negation of the mystic's stance in relation to his God. For the mystic, God chooses and disposes; for Emily, she has a choice – the very possibility of which would seem an arrogance to a mystic.

The second way in which Emily's poems are not characteristic of the mystical experience is that for all their passion and religious reference they do not seem to have that unique kind of mystic's ecstasy whose source lies in the actual or hoped-for defeat of the lures of the flesh and the triumph of the naked soul. The flesh plays its part in mystical poetry almost always as a temptation, as something to be denied, as a dangerous nostalgia. While the mystic thirsts for the ethereal, Emily's ecstasy in her visions still tastes of the sensual:

> Few hearts to mortals given
> On earth so wildly pine;
> Yet none would ask a Heaven
> More like this Earth than thine.

Nevertheless it must fairly be said that the impression of her communion with a world elsewhere which is conveyed in her poetry, with its frequent religious imagery, its ache for freedom from corporeal restraints, is strong enough to justify the contention that Emily had a relationship with mystical experience, if no blood kinship with it. Behind these poems lie powerful and unusual adventures of the imagination and spirit whose nature is elusive, disturbing and ubiquitous enough to have, in the end, wholly enveloped her thought and feeling. These forays of the imagination were 'spiritual' because they obviously took Emily beyond palpable time and solid earth towards eternity and the universe. They demanded from her an increasing dedication, and although there is no direct account of how this dedication affected her its profound results are amply displayed in *Wuthering Heights* and in the poems:

> O thy bright eyes must answer now,
> When Reason, with a scornful brow,

Is mocking at my otherthrow;
O thy sweet tongue must plead for me
And tell why I have chosen thee!

Stern Reason is to judgement come
Arrayed in all her forms of gloom:
Wilt thou my advocate be dumb?
No, radiant angel, speak and say
Why I did cast the world away;

Why I have persevered to shun
The common paths that others run;
And on a strange road journeyed on
Heedless alike of Wealth and Power –
Of Glory's wreath and Pleasure's flower.

These once indeed seemed Beings divine,
And they perchance heard vows of mine
And saw my offerings on their shrine –
But, careless gifts are seldom prized,
And mine were worthily despised;

So with a ready heart I swore
To seek their altar-stone no more,
And gave my spirit to adore
Thee, ever present, phantom thing –
My slave, my comrade, and my King!

We catch passing glimpses of the way in which Emily seemed possessed by external spiritual forces in comments by Charlotte, John Greenwood, and Ellen Nussey, the family friend. She had moments and periods of apparent withdrawal from the current of life, fixing herself to some secret anchorage while the world trafficked about her.

She would return from walks on the moors and seem to have a glow of transfiguration about her:

And thou art now a spirit pouring
Thy presence into all ...

A universal influence
From Thine own influence free;
A principle of life, intense,
Lost to mortality.

She would sit for hours in complete silence. She would enter a room full of people, obtain whatever object she was seeking and leave as if the room were empty. Her response to direct address and question was often a slow, remote, enigmatic smile:

Her extreme reserve seemed impenetrable, yet she was intensely lovable; she invited confidence in her moral power. Few people have the gift of looking and smiling as she could look and smile. One of her rare expressive looks was something to remember through life, there was such a depth of soul and feeling, and yet such a shyness of revealing herself.

The intensity of her withdrawal is confirmed in the effect made upon others by the contrast when, so to say, she revisited the world of people, and communicated:

... on one occasion whilst Charlotte's friend was visiting the parsonage, Charlotte herself was unable through illness to take walks with her. To the amazement of the household, Emily volunteered to accompany Miss Nussey on a ramble over the moors. They set off together, and the girl threw aside her reserve, and talked with freedom and vigour which gave evidence of the real strength of her character. Her companion was charmed with her intelligence and geniality. But on returning to the parsonage, Charlotte was found awaiting them . . . she anxiously asked Miss Nussey: 'How did Emily behave?' . . . It was the first time she had ever been known to invite the company of any one outside the narrow limits of the family circle.

The power whose presence Emily pines for is called by her the 'God of Visions', and in one of her poems she describes the effect upon her of one of the God's visitations:

Then dawns the Invisible, the Unseen its truth reveals;
My outward sense is gone, my inward essence feels –
Its wings are almost free, its home, its harbour found;
Measuring the gulf it stoops and dares the final bound!

Oh, dreadful is the check – intense the agony
When the ear begins to hear and the eye begins to see;
When the pulse begins to throb, the brain to think again,
The soul to feel the flesh and the flesh to feel the chain!

Yet I would lose no sting, would wish no torture less;
The more that anguish racks the earlier it will bless;
And robed in fires of Hell, or bright with heavenly shine,
If it but herald Death, the vision is divine.

But any predisposition to point to this description as proof of Emily's mystical experience must be considerably tempered by the fact that this poem is an avowed and documented Gondal poem – 'Julian M. and A.G. Rochelle'.

It is hazardous to attempt any close definition of this God of Visions without entering an area of fanciful speculation. In any case, it is probably more rewarding to record the two main effects that the God has. These dominate Emily's poetry, both Gondal and non-Gondal.

The first is her ecstasy at its presence. The ecstasy is not without its apprehensions, its pains, its fears, but these are subsumed in the excitement of an accompanying experience of release, absence from her own identity, and freedom. That word, freedom, repeats itself throughout the poetry, and it is the second result of the God of Vision's presence. The freedom, to put it simplistically, is to enable Emily to lose the constraints of self and become ecstatically identified with entities outside herself. The moors offered her the greatest opportunity; not only did they allow her the solitariness in which condition the God of Visions best made known his presence, but in their myriad animate and inanimate objects offered an endless reality in which she would lose herself. When John Greenwood saw her return from a walk on the moors, her face transfigured with a kind of glow, perhaps it was from this experience that she was returning:

> Methought the very breath I breathed
> Was full of sparks divine,
> And all my heather-couch was wreathed
> By that celestial shine.

> And while the wide Earth echoing rang
> To their strange minstrelsy,
> The little glittering spirits sang,
> Or seemed to sing, to me.

The quest for precise definitions and descriptions of Emily's experiences is fruitless. But we may perhaps ease ourselves a little further into her imagination if we regard her not as a latter-day medieval mystic but as a child of the Romantic movement. She shares with Shelley, Wordsworth and John Keats an aspiration to escape from the mere singularity of individuality. One general characteristic of the Romantic spirit is, indeed, a quest for freedom from the constraints of reason and flesh. The Romantic poets each sought their escape by different means, and in different directions, but all are characterized, to a degree, by the desire for, and attainment of, heightened states of experience in which apprehension, awe, mystery, self-surrender and visitation by a powerful Abstraction participate. So intense were these states for some poets, particularly Wordsworth, that he, like Emily, has been designated as a 'mystic' by some commentators. But it should be noted of him, of Keats, of Shelley, as of Emily, that none of the elements which participate in the heightened experiences involve the Christian God. Indeed, their kind of poetry seems to create its own theology, its own deistic authority, its own patterns of worship – all tending more towards the pagan and natural than the Christian and formalized, and all of them, very significantly, allowing the fullest licence to the sensuous, the palpable. Emily's God of Visions seems to be akin to Wordsworth's 'beloved Presence' in whom there exists:

> a virtue which irradiates and exalts
> All objects through all intercourse of sense.

Emily's aspirations for freedom are as devoid of chaste religiosity as are Shelley's,

> Panting to seize the wings of morn,

and her frequent yearnings for death, in whose bourne alone, in a paradox typical of the Romantics, the final reconciliation of body and spirit will take place, echo the poignant longings of John Keats:

> To cease upon the midnight with no pain.

But the most telling proof of Emily's identification with the poetry of the age immediately preceding her youth – the Romantic age – lies in a most obvious characteristic which she shares with them. For her, as for them, Nature is not merely a reality in which we live, not just the palpable context of our lives, but part of us. We are, in a sense, emanations of Nature, and our relationship to it has the intense and definitive intimacy of heart to body.

Therefore, whatever happens to and in Nature inevitably has its consequences in us. And the Romantic poets made the corollary peculiarly characteristic – whatever happens in and to us is reflected in Nature; our moods become hers in poignant parallel. The place of the moors in Emily's consciousness and imagination takes on an even more crucial intimacy, and a superficial reading of her poetry which sees it as mere description has to give place to an awareness of the oneness of the human soul and the spirit of Nature:

> Lady, watch Apollo's journey;
> Thus thy first born's course shall be –
> If his beams through summer vapours
> Warms the earth all placidly,
> Her days shall pass like a pleasant dream in sweet tranquillity,

but

> If it darken, if a shadow
> Quench his rays and summer rain,
> Flowers may open, buds may blossom:
> Bud and flower alike are vain;
> Her days shall pass like a mournful story in care and tears and pain.

The typical Romantic posture which was dubbed the 'pathetic fallacy' (the attribution of human emotions to natural objects) is very apparent in Emily:

> 'Tis evening now, the sun descends
> In golden glory down the sky;
> The city's murmur softly blends
> With Zephyrs breathing gently by.
> And yet it seems a dreary morn,
> A dark October morn to me,
> And black the piles of rain-clouds born
> Athwart heaven's stormy canopy.

For Emily, as for Keats and Wordsworth in particular, the elements of nature, the flora, the fauna, the weather, are familiars of her soul, and they all have a particular urgency of existence in her poetry because most of her experiences of them were gained so near to her Haworth home. The heather, bluebells, heather bells, mosses, ferns, and above all green grass were within sight of the parsonage. The skylarks, the deer, the winds, clouds and rain are cohabitants of the land and air of Haworth moor. Nature is as intimately 'domestic' to her as it was to Keats in his Hampstead garden listening to the nightingale or to Wordsworth proprietorially celebrating the daffodils in his beloved Lake District.

But Emily is un-Romantic in the manner of her expression. Her eye was keener than her ear and her rhythmical sense was under-developed (surprising in one with a reputation as a very accomplished pianist). Her poetry does not have the organized music of Keats's or Shelley's lyrics nor the sonorous grandeur of Wordsworth's philosophizing. It sometimes lacks a sense of spontaneous creation – it occasionally seems to come from resolution rather than inspiration, and seems built (sometimes awkwardly) in a matrix of prose:

> She was cruel in her fear;
> Through the bars, one dreary day,
> I looked out to see her there,
> And she turned her face away!
>
> Like a false guard, false watch keeping,
> Still, in strife, she whispered peace;
> She would sing while I was weeping;
> When I listened, she would cease.

Yet her irregular rhythms, uncertain rhymes, staccato movements and frequently a-tonal sounds, so often unbelievably combine into a kind of rugged perfection. It is often possible to say of a poem of

Emily's – that could be better written; but it is impossible to believe that it could ever have been written in any other way and still have its force and magic:

> If grief for grief can touch thee,
> If answering woe for woe,
> If any ruth can melt thee,
> Come to me now!
>
> I cannot be more lonely,
> More drear I cannot be!
> My worn heart throbs so wildly
> 'Twill break for thee.
>
> And when the world despises,
> When heaven repels my prayer,
> Will not mine angel comfort?
> My idol hear?

And just as the visionary experiences and metaphysical yearnings and speculations of the great Romantic poets penetrate, suffuse and influence their creative writings, so it is with Emily. Quite apart from her poems, *Wuthering Heights* is imbued with Emily's transcendental fusion of sensual and spiritual. It is nothing to Heathcliff that he is one entity, but it means everything to him that he could also 'be' Cathy. It is nothing to Cathy to remain Cathy – but her identification and identity with Heathcliff mean everything. The physicality of their relationship is obvious, and because it is careless of and impatient with mere separate identity it involves both love and hate, affection and sneer, violence and quietude. But its metaphysical thrust is equally apparent in Heathcliff and Cathy's awesome and sometimes harrowing mutual quest for death which, paradoxically, they expect to give them an eternal and total union without perturbation.

Any attempt, then, to explore Emily's imagination must be a journey into what is probably mostly unknowable or, at least, inexpressible, and remote from the familiar haunts of biography. But biography must return to the natural and familiar if only because it is equally true that Emily also did. She was no total and irrecoverable recluse, though she preferred her other world and, as time went on, sought its territory with ever-frequent urgency.

There can be no doubt that Emily had a 'personality' which etched itself very clearly on the family's and the neighbourhood's retinas quite separately from the slightly unnerving etherealism which many noted but could not give a name to. Emily's physicality was not always dedicated to metaphysical experience, and although she was never gregarious there seems to have been a deep, perhaps even at times boisterous, and certainly voluble relationship with the family. The boisterousness is reflected in yet another tale (there are no such tales of her sisters) told of her escapades on one Oak Apple Day – an occasion now defunct.

On this day children in many parts of the country, especially the ex-Royalist areas, would re-enact the events of Charles II's escape after the battle of Worcester, which involved his ignominious hiding in the branches of an oak tree. The Brontë version required the physically fearless Emily to climb, as the King, Mr Brontë's favourite cherry tree whose top branches were level with his bedroom window. Either Emily's weight or the tree's condition broke a branch. Emily escaped unhurt but the tree was conspicuously wounded. Tabitha Aykroyd was hurriedly summoned for help, and a bag of soot was found and the gash in the tree-trunk smeared with it. Mr Brontë was told of the mishap when he returned home – his reaction is not recorded.

Emily's forceful and excited zest for adventure seems to have had its wild side. Ellen Nussey records one of her early visits to Haworth:

> On the top of a moor or in a deep glen Emily was a child in spirit for glee and enjoyment ... A spell of mischief ... lurked in her on occasions when out on the moors. She enjoyed leading Charlotte where she would not dare to go of her own free-will. Charlotte had a mortal dread of unknown animals, and it was Emily's pleasure to lead her into close vicinity, and then to tell her of how and of what she had done, laughing at her horror with great amusement.

One recalls a similar disparity of personality in the poet John Keats, whose aesthetic appearance and obvious committedness to the passionate delicacy of lyrical poetry was paralleled in his early youth by a marked penchant for boxing and, later, for arduous physical exercise, until consumption weakened him. Indeed, great extremes of behaviour and activity are, it would seem, commonly found in the Romantic personality. Shelley displayed them, so did Coleridge. Only one feature of Wordsworth seemed alien to the Romantic character and for decades was employed as evidence to set him slightly apart from the rest – his apparent solemnity, and his utterly unremarkable and conventional personal life – until the full story of his French adventures and his affair with Annette Vallon pointed critical judgement in the opposite direction.

Emily stands apart from her family in a number of ways, but in none more certainly than in the various respects in which her work and her personality take their place alongside the Romantic poets. To see her as a latecomer in this distinguished company is, in a way, to make her less a loner, and certainly to dispel that freakish aura which still surrounds many people's image of her.

Reverend A. B. Nicholls, Charlotte's husband

Mary Taylor in later life

Ellen Nussey in later life

John Brown, sexton of Haworth: oil painting by Branwell

George Smith, Charlotte's publisher

W. S. Williams, reader to Charlotte's publisher

M. Heger

If we had none of Charlotte's letters we would still know that she had many acquaintances and at least two very close friends. One has the feeling that if we had as many letters of Emily's as there are of Charlotte's we would not know much more about her than we now do; she seems never to have committed herself to anyone other than her family sufficiently to make friends. Ellen Nussey appears to have liked her but it is doubtful if she understood her. Indeed many people in the Haworth neighbourhood liked her but found her strange, perhaps forbidding. There is no suggestion whatsoever that she encouraged any man to fall in love with her; there is no evidence whatsoever that she fell in love with any man – or indeed, any woman, for there is a small fringe opinion that can only explain the absence of a male lover by the proposition that there was a female one.

Charlotte excites the biographical instinct; Branwell incites a psychiatric curiosity; Anne encourages the human disposition to see critical justice done. But what of Emily? One feels that there is not much more significant biography to be known than what we have; one senses that psychiatry is powerless to explain the unique nature of her imagination; and as for critical justice, her creative work constantly eludes those prepared scholarly nets which are capable only of scooping in the expected shoals for grading, weighing and designation – *Wuthering Heights* glides away from them untouched.

To read *Wuthering Heights* is to enter a world for which there is no parallel, no comparison. Canons and principles of criticism which are so facilely applied to literature are left looking 'fractured and corroborate' as, with mordant comedy, Falstaff has it, when applied to this annunciation of one woman's imagination. To read it for the first time is to have the deepest nerves of your sensibilities set in strident motion; to re-read it and then again and again towards infinity does nothing to steady them down. You experience a kind of rich, excited unease from which you can never be free.

Anne Brontë (1820–1849) and Aunt Branwell (1776–1842)

Anne was the youngest, by all accounts the most pious, arguably one of the best-looking and perhaps unarguably the most spiritually courageous of all the Brontës. Overshadowed now and when she lived by her two sisters and their immense reputations she insists, nevertheless, upon a place in our minds, emotions and imaginations. Indeed she possessed that quality which seems to have been shared by every single one of them from mother and father onwards – she was not ordinary.

Her poetry was superior to Charlotte's, and even if her two novels lack depth of passion and width of experience compared with both Emily's and Charlotte's, within a limited area of observation her perceptions of human behaviour are as acute and sensitive, and she is as directly courageous as are they in treading territories of fiction considered out of bounds to women. She was, of all the surviving children, the most obviously and deeply religious.

Little documentary evidence about her life remains – it is possible that what existed was destroyed by Charlotte when Anne died. Perhaps, too, some of Anne's contributions to the Gondal legends of childhood were included in those papers that we know Charlotte sorted through after her sisters' deaths. Anne and Emily were very close – this we do know – and when they were children Anne became more a part of Emily's imaginative world than of Charlotte's and Branwell's.

Whether she was shy and retiring because she was the last to enter this volatile Celtic family cannot be known, but all reports suggest that, though not timorous, she lacked that extrovert behaviour that was endemic to Branwell, sometimes apparent in Charlotte and occasionally evident in Emily. She fell more under the influence of Aunt Branwell, who joined the family when Mrs Brontë died, than did the others – and Aunt Branwell, though probably lacking Anne's sweet contours of spirit, was herself a woman given to piety, prayer and privacy.

In fact Miss Branwell was a deeply religious woman. She had a missionary zeal, and though there was nothing to convert Anne from there was a good deal to direct her towards. Her influence was certain, for however much Anne's father loved his last-born, there can be no doubt that the death of his wife, followed closely by that of his two eldest daughters, drove him out of the company of, and out of total commitment to, this small child. He left Anne to the severe nonconformity of Miss Branwell, who was a native of Cornwall – one of the centres of the Wesleyan Methodist movement; indeed its Methodist circuit was regarded as one of the strongest in the country.

The religion to which she adhered with complete tenacity produced two quite starkly different kinds of devotee, but the popular notion held by non-Methodists was (and still is) that its adherents are of a gloomy, pessimistic, resigned disposition, eschewing all laughter and gaiety, and all the good things of life. This classic notion of the Wesleyan Methodist is of one so dedicated to the preparation for the next world, to contemplating the sins of this world, and to worshipping God, that there is neither time nor disposition to look around and experience and enjoy the beauties of life. In this conception, Sin is more prevalent than Good and eternal damnation much more real than temporal joy. All religions are vulnerable to misrepresentation, but Wesleyan Methodism seems to have incited an almost dramatic distortion of the nature of its hierarchy, doctrine, faith and observance.

Some fifty years after the birth of Anne, another artist who had experienced the full force of Cornish Wesleyan Methodism was to wrestle with the problems and terrors that such a notion of the religion into which he had been born had created for him. His name was Arthur Symons and he recorded the early influences and experiences of religion in his chapter of autobiography in *Spiritual Adventures* (1908). Symons eventually became one of the best-known, most prolific, and certainly one of the most typical of the decadent, fin-de-siècle poets of the 1890s. He was the finest chronicler of the entire Art for Art's sake movement of the late nineteenth century – indeed he ranks among the highest of the aesthetic critics of that century.

Symons's father had, at first, the greater parental influence because, his son said, he was a minister on the Cornish Methodist circuit. Symons describes that kind of Methodism which is so widely believed to be typical:

> My parents were deeply religious; we all went to church, a Nonconformist church, twice on Sunday; I was not allowed to read any but pious books or play anything but hymns or oratorios on Sunday; I was taught that this life, which seemed so real and so permanent to me, was but an episode in existence, a little finite part of eternity. We had grace before and after meals; we had family prayers night and morning; we seemed to be in continual communication with the other world.

But Methodism can accommodate those of much happier cast of mind, feelings and disposition, and the Brontës met many such. Willy Weightman, the poor doomed curate for whom Anne's heart seems to have yearned, and the rumbustious William Morgan, were far from being vinegar-faced prophets of doom, and Patrick Brontë himself was by no means averse to a tot of the hard stuff when he felt like it. Of this kind of Methodist we hear less. Arthur Symons had reason to be thankful that his Methodist mother walked in sunshine while his father gloomed in the shadows:

> She had the joy of life, she was sensitive to every aspect of the world; she felt the sunshine before it came, and knew from what quarter the wind was blowing when she awoke in the morning. I think she was never indifferent to any moment that ever passed her by; I think no moment ever passed her by without being seized in all the eagerness of acceptance. I never knew her when she was not delicate, so delicate that she could rarely go out of doors in the winter; but I never heard

her complain, she was always happy, with a natural gaiety which had only been strengthened into a kind of vivid peace by the continual presence of a religion at once calm and passionate.

Perhaps, indeed, the movement's greatest figure, John Wesley, embodies this very paradox. He fulminated against worldliness in every conceivable aspect of living but at the same time he both countenanced and realized the proselytizing value of the superbly joyous Methodist hymns which still, today, can be heard soaring in full-throated ease out of the doors of grim-walled chapels in Wales, Yorkshire and Cornwall.

Symons's vivid descriptions of the two aspects of the nonconformity he was brought up in are important not merely because they conveniently sum up a phenomenon, but because they embody a reality which can and did exist. Hell-fire and damnation are too powerful to be easily put down, heaven and salvation too fragile to be significant or to survive.

Symons abandoned both his father's and his mother's brand of Methodism, but it was his father's that haunted him all his life. One needs a superb sense of humour – far more developed than Symons had – to be able to put it firmly in its place, as Dylan Thomas did when, writing from nonconformist Wales on a wet Sunday, he described the Bible as opening itself at Revelations.

Anne Brontë never renounced her faith – it became, in fact, stronger as she grew older – but her own position relative to it may well have been made far more complex than it need have been by the presence of Aunt Branwell. Without loading on to her the entire responsibility for what was a dominant element in Anne's religious experience – that death lay around every corner waiting to deliver her unprepared into the maw of eternal damnation – it seems fair to claim that this joyless lady certainly did nothing to ease the frightening awareness of damnation and sin which possessed Anne. By comparison with the Symons's household the atmosphere in the Brontë home was liberal, but, by our permissive standards, it would have seemed oppressively authoritarian. A terrible gulf between heaven and hell was a groundnote to their lives. Death occurred in their time much more frequently in families than it does now, and, indeed, when one child died the other children who survived were inclined to believe it was because of some sin that child had committed. Although Anne escaped Emily's and Charlotte's exposure to the arrant cruelty of the Rev. Carus Wilson's threats of the imminence of hell-fire at Cowan Bridge School, there was much opportunity for her to become acquainted with terrifying possibilities. The religion that was assiduously taught to her in her father's sermons and talk, and by her Aunt's constant presence, was as menacing in its penalties as it was ecstatic in its promised rewards. Children fear at least as often as they enjoy, and one senses that any joy Anne felt was considerably darkened by the brooding warnings that were never far from her aunt's lips.

But Aunt Branwell was implacably opposed to the more extreme form of Methodism – Calvinism, and in particular to its emphasis on redemption only for a few elect. For her, salvation was open to all, but her apparently bleak personality was such that this comprehensive escape route was made to seem difficult to the point of being impassable. In one of her poems Anne says that when she looks back on childhood, she sees

> . . . a helpless child,
> Feeble, and full of causeless fears,
> Simple and easily beguiled
> To credit all it hears . . .

Neither did Aunt Branwell follow the Wesleyan edicts on dress – she wore shawls, lace and silk; and she indulged in an even worse lure to perdition – she took snuff. But she still presented a stern and gloomy aspect to the children. In none of their letters or diary-fragments is there any suggestion whatsoever that she ever had a happy day. No reference is made to her smiling; she is always a reproach, an admonition, a shadow on the sunlight.

She helped the children with money. She had a kind of frosty kindness, but she was perhaps so devoid and suspicious of any kind of intellectual stimulus (she was, for example, not known to read) that she was starved of mental activity: in this she surely did follow Wesley who spurned knowledge and its acquisition, and staked all on the development of character. She had nothing to turn her mind away from a predisposition to reside in life's shadows.

In mitigation is the fact that she had very probably abandoned all prospects of marriage by leaving her native Cornwall, where she was known, to come and live in Haworth, where she remained virtually unknown. This was an act of Christian charity, we must assume, but it may have embittered her without her conscious volition.

The only evidence about Anne's religion is in her poetry, and in references (which are scanty) to her in others' writings. It is clear that the poetry is dominated by a series of well-defined realities – these constitute her religion: (1) It was all-enveloping. (2) It did not depend on a blind faith or merely pious way of life and thought, for Anne had a keen and inquiring mind. She probed her religion as much as she accepted its total necessity for her. (3) She loved her God beyond herself and beyond the world and she was dedicated to finding communion with God:

> One hour, my spirit, stretch thy wings,
> And quit this joyless sod,
> Bask in the sunshine of the sky,
> And be alone with God!

(4) Many of her poems combine the sense of complete religiosity with intellectual query and are written in an attempt to reconcile the often conflicting demands of faith and reason. (5) Her religious consciousness started at a very early age. (6) By no means was her overall experience of religion invariably joyous. Sometimes she could not find her God. More often she became possessed of a fearful melancholy – sins, sorrows, hopes and fears combining:

> And yet, alas! how many times
> My feet have gone astray,
> How oft have I forgot my God,
> How greatly fallen away!

> My Sins increase, my love grows cold,
> And Hope within me dies,
> And Faith itself is wavering now,
> O how shall I arise!

(7) The melancholy was the result of her fear, almost anger, against the Calvinistic notion of salvation by selection:

> You may rejoice to think yourselves secure,
> You may be grateful for the gift divine,
> That grace unsought which made your black hearts pure,
> And fits your earthborn souls in Heaven to shine.

> But is it sweet to look around and view
> Thousands excluded from that happiness,
> Which they deserve at least as much as you,
> Their faults not greater nor their virtues less?

All the Brontës were against Calvinism. She was, very like her father, a dedicated Wesleyan. (8) There was a very strongly emotional factor in her detestation of Calvinism. (9) The width of Anne's religious experience can be demonstrated in her intense interest in hymns – she wrote them and collected them in a music manuscript book extant at Haworth Parsonage Museum – and in the many references to the Bible in her novels. Three of her hymns are in the Methodist Hymnal.

In Chapter 17 of *Agnes Grey*, the heroine is made to say:

When we are harassed by sorrows or anxieties, or long oppressed by any powerful feelings which we must keep to ourselves, for which we can obtain and seek no sympathy from any living creature, and which we cannot, or will not wholly crush, we often naturally seek relief in poetry – and often find it too –.

This, succinctly, not only gives a motive for her writing of poems but also gives justification for our regarding many of them as spiritual autobiography. There is nothing forced or dilettante about Anne's poetry. It has a direct and honest simplicity without lacking force and urgency and control. Its sweetness is not that of added sugar but of a natural essence of a kindly, submissive, gentle creature. Some poetry is a mirror of a vision, Anne's is a window into her soul.

But not all of her poems are religious. Seven or more of her published poems are almost certainly a record of her feelings about her father's curate, William Weightman, who arrived in Haworth in the later summer of 1839, and died in a cholera epidemic there in 1842.

Weightman was a well-liked, cheerful, friendly man, with a flirtatious eye and manner for the ladies – he seems, at one point, to have directed his gaze towards the redoubtable Ellen Nussey. Charlotte at first like him enormously. He was a 'cheerful, chatty kind of body', but she later regarded him with a good deal of suspicious reserve and declared him to be 'a thorough male flirt' – with which judgement the Haworth district community would have heartily agreed. In successive years, indeed, he sent Valentines to all three Brontë sisters and to Ellen Nussey. The first one prompted a poetic reply from Charlotte, part of which runs:

A Roland for your Oliver
We think you've justly earned;
You sent us each a valentine
Your gift is now returned.

We cannot write or talk like you;
We're plain folks every one;
You've played a clever jest on us,
We thank you for your fun.

Believe us when we frankly say
(Our words though blunt are true)
At home, abroad, by night or day
We all wish well to you.

And never may a cloud come o'er
The sunshine of your mind;
Kind friends, warm hearts, and happy hours
Through life we trust you'll find.

Anne was, therefore, by no means his one and only 'love', but her emotions and her desires were deeply stirred by him. Probably she was not the only one, and Charlotte's eventual ambiguous dismissal of him may hide a personal hurt:

> ... for all the tricks, wiles, and insincerities of love, the gentleman has not his match for 20 miles around. He would fain persuade every woman under 30 whom he sees that he is desperately in love with her ...

What was a steadfast soul like Anne doing to fall in love (for her poems and the scraps of evidence of her behaviour persuade us that she apparently did) with such a flighty man? His eye may have been roving and his favours easily dispensed, but Weightman seems simply to have been indulging the prerogative of youthful verve. There is some indication that he would have settled down. Patrick Brontë's view of him as a curate is a fine corrective to Charlotte's perhaps biased assessment:

> His character wore well ... the surest proof of real worth. He had, it is true, some peculiar advantages. Agreeable in person and manners, and constitutionally cheerful, his first introduction was prepossessing. But what he gained at first, he did not lose afterwards ...

Perhaps this was what Anne's cool mind perceived as her warmer emotions responded. If it is true that Weston, the curate in *Agnes Grey*, is a portrait of Weightman, then it is a confirmation that Anne agreed with her father's appraisal.

Poor Anne – a sort of solitariness dogs her life and her death – she was away when Weightman died, and heard by letter, and mourned alone. If we can believe that what she said about the efficacy of writing poetry was true about her religion, then it is equally true of perhaps her only experience of love. Some considerable time after Weightman's death she turned to poetry to express and to help to exorcize the harassment by sorrows, by anxieties, by powerful feelings 'which we must keep to ourselves'. The result is a touching reflection of her grieved heart:

> Severed and gone, so many years!
> And art thou still so dear to me,
> That throbbing heart and burning tears
> Can witness how I clung to thee?
>
> I know that in the narrow tomb
> The form I loved was buried deep,
> And left, in silence and in gloom,
> To slumber out its dreamless sleep.

Nothing became Anne's life more splendidly than her departing it. To the cynical the precise details of its dignity, courage and gentleness will seem like a fiction; to the sympathetic an affirmation of the power of her religion and of her devotion to it:

Then – my sister died happily; nothing dark, except the inevitable shadow of death overclouded her hour of dissolution – the doctor – a stranger – who was called in – wondered at her fixed tranquillity of spirit and settled longing to be gone. He said in all his experience he had seen no such deathbed, and that it gave evidence of no common mind. Yet to speak the truth – it but half consoles to remember this calm – there is piercing pain in it. Anne had had enough of life such as it was – in her twenty-eight years – she laid it down.

She is buried at Scarborough – the only one of her family not to have been put to rest at Haworth. The loneliness we have noted above is given an image by the photographs of her gravestone, and there is somehow an extra catch of pathos in the date error on its inscription.

Until quite recently critical opinion in general was that Anne walked into posterity on the apron strings of her sisters. Some have even concluded that without the existence and reputation of her sisters we would never have heard of her. Who knows, indeed, whether the answer to that is yea or nay. It is time, however, to take a less emotionally charged view of Anne's status as an artist.

The quality of her poetry speaks for itself – but that quality is not strongly enough served by Charlotte's description of it as having a 'sweet sincere pathos'. It is minor poetry of excellent quality. Indeed, one should perhaps employ the word 'minor' in the sense in which it is often used of certain lyricists of the sixteenth and early seventeenth centuries, not so much to imply inferior quality as to designate a particular category of poetry. A 'minor' poet is often deliberately so, in that he or she is not concerned with confronting the great issues of life – death, time and eternity on an epic or large scale – but with commenting upon, reacting to, the minutiae or the flotsam and jetsam, which demand attention from the imagination, without becoming its constant master. For Anne, the writing of poetry had two motivations. Some she wrote, as she indicates, as a kind of therapy; poetry becomes a way of laying a ghost or easing a worry or giving balm to a hurt mind. But some she wrote – her hymns, that is – as a joyous response to the need to worship.

Like that of the best 'minor' poets Anne's poetry, of whichever category, is characterized by a kind of pointilliste precision of word and form, and by a delicacy of tone and manner. One never feels one is being beleaguered by profundity either of matter or manner; on the other hand one equally never feels one is likely to be affronted by coarseness of either expression or style. Her sincerity can, so to speak, be taken for granted – indeed, the very fastidiousness of her verse bespeaks honesty of emotion and thought:

> I love the silent hour of night,
> For blissful dreams may then arise,
> Revealing to my charméd sight
> What may not bless my waking eyes!
>
> And then a voice may meet my ear
> That death has silenced long ago;
> And hope and rapture may appear
> Instead of solitude and woe.
>
> Cold in the grave for years has lain
> The form it was my bliss to see,
> And only dreams can bring again
> The darling of my heart to me.

Some find in Anne's poetry echoes and influences of Cowper, whom she had read and obviously absorbed. Without denying his presence and effect, it ought to be recorded that there is also in her poetry something of the spirit of George Herbert, the seventeenth-century divine. It consists of a kind of direct purity of vision, an uncluttered sight of what, to many, is unseeable – the distant horizon of heaven. And like Herbert's, Anne's poetry, even in its most despondent states, never loses a sense of worship; it is, therefore, most un-selfindulgent in its moods.

Her novels have a similar personality to her poetry but, because of the greater opportunity their longer form gives us for study, it is apparent that hers was a mind which was dominated by an impulse for correctness and felicity. She is a far more efficient constructor of a narrative than Charlotte and can juxtapose incidents and episodes with the same kind of skill that Emily shows in *Wuthering Heights*. Her style is free of that curious lurching between what one can only describe as the ad hoc, and the superbly designed that characterizes Charlotte's. But Anne's style, though smoother, is not bland. It indulges in shafts of satire, in broad comic blows and is blessedly capable of sentiment without sentimentality.

Although, then, there is much in *Agnes Grey* and in *The Tenant of Wildfell Hall* which might alert one to the blood relationship of Anne to Charlotte and Emily, her novels should never be judged as mere off-shoots on luxuriant plants which only sentimentality stops from being pinched out.

In many ways *The Tenant* is a fiercer novel than any of Charlotte's in its moral condemnations and assertions, and in its merciless exposure of the sickening and widespread effects of dissipation. In some ways its depiction of the sacrifices of love is more credible than Charlotte's and more naturalistically effective than Emily's. There are very few Victorian women novelists who, at the age of twenty-eight, wrote, or would have dared to write a novel more calculated to offend public sensibilities by its relentless naturalism.

Had she lived Anne Brontë might well have provided much more and conclusive evidence that she was not her sisters' shadow.

Patrick Branwell Brontë (1817–1848)

Of the large Brontë family two stand out in presenting a different kind of image to the world from the others. They are Emily and Branwell. They both have something of an unreal quality about them. Emily seems more spirit than flesh, however much we are impressed by her practical, down-to-earth qualities as a good manager of the Haworth household in times of necessity, as a possessor of quick wits as is shown in the story of how she cauterized a possible rabid dog-bite on her arm with a red-hot poker, and of how she saved her brother from the flames of the bed he had, probably accidentally, set on fire. As a real person, she eludes us; when we think we have her and know her she seems to turn to a less palpable element even as we look.

Branwell's image also has a fictive aura, but of a different order. If Emily's has a spiritual quality, his is fantastic. Branwell's short life, in many of its aspects, was larger than life. From a very early age most of what he did veered towards the happenings sometimes of a kind of nightmare, sometimes of a sensational daydream.

Whatever inherited characteristics contributed towards this persona, there seems to be little doubt that his early environment had a large, lasting and almost certainly unsettling effect on him. He may have been, to an extent, predisposed by temperament to become what he became and do what he did, but Branwell also suffered from events which happened early in his existence. He was an only son in a family of six, his mother died when he was four years old, his two eldest sisters Elizabeth and Maria died, tragically young, when he was in his ninth year.

These dark events in themselves would be sufficient to dull the bright avenues of childhood, and since he was the imaginative and sensitive child of Celtic parents, the shadows would have been deep. Maria's death, in particular, seems to have been recapitulated in his memory and imagination, and a sense of loss had constant occupation of his soul. But there were other, more insidious strains at work.

Branwell shared with other only boys in large families the mixed blessing conferred by the conventional adulations of and expectations for the male in a largely female environment. That these were conventional in a century where the economic and prestige value of the son in a family of daughters was crucial did not mean that they were also perfunctory and artificial – certainly not in Branwell's case. He seems to have been deeply loved, and looked up to by his sisters and his aunt, while his father spared nothing in time, energy and money in his attempt to lead and bring the boy on to a noble, proud and worthwhile manhood. The girls, especially Charlotte, eventually lost all hope for and patience with Branwell, and with them some love leaked away. Only when he was on his death-bed does the strength of the family bond of affection and shared childhood seem to have returned and, indeed, joined again with the father's anguished love – which he had never lost. Charlotte expresses it:

> I do not weep from a sense of bereavement – there is no prop withdrawn, no consolation torn away, no dear companion lost – but for the wreck of talent, the ruin of promise, the untimely dreary extinction of what might have been a burning and a shining light . . . Nothing remains of him but a memory of errors and sufferings. There is such a bitterness of pity for his life and death, such a yearning for the emptiness of his whole existence as I cannot describe . . .

The anguish which the family felt on his death was in excess, so to speak, of simple bereavement. They grieved over unfulfilled promise, but, as Charlotte so clearly implies, they also felt a kind of exhausted despair at the fretful, often violent, morose last months of his life – a life which, in its excesses, had for so long seemed wedded to flamboyant disaster.

What we can never know, and perhaps what even Charlotte for all her perceptive curiosity and precise memory never knew, is whether it is true that Branwell's life was entirely unfulfilled. Branwell had done more than a little painting at a time when it was thought that it would be both the chosen and the right career for him – but it is the painting of a gifted amateur. He had written a great deal of poetry, as well as stories and an incomplete novel, over a long period of time, in pursuit of what he often felt (and expected) was his bent, that of a man of letters. It is the writing of a man of prodigious energy, fervent enthusiasm, huge but wayward imagination, untutored style and fitful intellectual discipline. But it is what lies inside this flourish of writing that prompts the doubt about the totality of Branwell's lack of fulfilment.

If Branwell's life, which had so much the ambience of fiction about it, is, demonstrably, larger-than-life in its attempts and excesses, so is the major fiction-writing of his two elder sisters – in particular *Wuthering Heights* and *Jane Eyre*. Moreover, even the less resonant, aesthetically thinner work of Anne seemed to her literary generation to cock a somewhat brazen snook at the accepted mores and modes of polite fiction-writing, and to be highly coloured. There may well be a potent connection between the apparent tuppence-coloured of Branwell's life and imagination, and the beaten gold of his sisters' literary achievement. The question arises – is Branwell fulfilled in the work of his sisters, not merely in the beaten sentimental way of family relationship, but in a more positive sense? Many things bound the Brontës together, but not the least were the common sources, shape and timbre of the imaginative world which dominated their childhood – designated separately as Gondal and Angria but, in essence, one common stock of ideas, characters, images and fables. One would be hard put to it to allocate fairly to Charlotte, Emily, Anne or Branwell their share in the invention of the legends of Angria and Gondal. It would be easy to be unfair about Branwell's contribution to the saga, simply because he never successfully formalized or employed Gondal and Angria in published work.

No one can tell precisely where the Glasstown Confederacy had its first inception, or Gondal or Angria. And though the origins and originals of many of the places and characters who populate their legends are known, it remains a mystery in which child's 'spinning-place' of the imagination their relationship to the whole intricate story was woven. It has become customary to attribute most of the invention to Charlotte, partly because we know more about her, because she wrote more, lived longer, and, in her assiduous correspondence, recorded a good deal (though not enough) about that childhood world. But we should not be magnetized by Charlotte's ample persuasiveness.

Branwell's *History of the Young Men* (started 1830) is a comparatively early account of the world which was later to be further explored and developed by all of them, but notably by Charlotte. Again, the early and crucial involvement of Branwell may well be signalled in the existence of his copy, in his own hand, of a map from *Blackwood's Magazine* of the west coast of Africa from the Gulf of Guinea northwards. This map still survives and the frisson one gets in looking at its childish, if faded, urgency may well be accompanied by the reflection that this, in Branwell's hand, was among the first indices of names – Ashantee, Etrei, Calabar – which became inextricably part of

Angria. Some places do not appear in *Blackwood's* or any other professional piece of cartography; Stumps Land, Monkey's Land, Frenchy Land, are someone's invention. There is no reason to suppose it was anyone else but Branwell.

But more important than the attribution of detailed invention to one or other of the children is the evidence not only of Branwell's complete involvement in this imaginary world which so dominated them all but of the influence of his interests and predilections on the whole body of the fictional material that came out of it. It was, for example, almost certainly he who suggested that Haworth parsonage should publish its own magazine, modelled on the beloved and precious *Blackwood's Magazine*; certainly, the first numbers bore his name and were called *The Magazine*. With that relentless assumption of leadership which seems to characterize so much of Charlotte's relationships with her family, she took over the magazine after the third number.

Again, Branwell's participation is exemplified in the extent to which so many elements of the world of Angria are fashioned out of the real world. This is particularly true of many of the characters whose personalities and activities at times turn what would in any event be bizarre narrative into a kind of vaunting and passionate drama. Branwell had also received the benefit of his father's liberal determination to allow his children to know as much as possible of the world outside – particularly the world of military men and politicians – by reading both books and whatever magazines and newspapers they could lay their hands on. The direction Branwell's interests took was not only definite but seems to have elicited an accompanying response from Charlotte and perhaps even guided her towards certain destinations. For Branwell had an excited and deeply detailed interest in history – virtually contemporary history.

For the Brontës the air of recent history was full of heroes and villains, but mostly heroes. Branwell was born only two decades after the French Revolution, twelve years after the battle of Trafalgar, and two years after Napoleon's defeat at Waterloo. Where Charlotte fashioned a hero out of expected material (the Duke of Wellington) Branwell fervently went for the unexpected – Napoleon Buonaparte at first, then one of his generals, Marshall Soult. But both children, mutually inspirited or not, were unexpected in the way they turned reality into fiction.

Charlotte signalled her intention of avoiding both Waterloo and too obvious an identity with the Iron Duke by metamorphosing him into his two sons (Arthur Augustus Adrian Wellesley and Lord Charles Albert Florian Wellesley); both appeared either as protagonist or hero in many of her stories. Branwell announced the influence of, and his admiration for, Soult (who had behaved with special chivalry by ordering a French salute of guns at Sir John Moore's burial in Corunna) by inventing a character often called 'Young Soult the Rymer'. He very closely identified himself with the character in the sense that Young Soult's son's name appeared frequently (as, for example, in *Young Soult's Poems*, 1829) as the author of a number of works written by Branwell himself:

> This truly great poet [writes Charlotte] is in his 23 year. . . His apparel is generally torn and he wears it hanging about him in a very careless and untidy manner. His shoes are often slipshod and his stockings full of holes . . . He appears constantly labouring under a state of strong excitement, occasioned by excessive drinking and gambling to which he is unfortunately much addicted. . .

The acceptance of the fictionalized heirs of a British and a French General by both Charlotte and Branwell, leading to a constant cross-fertilization of inventiveness about their personalities and fortunes, is an important example of the extent of mutual commitment that the Brontë children made to the common pool of imaginative experience. There is no reason to believe that Emily and Anne were less committed (certainly Emily's 'Gondal' poems exhibit a strikingly similar energy and imagination), but specific evidence is slender.

There was nothing slender about Branwell's contribution. He played a major part in recording the history of the Glasstown Confederacy, the story of whose society and people dominated his own and Charlotte's early writings. In character-sketches, poems, narrative accounts, dialogues, records of political and governmental meetings, he matched Charlotte's own prodigious outpourings quantitively if not qualitatively.

From the midst of this impressive display of application, imagination and energy there gradually emerged perhaps Branwell's most nearly distinguished single artistic creation. Its nature and form are important to an understanding of Branwell's image of himself and probably of his sisters' image of him. Moreover, the part it plays in the early childhood sagas is of a kind which suggests the nature of their relationships, particularly those of Charlotte and Branwell.

The character of Alexander Rogue was one which he seems to have begun seriously to develop at a time when Charlotte was away at school from January 1831 to May 1832. Her absence, and therefore the abatement of her direct influence, is worth emphasizing – Branwell gave depth to this character when Genius Tallii was not there to conspire with him or to interfere. Rogue eventually became infamous as Alexander Percy, Viscount Ellrington (through marriage with the ravishingly beautiful Zenobia Ellrington), and was created Earl of

Northangerland. He had been Rogue by name and was indeed arrant rogue by nature. He incited civil war, was involved in both political and personal intrigue, totally lacked moral fibre and was eventually sentenced to the firing-squad.

Northangerland is emblematic of some important interrelated matters which concern Branwell. He testifies to Branwell's ability (however fugitive and unpredictable) to create character out of his own mind and application; he can refute, by the dramatic, if somewhat bizarre, effectiveness of his existence, any suggestion that Branwell was absolutely incapable of cogent artistic creation; he is further proof of the major part played by Branwell in the early combined work of the children. Yet Northangerland is more important as an indicator of the nature of Branwell and of his postures, both conscious and unconscious, in relation to his family.

As a character in a fiction Northangerland both represents and, to an extent, motivates a spirit of immorality, destructiveness and deceit. He stands for the almost exact opposite of the spirit that Charlotte generates in her Glasstown writings. The society she pictures is not devoid of its multiplying villainies but their effect is subsumed by the power of right action, right thought, right feeling. The moral core of Charlotte's world is strong and sound, the sentiments are placatory and mild, the society is one which tends conspicuously towards good. Atmospherically, her juvenile world is redolent of and dominated by the kind of high-life society we have long associated with accounts of that dramatic ball, from which high and low ranking officers disappeared with tactful deliberation, then headed, under orders, for the field of Waterloo. Charlotte's Glasstown was a sophisticated haven of the nobility, frequently on show, en masse, in fine military raiment or the latest in feminine adornment. The chief occupation was either gossip about or indulgence in intrigue – political, domestic and amorous.

The spirit of Branwell's Glasstown seems nearer that of the darker areas of those Gothic novels, so popular at the beginning of the nineteenth century, where terror, torture and treachery weave in and out of sentimentality, romance and adventure. But there is the significant difference that in Branwell's Glasstown stories and narratives there is an access of violence, blood, deceit and death which seems obsessive in its intensity, detail and extent and which appears to be under the direct control of the satanic figure of Northangerland:

> But tall and solemnly, with his head uncovered and the high bald
> forehead pale features and sunken eye – my sight almost grew dim
> while I felt in my mind that I saw before me the immortal Alexander
> Percy – immortal for his greatness and crimes... His lordship was

attired in black frock coat, light trousers and the red ribbon round his neck while his profuse dyed whiskers and scarlet lips contrasted strongly with his fork beard and eyes. . .

The very last picture we have of Branwell Brontë is uncannily redolent of the fantastic ambience which surrounds Northangerland. His friend Grundy, an engineer, invited him to dinner at the Black Bull. He waited and

> Presently the door opened cautiously, and a head appeared. It was a mass of red, unkempt, uncut hair, wildly floating around a great, gaunt forehead; the cheeks yellow and hollow, the mouth fallen, the thin white lips not trembling but shaking, the sunken eyes, once small, now glaring with the light of madness – all told the sad tale but too surely. I hastened to my friend, greeted him in my gayest manner, and, as I knew he best liked, drew him quickly into the room, and forced upon him a stiff glass of hot brandy. Under its influence, and that of the bright, cheerful surroundings, he looked frightened – frightened of himself. . . When at last I was compelled to leave, he quietly drew from his coat sleeve a carving-knife, placed it on the table, and holding me by both hands, said that, having given up all thoughts of ever seeing me again, he imagined when my message came that it was a call from Satan . . .

This description was written by one who there is no reason to believe had any knowledge whatsoever of Angria or Gondal: yet he might well be reporting an encounter with one of the fictional inhabitants of those legendary and fabulous worlds. It is tempting to indulge in some fancy and to see this Branwell, sick with excess and indulgence, as a desiccated, decayed hero-villain of the Glasstown conspiracy.

Long before he died Branwell had become a trial and tribulation to his family, and a terrible disappointment to the very expectations which his own incandescent creative qualities helped to arouse. But his status in the family's life was much more subtle than this. What Branwell represented haunted the pages of Charlotte's work, and certainly Anne's. Indeed, the depiction of profligacy, drunkenness and unreliability in *The Tenant of Wildfell Hall* could not possibly have possessed their authenticity if Branwell had not existed or had been a different kind of man.

Angria and Gondal surfaced into real life through the personality of Branwell. Everything he did was done with a reckless panache, a larger-than-life intensity which we usually associate with high fiction, not everyday life. It is tempting to conclude that he was, to a degree, living out a fiction: his letters often read like reports written by someone else about Branwell himself:

My appetite is lost; my nights are dreadful, and having nothing to do makes me dwell on past scenes – on her own self, her voice, her person, her thoughts, till I could be glad if God took me. In the next world I could not be worse than I am in this.

I am not a whiner, dear Sir, but when a young man like myself has fixed his soul on a being worthy of all love, pardon him for boring a friend with a misery that has only one black end.

When you place such speculation about Branwell's personality into the context of the hard biographical facts it is, amazingly, usually confirmed – even its most apparently exaggerated flights. His life was a chapter of bizarre incidents, unpredictable behaviour and self-destructive activity. And all this was embarked upon with flamboyance and emotional fervour; even braggadocio. Examples abound to confirm the reflection that, in him, fiction and reality rarely had clear boundaries.

As early as 1835 Branwell, who had shown promise as an artist, was to go to London to seek admission to the Academy School. He went by coach, but as soon as he arrived there he seems completely to have lost heart and will. He never darkened the portals of the School's headquarters at Somerset House, and never had his letters of recommendation delivered. He went to the Embankment, gazed at the river's traffic and became more and more depressed. This did not prevent his indulging in sightseeing and in lengthy sessions at the Castle tavern in High Holborn, which was kept by a famous boxer; he seems to have become very quickly accepted there as a loquacious 'character'. When he returned to Haworth he announced that he had been robbed!

The impression of self-dramatization here is strongly supported by the existence of a highly coloured account of a visit by an Angrian hero – Captain Henry Hastings – to Verdopolis, the capital of Angria. Hastings has too much of Branwell in him not to be easily identifiable, and Verdopolis is uncannily like the London that Branwell experienced.

In Haworth, Branwell was a very strict Sunday School teacher, a part-time secretary of the local Masonic Lodge, and a full-time official of the local Temperance Society. He sent the most extraordinary letters to the editor of the prestigious *Blackwood's Magazine*, one of which made the claim that he was 'in possession of something, the design of which, whatever might be its execution, would be superior to that of any series of articles which has yet appeared in *Blackwood's Magazine*', and sent examples of his poems to Wordsworth – who never replied.

In May 1838 he had acquired an artist's studio in Bradford. His father, and several friends, had gone to some trouble to obtain what they hoped would be the right environment for the development of his talent. To be fair to Branwell he wasted no time in making the acquaintance – indeed, in some cases the close friendship – of men who might well be of help to him in the world of art and letters. J.B. Leyland, the notable sculptor, became a firm friend, as did the mezzotint expert W.O. Geller, and Coleridge's son, Hartley, whose temperament in some respects closely resembled Branwell's. But the heady world of Bradford cultural life and the insistent allure of the pubs and hotel snugs and lounges proved too much for Branwell's sense of balance. His work deteriorated, he spent more time talking than creating, he became locally renowned as a 'character' rather than widely recognized as an artist: perhaps it might be said that he displayed something of the Dylan Thomas syndrome – but Thomas was no failure.

From 1836 onwards confirmation of the quite unusual way in which fiction and actuality pendulumed in Branwell's life and personality is to be amply found in Charlotte's Angrian writings. In her character Patrick Wiggins, and in her versions of Captain Henry Hastings, her brother's body, soul and spirit are curiously but obviously mixed, and admiration and apprehension vie with one another in Charlotte's reflections on the result.

Branwell became tutor to the Postlethwaite's sons at Broughton-in-Furness in early 1840. While there he translated some of Horace's Odes, and sent them, together with a poem, to Hartley Coleridge. (The result was an invitation to spend the day at Rydal Water, in the Lake District, which he accepted.) Again, hospitality, vanity and emotional exhilaration attacked his sense of fitness and he neglected his tutorial duties. By the end of August, this extraordinary young being had become assistant clerk at the new railway station at Sowerby Bridge on the new Leeds/Hebden Bridge line. Early in 1841 he was promoted and became station master at Luddenden Foot, a mile further up the line towards Hebden Bridge. The body of William Grimshaw the famed predecessor of Patrick Brontë at Haworth Church lay in Luddenden churchyard barely a stone's throw away from the Lord Nelson inn – whose cosy presence contributed to Branwell's downfall in his new career of railway employee. J.B. Leyland lived nearby and he saw a great deal of him; he wrote poetry, some of which was printed in the *Halifax Guardian*; and he spent his substance at the Lord Nelson. In March 1842 he was dismissed because a deficit of £11 was discovered in his railway accounts. It is impossible to know how the money disappeared – embezzlement? forgetfulness? inefficiency? His notebooks which he kept at this time give credence to the possibility of total administrative chaos – they are a testament of disorganization.

Anne, his sister, then found him employment as a tutor to the Robinson family of Thorp Green Hall, between Ripon and York. This is where one of the most sensational examples of Branwell's dramatization of his life begins and ends. He stayed there for two-and-a-half years and for most of that time seems to have conducted himself reasonably well, though the reasons for his departure, when it came, must have cast their shadows ahead. At some point, Branwell appears to have convinced himself that he was in love with the lady of the house, Mrs Robinson, and that she reciprocated.

Perhaps he received some encouragement, for she may well have been a flirt and while not aiming could have scored a decisive hit on the impressionable Branwell. It is quite impossible to know the truth of what happened, and for how long, at Thorp Green. Perhaps only Anne Brontë, who was, of course, present throughout the whole time as governess, could have provided reliable evidence, but she left none that was direct. *Agnes Grey* obviously draws upon Anne's memories of her life at the Robinsons' – there is, for example, in the precise description of Rosalie Murray's appearance, what many believe to be a portrait of Mrs Robinson – but what the novel lacks is a red-haired tutor! Biography filtered through the artistic imagination is likely to change considerably: Anne's indirect evidence cannot be used too closely.

But from the letters he himself wrote, it might well be concluded that Branwell was not entirely driven by the rages of love. Is it not possible that a young man, always short of money, fond of spending it, given to revel in the high life, disposed, on his record, to be more interested in the pursuit of civilized (if extravagant) leisure than the slow acquisition of status, might have seen the main chance at Thorp Green? Mrs Robinson was beautiful, perhaps neglected, probably bored, and wealthy. Her husband was ailing. It was a situation for a Percy of Angria or a Branwell Brontë of Haworth to exploit with enthusiasm. His letters to his friends vibrate with enthusiasm, and the effects of his delusion obviously communicated themselves very strongly to his friends; one of them, Francis Leyland, writes that Branwell, for a time, could talk of nothing else but the woman to whom he felt so attached: 'This lady, he said, loved him to distraction. She was in a state of inconceivable agony at his loss.'

But whenever Branwell writes of this affair there is, inevitably, a fictive aura in everything he says – though the careful reader will not fail to notice in this letter to Grundy the plain reference to Mrs Robinson's estate:

> I have lain down during nine long weeks utterly shattered in body and broken down in mind. The probability of her becoming free to give me herself and her estate never rose to drive away the prospect of her decline under her present grief.

On 17 July 1845, when Branwell was at Haworth, he received an unexpected letter from Mr Robinson dismissing him from employment. There exists no explanation for the apparent suddenness of this decision. His own subsequent comments stress that the lady and he had been intensely in love from the very beginning; that she had sent her coachman to Haworth to inform him that by her husband's will she stood to lose all her fortune if she married him (Robinson died in May 1846); that the doctor who attended Mr Robinson in his last illness had declared that his wife's conduct (i.e. her affair with Branwell) contributed to her husband's death; that Mrs Robinson (in token of their liaison) sent him (Branwell) sums of money at intervals.

None of Branwell's allegations have any confirmation whatsoever, and there is nothing that suggests any kind of discord between Mr and Mrs Robinson, nor any reason why the doctor should write to Branwell. Perhaps Branwell invented the episodes to engage the sympathy of friends in an attempt to borrow money from them in his abandoned and shattered state, or perhaps, by now, the spirit of Percy Northangerland had taken him over and he no longer made any effort to distinguish between fiction and fact.

There is some doubt about the date when Branwell began writing his novel *And the Weary Are at Rest*, but there is no doubt about its possible relationship to the extraordinary Robinson affair. Percy, Earl of Northangerland (Branwell's alter ego) is the hero, and the heroine is Maria Thurston. He arrives to stay with Mr and Mrs Thurston at their country estate on the moors in time for the beginning of the grouse-shooting season, but is less concerned with destroying grouse than seducing Maria. She eventually yields.

Throughout the novel the identification between Branwell's idealized conception of himself as Percy and his version of the Robinson story as an Angrian narrative is close. Moreover, Mrs Robinson becomes an Angrian heroine – Maria Thurston. The pendulum between fiction and reality which had, so to speak, counterpointed Branwell's heartbeats for all of his conscious life swings with unabated vigour.

After Robinson's death and what appears to have been an amplification of his dismissal as tutor by his banishment from Mrs Robinson's ambience, Branwell went from bad to worse. He drank heavily, took opium, spent days in a stupor, and his unpaid bills arrived to plague his father even further. He seems to have known nothing of his sisters' publishing success – though J.B. Leyland believed otherwise – and rapidly descended to the day of his early death on 24 September 1848.

It is easy to dismiss Branwell Brontë's life as incandescent and wasted. In material terms he achieved nothing and expended a great deal. He brought untold grief to his father and family. He perplexed his friends. There is nothing uncommon about his kind of profligacy – many families, both now and in the past, knew and know the torment of having in their midst someone who constantly promised much and equally constantly dissipated expectations in the most sensational way.

But any serious consideration of Branwell must leave a nagging doubt that he does not quite fit into this pattern. There is too much of Branwell in Angria and too much of Angria in the crowning literary successes of his sister to conclude that his was a totally unfulfilled existence. And the realist who might sardonically point out that it is one thing for an uncommitted commentator writing over a century later to say this, and quite another for Branwell to know it, ought to reflect on the possibility that, both to himself and to his sisters, Branwell was, in a sense, a living embodiment, the only living embodiment, of an imaginary childhood world which was, to them, as real as that world where in actuality he wasted so much of his substance.

Glossary of Family, Friends and Relatives

[Known, or rationally conjectured, fictional characters in the novels that are based on an actual individual are given in brackets.]

Acton, Eliza. Successful poet, 1777–1859; Ae.'s pen name.

Andrews, Miss. Harsh teacher at Cowan Bridge School. (Miss Scatcherd, *J.E.*)

Arnold, Mrs. Dr Arnold's widow; mother of Matthew.

Atkinson, Rev. Thomas. Curate at Thornton; married Frances Walker.

Aykroyd, Tabitha (Tabby). Came to work for the Brontës in 1824; stayed, with a few breaks for illness, until her death in 1855.

Aylott and Jones. Publishers of *Poems* by Currer, Ellis and Acton Bell.

Batley, Dr. Doctor at Cowan Bridge School. (Mr Bates, *J.E.*)

Bell, James Adamson. Mr N.'s cousin.

Bennock, Francis. A patron of authors who calls on C.

Black Tom. The parsonage cat; died June 1841.

Blackwood's Magazine. Popular journal of the time lent to the Brontës by Dr Driver; greatly influenced their juvenile writing.

Blanche, Mlle. Resident teacher at the Pensionnat Heger. (Mlle Zéphyrine, *The Professor*; Mlle Zélie de St Pierre, *V.*)

Bradley, Rev. James Chesterton. Curate of Oakworth, near Haworth. (David Sweeting, *SH.*)

Branwell, Charlotte. M.B.'s sister; married Joseph Branwell, a cousin.

Branwell, Elizabeth. M.B.'s sister; stays with P. and M.B., 1815/6; returns after M.B.'s death, 1820/1, to look after the children; died 29 Oct. 1842, leaving her estate to be shared between C., E. and Ae. and their cousin, Elizabeth Kingston.

Branwell, Joseph. Of Cornwall; married Charlotte Branwell, his cousin.

Branwell, Thomas. Father of M.B.

Brontë, Anne. Born 17 Jan. 1820; attended Roe Head School, Oct. 1835–Dec. 1837; governess to Mrs Ingham, April–Dec. 1839; governess to Mrs Robinson, (May?) 1840–June 1845; author of a selection of poems in *Poems,* 1846, and two novels – *Agnes Grey,* 1847, *The Tenant of Wildfell Hall,* 1848; died 29 May 1849 and buried at Scarborough.

Brontë, Charlotte. Born 21 April 1816; pupil at the Clergy Daughters' School, Cowan Bridge, Aug. 1824–June 1825; pupil at Miss Wooler's school, Roe Head, Jan. 1831–June 1832; teacher at Roe Head, July 1835–May 1838; governess to Mrs Sidgwick, Stonegappe, June –July 1839; governess to Mrs White, Rawdon, March–Dec. 1841; pupil at the Pensionnat Heger, Feb.–Nov. 1842; teacher at the Pensionnat Heger, Jan. 1843–Jan. 1844; married the Rev. Arthur Bell Nicholls, 29 June 1854; died 31 March 1855; author of a selection of poems in *Poems,* 1846, and four novels – *Jane Eyre,* 1847, *Shirley,* 1849, *Villette,* 1853, *The Professor,* 1859 (posthumous).

Brontë, Elizabeth. Born 9 Feb. 1815; died 15 June 1825; P.'s second daughter.

Brontë, Emily Jane. Born 30 July 1818; pupil at the Clergy Daughters' School, Cowan Bridge, Nov. 1824–June 1825; pupil at Miss Wooler's school at Roe Head, July-Oct. 1835; teacher at Law Hill School, Oct. 1836–?; pupil at the Pensionnat Heger, Feb.–Nov. 1842; died 19 Dec. 1848; author of a selection of poems in *Poems,* 1846, the novel *Wuthering Heights,* 1847, and poems published posthumously. (Shirley Keeldar, *SH.*)

Brontë Hugh (Brunty). Father of Rev. Patrick Brontë, lived in Ireland.

Brontë, Hugh. P.'s brother, lived in Ireland.

Brontë, Maria. *Née* Branwell. Born 1785 in Penzance, Cornwall; married P., 29 Dec. 1812; six children – Maria, Elizabeth, Charlotte, Branwell, Emily and Anne; died 15 Sept. 1821.

Brontë, Maria. P. and M.B.'s eldest daughter; christened 23 April 1814; died 6 May 1825. (Helen Burns, *J.E.*)

Brontë, Rev. Patrick. Born March 1777 at Emdale, County Down, Ireland; attended St John's College, Cambridge; married Maria Branwell, 29 Dec 1812; moved to Haworth as curate, April 1820, remaining there until his death in 1861; author of *Cottage Poems,* 1811, *The Rural Minstrel,* 1813, *The Cottage in the Wood or The Art of Becoming Rich and Happy,* 1815; *The Maid of Killarney,* 1818; *The Phenomenon,* 1824; *The Signs of the Times,* 1835.

Brontë, Patrick Branwell. Born 26 June 1817; P. and M.B.'s only son; to Bradford as a portrait painter, May 1838; tutor to Edmund Postlethwaite, Dec. 1839–June 1840 (dismissed); railway clerk at Sowerby Bridge, Aug./Sept. 1840 moved to Luddenden Foot Station, April 1841; dismissed, March 1842; tutor to the Robinsons, Jan. 1843–June 1845 (dismissed); died 24 Sept 1848; author of much unpublished writing; poems published – *The Afghan War,* 7 May 1842, in the *Leeds Intelligencer; On the Callousness Produced by Care . . .* and *Peaceful Death and Painful Life,* 7 and 14 May 1842, in the *Halifax Guardian.*

Brown, Dr. Phrenologist C. and George Smith consulted as Mr and Miss Fraser.

Brown, John. Stonemason; father of Martha; Master of the Masonic Lodge at Haworth; B.'s friend; died 10 Aug. 1855. (John Green, *J.E.*)

Brown, Martha. Born 1828; servant to the Brontës.

Brunty, Hugh. *See* Brontë, Hugh.

Bryce, Rev. David. Curate; proposed to C. on a brief visit to the parsonage.

Buckworth, Rev. J. Friend of P.

Burder, Mary. Of Finchingfield Park, Essex; P. proposed to her first in 1806/7; then again in 1823.

Cartwright, William. Owner of Rawfolds Mill. (Robert Gerard Moore, *SH*.)

Clapham, Ann. *See* Nussey, Ann.

Colburn, Henry. Publisher; rejected *The Professor, W.H.* and *A.G.* when sent to him in 1846.

Coleridge, Hartley. Son of S.T. Coleridge, the poet, whom B. met May 1840, and to whom both he and C. sent examples of their writing for comment.

Crosby, Dr. Conveyed information (and possibly money) from the Robinson family to B.

Currer, Frances. Book collector; well-known member of the Keighley Mechanics Institute; friend of P.; C.'s pen name.

Dearden, William. Schoolmaster, author, critic; friend of B. at Halifax; believed B. to have been either whole or part author of *W.H.* (see *Halifax Guardian*, 1867).

De Quincey, Thomas. Writer; on staff of *Blackwood's Magazine*; C. sent him one of the unsold copies of *Poems*, 1846.

Dixon, Abraham. Of Gomersal; industrialist; two sons – George and Tom – one daughter – Mary – with whom C. was friendly when in Brussels, where Abraham visited on business; uncle of the Taylors.

Dixon, Mary. Daughter of the above; drew a likeness of C. to send to Mary Taylor.

Drury, Isabella. Of Keighley; rejected P.'s proposal of marriage, 1822.

Evans, Miss Anne. Superintendent of Cowan Bridge School. (Maria Temple, *J.E.*)

Feather, Samuel and James. Post Office manager and postman respectively at Haworth.

Fennell, Jane. Married William Morgan; died 24 Sept 1827.

Fennell, Rev. John. Of Todmorden; M.B.'s uncle; Governor of Woodhouse Grove Academy (for sons of Wesleyan clergymen); died Oct. 1841.

Ferrand, W. Busfield. Landowner; lived at Harden Grange, near Haworth; called on C. with his wife and sent P. a present of game.

Finden, William. Painter and illustrator, 1787–1852; C. and E. copied his pictures.

Firth, Elizabeth. Born Jan. 1797; lived at Kipping House; great friend of P. and M.B. and Aunt B. when they lived at Thornton; kept a diary of their social activities of this period; possible P. proposed to her after M.B.'s death; married Rev. James Franks, 21 Sept 1825; died 11 Sept. 1837.

Flossie (y). Dog given to Ae. by the Robinsons, June 1843.

Flossie, Little. Flossie's puppy given to E.N.

Forster, W.E. Liberal MP for Bradford; married Matthew Arnold's sister; visited Haworth 1852.

Franks, Elizabeth. *See* Firth, Elizabeth.

Franks, Rev. James. Vicar of Huddersfield; married Elizabeth Firth.

Garrs, Nancy. Appointed as nurse to the Brontë children after the birth of C., 1816; left to get married 1824.

Garrs, Sarah. Nancy's younger sister; joined the Brontë household in 1818; left with her sister, 1824.

Gaskell, Elizabeth. Novelist, 1810–65; friend and biographer of C. Her *Life of Charlotte Brontë*, written at P.'s request, published 1857.

Gasper. Parsonage dog, 1831–7/8; drawn by E., Jan. 1834.

Graham, T.J. Author of *Modern Domestic Medicine*, 1826, used by P., in which he entered his own remedies as well as commenting on those printed.

Grant, Rev. Joseph Brett. Headmaster, Haworth Grammar School, 1844. (Joseph Donne, *SH.*)

Greenwood, John. Organist at Leeds; inaugurated the new organ at Haworth Church, May 1835.

Greenwood, John. Stationer of Haworth; kept a diary with references to the Brontës.

Grundy, Francis Henry. Railway engineer on the Halifax–Leeds line; recollections of B. given in his *Pictures of the Past*, 1879; believed B. wrote a great part of *W.H.*

Halifax Guardian. Newspaper, edited by Mr Leyland, snr; B. had two poems published in it, 1842.

Hannah (Brown). Helped in the parsonage; left June 1843.

Heald, Margaret. Sister of William Heald. Called *J.E.* a 'bad book'. (Margaret Hall, *SH.*)

Heald, Rev. William Margetson. Vicar of Birstall. (Cyril Hall, *SH.*)

Healds House. Dewsbury Moor; Miss Wooler moved her school there from Roe Head, 1837.

Heatons, the. Farming family; four brothers; lived at Ponden Hall, near Stanbury; owned a large library; Robert married Alice Midgley, 1821; trustee of Haworth Church.

Heger, Constantin Georges Romain. Born July 1809; married Claire Zoé, 1836; by 1842, when C. and E. at the Pensionnat Heger, had four children; two others born in 1842, 1846; Professor, then Principal at the Athenée Royal, leading boys' school in Brussels; also taught at the Pensionnat; C.'s 'black swan' with whom she corresponded, growing increasingly miserable at the lack of response from him, after she left Brussels. (Paul Emmanuel, *V.*)

Heger, Madame. Wife of above, whom C. grew to dislike and distrust. (Possibly Marie Modeste Beck, *V.*)

Hero. E.'s hawk; disappeared while she was away in Brussels.

Hodgson, Mr. P.'s curate, 1836–9, who had haunted lodgings in Haworth.

Hogg, James. Poet, 1770–1835, called the 'Ettrick Shepherd'; wrote for *Blackwood's Magazine*.

Hudson, John and Sophia. C. and E.N. stayed with them at Easton House (which C. sketched) on their visit to Bridlington.

Ibbotsons, the. Mr and Mrs J., Miss M., and Mr Tom – all friends of P. and M.B. at Thornton.

Inghams, the. Of Blake Hall; Ae. governess to their children, Joshua and Mary, April 1839. (The Bloomfields in *A.G.*)

Jenkins, Rev. Evan. Resident Chaplain of the Chapel Royal, Brussels; gave P. and C. advice about schools in Brussels; escorted P. and C. to the Pensionnat Heger in Feb. 1842.

Kavanagh, Julia. Novelist, 1824–77; published by S/E; C. felt sorry for her (she was a dwarfish creature who supported her mother by her writing) and helped with money.

Keeper. E.'s dog, 1837–51; her drawing of him, 24 April 1838.

Kingston, Elizabeth. Cornish cousin, with whom C., E. and Ae., shared Aunt B.'s legacies.

Kirkby, Mr and Mrs. Of Bradford; B. lodged with them; painted their portraits, 1839.

Leopold 1st of the Belgians, King. (King of Labassecour, *V.*)

Louise, Queen of the Belgians. (Queen of Labassecour, *V.*)

Lewes, G.H. Novelist, 1817–78; reviewed C.'s novels; corresponded with C.

Leylands, the. Father, sometime editor of the *Halifax Guardian*; sons: Francis – antiquarian, author of *The Brontë Family*; Joseph Bentley – sculptor, exhibited in Leeds, 1834; friend of B. with whom he corresponded.

Little Dick. The parsonage canary, acquired 1841.

MacTurk, Dr. Attended Ae. (and E.?). (Dr MacTurk, *SH.*)

Major, The. Name given to E., known by E.N. – possibly as the result of E. protecting her from the flirtatious William Weightman.

Martha. *See* Brown, Martha.

Martin, John. Well-known artist; his pictures, or engravings of them, copied by B. and influenced C.

Martineau, Harriet. Writer, critic, 1802–76; with whom C. corresponded until 1853 when she disagreed with her religious views.

Masons, the. Society of Freemasons; B. joined the Three Graces Lodge of Haworth of which John Brown was Master, attending meetings and acting at times as secretary, 1836–8.

McClory, Alice. Married Hugh Brunty; P.'s mother.

Midgley, David. Of Withens End; left money for clothes for ten poor children of the parish.

Morgan, Jane. *Née* Fennell; daughter of Rev. John and Mrs Jane Fennell; married William Morgan when P. married M.B.; died 1827.

Morgan, William. Fellow curate with P. at Wellington, Shropshire; became Vicar of Christchurch, Bradford; married Jane Fennell, 29 Dec. 1812; married Mary Gibson, 1836; exchanged livings with the Rector of Hulcott, Bucks, 1851; died 1858; he and P. remained friends until his death. (Dr Thomas Boultby, *SH.*)

Newby, T.C. Unsatisfactory publisher of E.'s *W.H.*, Ae.'s *A.G.*, *T. of W.H.*; used C.'s fame, after the publication of *J.E.*, to further the sale of E.'s and Ae.'s novels by pretending all the novels were by the same person; eventually *W.H.* and *A.G.* republished under the auspices of S/E to C.'s satisfaction.

Nicholls, Rev. Arthur Bell. Appointed P.'s curate, May 1845; married C., 29 June 1854; after C.'s death remained with P. until P.'s death; returned to Ireland where he remarried.

Nicholson, T.W. Proprietor of the Talbot Inn, Halifax; threatened B. with a court summons for debt.

Northangerland. B.'s pseudonym, used for his newspaper publications which Mrs Robinson recognized.

Nusseys, the. Family of cloth manufacturers; father, John, married Ellen Wade; thirteen children, including Henry, who proposed to and was rejected by C., 1839; John, who was a court physician; Ann, who married Mr Clapham, 26 Sept. 1849; Mercy, with whom C. occasionally corresponded, giving her a copy of Felicia Hemans's poems; Sarah, whom C. disliked; George, who suffered a mental breakdown; and Ellen, the youngest, born 22 April 1817, who was C.'s friend and correspondent from the time of their first meeting at Roe Head School, 1831, until C.'s death, 1855; much of our information about C. and her activities comes from the many letters she wrote to E.N., which E.N. kept; the family lived first at Rydings, then at Brookroyd. (E.N. – ? Caroline Helstone, *SH*.; H.N. – St John Eyre Rivers, *J.E.*)

Outhwaite, Fanny (Frances). Ae.'s godmother; let her £200, which Ae. used for her last visit to Scarborough when she died.

Pastoral Visitor, The. Magazine issued by William Morgan, to which P. contributed.

Patchett, the Misses. Kept a school at Law Hill, Halifax, where E. went as a teacher.

Postlethwaite, Mr and Mrs. Of Broughton House, Ulverston; B. tutor to their sons, John and William, Jan.–June 1840.

Rachel. French actress, 1821–58; famous for her acting of Adrienne, in *Adrienne Le Couvreur*, and of Camille.

Redhead, Samuel. P. replaced him as curate in Haworth.

Ringrose, Amelia. Engaged to George Nussey; married Joe Taylor; corresponded with and visited C.

Robertson, Rev. Hammond. P.B.'s predecessor at Hartshead. (Rev. Matthewson Helstone, *SH*.)

Robinsons, the. Rev. Edmund, his wife Lydia (later Lady Scott), lived at Thorp Green; B. tutor to their son Edmund, 1843–5; B.'s relationship with Mrs Robinson, whether real or imagined or a mixture of both, caused him and his family much anguish.

Robinson, William. Leeds artist and portrait painter; engaged to give B. lessons.

Shuttleworth, Sir Kay and Lady. Lived at Gawthorpe Hall, near Burnley, Lancs; as a guest at their holiday home at Windermere C. met Mrs Gaskell.

Sidgwick, Mr and Mrs. Of Stonegappe, Lothersdale, near Skipton; C. their governess, 1839.

Smith, Elder and Co. C.'s publishers, who later also reissued *W.H.* and *A.G.*

Smith, George Murray. Owner of S/E whom C. visited and corresponded with. (John Graham Bretton, *V*.)

Smith, Rev. J.W. P.'s curate, 1842–4, whom he did not trust. (Peter Augustus Malone, *SH*.)

Smith, Mrs. George Smith's mother, with whom C. stayed. (Mrs Louisa Bretton, *V*.)

Southey, Robert. Poet Laureate, 1774–1843; C. consulted him about her writing, 1836.

Sowden, Sutcliffe. Mr N.'s friend who officiated at C.'s wedding.

Sugden, Mr. Landlord of the Black Bull, Haworth.

Sugden, Mrs. Proprietress of the Black Bull, Haworth, where B. had a 'fainting fit'.

Sunderland, A.S. Organist at Keighley Parish Church; taught E., Ae. and B. music – C. too shortsighted to learn.

Tabby. *See* Aykroyd, Tabitha.

Taylor, James. Member of the S/E firm; a 'little man'; left for India, 1851, returning 1856 after C.'s death; C.'s letters suggest she once thought of marrying him.

Taylors, the. Father, Joshua; mother, Anne; son, Joe, married Amelia Ringrose; daughters, Mary and Martha, friends of C. from her school days at Roe Head; Martha, 'little Miss Boisterous', died of cholera in Brussels, 1842, buried at the Protestant Cemetery there; Mary emigrated to New Zealand, from where she corresponded with C., but unfortunately destroyed C.'s letters; a very determined and independent-minded person; author of a series of articles on *The First Duty of Women*, 1865–70 (later published in book form); *Swiss Notes* by Five Ladies; *Miss Miles or a Tale of Yorkshire Life Sixty Years Ago*; the family lived at The Red House, Gomersal, until the death of Joshua, when it broke up. (Joshua – Hiram Yorke; Martha – Jessie Yorke; Mary – Rose Yorke; Mrs Taylor – Mrs Yorke; Joshua T. junior – Matthew Yorke; Joseph – Martin Yorke; John – Mark Yorke, *SH.*)

Temperance Society. P. was president, B. secretary of the Haworth branch.

Thackeray, Anne. Thackeray's daughter, later Lady Ritchie; recorded her meeting with C. in 1860.

Thackeray, William Makepeace. Novelist, 1811–63; at first hero-worshipped by C. as the moral giant of his age, to whom she dedicated the 2nd edition of *J.E.*; C. attended his *Lectures on the English Humorists of the Eighteenth Century* and tempered her earlier opinion of him as she grew to know him better.

Thompson, John H. Fellow-pupil with B. of William Robinson; fine draughtsman.

Tiger. Parsonage cat, died March 1844.

Upjohn, Rev. Francis. Vicar of Gorleston, Suffolk; he and his wife wished to 'adopt' E.N. – she was to become their heir in return for her looking after them in their old age; both C. and Mary Taylor against it.

Walker, Amelia. Mrs Franks's cousin; daughter of Joseph, of Lascelles Hall, Kirkheaton, near Huddersfield; C. visited her.

Walker, Fanny (Frances). Married the Rev. Thomas Atkinson.

Weightman, William. Became P.'s curate, Aug. 1839; died of cholera, 6 Sept. 1842; C. describes him – 'bonny, pleasant, lighthearted, good tempered, generous, careless, fickle, unclerical'; sent C., E., Ae. and E.N. valentines.

Wheelwrights, the. Dr Thomas Wheelwright had five daughters who attended the Pensionnat Heger as boarders; E. taught music to the younger ones; Laetitia, who disliked E., remained friends with C.; Julia died of cholera in Brussels, 1842, age seven; the family left Brussels, 1843.

Whites, the. C. was governess to them, March 1841; lived at Upperwood House, Rawdon, near Bradford.

Williams, William Smith. Reader for S/E; C.'s correspondent; married, with daughters about whose earning future C. gave advice.

Wilson, Rev. Carus. In charge of the Clergy Daughters' School, Cowan Bridge. (Mr Brocklehurst, *J.E.*)

Wood, William. Carpenter and odd job man of Haworth; Tabby's nephew.

Woolers, the. Two brothers and five daughters, of whom Margaret, the eldest, ran Roe Head School, which C., E. and Ae. attended, and gave C. away at her wedding. (Margaret–?Mrs Pryor, *SH.*)

II The Juvenilia

Introduction

There are two main problems that arise when dealing with the childhood writings of the Brontës – the dispersal of the manuscripts, and the nature of the manuscripts themselves. After the death of Charlotte they presumably remained in the Haworth parsonage with her father and her husband. When her father died, however, Mr Nicholls removed himself to Ireland, where he later remarried. There he was visited by Clement Shorter who purchased on behalf of T.J. Wise the children's MSS. Wise selected some of these to edit and publish, others he sold and disposed of as he wished. As a result the MSS are scattered over many places both in England and in the United States. Some were acquired by the British Library after the death of the second Mrs Nicholls, and many have been bought by or donated to the Brontë Parsonage Museum, but a large proportion are still in America. Further problems arise because the pages of some MSS have become separated, so that while some pages may be in one collection, the rest may be elsewhere. This is particularly true of Branwell's early writings.

The second difficulty is that there is still no one complete and accurate edition of all these MSS. Many are in the tiny print-writing the Brontë children adopted to make their scripts look as much like real printed books as possible. Some have been transcribed and editions published, but by no means all of them, particularly in the case of Branwell's writing. Moreover, what has been published is not always easily accessible. Some volumes are either out of print or so large and expensive that they are beyond the pocket of the ordinary book-buyer. Some that have been reissued or re-published are, sadly, not updated in the light of more recent knowledge and are often unreliable, with material omitted, misdated or misread. There are also references to some manuscripts, by title, that seem no longer to exist at all – or are being held back, wittingly or unwittingly, their location and/or the history of their acquisition shrouded in mystery. As there is, therefore, no single complete and accurate source for the scholar or the interested amateur to go to and browse through, it has not yet been possible to feel the full impact of the vast amount of writing that Charlotte and Branwell accomplished during their early childhood and teenage years. There is a world here rich and varied and fascinating, an 'epic' world, where the reader can walk and talk, eat and drink, gossip and mock, live and die with the heroes and heroines, their friends and their progeny. Even the earliest of the writing is never totally childish or banal; and even though vocabulary and expression may later ape and copy elders and betters, the sense of the reality of this imagined world and of the authors' commitment to it are so wholly engaging that the reader can lose his or her heart to it as readily as Charlotte and Branwell did theirs.

In this section on the Juvenilia we can deal only with the peripheries of all this, for the stories of the Glasstown Confederacy and Gondal as narratives are just a small part of that imaginary world. What we have touched on here may give some indication of the greater and more intricate whole that, perhaps, readers may enjoy for themselves at some time in the future, when drawings, sketches, maps, articles, stories, poems, letters, social and political reports, even advertisements, may all be allowed to complement each other and bring to life the saga that grew over the years in the parsonage in that 'miserable little village, buried in dreary moors and moss-hags and marshes'. (Charlotte Brontë, *My Angria and the Angrians*.)

The Glasstown Confederacy

The Origins

The beginnings of this all-enveloping 'game' are well documented. Charlotte in her *History of the Year 1829* and Branwell in his *History of the Young Men* have both given their versions of what happened. Branwell goes back to the beginnings as he remembers them. In the summer of 1824 he asked his father to buy him a box of soldiers from Bradford. He got a box of twelve, costing 1s. 6d. – 'they were the best I ever had'. Soon after, he had another set from Keighley, which lasted about a year and then were either burnt, destroyed or lost. He then bought a set of Turkish musicians from Keighley, which he managed to keep until the summer of 1825. All this time he had been playing with his toy soldiers by himself, for between July 1824 and June 1825 his sisters (with the exception of the four-year-old Anne) had been away at school. By the time they got home, Branwell had only a few remnants left, and then for ten months, he records sadly, he had no soldiers at all. Papa came to the rescue. On 5 June 1826, at Leeds, he bought a new set as a present for Branwell's birthday the next day. These became the basis for the 'Twelves'. Branwell writes, 'I first saw them in the morning after they were bought. I carried them to Emily, Charlotte and Anne.' Each of them took up a soldier and gave it a name 'which I consented to, and I gave Charlotte, Twemy [Wellington], Emily, Pare [Parry], to Ann, Trott [Ross], to take care of'. At first they were on a kind of extended loan, Branwell still having the last say in what should happen to them, but later he gave them to his sisters as their own.

Such is Branwell's sober account, befitting a history of the beginning of a nation. Charlotte's record is a more intimate and eventful one. She and Emily 'jumped out of bed' and Charlotte 'snatched up' one of the soldiers and exclaimed, 'This is the Duke of Wellington! This shall be the Duke.' Emily, likewise, took a soldier, a 'grave-looking fellow called Gravey', and Anne's was a 'queer little thing, much like herself' called 'Waiting-boy'; Branwell's choice was Buonaparte. The discrepancy in the names in the two accounts suggests that the little soldiers had descriptive as well as given names, and that they doubled up according to the game, the 'play' as Charlotte calls it, that the children were engaged in.

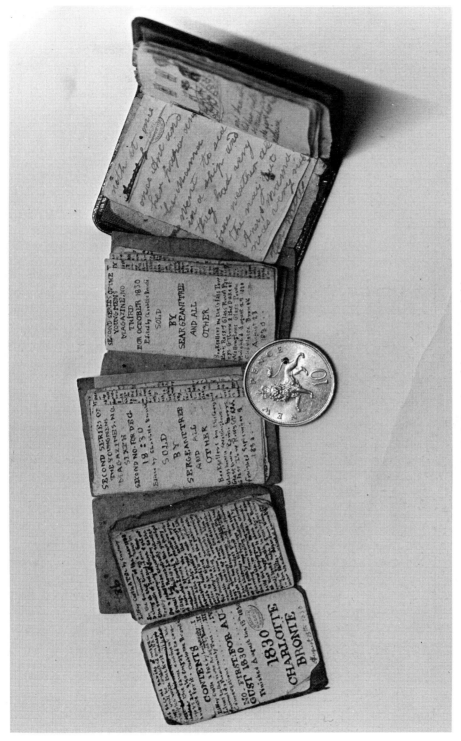

The little books of the Brontë children

Branwell's drawing of Zamorna,
a character from the juvenilia

Charlotte's watercolour of an unknown
girl (possibly Caroline Vernon from
the juvenilia)

Pen and ink sketch from a letter by Branwell

Emily's and Anne's 'diary paper', 1837

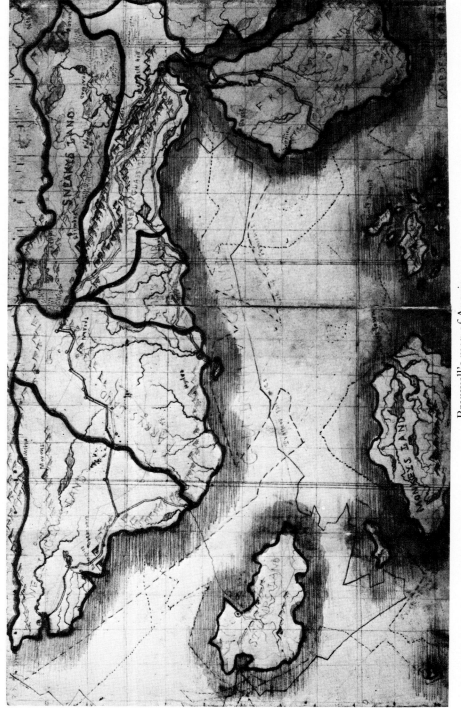

Branwell's map of Angria

The soldiers – those in ceremonial dress – had coats and sailor-like jackets and light pantaloons all painted scarlet, and black caps with 'hierogliphical figures' on them; others were in the ordinary 'regimental dress of the day'; common to all, however, was the curious footwear. 'This shoe, for each man had only one, was like a round flat cake with two holes in the middle into which his feet were inserted as in a stocks' – the 'curious shoe', Branwell's footnote explains helpfully, 'was the little stand which each soldier had to keep him from falling'. Neither he nor Charlotte gives any description of the set of ninepins bought at the same time as the soldiers, nor do they record for whom they were bought. However, as it seems these ninepins became the black Ashantees, the savage inhabitants of the area of Africa to which the Twelves sailed, perhaps they had something of a 'gollywog' appearance like that depicted on early sets of children's playing cards.

No time was lost in creating make-believe games with these toys. The 'play' of the Young Men, or the 'Twelves' as they became known, was begun, Charlotte tells us, in June 1826. In 1827 Branwell acquired from Halifax a second band of Turkish musicians, and by July 1827 the 'play' of *Our Fellows* was established, based, Charlotte explains, on Aesop's *Fables*. In the O'Deays 'play', each of the children pretended they had an island inhabited by people six miles high, with their 'Cheif [sic] Men [Hay Man, Charlotte's; Clown, Emily's; Hunter, Anne's; and Boaster, Branwell's] ten miles high, except Clown who was only four!'

At the end of the year, however, interest in both the Young Men and the Fellows as playing material seems to have been flagging. On a cold winter's night in December, when they were all sitting by a blazing fire, complaining they didn't know what to do, Tabby, the servant, turned on them with a sharp, 'Wha ya may go t'bed.' This advice was obviously rejected, for Branwell replies, 'I would rather do anything than that.' Charlotte then had an idea: let each of them adopt an island. She started by choosing the Isle of Wight, Emily chose that of Arran, Anne, Guernsey, and Branwell, the Isle of Man. Then, boredom forgotten, as the 'play' of *The Islanders* developed the 'making out' took wing. Each chose his or her own pet heroes to put on the island, their choice ranging through military or political heroes (the inevitable Duke of Wellington is included), political reformers, editors, poets, novelists and biographers, famous surgeons and physicians of the day. At that point, alas, the clock struck seven and they were bundled off to bed. Even there, however, matters did not rest, for there were also 'bed' plays. 'Bed plays', Charlotte explains, meant 'secret plays'. Hers and Emily's were first established on 1 December 1827, and others followed in March 1828. As these were presumably a result of the sleeping arrangements at the parsonage, when Emily and Charlotte as children shared a bed (Anne when small slept in Aunt Branwell's room) it seems that neither of the other two, Branwell and Anne, made up 'bed plays'. What these secret plays were about we are not told, but if Charlotte's early writing is any indication, there must have been a large element of magic, mystery and 'spookiness' about them.

Branwell's final box of toy figures, one of Indians, was bought in Haworth itself in 1828. By 1831, he records, he still had this group, and the Turkish musicians, and two or three of the soldiers left. By then, however, the reality of the presence of the toy figures probably mattered less, for in 1828 an important development took place. Instead of, or more likely, as well as actively playing games with the figures, the two eldest children began not only writing about them but, what is perhaps more important, writing as though they were the characters themselves. And, as they did in their games, Charlotte identified herself with the Duke of Wellington and the Wellesleys, and Branwell with the Sneachies (Buonaparte's close allies) and later with the Percys. Although Emily and Anne were not old enough to make their contribution to a written record, as they did to the 'plays', they were certainly given their place in the scheme of things. It seems that the Brontë children learned early in life to help and entertain each other, the older ones looking after, teaching, drawing pictures, or making out stories for, the younger. In 1826, both Charlotte and Branwell were making sketches of cottages, castles or ruins for Anne, and Charlotte's earliest extant MS is 'There was once a little girl and her name was Ane [sic]', a story about and for her six-year-old sister.

Branwell's earliest extant MS is one of the well-known 'little books'. These are 'books' made out of sheets of paper, about 5 × 4 cm, sewn together, with a coarse cover that seems to have come from a discarded sugar bag or the wrappings from purchases made at the chemists. Inside, the script is small and print-like. Each booklet was got up to look as nearly like an actual published book as possible with a title page, including author, printer, place of sale, and sometimes an ornamental device as well. The first one of Branwell's that is extant, dated 12 March 1827, is about the battle of Washington and consists of drawings, partly coloured, of incidents in the battle. These drawings probably owe much to a series of illustrations about the campaign of the British Army at Washington and Orleans in the American War which was published in *Blackwood's Magazine* in March and April 1827. Although Branwell's drawings are of stiff little soldiers, there is a sense of character and immediacy about them, qualities that enliven also many of his later sketches. His second manuscript – *A History of the Rebellion in* —— (my army? Fellows? Twelves? – the title is unclear and incomplete) relates to the activities of Branwell's Fellows. Here two villains, Goodman and Boaster, with an army of 10,000 foot and 11,000 horse, declare war on 'little Branwell'.

By the early months of 1829, writing is in full swing. In April Charlotte writes her account of the voyage of the Twelves to Africa, while between December 1830 and May 1831 Branwell writes his *History of the Young Men Volume I in Six Chapters*. In general outline, both are the same. Charlotte's account is shorter and has more of the element of strange magic about it, while Branwell's is more matter-of-fact, and precise in 'historic' date and detail. In fact, even here in this, the beginning of their juvenile writing, the accounts of their imaginary world complement each other. Branwell is more concerned with martial adventure, colonization, and, later, with political parties, speeches, rebellions and revolutions, whereas Charlotte's interest is with the places and people, their social and amorous adventures.

The Saga of the Twelves

The story of the Twelves, which is first the story of the Glasstown Confederacy, then the story of Angria, falls roughly into three stages. *Stage I* from about 1829 to 1832 is concerned with the Twelves' voyage to Africa; their settling in in their kingdoms of Wellingtonsland, Parrysland, Ross's land, and Sneachiesland; the formation of the Glasstown Confederacy; and Rogue's rebellion and death in March 1832. *Stage II* covers the period from about 1833 to 1837 and deals with the second generation, particularly the Marquis of Douro and Lord Charles Wellesley (the Duke of Wellington's two elder sons) and Alexander Percy (first known as Rogue, later the Earl of Northangerland); their affairs, both military and amatory, reflecting the developing complexity of their characters; the founding of Angria; Northangerland's Revolution; Zamorna's exile and return home. *Stage III*, from 1838 onwards, is concerned with the third generation in the colony, trading, businessmen, and ordinary misters and misses rather than kings and queens. This stage finds its most complete expression in Charlotte's, Emily's and Anne's publications and Branwell's desultory *And the Weary Are at Rest*.

Over a period of ten years, then, the Glasstown Confederacy, starting in a fairy tale world of childhood imagination, draws, as time goes on and the children get older, closer to the life in the Yorkshire mill and wool towns and villages. This is a development, however, not an unexpected about-turn, for one is to some extent prepared for the growing encroachment of the 'real world' by the numerous small realistic details that abound in the earlier, more fanciful flights of imagination: the explanations of the 'archeological' problem, of the one-footed shoe, for example, or the episode of Pigtail's disappearance. Pigtail is being tried by Napoleon, who is seized with a sudden cataleptic fit; he walks to the fireplace, holds up the mantelpiece, and lays himself down in the hole inside, and is not found until two weeks later when, Branwell tells us, the 'Emperor and his party' were 'springcleaning'! It is Branwell who gives the prosaic reason why Frederick Guelph, the first King of the Twelves, had to be made dead 'so as not to be got alive again' because he and Stumps were the same toy soldier.

These glimpses, haunting and provoking as they are, of the inter-relationship between life and imagination in the Brontë children, are fairly frequent in the first stage of their saga. When Charlotte uses them later, she often does so to make capital out of their comic or satirical effect.

As the saga progresses these 'lapses' into the real world are joined by another kind of 'reality' – the imitations of language and attitude picked up by the children from their reading. Echoes of Milton, Byron, Cowper, as well as Scott and the magazines of the time, haunt the pages. Political speeches, especially Northangerland's in Branwell's writing, have the same kind of oratorical and rhetorical devices as Milton's Satan and his colleagues debating in Hell; Charlotte's flashing sardonic hero, Zamorna, develops a strong Byronic strain, and the simple charm of a Cowper lyric finds its way into many of the songs that intersperse the prose stories. Charlotte's and Branwell's own *Blackwood's Young Men's Magazine* and the 'publications' in Glasstown of plays, stories, biographies, articles and poems reflect the contents and publishing habits of the real *Blackwood's* and *Fraser's* magazines.

Stage I (1829–1832)
'*A marvellous fiction*' (*Shirley*, ch. 7)

The Founding of Glasstown

On 5 February 1770 (according to Branwell), 1 March 1770 (according to Charlotte), the Twelves set out from England with a fair wind and fair weather. The crew names differ slightly (*see* Glossary to Glasstown), Branwell taking a more practical view of the composition of his ship's crew of thirteen than Charlotte does with hers of twelve, but both crews set sail on the *Invincible*, a 74-gunner. They come first to the coast of Spain, then, driven by storms, to Trinidad and finally to

Ascension Island where, in Branwell's account, several, including Stumps, die on 18 May after a fight with the Dutch. All the dead, however, are brought alive again and they sail on to reach the African coastline on 2 June. There Charlotte's crew lands, and to its great surprise finds the country inhabited and cultivated. Branwell's crew sails on round the coast – for his country (Sneachiesland) is further to the west and further inland than Charlotte's Wellingtonsland – until, on 5 June, they reach the bay (later called the Great Glasstown Bay) where they anchor. From the time of arrival, Charlotte's and Branwell's accounts begin to differ.

Charlotte's Account. Charlotte's landing forces, after marching twenty miles inland, find themselves fighting the Ashantees, the local inhabitants. They take the Ashantee Chief prisoner, and, using him as hostage, they make advantageous peace terms. Then they settle in to building their city – Twelves Town (later Great Glasstown).

At one point in an early manuscript, Charlotte tried to express how these creations of her imagination came about. Lord Charles Wellesley, the speaker in the story, explains that existence is a kind of reverie, a dream, a figment of someone's brain. There is a 'real' world and an 'idea' world. The minds and bodies of the 'real' world can exist without the 'ourselves' of the 'idea' world, but only as shadows. It's as if, he adds, there were, at the end of a long vista, beings who live in tangible shapes, who are called by our names and from whom we have been copied by someone or something. The true world is the 'idea' world, the other only coming fully alive when it is one with the 'idea' world. This is surely as true for Charlotte as it is for her character, Lord Charles, and there is a touch of irony in the fact that she is as much at the end of his 'long vista' as he is at the end of hers. It is a complex line of thought, but probably reflects less Charlotte's powers of ratiocination than the overwhelming power of her imagination.

She describes this power more fully in several separate manuscripts – some dated, some not – that she wrote when she returned to Roe Head, in 1837, as a teacher. In one fragment, dated 11 August (1837), she wrote, 'All this day I have been in a dream, half miserable and half ecstatic', miserable because of the interruptions, ecstatic because she saw in the 'vivid light of reality the ongoings of the infernal world' (i.e. the Glasstown world). After the 'interruption' – a lesson on parsing – is over she goes to the window, throws up the sash, and looks towards the south where 'Huddersfield and the hills beyond it were all veiled in blue mist, the woods of Hopton and Heaton Lodge were clouding the water-edge and the Calder silent but bright was shooting among them like a silver arrow'. When she goes back to her seat there comes rushing on her 'impetuously all the mighty phantasm that we had conjured from nothing to a system strong as some religious creed'. Later she adds, 'What I imagined grew morbidly vivid', and she describes a handsome lady, with black curls and dark anxious-looking eyes, dressed in muslin, coming into the hall of a gentleman's house with a flat candlestick in her hand, and, as the door opens, she sees beyond it to the moonlight on the lawn and the twinkling lights of the distant town. Another time, she sees 'a tall man washing his bloody hands in a bason [sic] and a dark beauty standing by... I grew frightened at the vivid glow of the candle, at the reality of the lady's erect and symmetrical figure.' She describes the agony of wrenching herself away from this 'vision' – 'At last I became aware of a heavy weight lying across me. I knew I was wide awake and that it was dark and moreover the ladies were now come into the room to get their curl papers they perceived me lying on the bed and I heard them talking about me. I wanted to speak, to rise it was impossible ... I must get up and I did so with a start...' and, as in earlier years when the clock had struck seven and she was sent to bed, so here at Roe Head, 'tea's ready Miss Wooler impatient'. The intensity and sharp vividness of her description of what she experiences bear witness to her earlier explanations as to which, for her, is the 'real', and which the 'imaginary' world. This powerful, rapt concentration, if that is not too negative a word for such 'visions', finds expression later in the intensity and sense of immediacy of *Jane Eyre, Shirley* and *Villette*. No wonder she wrote to W.S. Williams that much as Smith, Elder and Co. might disagree with what she had written she could not alter it in any way. She had to remain true to her 'visions'.

In Charlotte's account, a month after landing, when the building has been going apace, the Twelves have their first encounter with the Genii. These Genii are the four children – Talli(i) (Charlotte), Emmi(i), Anni(i) and Branni(i) who are the guardians and protectors of the Twelves, each especially over the particular soldier he or she has chosen. The genius the Twelves encounter is the Genius of the Storm, who is about to destroy them all, when an even greater Giant Genius appears and commands him to forbear. Here again, reality, it seems breaks in – for in a letter written by their father to Mrs Gaskell after they were all dead and her *Life of Charlotte Brontë* was in preparation, he records that, at times, he had to act as referee in their games. Undoubtedly he would have made a spectacular Giant Genius, and as the Genius of the Storm is referred to as 'he', whereas the Genius who seizes the Duke of Wellington is 'she', one might be forgiven, perhaps, for seeing in this account a bullying Branwell out to destroy all Charlotte's adventurers, and Papa, being called upon, forbidding it.

After this encounter, the city building continues. Then Arthur Wellesley, at this time a mere Trumpeter, persuades the older and more experienced of the Twelves to let him go back to England with the news of the colony. Before he can leave, however, the Genii send for the Twelves and lead them to a magic palace with a hall of sapphire and thrones of gold, on which sit the four Genii themselves. Immediately one of the Genii jumps up and seizes Arthur Wellesley crying, 'This is the Duke of Wellington!' and she goes on to prophesy all the fame and glory he will achieve. Then, with music, as the Genii and their attendant fairies join in one grand chorus, the palace disappears and the Twelves, somewhat bewildered, return to Twelvestown.

The next morning, after a sharp attack from the Ashantees which they repel, the Twelves find a group of Englishmen shipwrecked on their shores. They take them in, and a fortnight later, after their ship has been refitted, they sail back to England, accompanied by Arthur Wellesley. For the next ten years the Duke of York, Frederick Guelph, and the Twelves remain at war with the Ashantees, then there is peace for ten years with, as Charlotte laconically puts it, 'nothing much happening'. On 16 May 1816, however, a large fleet appears off Twelvestown. Fearful of attack, the Duke of York and his company hide in the Great Tower until it is discovered that with the fleet is none other than the now-famous Arthur Wellesley, the Duke of Wellington – 'conqueror of Buonaparte and deliverer of Europe'. The Duke of York decides to return to England, and so, on 14 June 1816, the whole nation (for other settlers had arrived with the fleet) is assembled in the Palace of Justice and there Arthur Wellesley, Duke of Wellington, is chosen as their king.

Branwell's Account. In Branwell's account, as soon as the Twelves land on 5 June, they choose Frederick Guelph, Duke of York, as their first king; the next day, 6 June (Branwell's birthday), he leads an expedition into the desert, where the encounter with the Genii takes place – this time, however, with Branni as chief Genii holding Crashey in his hand. Of the other three Genii, the tallest (Talli) takes up Arthur Wellesley, the next (Emmi) takes Parry, Anni, the smallest, taking Ross. Then, as the building of the town starts, Crashey, the oldest and most venerable of the Twelves (a remnant, perhaps, from an earlier set of toy soldiers – hence Branwell's crew of thirteen), disappears. A search party is sent out, meets and fights with the Ashantees and takes prisoners. The Genii appear to the Twelves, promising them their protection against their enemies. There follow eight years of peace with Kashna Quamina, the kindly king of the Ashantees, but at his death, in 1779, his son Sai Tootoo takes over, and war begins again, ending in the sacking of

Rossendale Town and the death of King Frederick I at the battle of
Rossendale Hill (at the same time, Branwell informs us, as the 'real'
Duke of York died). Helped by the Genii the Twelves overcome the
Ashantees. A new king – Stumps – is elected as King Frederick II. The
Ashantees reorganize and invade Twelvestown but, again helped by the
Genii, the Twelves win a 'bloody' war, sacking Coomassie, the
Ashantee capital, and killing Sai Tootoo. Arthur Wellesley adopts
Quashia, Sai Tootoo's son, to be brought up with his own children,
then goes off to England, later returning to Glasstown with the second
Twelves. In honour of his great exploits he is given the crown by
Stumps and becomes king.

The Glasstown Confederacy

By 1829/30 the Twelves share a large area of Africa, along the coast of
Guinea, westwards to the Atlantic Sea, eastwards to the desert,
northwards to the J(G)ibble Kumri Mountains, and southwards to the
Gulf of Guinea. This is divided into five areas each with its own capital
called Glasstown. Wellingtonsland is Charlotte's country on the west
coast, with the Duke of Wellington as its king; next, moving
eastwards, is Emily's Parrysland, with John Parry in charge; then
Anne's Rossland, with Trott in charge; then Nigrilis, the central area,
where the Great Glasstown itself is; finally, to the north-east of that,
Branwell's Sneachiesland, where Alexander Sneachie (Sneaky) is king.
These areas together with Monkey's and Stumps' Islands form the
Glasstown Confederacy, in which each king has control over his own
country, but is subject to the control of the combined kingdoms in the
Confederacy. Beyond the Confederacy, always threatening or ready to
take the chance of attacking when Ashantees are causing trouble, or
even allying with them to cause trouble, is Frenchland, an island with
Paris as its capital, and where, of course, Buonaparte himself rules.

In these early years of writing, however, while the Twelves and their
adventures are never totally forgotten, they do not dominate the scene
to the exclusion of all else. In fact, at this time, Charlotte's imaginary
world is more often concerned with fairies, magic, and above all the
Duke of Wellington. On 12 March 1829 she starts her *Tales of the
Islanders*, stories presumably connected with the 'play' established in
July 1827. Certainly in these first years of writing much of what seems
to spring so easily, fully grown, from the children's pens must have
been backward-looking, towards the 'plays' that had been going on for
one or two or even more years. In the stories themselves, incidents that

are strangely, even comically, realistic occur in the most fantastic situations. In Charlotte's *Tales of the Islanders* – about the Duke of Wellington, his two young sons and the dream-like magic of Vision Island – the Little King (Branwell) and Queens (Charlotte, Emily and Anne) themselves take part. The series ends, 30 July 1830, with the story of the *Three Washerwomen of Strathfieldsaye*. These three women are first encountered by the Little King as he is picking violets, and are taken back to the palace (?the parsonage) to be engaged at ten guineas a year if they are suitable. At first they work well, then they get lazy and begin to fight. They make an appearance one night deep in the dungeon of the castle in three coffins, with a black canopy swaying beneath them. Then suddenly they disappear, never to be seen again. Charlotte's other stories – *A Search after Happiness* (1829), *Leisure Hours* (1830), *Anecdotes of the Duke of Wellington* (1829), *The Adventures of Mon Edouard de Crack* (1830), *The Adventures of Ernest Alembert* (1830), are concerned with similar material, where the Duke of Wellington and his family, household activities at the parsonage, and magic, rub shoulders happily together.

However, her *Characters of the Eminent Men of the Time* (December 1829) and her two volumes of *Visits in Verreopolis* (December 1830) are more directly connected with the Glasstown Confederacy. These two books contain character sketches of some of the more interesting inhabitants of Glasstown: the Duke of Wellington, his two sons – Arthur, Marquis of Douro and Lord Charles Wellesley – Captain Bud, Young Soult the Rhymer, Sergeant Bud, Rogue, Young Man Naughty, Dr Hume Badry, Pigtail, and the painters De Lisle, Le Brun, Dundee and Vernel; and visits are made to Lady Ellrington, Captain Bud, Young Soult, the Rotunda, and Bravey's Inn. Charlotte is, in fact, beginning to put flesh on the skeleton of the 'plays', to weld together the 'real' and the 'imaginary' and to explore in written form the people, relationships and situations that crowd into her restless imagination.

Meanwhile Branwell completes (1829) two volumes of poetry and two dramatic poems under his pen-name, Young Soult. Then, under the name of James Bellingham, an Englishman who is on a visit to Verdopolis, he writes his *Letters from an Englishman, 1st Series* (6 September 1830), in which he describes life in the Glasstown Confederacy where strange things can happen. Bellingham, for example, receives a mysterious warning – to leave the place, or he will end up as other Englishmen have. This arouses his fear and curiosity. He visits Dr Hume Badry's house, where he discovers a bodysnatching group in action, and, as he himself is about to be killed for dissection, he swoons. When he comes to, he finds himself bound to a table that is covered in dried blood, in a room where 'darkness visible' shows him a Frenchman putting away a coffin and a dead body. Luckily he is saved in the nick of time by the Duke of Wellington, his son (Charles), and his estate manager, Ned Laury, who send Dr Badry and the Frenchman off to prison for their nefarious activities. This bizarre sepulchral atmosphere permeates much of Branwell's early writing.

In the *Second Series of Letters from an Englishman* (June 1831), Bellingham accompanies the Marquis of Douro, Lord Charles Wellesley and Young Soult, the Rhymer across Twelvesland to visit Glasstown in Wellingtonsland. They enjoy the moorland scenery, suitably described by Bellingham for the recipient of his letter, but, as before, bizarre events follow. They encounter a herd of mountain bulls; one, a monstrous brute, 12ft. long and 6ft. high, rushes past the carriage, tosses and kills the drover. The man in charge of these fearsome beasts has an ugly, savage face, and long, crooked legs with misshapen feet. He is recognized as Pigtail, the champion of Frenchmen, and when he tries to stop the travellers the Marquis of Douro cuts off his hand.

They journey on, and Bellingham is told the unsavoury history of Pigtail – how he killed his landlord, 'Monsieur-who-lives-and-dies' ('you know,' Douro adds, 'the ridiculousness of these French names'!); how he disappeared behind the mantelpiece, to be found again only when the room was spring-cleaned; how he set out, with the Marquis of Douro, to sail to the sun in a balloon, and a 'terrible time' the Marquis had with him; how he joined up with Monsieur Skeleton (Sheckleton), both going off to the mountains of Nawhalgerii in India and returning two years later to trade in stray children, selling them to the mills, or for torturing to death for entertainment; at present his business is stealing cattle from the fields to sell, having already stolen three from his own father who buys them back for 3d. which, had his father gone to law, would have cost him 30d!

As the landscape around the travellers changes into moorland, with ceaseless seas of heather, evening approaches, and with it a storm, about which Young Soult immediately composes some verses; they take shelter, spending the night in Naughty's cottage. The next day they see Rossendale Hill, the scene of the great battle, and they go down into Rossendale town which once had 500,000 inhabitants but is now deserted, the haunt of tigers and owls. Then suddenly a chariot dashes up. Inside are the Duke of Wellington and William Sneachie, son of King Alexander Sneaky, who tell Douro his presence is needed in Great Glasstown as a revolution is about to break out. Anxiously all return to the capital.

In the third volume of these series of letters (11 June 1831),

Bellingham describes their re-entry into the city on 15 March 1831. Everywhere is shut up, the streets deserted, with only groups of Rare Lads (ruffians and ne'er-do-wells) about. A meeting is held in the House of Representatives, where Rogue, who is as usual behind all the trouble, makes an insolent speech, is ejected and, by 16 March, gunfire is heard in the streets. In George Street 30,000 men fight the militia who are trying to control the situation. On 17 March, the battle of Great Glasstown takes place, and Glasstown is left in the hands of Rogue who sets up a provisional government. Bellingham himself is taken prisoner, is tried by Rogue, and is just about to have his head chopped off for supporting the Twelves when a shout is heard that the Twelves are coming. Rogue and his followers flee. Bellingham is saved. Then Crashey (Papa?) dashes up in his carriage and appeals to all to stop fighting. They agree, but decide that Rogue and his followers must be punished. Crashey, at the head of the crowd, goes into the city, releases the prisoners, including Bellingham, and all unite in helping to make alive the dead and restore the city. By 23 March all is sufficiently restored to hold the first African Olympic Games, where before an assembly of five or six million, with an orchestra of 10,000, an Ode in praise of the Twelves is performed, which reduces them all, even the Rare Lads, to tears.

This series of letters is taken up again by Branwell on 3 August 1832. Bellingham returns to Glasstown a year afterwards, then sets off again, this time to Sneaky's Glasstown and the Greygarach Mountains where Rogue is found once more stirring up trouble, exhorting a group of people, including some Rare Lads, to rebel against the Duke of Wellington and the Twelves. Rogue orders the Marquis of Douro and Bellingham to be arrested and kept prisoner underground (the parsonage cellar?). Then Rogue and his followers march off, picking up supporters as they go, and on 8 March 1832 capture 300 of Sneaky's soldiers, who are all shot, their bodies thrown into Red River. Some of the troops move on to Fidena, while the others sit down to watch them and eat their dinner! In the subsequent, very bloody, battle of Fidena, Rogue loses 156,000 out of his army of 706,000; Sneaky with his 845,400 loses 46,950. Rogue takes Fidena and is about to court-martial one of his follower, O'Connor, when a wild man appears and frightens them all – it is Lemuel Gulliver. The armies under the Duke, Sneaky, Parry and Frederick Stumps re-form and a fierce battle takes place at Haslingden on 16 March 1832. The kings win, Rogue is taken and shot by a firing squad. It is not, of course, the end of him, since the toy soldier dead are always (unless there are circumstances beyond the control of the Genii, as in the case of King Frederick Guelph) 'made alive again'.

These manuscripts by Branwell are a mixture of many things, the childish, the comic, the exciting and the intriguing. The hints as to what really happened in the 'making out' of stories like these are tantalizing, mere glimpses round corners. However there can be no doubt about one thing – that is the freedom allowed to this small self-contained family in its remote parsonage on the edge of the moors, to give rein to their imaginations, to create and act out their own worlds. What today might be considered deprivation, they turned to advantage.

Stage II (1833–1837)
'Elfland and the Shores of Reality'

The Shores of Reality

During this period of writing decisions were made that were to have far-reaching effects on both Charlotte and Branwell. On 5 July 1835 Charlotte wrote to Ellen Nussey about family plans – she and Emily were to go to Roe Head, she to teach, Emily as a pupil, and Branwell was to try for the Royal Academy of Arts in London. Charlotte's return to Roe Head, besides making her aware of her own responsibility for earning some kind of living for herself and even helping to support her younger sisters, also undoubtedly affected her output as far as the 'infernal world' was concerned. In the next two years, she produced only about six MSS, several of which are not only brief but 'bitty'. The better ones were written in the summer half-yearly holidays or in the Christmas break, and it was not until 1839 (she left Roe Head in May 1838 in a state of nervous depression) that she really got going again. What pieces were written, she collected in a 'Scrapbook'. About the time of the 1835 Christmas break (19 December), she composed one of her best-known poems, 'We wove a web in childhood'. The tone of sad nostalgia in this poem for childhood's fragile 'web of sunny air' and the unfruitful 'mustard seeds' sown in youth, suggests time was bringing about its own changes and that happiness was becoming a backward-looking process:

> We are now grown up to riper age –
> Are they withered in the sod?

she asks rather wistfully.

The ecstasy of the vivid scenes she saw while at Roe Head and her agony at the interruptions caused by the claims of her position as teacher suggest that the 'real' world was pressing in on her and time was growing short for the Glasstown world. Certainly the MSS of 1838 onwards are moving more surely towards the themes, the style and manner of *The Professor* and *Jane Eyre*, rather than lingering within Glasstown's 'web of sunny air'.

The decision that Branwell should attempt to get into the Royal Academy is related in both Papa's letter to Mrs Franks of 1 July 1835, and in his letter of 7 September to William Robinson, where he informed Robinson that Branwell would be finishing his course of lessons with him at the end of that week. There is also extant a draft of an undated letter of Branwell's to the Royal Academy asking where he should present his drawings, and when – in August or September? The next move, as far as his career is concerned, is Branwell's arrogant letter (7 December 1835) to the Editor of *Blackwood's Magazine*, 'Sir – Read what I write . . .' asking that he be allowed to replace James Hogg, the poet who wrote for the magazine and who had recently died. It seems likely, therefore, that some time between 7 September and 7 December he had been up to London, and for some reason or other had failed to be accepted for the Academy. The guesses as to the reasons are many and varied, but perhaps the most intriguing comment we have is in the account Branwell writes (May 1836) of Charles Wentworth (i.e. himself) visiting Verdopolis (London). Charles Wentworth 'threaded the dense and bustling crowds and walked for hours, never staying to eat or drink, never calling a coach or attending to personal appearance . . . his mind was too restless to stop and fully examine anything. . . Here is what he was doing. He was going about striking sparks from his mind by a contact with scenes connected with glorious events, associations, persons.' At one time, as Wentworth was leaning over a parapet looking down on the quayside wharfs 'on a sudden, tears came, starting into his eyes, and a feeling like a wind seemed to pass across his spirits, because now he felt that not even the flashes of glory which these streets and buildings had struck from his soul, not even these feelings which he had reckoned as something to supply his years of dullness, could preserve his thoughts from aimless depression'. The contrast between the simplicity of his lonely home and the stir and complexity of Verdopolis drove him back to his hotel, where 'he stretched himself on a sofa, and listlessly dreamed away his time till dark'. He visited St Michael's Cathedral (St Paul's?) where 'he looked, till to his dimmed eyes it seems to rise and soar beyond his sight. He lay down on the pavement and still looked, till he thought it would thunder down in ruins on his head.' The next day found him 'still unknown and unvisited' and 'restlessly and aimlessly, and with the same anxious face, feeding his feeling with "little squibs of rum"', 'perfectly aware they would only the more depress him afterwards'.

That night at midnight 'there came upon his mind the word Anticipation and he remembered all his present feelings were those of
anticipation. How anxious and impatient and incomplete was his
greatest pleasure, and was it all there was to be? For those who
possessed what he *thought about*, in reality were they happy?' He left
Verdopolis abruptly.

This account of Charles Wentworth's visit cannot, of course, be
taken as a literal account of Branwell's visit to London. It seems that
Branwell spent at least some of his time in the Castle Tavern, High
Holborn, the haunt of pugilists, an art in which Branwell and other of
the 'Rare Lads' of Haworth were interested. However, one can hardly
doubt, considering the inter-relationship between 'real' events and
'imagined' ones in both his and Charlotte's writing, that at least
something of the spirit of this account is pertinent to Branwell's failure
to become a student at the Royal Academy.

As to the similarity of Charles Wentworth's personality to that of
Branwell's, Charlotte, in her *My Angria and the Angrians* of 14 October
1834, provides support. In her depiction of Patrick Wiggins, she gives a
shrewd, satirical portrait of her brother at that time, and in Patrick
Wiggins can easily be seen a somewhat younger Charles Wentworth –
'a low slightly built man attired in a black coat and raven grey trousers,
his hat placed nearly at the back of his head, revealing a bush of carroty
hair so arranged that at the side it projected almost like two spread
hands, a pair of spectacles placed across a prominent Roman nose, black
handkerchief adjusted with no great attention to precision, and, to
complete the picture, a little black rattan flourished in the hand'. His
bearing was 'tolerably upright and marked with that indescribable
swing always assumed by those who pride themselves on being good
pedestrians. . .' Meeting Lord Charles Wellesley, he will, he says, 'be
proud of your company, that is if you can keep up with me'. Lord
Charles, amused, asks him if he is going to the end of the world for that
is what his gait suggests. Wiggins replies blandly, 'Not quite to the end
of the world, that is not altogether.' He has walked from Verdopolis
which 'is thirty miles and I did it all in twelve hours – indeed it's more
than forty, nearer fifty. O, yes and above sixty I daresay, or sixty-five.
Now Sir, what do you say to a man's walking sixty-five miles in one
day?' Asked where he was born, he replies, 'I was born partly in
Thorncliffe, that is after a fashion, but then I always account myself a
native of Howard, a great City among the Warner Hills.' Lord Charles
refutes this – 'None of your humbug, Wiggins . . . I know well enough
Howard is only a miserably little village, buried in dreary moors and
moss-hags and marshes. I question whether it has one church or
anything nearer an Hotel than that wayside Ale-house you are now

eyeing so longingly. . .' Wiggins dashes into the alehouse, saying he is going for a pot of porter or a tumbler of brandy and water. When inside, however, he asks the fat landlady, 'If you please ma'am will you be so kind as to give a ha'penny'orth of milk, or a gill of whey, or even a draught of ditchwater, if it would be too much trouble to procure the other liquids for such a mere Tom-cat as I am.' When, after taking tea and bread and butter, he rejoins Lord Charles, he boasts to him that he has downed two bottles of Sneachie's Glasstown ale, a double quart of Porter, with cheese, bread and cold beef, which is what he calls 'doing the thing in a handsome way'. Replying to Lord Charles's query about his relatives – Wiggins says, 'In a way I may be said to have no relations. I can't tell who my father and mother are no more than that stone. I've some people who call themselves akin to me in the shape of three girls, not that they are honoured by possessing me as a brother, but I deny that they're my sisters . . . Charlotte Wiggins, Jane Wiggins and Anne Wiggins . . . They are miserable creatures not worth talking about. Charlotte's eighteen years old, a broad dumpy thing, whose head does not come higher than my elbow. Emily's sixteen, lean and scant, with a face about the size of a penny, and Anne is nothing, absolutely nothing.' 'Is she,' Lord Charles inquires, 'an idiot?' 'Next door to it,' is the abrupt reply. His own mind, Wiggins declares 'was always looking above my station. I was not satisfied with being a sign-painter at Howard, as Charlotte and them things were with being sempstresses . . . I traced a path for my own feet . . . which terminated at the door of a splendid Palace situated on a Cock-hill.' In fact, the tomb to be erected there in his memory is to be engraved 'as a Musician he was greater than Bach, as a Poet he surpasses Byron, as a Painter, Claude Lorraine yielded to him, as a Rebel he snatched the Palm from Alexander Rogue, as a Merchant Edward Percy was his inferior, as a mill-owner, Grenville came not near him, as a Traveller De Humbolt, Ledyard, Mungo Park etc. never braved half his dangers. . .' Finally he tells Lord Charles of his encounter with Mr Greenwood, when 'a fine full new Horgan was hoppened in Howard Church' and he behaved like a 'thorough going toadie'.

It seems Charlotte, writing as Lord Charles, has few illusions about the appearance of herself or Emily, or about the character and nature of her brother – foolish, a braggart, a 'thorough going toadie', a bletherer, all talk and little else, as full of blarney and wordmongering as his double Celtic heritage, Irish and Cornish, could make him. The tone is light and bantering, but the picture painted, as far as the future of Patrick Wiggins is concerned, is a dismal one. It seems that at least one of the four young Brontës was already aware of the harsh shores of reality.

Elfland

During the years 1833–7 the greater part of Charlotte's and Branwell's juvenile compositions was written and a formidable amount of words it adds up to. Both return to the (Glasstown) past, and the present-tense reality of the characters is given solidity by stories dealing with their earlier life.

Charlotte's Account. Charlotte attends to Wellington's eldest son, Arthur Adrian Augustus Wellesley, the Marquis of Douro, Duke of Zamorna. In 1832 she had written *The Bridal*, the story of Douro's love for and marriage with Marian Hume. Now in 1833 she recalls the childhood betrothal of Marian to Henry Percy, Alexander Percy's eldest son. In *The Secret* Marian's and Douro's enemies try to break up their recent marriage by telling Marian that Henry is still really alive – his father had given him as a young man to S'Death to get rid of – and has come home. However the treachery is discovered and all ends happily, with Douro even more deeply in love with his childlike Marian. Douro's own boyhood relationship with Helen Victorine, the Lily of Sunart, is told in *The Spell* (1834). Helen dies at the birth of their son, Ernest Edward Gordon, whose destiny, it is prophesied, will not be a happy one – he is later brutally murdered by Quashia. In *The Foundling* (1833) Edward Sydney sets out to discover his own background, and *Lily Hart* (1833) is the story of Miss Hart's young love for Henry Sneachie, son of King Alexander Sneachie, who is wounded in Rogue's rebellion of 1831, and of their secret marriage a year later. Percy's attendance at the Great Olympic Games held in 1831 after his rebellion, and his abduction of Lady Emily Charlesworth is told in *The Green Dwarf* (1834).

There are also two volumes containing a medley of stories dealing with past and present affairs, collected together by Charlotte in *Arthuriana* (1833) and *Corner Dishes* (1834). Amongst these is one tale in which Marian is shown at the mercy of a drunken Northangerland (Percy) over whom, to sober him up, someone pours boiling water. In another, Patrick Wiggins appears accompanying Mr Greenwood when he comes to give his music lesson to the Queen. He is floored by the Queen (Emily?) after commenting on her large nose and trying to touch it.

Some of the references in these manuscripts of Charlotte's for 1833–4 give rise to speculation – the drunken Northangerland, for example, and in *The Foundling*, Crashie creates a fluid 'so pure, so refined, so ethereal, that one drop of it distilled in our mortal clay penetrates the soul', freeing 'it from all grosser particles', raising it 'far above worldly troubles', rendering it 'capable of enjoying the calm of heaven amid the turmoil of earth'. And in the same story are the following lines –

Eamala is a gurt bellaring bull
Shoo swilled and swilled till shoo drank her full;
 Then shoo rolled abaat
 With a screeaam an' shaat
And aat of her pocket a knoife did pull.

An' wi' that knoife shhoo'd a cut her throit
If I hadn't gean her a strait waist-coit;
 Then shoo flang an' jumped
 And girned and grumped,
But I didn't caare for her a doit.

These references suggest that, by 1834, Charlotte was well aware of the ill effects of drinking too much and of drug-taking. It is noticeable that each of these experiences is described from the onlooker's point of view, and each has the mark of a real, not a literary or imagined, experience about it – the effectiveness of a kettle of boiling water for sobering up, for example, or the way in which Eamala (Emily?) is left to sleep it off!

Branwell's Account. With Branwell it is Alexander Percy (known at various times as Rogue, Ellrington, Northangerland) who figures largely. The outline of the continuing story of Glasstown is given in his *Historical Narrative of the War of Encroachment* (1833), *History of Angria* (a medley of manuscripts, 1834–7), *The Wool Is Rising* (1834), *Narrative of the First War* (1836), *A New Year Story* (1836), a life of Percy (untitled), 1837, and a Baron Richton Story (untitled), 1837. In *A New Year Story*, for example, he writes of the founding of Glasstown, its conception and creation, up to 1782, when the Verdopolitan Union (i.e. the Glasstown Confederacy), as Branwell later calls it, is formed – 'with its kingdoms four, its customs one'. He tells of Percy's place in it and then turns aside to fill in Percy's biographical background (*see* Glossary – Percy, Alexander).

With his *Politics in Verdopolis* (November 1833) a new era in the Glasstown Confederacy begins. Percy brings Mary, his daughter, to Verdopolis where she meets Douro, now known as Zamorna, and they fall passionately in love. Zamorna returns home to tell his wife, Marian, that if she really loves him she will not make him suffer by standing in his way as far as Mary is concerned. Marian agrees to step aside, and eventually dies of a decline (Charlotte in 1834 writes the *Last Will and Testament of Florence Marian Wellesley*, as, in April 1833, Aunt Branwell had made hers). Marian's child, born that year, is given into the care of Mina Laury, Zamorna's most faithful and ardent follower, and later dies of consumption.

Although for Charlotte, Marian Wellesley always remains a 'green and white maiden of snowdrop purity' the saga cannot stay still for long – Branwell sees to that – and in May 1833 Zamorna marries Mary in St Michael's Cathedral, Verdopolis. The following years, 1834, 1835 and 1836, are years of considerable activity in Glasstown, for the next great event is the founding of Angria, described by Baron Richton in *The Wool Is Rising*. Zamorna, speaking in the House of Commons in Verdopolis on 8 February 1834, reminds members of how courageously he has been fighting on their behalf and that, as he too is a son of a Twelve, he like the others should have a kingdom of his own. He is given Angria, on the understanding that it remains within the Confederacy under the same terms as the other kingdoms. Angria is a broad fertile region, 400 miles by 300, stretching from the Gordon Mountains in the north to the Calabar river in the south, and is to the east of the Niger river. Northangerland, however, who had supported Zamorna's appeal, is dissatisfied with this, feeling that Zamorna, powerful as he is at this time, could easily have become the sole king of Verdopolis – of the Confederacy in fact – and, as a result, Northangerland would also have done better for himself.

The actual coronation of Zamorna as King of Angria takes place on 14 February 1834, with the singing of the National Song of Angria – 'Sound the loud trumpet' – and the Anthem of the Coronation, both composed by the poet of Angria, Henry Hastings (Branwell). During the first month Angria's new capital is built, and people, urged on by Northangerland, leave Verdopolis for the new Adrianopolis. The constitution is worked out and a government formed with Northangerland as Prime Minister. Meetings are held in the provinces, Zamorna himself addressing the Angrians. On 20 September the first Angrian Parliament is opened, with an Ode – 'The Angrian Welcome', by Henry Hastings – to commemorate it.

By the end of 1835, however, Northangerland is again causing trouble, despite Zamorna's warning that if he continues in this way, he, Zamorna, will abandon his wife Mary (Northangerland's daughter) and send her back to Alnwick – a separation he knows will cause Mary, and through her Northangerland, distress. Northangerland, disregarding his warning, rallies support for himself on all sides, and, on 26 June 1836, starts a revolution. In the ensuing battles Zamorna is defeated and his son, Ernest, horribly blinded by Quashia, later dying in Warner Howard Warner's arms. Zamorna himself is eventually captured, tried and sentenced to death, but Northangerland, in the face of opposition, allows him to sail away in *The Rover*, Northangerland's own boat, to the safety of exile. At Marseilles, Zamorna learns of the death of his son, Ernest. He swears that to revenge himself against Northangerland he will cause Mary's death, despite the fact that he will be killing the one thing in life he loves. At Marseilles he meets Mina Laury, whose devotion and love help restore his spirits at this time. He rallies both himself and his troops, and, with the help of Mina and Warner Howard Warner, he returns to retake his kingdom.

Many of Branwell's manuscripts dealing with these events have yet to be transcribed. Until they have all been deciphered and put into proper order, difficulties arise – in the first place concerning details of the development of the Glasstown saga itself, and, in the second, over any critical evaluation of Branwell's writing. However, it is plain that the quality of his writing as a whole varies from the exciting to the verbose and arrogant. Much of its value lies in the fact that it provides us with a skeleton which Charlotte fleshes with such a multiplicity of stories and characters. Branwell is always pushing the story forward, so that his characters change and age, as for example in the untitled script of 1837 where Northangerland is shown growing old and peevish. Charlotte, on the other hand, is happy to go on weaving her web around people and places as they are, with little thought to the differences time and change may make upon them. Her concern is always with the present tense.

Charlotte's MSS. In Charlotte's work of this period there are three areas of interest, all of which are connected, not only with her later writing as a novelist, but also with the work of her sisters, particularly of Emily in *Wuthering Heights*.

(1) *The development of the relationship between Zamorna and Northangerland.* Charlotte's growing attention to, and sensitivity for, the complexity of this relationship is remarkable. At first the two are related only by ties of companionship – a loving rivalry – between the young boy, Arthur Wellesley and the older Alexander Percy. The solidarity of this early relationship is never in later years forgotten. When they become political opponents, engaged in a struggle that erupts into open rebellion and revolution, they still find themselves unable to destroy each other. A strange liaison of honour and treachery, commitment and cunning, love and hate marks their relationship, becoming more complex as it is more finely drawn. It is a relationship which belongs to a 'man's world', on which the passionate, adoring, sometimes petty, often empty-headed, women of the saga have little effect. They do not understand it, neither do they try to. It becomes, finally, a relationship in which each character is a necessary part of the other. This has nothing to do with the fact that Zamorna marries

Percy's daughter, or that he extends the love he has for Mary to her father. In actual fact, he more often uses Mary as a stick with which to beat Percy. Both Zamorna and Percy recognize the ties of this 'blood and spirit brotherhood', which can be neither forgotten nor rejected, no matter what each may do to the other. It seldom acknowledges itself openly and is much of the time lax and easy-going, but occasionally it flares up into a degree of intensity that results in anger, fisticuffs or war. It seems to find its most passionate expression in hatred rather than in love and compassion, although the hatred itself is really one aspect of the love. One is reminded very much of the Heathcliff/Cathy relationship (*Wuthering Heights*), with its strange asexual depths and the completeness of its commitment, and of Cathy's cry, 'He is more myself than I am'.

(**2**) *The relationship of death to life, of death to love.* In July 1836, Charlotte wrote a long poem now called *Zamorna's Exile*, adding further stanzas to it in January 1837. It expresses, in a kind of soliloquy, the thoughts of Zamorna as he sails away into exile after the revolution. He laments over his dead son, for

> that which now beyond the power of waking
> Sleeps in its gory grave. There's Heaven above,
> And Earth around me, and, beneath me, shaking
> With crimes of the tormented, Hell may move.

But

> neither from Hell nor Earth nor Righteous Heaven
> Can rest or comfort to my heart be given.

He is left with

> ... nothing but revenge to think on now.

As Northangerland had caused Zamorna's child, Ernest, to be destroyed, so Zamorna will destroy Northangerland's child, Mary, despite the fact that in doing so he will bring down the curses of the 'Most High' on his own head. In marrying Mary he swore

> that if your father drew
> His hand from mine, I'd give him back his gift
> Of happiness and hope and fame bereft.

Despite Mary's cry, 'You love me, yet you'll kill me!', he is determined to carry out his threat. She tells him that although he is

> as cruel as the fiend that crushes
> Its victim after snaring it in toils,

he has given her

Glimpses of all on earth that's worth possessing

and begs him not to leave her. He, however, does not expect her to die

> and that forever
> The grave would hide her from me? Did I deem
> That after parting I should never, never
> Behold her save in some delusive dream.

He asks if she is really dead –

> Will no voice answer 'No'? Will no tongue say
> That she still lives and longs and waits for me?

He imagines her dying

> Conscious that death was near, her spirit led –
> While her soul waved its wings, prepared to soar –
> Back to the days she never might see more,

and watching, can only think of the success of his revenge over Northangerland

> whom in spite of blood and crime
> I loved intensely, dark thy doom is sealing!
> Am I not well avenged? . . .

Her father may try to call her back, in vain,

> She's gone. Aye, shudder. Stoop lower.
> Speak, call her back! The winged spirit may hear!

But the spirit does not, and Northangerland is left to grieve. Zamorna, too, must try to forget, but he keeps seeing her 'along the pathway she has taken', 'like an apparition beckon' to him, for

> Had she but known all the love that I bore her . . .
> Then, when the wing of the spectre swept o'er her,
> Her death-frozen features had fixed in a smile.

The attitude towards death expressed here, its connections with hell rather than heaven, the attempt at the moment of death to recall the dying, the search for and the meeting with the lingering ghost, recall both Heathcliff with the dying Cathy and the dying Heathcliff himself in *Wuthering Heights*:

> His eyes met mine so keen and fierce, I started; then he seemed to smile. . . . I tried to close his eyes . . . they would not shut; they seemed to sneer at my attempts; and his parted lips and sharp white teeth sneered too! . . . 'Ech! what a wicked un he looks grinning at death! . . . (Heathcliff's death, *Wuthering Heights*.)

The wild vehemence of the language here, in both Charlotte's poetry and Emily's prose, betokens a world free of the shifts of morality and law, neither hidebound by, nor compromising itself to, any particular social or religious mores. The 'enthusiast', as Charlotte calls Zamorna, is both untamed and untameable; he is untrammelled, his own law-maker and law-breaker. This is certainly not the world of Jane Eyre or Lucy Snowe, though both these heroines at times hover on its boundaries. It is very much the amoral world of *Wuthering Heights*, in essence and approach, if not in the romantic immaturity of its expression.

(3) *The relationship between Zamorna and Mina Laury*. In 1836 Charlotte introduced into *Passing Events* a character, Mina Laury, who figured in the earlier scripts of both Charlotte and Branwell. Mina, born the same year as Zamorna, brought up on the Wellesley estates with him, is companion to his first wife Marian, and entrusted with the care of their son. In the poem, *Zamorna's Exile*, Charlotte further explores Mina's devotion to Zamorna, which results in her following him into exile. It is the quality and kind of this devotion that recurs in Charlotte's published novels, and is explored and worked upon in the 'novelettes' of 1838/9. In the poem, Mina worships the very ground Zamorna treads on:

> This moment like a faithful dog she's lying
> Crouched at my feet, for with sad, subdued,
> Untiring constancy she's ever trying
> To gain one word or even one look, imbued
> With some slight touch of kindness. There, then, take
> A brief caress for all thy labour's sake.

Both the need to love deeply, passionately and faithfully – though often silently and secretly, because of some moral impediment to the happy conclusion of that love – and the need to be loved, if only carelessly and fleetingly, hallmark Mina's relationship with Zamorna. Adolescent, immature, romantic, even Byronic though this may be as an expression of love, it dominates Charlotte's juvenile writing from about 1836 onwards. It is almost as though, having mounted this particular love (sexual is far too harsh a word for it) carousel, she could neither dismount from nor stop it.

Stage III (1838 onwards)

'Love's troubled waters'

Branwell's MSS, 1838–c.1845

By 1838/9 much of the coherence of the Glasstown saga has gone. Branwell's manuscripts, with the exception of several fragments dated February and April 1839 ('Love and Warfare') and a prose manuscript of 1840 about Alexander Percy, are mostly poetry. The poems are no longer merely decorative pieces for the prose stories, but are often long and complete in themselves. Branwell published very little, but did send his poetry to others for comment – to Hartley Coleridge, De Quincey, Wordsworth, for example. Little came of it, although Hartley Coleridge did, in an unfinished, unposted letter, commend Branwell's abilities as both a versifier and translator, based on the translations of the Odes of Horace that Branwell sent.

The first of the poems written between 1838 and 1843 is *Harriet II* which harks back to themes he has been dealing with since 1837 – the sisters Harriet and Caroline, the death of Caroline and the visit of Harriet to see her in her coffin. Harriet grows up to love Alexander Percy, but is married off to Hector Montmorency. In *Harriet II* that love becomes a distracting passion to the exclusion of all else, resulting in a wild, feverish poem.

The other poems, *Sir Henry Tunstall* (1840), the poems in the Luddenden Foot notebook (1841–2), *The Afghan War* (1842) and *Azrael* (1842) are all public pieces in the sense that they are either to be read at meetings or sent in letters to friends, or are to be offered for publication in newspapers. They are not longer a necessary part of the 'web of childhood' and there is no aura of privateness about them. Similar themes to the old ones occur – *Sir Henry Tunstall*, for example, is about the return of an outcast. The Luddenden Foot notebook, kept by Branwell when he was working on the railway, is a mixture of drafts of poems and of railway business. Of the shorter pieces some – *On the Callousness Produced by Care* and *Peaceful Death and Painful Life* – found their way into the *Halifax Guardian* pages. Others, the longer ventures – *Lord Nelson* (later known as *The Triumph of Mind over Body*) and *Azrael* – were read and discussed by Branwell and his drinking cronies. One thing however seems clear from this – Branwell was making a deliberate attempt to write poetry for publication, perhaps even trying to build up some kind of career for himself as the James Hogg of Yorkshire. An occupation such as a clerkship on the railway would give him enough ready cash to rub along with and enough time to jot down the odd poem to be worked upon later when he was off duty.

During his years at Thorp Green (January 1843–June 1845), however, his writing seems to have come almost to a halt. He produced only one known prose manuscript – *And the Weary Are at Rest* – and several poems, *Real Rest* (1845/6), *Morley Hall* (in October 1846 it was, according to Branwell, in the 'last month of its pregnancy') and *Percy Hall* (1847). Of these *Morley Hall* was written for J.B. Leyland, about a member of the Leyland family, one Anne, who eloped with Edward Tyldesley by putting a rope about her waist so that her lover could pull her across the water in the moat. *Percy Hall* is a retelling of the story of the death of Alexander Percy's consumptive wife, Mary. Only *Real Rest* has any power, with its yearning for the peace of death and the rest that the grave alone can give.

Many of the poems of these years are restless, marked by an acute awareness of death and physical decay, of being deserted, unwanted, of the despair that comes from both the frustrations of life here and the denial of any life hereafter. They are seldom the bland poetizing of a comfortable mind. Shafts of agony cut through them and they seem to bear witness to an experience of suffering which can also be seen in Branwell's letters of the time. 'I am too hard to die and too wretched to live,' he writes to J.B. Leyland, adding to the letter sketches that cruelly caricature his misery. This misery may at times seem exaggerated. However, to want so feverishly to give all one's youth and health to become a corpse, because death alone brings, if not peace at least annihilation of suffering, seems hardly at the age of twenty-nine to be merely adolescent folly, especially when, in these last years, as he must well have realized, his manner of living was making him his own executioner.

What is probably his last prose manuscript, *And the Weary Are at Rest*, is undated. Some have put it as early as 1842, although the bulk of it seems more likely to have been written after his return from Thorp Green in 1845, or perhaps started during his time there. It concerns the further adventures of Alexander Percy, now getting older and dreading the threat of physical decay, when the 'firm foot can no longer tread the heather, this warm blood no longer thrill to a woman's touch ... this working brain no longer teem with thick coming fancies, this omnivorous stomach no longer bear its three bottles or twenty tumblers...' Percy is staying with a Mr and Mrs Thurston at the opening of the grouse season. He shoots on the moors, then, evading his companions, returns to the house to find his hostess Maria Thurston who, as a neglected and pretty lady, he regards as fair game. She is attracted by him and his swashbuckling approach, but is fearful of her husband. To persuade her of his uprightness, Percy calls a meeting at the local chapel where he preaches, appealing for funds for missions to

Africa, Asia, America, Europe and England! Next morning knowing that she will have heard about the service, he returns to the house to further his cause. He persuades her into the shrubbery, from where she returns with her 'raven tresses' 'disordered'. When his companions come in, the guilt of their close association reveals itself, and the story ends, incomplete, with Maria's thoughts on what she has done – how can she 'shake off what my heart clings to'? God, she argues, has caused her to have such feelings, so if she has them about the wrong person, it is hardly her fault. She leaves the outcome in His good hands. (One cannot help but speculate – was Branwell merely imagining all this, or was he drawing on his own experience with Mrs Robinson, or even Charlotte's with M. Heger?)

The liveliest part of the story is the odd section that seems to have been slotted in willy-nilly, in which Branwell ruthlessly satirizes the nonconformist church, its cant and hypocrisy, the conning of the more simple honest members by their more intelligent elders and betters, the wildness of the 'conversion' meetings and the Bible-thumping that goes on in them. It is vivid, comic, often distasteful. The whole story, in fact, exudes a kind of suppressed hysteria, a straining at the humorous that makes one feel that in it we are witnessing more than anything else the death struggles of a worn-out talent.

Charlotte's MSS, 1838–1839

Between 1838 and March 1841 when Charlotte left her position as governess with the Whites at Rawdon prior to going to Brussels, she wrote four very substantial manuscripts. Two are signed and dated by her – *Mina Laury*, 17 January 1838, and an untitled script about the life of Alexander Percy, 21 July 1838. The other two – one untitled (usually called *Henry Hastings*), and *Caroline Vernon* – contain dates in the stories themselves, but are neither signed nor dated. The dates in *Henry Hastings* are autumn – partridge shooting time – 1838 and 26 March 1839, and the manuscript is signed with the name of Charles Townshend; the dates in *Caroline Vernon* are 1 July at the beginning and 7 December at the end, though no year date is given.

Between the end of May 1838 and June 1839, and again from mid-July 1839 onwards, Charlotte was at home at the times when these scripts must have been written, for there would have been little time for writing at all, let alone scripts as long as these, when she was 'governessing'. As Charlotte seldom wrote stories in which the dates mentioned were ahead of the date when she was actually writing them, we think it can be accepted that in all probability the *Henry Hastings* story and *Caroline Vernon* were written, in that order, in 1839.

Mina Laury (17 January 1838). The events of Mina Laury take place a year after the Revolution, when Zamorna is restored to his kingdom and Percy has become a restless private individual passing his time at Alnwick, the Percy country residence, where his daughter Mary and his son-in-law Zamorna visit him. It is the love story of Zamorna and Mina, the culmination of a relationship that goes back to their childhood days together. For Zamorna, Mina rejects Lord Hartford, and Zamorna, becoming increasingly aware of her passion for him, finally packs his wife off to Verdopolis, telling her he will follow her the next day, and presumably spends the night with Mina – although this is not made blatantly obvious.

There are three elements of interest in this story. The first is Charlotte's continuing exploration of the relationship between Zamorna and Percy – here known as Northangerland. Zamorna's fidelity to him after the revolution which Northangerland had himself brought about – allowing him to remain in the country as a private citizen rather than be executed or exiled as a traitor – is not in the least a 'kiss and make friends' kind of forgiveness, or even a quid pro quo for Northangerland's having earlier saved his life. His 'mercy' is of the same quality as his love and hate. It exists because neither Percy nor Zamorna 'could find a substitute for the other in the whole world besides'. Each of these two, whether in triumph or defeat, needs – is a necessary part of – the other. Each is, in Charlotte's own words, the other's 'anti-type'.

The second element of interest is that some of Zamorna's former attitude towards the dying Mary (*see* Stage II) is now directed towards the living Mina. He would, in fact, 'rather see Mina in her coffin' than let anyone else have her. Again one is reminded of Emily's depiction in *Wuthering Heights* of the Heathcliff/Cathy relationship where equally 'neither could find a substitute for the other in the whole world besides'. Certainly Heathcliff would rather see Cathy in her coffin than that anyone else should have her love.

The third element of interest is concerned with Mina's attitude towards Zamorna. It is a continuation and development of that expressed in *Zamorna's Exile* (*see* Stage II) and it is a way of loving that Charlotte gives expression to in her later novels and which led to her quarrel with Harriet Martineau. She vehemently denied Miss Martineau's criticism of her attitude towards love – 'I know what love is as I understand it' – and certainly for Mina in Zamorna's arms everything else fades away and, while not totally losing her own personality, she readily suppresses it, a submission demanded, and gladly accepted as legitimate, by the overwhelming power of that love.

Again, in this script of 1838, the two worlds of Zamorna and

Wuthering Heights rub strangely together, for whereas Jane Eyre bows to the social and moral conventions of her society, Mina, Cathy and Heathcliff never do.

Henry Hastings. This is the story of the capture and trial of Henry Hastings for the attempt he makes on Zamorna's life, of the efforts of his sister, Elizabeth, to save him, and of her subsequent relationship with Sir William Percy, Alexander Percy's son and the officer in charge of the Hastings affair. The story is in two parts. The first deals with events up to the time of Henry's capture on 24 February 1839, when he is in hiding at the Moore's country house, where Elizabeth is engaged as governess/companion to the beautiful Jane Moore. The second part is about Elizabeth – her pleas for her brother's life, and her love for Sir William Percy whom she first meets when he comes to arrest Hastings. Sir William engineers it so that he meets Elizabeth again when she is out walking on the moors. There he asks her quite bluntly to become his mistress. In the first part of the story he has not been presented as a particularly likeable man – he is harsh, ruthless, self-centred (a true son of Alexander Percy in fact), and finds it 'mighty convenient to be in love with French women – one's passion never interferes with one's comfort'. His tricky way of getting Elizabeth on her own suggests hypocrisy and deceit. Unfortunately Elizabeth falls desperately in love with him. With all three heroines of this time – Mina, Elizabeth and Caroline – the reader is never left in any doubt that the love they feel and offer has a value far beyond that offered by the recipient. Zamorna's and Sir William's careless acceptance of this golden gift of true love only adds to the painfulness of the situation. However, whereas Mina and Caroline accept their lot as Zamorna's mistresses (merely two in a long line), Elizabeth refuses Sir William's offer as briefly and directly as he himself had put it – 'No'. She then runs away from him, and Sir William – for whom, the reader realizes, Elizabeth would have been a mere passing fancy – retires scowling, without even having the decency to see her safely home in the darkness of night that had gathered around them.

Henry Hastings is one of the most fascinating of all Charlotte's juvenilia, certainly as far as her development as a novelist is concerned. Her choice of narrator is a good one – Charles Townshend (alias Charles Wellesley) who is now a writer by profession, and varies his style according to his mood or the situation he is writing about. He can be endearingly sharp and amusing, and, at other times, romantic and mysterious. In some of these romantic passages one feels Charlotte, herself, is mocking him by the very words she puts into his mouth, but as a keen observer of, and commentator on, life, Charles Townshend is often a match for Jane Austen.

Not all the story is told by him, however, and in the second part, which is increasingly dominated by Elizabeth, a kind of glow suffuses the prose, in keeping with the love theme of the story. Sir William comments on the place where he and Elizabeth are walking:

> I've seen these hedges bright as they are now in sunshine and throwing a dark shade by moonlight – if there were such things as fairies I should have met them often – for these are just their haunts – fox-glove leaves and bell-moss like green velvet – mushrooms – springing at the roots of oak-trees – thorns a hundred years old. . .

Charlotte's technique in the presentation of character is becoming more skilful. In herself Elizabeth is, as Jane Eyre so obviously is, an 'extract' of Charlotte herself, with Charlotte's awareness of her own plainness, her sense of social inadequacy and her depth of hidden feeling. It is the reprobate Charles who sees into the heart of this creature and feels at least some sympathy for her.

There are two things, however, that Charlotte does not achieve in this story with which she has more success in *Caroline Vernon* – both are concerned with the continuity of the story-telling.

Caroline Vernon. This is the last known piece of Charlotte's juvenilia. The next piece of complete writing extant is *The Professor*, first sent to the publishers in 1846. *Caroline Vernon*, however, can hardly be seen as a triumphant climax to all that has gone before and a clear pointer to the future – to *Jane Eyre*, *Shirley*, and *Villette*. It is the story of Zamorna's relationship with Caroline, the illegitimate daughter of Alexander Percy and Louisa Dance/Vernon. When, after his exile, Zamorna wins back his kingdom, Louisa Vernon and her daughter are put into Zamorna's guardianship. When Percy returns to Angria, he decides it is time he took an interest in his own daughter, giving her some kind of place in society and introducing her to the ways of the world in both France and Verdopolis. Reluctantly Zamorna agrees. However, after a brief sojourn in Paris and Verdopolis with her father, Caroline returns to seek out Zamorna, with whom she has fallen in love, to become his mistress.

It is in some ways a disappointing story. In the first place, the note of sincerity and urgency that marked *Henry Hastings* is missing, partly because the narrator is no longer Charles Townshend. The teller of this tale is both faceless and monotone. What it loses in this way, however, it gains in continuity. It is not merely a series of dramatic scenes jostling together. Charlotte's efforts to achieve this ease of continuity, and at the same time to maintain the tension, can be seen in the changes she made in a second version where the reunion of Caroline and Zamorna is the final climax towards which the story builds. This ensures not only that it holds together far better but that the tension never lessens. It is, in fact, even if it does lack the sense of immediacy of *Henry Hastings*, a very neat and tidy story.

The six years or so between the writing of *Caroline Vernon* and that of *The Professor*, with, between, all Charlotte's new experiences abroad and at home, naturally add much to the authority and sophistication of her writing, which is shown in *Jane Eyre*. However, it is clear that by 1839 she is already familiar with the tools of her trade and experienced at using them to express what she herself knows and feels. For her, at least, one feels that 'elfland' and 'the shores of reality' were beginning to draw closer together.

Some Events in the History of Glasstown

This table of events is offered as a guide for those who may wish to browse through the childhood writing of Charlotte and Branwell. It should be noted that the dates given here are not the dates of composition of the manuscripts. They are those of the Glasstown Confederacy saga, taken from many manuscripts over a period of ten years or more. They were not worked out systematically as 'historical' dates by Charlotte and Branwell, who certainly had no kind of card-index approach to the continuing development of their imaginary world. New facts and figures, sometimes conflicting, were added as the occasion arose. This is merely an attempt to put the events of the stories into some reasonable order, even though they do not always have a logical sequence. Dates have been given where they exist or can be deduced.

1770 Feb. 5– Mar. 1	The Twelves set out from England for Africa.
	May 19	They arrive at Ascension Island; Stumps and others are killed but brought back to life again.
	June 2–5	They arrive in Africa.
1779		Death of K(C)ashna Quamina.
1782		The Foundation of the Confederacy of the Four Kingdoms – Wellingtonsland, Parrysland, Ross('s)land and Sneachiesland.
1792/3		Alexander Percy born.
1809 May		Pauline Louisada Ellrington writes to Robert King that Alexander Percy is restive and she needs more money for him.
1812		Augusta di Segovia either marries or becomes the mistress of

	Percy; he is sent by his father to the Philosopher's Isle; writes poetry to Augusta.
1812–13	Percy returns from the Philosopher's Isle, falls in love with and marries Mary Wharton.
	Arthur, Marquis of Douro born.
1814 June 4	1st African Olympic Games.
1815	Mary, Northangerland's wife, dies.
1816 June 14	Arthur Wellesley, Duke of Wellington chosen as king.
1818	Percy leaves Africa – for ever.
1827	Death of Frederick Guelph – the year the 'real' Duke of York died.
1829(?)	Percy – now known as Northangerland – is ruined and imprisoned.
1831 Mar. 16–18	Rogue's (i.e. Percy's) rebellion.
Mar. 17	Battle of Glasstown.
Mar. 23	First African Olympic Games.
1831	The Marquis of Douro and Marian Hume married.
1832	Rogue raises the Great Rebellion; is captured and executed, but brought back to life – and has his property confiscated; becomes a pirate.
1833	Rogue marries Lady Zenobia Ellrington; opening of the 1st Verdopolitan Parliament with Crashey's prayer to the Genii; birth of a son to Douro and his wife, Marian; Mary, Percy's daughter, meets Douro who persuades Marian to release him from his marriage; Napoleon and the French invade the wild eastern territories of Glasstown; Douro fights and defeats him and is created Duke of Zamorna. War against the Ashantees – Rogue becomes Colonel Alexander Percy, a brilliant young soldier.
Dec. 4	Battle of Velino.
1834 Feb. 4	A meeting of the Peers in Verdopolis; Zamorna asks for a kingdom of his own.
Feb. 8	The bill to confer a kingdom on Zamorna passed.
Feb. 18	Coronation of Zamorna as King of Angria.
Sept. 3	Grand provincial meeting held in the County Field in the City of Zamorna.
Sept. 11	Meeting in the Grand Square of Adrianopolis.
Sept. 17	Meeting at the Ings, near Falls, of the Douronians.
Sept. 20	1st opening of the Angrian Parliament with a speech by Zamorna.
1834–5	Northangerland (Percy) is stirring up trouble between Zamorna, his ministers and the people.

1836	Dismissal of Northangerland.
June 22	Rumours in Verdopolis of trouble at the opening of Parliament.
June 23	Colonel Gre(n)ville, the Mayor, calls out the Metropolitan Volunteers.
June 24	Directions given for arming the police.
June 25	5,000 cavalry with Sir John Fenton and seven regiments of foot enter Verdopolis from Edwardston and Zamornaland; 100 guns from the Island Fleet sent to the Citadel Hill, Parliament Square, St Michael's Square.
June 26	The Revolution begins – Northangerland is taking his breakfast of hot green tea and dry toast when his mother comes to tell him his daughter Mary, Zamorna's wife, is very ill.
June 27	The battle of Edwardston in which Zamorna is defeated and chased by MacTerrorglen from Verdopolis to Adrianopolis; the fleet is sent up the Calabar to blockade Adrianopolis; there are engagements at Westbeach, Ludlow, Grantly and Avondale; Zamorna is forced to withdraw across Angria and into the Warner Hills; there is pillaging and killing throughout Zamorna, Arundel and into the Gordon Mountains.
July 1	Zamorna's son is snatched from Mina Laury, blinded by Quashia, dies in Warner's arms; Zamorna is captured, tried and offered a pact by Northangerland – to join him in power and to destroy Angria; Zamorna refuses; he is put on board *The Rover* (Northangerland's boat) and banished 2,000 miles off the rocky coast of Ascension Isle; he meets Mina Laury at Marseilles; Northangerland sets up the Grand Provisional Directory.
Aug. 1	Grand public entry of the new government into Zamorna with a great display of military force; people are ordered to take an oath of allegiance to the new government or die. Meanwhile Fidena masses 70,000 troops on the frontiers of Angria and Warner sets out to join him. Northangerland sends orders to crush them; Lady Georgiana Greville asks Northangerland to restore Zamorna; Northangerland is in despair because Mary (his daughter, and Zamorna's wife) is dying at Alnwick, where she was sent when the Revolution began, and his friends are beginning to desert him and plot against him; Warner appeals to the Angrians to rise against Northangerland; with the help of Mina Laury, Zamorna returns and rallies his supporters; Northangerland flees; Zamorna reviews his troops at Gazemba; the Revolution ends with much bad feeling against Northangerland, but he is allowed by Zamorna to live on as a private individual provided he keep out of politics; he becomes an irritable and restless private citizen.
1837–8	Northangerland seeks out his daughter Caroline, age 15, who

with her mother, Louisa Vernon, is kept under house arrest by Zamorna, and travels abroad with her; she meets Zamorna, and later (age 16), becomes his kept woman.

Glossary to Glasstown

A glossary of the main references

[It should be noted that Charlotte and Branwell are not always consistent in their use of their characters.]

Abercorn. General in Zamorna's army; his estate, including Brushwood Hall, purchased by Mr Smith; a fop and a coxcomb.

Ac(e)rofcroomb. City and province of Ashantee, with ten cannibal chiefs who roast and eat Cheeky, Crackey and Gravey; destroyed by King Frederic and Arthur Wellesley.

Adrian, Emperor. *See* Wellesley, Arthur A.A.

Adrian, Fort. Opposite Adrianopolis on the Calabar.

Adrian, Prince. Son of Emperor Adrian; m. Zorayda.

Adrianopolis. Emperor Adrian's city, on the banks of the Calabar; capital of Angria and seat of the government; 150 miles from Verdopolis; destroyed by Zamorna himself to prevent it falling into Northangerland's hands during the Revolution.

African Olympic Games. *See* Olympic Games.

African Queen. Quashia's mother.

Agar, Richard. Owner of a rabbit warren.

Agars, the. W.H. Warner's clan; Zamorna's supporters.

Agnes. Countess of Seymour's daughter.

Alanna. King of the Inward Tribes – Quashia's ally.

Albert, Lord. Loves Maria; dies of wounds in battle.

Albion. Name given to the Marquis of Douro in C.'s story *Albion and Marina*.

Alderney. Wood near Selden Hall.

Alderwood. Where Edward Ernest Gordon Wellesley b.; where the bell tolls for men on the eve of battle.

Alembert, Ernest. Visits the Land of Faery.

Alexander, Grand Duke. *See* Ravenswood.

Alexander Percy. *See* Percy, Alexander.

Alford, Dr. Attends the birth of Zamorna's twin sons.

Alhamas, Emily Marchioness of. Wife of Ernest.

Alhamas, Marquis of. *See* Wellesley, Ernest Julius Mornington.

Allen, Louisa. Thornton's cousin. Louisa Vernon's acting name (*see* Vernon, Louisa).

Almeida, Lord Julius, Marquis of. Son of Zamorna and Marian; dies age six months. (Wellington's Portuguese headquarters in Peninsular War.)

Alnwick House. The Percy family home in Sneachiesland; on banks of the Derwent; where Mary Henrietta, sent by Zamorna, becomes ill and dies.

Alpha. A Geni; reminds Zenobia of her promise to open Northangerland's coffin twenty years after his death.

Alured, Sir. Lives at Oakwood House.

Amelia. Lady of Annersley Estate.

Andrew. St Clair's page; a printer's devil; eventually Capt. Tree, a writer of 'snivelling rhymes and snivelling tales'.

Angria. Kingdom created in 1834 for Zamorna to the east of Glasstown; 80 by 180 miles; capital Adrianopolis; has 7 provinces – Zamorna, Edwardston, Sydenham, Northangerland, Arundel, Howard and Warner, each with its own capital.

Angria House. W.H. Warner's residence.

Angria Wars. (1) Against the local natives on landing in Africa; (2) against the Ashantee chief, Quashia, stirred up by Rogue and helped by the French; (3) an insurrection raised by Rogue in 1831 and a rebellion in 1832; (4) the Great Revolution raised by Northangerland against Zamorna, 26 June 1836.

Angus, Sir Alured. Otherwise Hume, in *Albion and Marina*.

Angus, Marina. Otherwise Marian Hume in *Albion and Marina*; d. 18 June 1815 at midnight in C.'s story.

Anni(i). One of the Genii, protector of Ross – i.e. Ae.

An(n)vale. Woods of fir and pine; site of battle.

Aornos. Mountain, abode of the chief Genii.

Ape of the Hills. Donald the Standard, age 110; lives in Elimbos, the leader of tall wild men; helps Rogue in the Rebellion of 1832 and becomes one of the 42nd Regiment of Highlanders.

Aragua. River near the Elboros Mountain.

Arbor. Capt.; literary figure and singer.

Ardrah, Marquis of. Arthur Parry (E.'s soldier), Prince of Parrysland; leader of Reformers; ally of Northangerland; defeated by W.H. Warner.

Ardsley Hall. Where George Turner lives; Zamorna wins a victory there; used by grouse shooters.

Arniston, Lady Emma. Lord Hartford's sister, has dark eyes, black hair.

Arno. River running through Hawkescliff forest.

Arthur Julius. *See* Julius, Arthur.

Arthur's Peaks. Near the Great Red River.

Arthurstown. Capital of Senegambia (Wellingtonsland).

Arundel. Province of Angria; 165 by 90 miles; capital Seaton; pop. 971,000; Lord Lieutenant – the Earl of Arundel.

Arundel, Lady. Edith Sneaky, wife of Lord Arundel; 'tall and stately'; had two flaxen-haired children – one called Amelie.

Arundel, Lord. Lord Lieutenant of Arundel; a 'gallant courteous Chevalier' with 'fair locks'.

Ascension Island. Where Twelves fight the Dutch and where Zamorna exiled after Northangerland's Revolution.

Ash, Reuben. A Methodist class leader.

Ashantee. Large area of Africa colonized by the Twelves – to east, the desert; west, the Atlantic Sea; south, Gulf of Guinea; north, the Gibbel Kumri Mountains.

Ashantees. Natives of Africa against whom the Twelves fight. (Ashanti – on African Gold Coast.)

Ashburnham Villa. Zamorna's belongings auctioned there.

Ashfield. In Angria, where line of 20 gibbets erected after the Revolution.

Ashura. Powerful faery.

Ashworth, Brother. Alias Alexander Percy – preaches at the Slug Street chapel.

Ashworth, Mrs. Alias Louisa Dance.

Augustus, John. *See* Sneaky, John Augustus.

Avon, Sir James (Jemmy). Engaged to Lady Julia Wellesley; nephew to the Earl of Cathcart; m. Lady Selina Cathcart.

Azalia Bower. Louisa Vernon's home.

Azrael. Angel (of death and destruction).

Bad(r)y, Duke of. Originally Dr Hume; in league with bodysnatchers; one of the Twelves; physician to the Duke of Wellington; expires of apoplexy. (Thomas Hume, physician 1769–1850.)

Balcastro, Nicholas. Colonel in the Angrian Army; Henry Hastings sent to him after being cashiered.

Banbarren. Town on the way to Sneachiesland.

Banner. Evening newspaper.

Bany. Chief Genius – Branni(i) – B.

Barlow. Clergyman on the Verdopolitan circuit.

Beaufort, Duke of. Rogue his nephew and heir until Beaufort has two sons.

Bell. Zamorna's dog.

Bellingham, James Everard. A London banker who visits Glasstown; 'writer' of *Letters from an Englishman* (B.); narrator in *The Pirate* (B.).

Benguela. River with marshes. (Province in Angola.)

Benini. Eredi's brother, an Ashantee; Sai Tootoo's counsellor.

Benini Palace. In Verdopolis; entered by the escaping Quashia and Jordan after the Revolution.

Beresford. Duke of Wellington's companion; messenger from England. (Viscount Beresford, general in Wellington's army.)

Bertha. Withered old hag, keeper of the castle to which Northangerland abducts Lady Emily Charlesworth.

Bessie. Mrs Hart's servant.

Biblio Street. Street where Tree has his publishing firm.

Blanco. Duke of Wellington's horse.

Bland, Mr. Surgeon.

Bleachum, Mrs. Washerwoman.

Blood, Sergeant. Sells copies of *Blackwood's Young Men's Magazine* in August 1829.

Blucher. (Head of the Prussian army.)

Boaster, Advising. B.'s chief man in *Our Fellows*; helps B. against Goodman's rebellion, losing the battle of Lorraine, winning that of Loo: made Duke of Bas.

Bobadil. One of Wellington's officers.

Body. *See* Bady.

Bottomley, Timothy. Character in B.'s *And the Weary Are at Rest*.

Boulsworth. Hill, near Haworth.

Boy, Bingo. Leader of negroes with King Jack.

Boy, King. Character in B.'s *And the Weary Are at Rest*.

Branni(i) (Brany, Bany). A Geni, protector of Crashey – i.e. B.

Branni(i) Hills. Chain of 'black untraversed mountains'.

Bravey, Sir William. One of B.'s Twelves, co-founder of Glasstown; President of the African Olympic Games, 4 June 1814.

Bravey's Inn. Inn in Glasstown, kept by Bravey where Wellington and his sons and friends meet to gossip and discuss war, politics, literature.

Broadbent. Steward of the Methodist circuit.

Bromley, Mr. Minister of Slug Street Chapel.

Brunswick, Frederic. *See* Guelph.

Brushwood. Hall.

Bud, Capt. 'Author' of *The History of the Young Men* (B.) and other works. (C. uses him to satirize B.'s style of writing.)

Bud, Sergeant. Capt. Bud's son – 'a clever lawyer and great liar'.

Buonaparte. Name given to B.'s soldier.

Butler, John. A Methodist class leader.

Byson. A breed of bull in Angria.

Cahin. Village.

Calabar. Province; 190 by 130 miles; capital Gazemba; pop. 59,000; river in Angria where Adrianopolis situated. (West African river.)

Camalia. A plain, scene of a battle with the Ashantees.

Cameron. Marshy river.

Cameron, Eugene. One of C.'s Twelves.

Camingo Quacco. King Jack, negro leader.

Carey, Lucius. Captain; Rogue's minion; guards the Marquis of Douro and Lord Charles Bellingham in the battle of Fidena.

Caroline. Harriet's dead sister, whom Harriet is taken to see in her coffin. (*See also* Vernon.)

Carter. Boaster's supporter.

Cartington, Earl of. Marquis of Ardrah's supporter; Northangerland's guest after the Revolution.

Cartwright, John and Margaret. Of Derbyshire; found Edward Sydney on their doorstep.

Caseputh. Mountain of the North.

Cashna. *See* Kashna.

Castlereagh, Lady. Harriet, *née* Montmorency, Lord Castlereagh's wife; leaves him for Northangerland, who deserts her.

Castlereagh, Lord. Frederick, Lord Lieutenant of Zamorna; a 'noble, dashing dandy'.

Castleton. Assembly point for troops.

Cathcart, Selina, Lady. m. Sir James Avon.

Caversham, George Frederick, Lord. Governor of Arundel; Mrs Young leaves her husband for him; joins plot against Zamorna.

Cecil(l)ia. Countess of Seymour's daughter; plays harp.

Cena Gabrielle. Italian singer.

Central Market Square. In Zamorna; place of execution.

Central Square. In Verdopolis.

Chantr(e)y, Sir Henry. A sculptor, patronized by Zamorna.

Charlesworth, Emily, Lady. Bravey's niece; abducted by Percy on the eve of her marriage to Lord St Clair.

Charlesworth, Marquis of. Uncle of Emily; one of Wellington's officers.

Château de Bois Orleannois. Residence of Madame Lalande.

Chateaubriand. Napoleon's valet; critic of Young Soult's poetry.

Cheeky, Alexander. Surgeon; one of B.'s Twelves.

Cheshunt. Near Girnington Hall.

Chevalier. Napoleon's valet.

Churchill. Warner's headquarters in the Revolution.

Girnington Hall. Where General Thornton, wife Julia and four children live.

Cirhala. River on which Evesham situated.

Citadel Hill. In Verdopolis.

Clarence Wood. Property of Sir John Clarence; Zamorna's headquarters at the battle of Evesham.

Clarges Street. Street of lodging houses.

Clay, Samuel. A Methodist class leader.

Clifton, Amelia. Mary Henrietta's maid; looks after Zamorna's children – Frederick, Edward and little Arthur.

Clinton, Henry. One of C.'s Twelves. (Sir Henry Clinton, 1771–1829, aide-de-camp to the Duke of York.)

Clown. E.'s character in *Our Fellows*.

Cludesdale Castle. Seat of the Marquis of Charlesworth.

Colne Tarn Moor. Where Henry Hastings' father lives. (Colne, near Haworth.)

Conqueror Mail Coach. Coach to Adrianopolis.

Conway, Mr and Mrs. Valet and housekeeper at Brushwood Hall.

Coomassie. Ashantee capital at foot of Mount Aornos destroyed by the Twelves. (Kumasi chief town on the then African Gold Coast.)

Cooper, Dr. Attends the duel between Zamorna and Lord Hartford.

Corbett, Angelica. Of Melon Grove, an heiress.

Cornelius, Lord. Name given to Charles Wellesley in *Albion and Marina*.

Corelli, Julia. Finest 'figurante' in Verdopolitan opera.

Cortez, Ferdinand. One of C.'s Twelves.

Council. Held on 14 June 1816, when Arthur Wellesley elected king.

County Field. Opposite Edward Percy's mill in Zamorna.

Courier de Français. Newspaper.

Cowper, Sir Ashton. Attends Mary Henrietta's 'deathbed'.

Crabbe. Gamekeeper at Selden House.

Crack, Mon Edouard de. Hero of C.'s story.

Crack(e)y. A middy, one of B.'s Twelves; later David Cracks.

Crack-skull, Dick. Poacher.

Cracone. Mines.

Crashey, Butter, Capt. One of B.'s Twelves; 140 years old; the Patriarch; brings peace after Rogue's rebellion, March 1831; mediator for the Twelves with the Genii; President of the Secret Society on Philosophers' Isle; discovers a fluid that 'freed [the soul] from all grosser particles and rendered it capable of enjoying the calm of heaven amid the turmoil of earth' (laudanum?).

Cruachan, Earl of. His home visited by Albion.

Crumps, Colonel. An apparition.

Curier. French supporter of Northangerland.

Cutehead, Tom. Owns a pothouse in Glasstown.

Dahomey. Northern plain. (Place in West Africa.)

Daitura Arbora. Expensive tree brought from India by Zamorna as a bridal present for his wife; later auctioned for £3.

Dampier, Capt. His troops called 'the bloodhounds'.

Dance(i), Louisa. *See* Vernon, Louisa.

Dancetown. Where Kirkwall and Zamorna fight the French.

Danhasch. Son of Schemhourasch. (Character in the *Arabian Nights*.)

Danvers, Lady Isabella. Wife of William.

Danvers, Sergeant William. Also called Fearnothing; Lady Dunally's brother.

Darrow. A maker of fire-arms.

Dash. Charles Wellesley's/Zamorna's pointer dog.

D'Aubigne's Hotel. In Verdopolis where Northangerland takes his pre-Revolution breakfast.

De Brunette. Publisher of Young Soult's poem in Paris.

Delancy, Alexander. Accompanies Henry O'Donell in his search for happiness; becomes a rich merchant in Paris; also called Monsieur Like-to-live-in-lonely-places.

De La Pack. Publisher of Young Soult's poems in Paris.

De Lisle, Frederick. Painter and engraver of Angria; wife Matilda; 'great in the beautiful'.

Delph, Victoria. An heiress, with a steam packet travelling between Doverham and Calais named after her; Northangerland's mistress.

Demrys Hotel. Headquarters of Madame Lalande.

Denard. River nearly 200 miles long, joined by Red River and flowing into the Niger; town.

Denard, Sir John. Watches over Caroline Vernon at Eden Cottage; Northangerland's guest.

De Rothesay, Felix. One of B.'s Twelves.

Derrinane, Lord. *See* Montmorency, Hector.

Dimdims Square. In Verdopolis, where Northangerland resides.

Dimdims Throne. Chain of Mountains near the Lake of the Genii.

Dinard, Sir John. Cavalry general, supporting Northangerland.

Donald of the Standard. *See* Ape of the Hills.

Dongola (Dougola). Fort on the river Etrei, where a massacre occurs. (Province in Egypt.)

Dorn, Capt. C. Commander in Northangerland's army.

Dorn, Fanny. The captain's daughter.

Dorn, First Lieutenant. (Same person as Capt. C?) Accompanies Arthur Wellesley to England.

Douglas, Capt. MP of Verdopolis; Northangerland's supporter.

Douro. Province; 130 by 100 miles; capital Douro; pop. 71,000; Lord Lieutenant, the Earl of Jordan. A river of Angria. (River in Spain.)

Douro, Marquis of. *See* Wellesley, Arthur Augustus Adrian.

Douro Villa. Near Girningham Hall.

Doverham. Port of embarkation for Calais; where rear of French army assembles.

Dragonetti. To whom Patrick Wiggins toadies.

Dreams, Island of. Where in June 1828 a school set up for 1,000 children of noblemen; chief Governor, the Duke of Wellington; the Guardians of the

children are his sons, the Marquis of Douro (Zamorna) and Lord Charles
Wellesley; 'a work of enchantment rather than sober reality'.

Ducie, Lady Beatrice. Widow of Lord Ducie.

Ducie, Lord. (2nd Lord Ducie, 1802–53; free trade advocate; breeder of
shorthorns.)

Dunaley (Dunally, Dumally), Gustavus. Captain; one of C.'s Twelves;
wealthy; m. with three children – Augusta Cecilia, given to being mystical,
Henry, a 'wick-will boy' (sic) and Gina Rosaline, 'a pet'.

Dunaley, Lady. Wife of Gustavus.

Duncombe, Dr. Prelate; attends Mary Henrietta's deathbed.

Dundee, Sir Martin. Painter of Angria; 'author' of *Scenery of Glasstown*; 'great in
the sublime'.

Dundin. Mountain.

Dupon. French supporter of Northangerland.

Dwarf, Green. Helps abduct Lady Charlesworth.

Eagle, Black. Horse ridden in the battle of Zamorna.

Eamala. 'A gurt bellaring bull' who drinks until she is so drunk she tries to cut her
throat – then passes out.

Eastern Highway. Road out of Verdopolis to Adrianopolis.

Ebor Terrace. Wide splendid street in Verdopolis.

Eden Cottage. Louisa Vernon's house at St Cloud, given her by Northangerland.

Eden Hall. Northangerland's house in the North.

Edwardston. Province with chief manufacturing town of Angria, founded by
Edward Percy; Zamorna defeated there by Northangerland.

Edwardston Hall. Edward Percy's home, at the edge of Girningham Park.

Edwardston Mail. Mail coach.

Edwardston Village. Near Girningham.

Elah. Valley with palms.

Elboros(us). Mountains near the Great Lake of the Genii.

Elbruz. (Same place?) Snowy area of the Caucasus. (Elbrus Mt, Russia.)

Eli(y)mbos. Mountainous northern area; home of the Ape of the Hills.

Eli(y)mbos Palace. Residence of King Alexander Sneaky.

Elinor. Gilbert's wife.

Elise (Touquet). Louisa Vernon's French maid.

Eliza. Fitzgeorge's sister.

Elizabeth. *See* Hastings, Elizabeth.

Ellibank. The hills of, where Zamorna and Mina Laury 'loved'.

Ellrington, Alsana. Lord Orleans, Zenobia's brother.

Ellrington, Graeme. Lived at 12 Chapel Street, Verdopolis.

Ellrington House. In Victoria Square, Verdopolis; Northangerland's home.

Ellrington, Pauline Louisada. Earl of Ellrington's wife; mother of Zenobia; a
Spaniard with raven locks.

Ellrington, Surena. A linen draper from whom Charles Wellesley rented
apartments.

Ellrington, Viscount Lord. Rogue's title on marrying Zenobia.

Ellrington, Lady Zelzia. Name given to Zenobia in *Albion and Marina*.

Ellrington, Lady Zenobia. Rival to Marian Hume for love of the Marquis of
Douro; married Alexander Rogue after being abducted to his ship; 'the most

learned woman of the age', 'the modern Cleopatra', 'the Verdopolitan de Stael'. (Tragedy, by Arthur Murphy, produced at Drury Lane, 1768.)

Elm Grove Villa. Lily Hart's residence after her marriage to Mr Seymour.

Emma. Sister to Jane; dies.

Emmi(i). One of the Genii, protector of Gravey. Parry – i.e. E.

Enara, Henry (Henri) Fernando di. Baron of Etrei and Lord Lieutenant; 'the Italian', also known as 'the Tiger'; undefeated supporter of Zamorna in the Revolution; carries great black and silver banners; has four little daughters, one named Maria.

Ennerdale. Solitary place where Zamorna goes after Mary Henrietta's death.

Eredi. Benini's brother, an Ashantee rebel; Sai Tootoo's counsellor.

Erin, Grenn. In Angria; served by Verdopolitan mail coach.

Etrei. Province; 120 by 95 miles; capital Don(u)gola; pop. 4000; Lord Lieutenant, Henri Fernando di Enara. (District of Ethiopia.)

Etrei River. A 'wild eerie' river marked with a 'vein of negro blood'.

Etty, Sir William. Angrian artist; supposed son of Northangerland by his first wife, Maria di Segravia; daughter – Zorayda. (Sir William Etty, RA, 1787–1849.)

Eve(r)sham. In Edwardston province, on river Cirhala; fortified by Revolutionary troops; taken by General Thornton.

Faction du Manège. Faction led by Jean, Prince of Ponte Corre.

Fala. Plain with town on the North Calabar where Greenwood hopes to install an organ.

Fala, Sir Frederic. Friend of Charles Townshend; has a box at the theatre.

Fanny. Servant at hotel.

Fateconda. On river Senegal where the Verdopolitans defeat the Ashantees.

Fenton Hall. In Twelves Town, where the Duke of Wellington's victories are portrayed.

Fenton, Sir John (Joseph). Cavalry leader; leads two French cavalry regiments in the opening procession of the Grand Provisional Directory.

Fernando, Henri. *See* Enara.

Fidena. Large city on the Fidenaz in Sneachiesland; 300 miles from Verdopolis; first taken by Northangerland, then by the Duke of Wellington.

Fidena, battle of. 13–15 March 1832; after his defeat there, Rogue is shot.

Fidena, Duke of. *See* Sneaky, John, 1st Marquis of Rosendale.

Fidena, Prince of. *See* Sneaky, John Augustus.

Fidenaz. River flowing from Greygarach into the Great Red River.

Figgins. Member of firm of merchants, Figgins, Smith & Co., of London; has wife and five children.

Figgs, Sudbury. Music teacher.

Finde(a)n, Edward. Engraver of De Lisle's portrait of Zenobia. (Edward Finden, 1791–1857, famous engraver.)

Finic(k). Zamorna's dumb dwarf; guards Mary Henrietta.

FitzGeorge, Harold. One of C.'s Twelves – Lady Seymour's son.

Flanag(h)an, Maurice. Marquis of Douro's protégé boxer.

Fleshbotham, Appolos. Character in B.'s *And the Weary Are at Rest*.

Flower, John. Capt.; became Baron Flower and Viscount Richton; 'author' of *Letters from an Englishman*, *Real Life in Verdopolis* and *The Wool Is Rising*;

ambassador plenipotentiary to the court of Angria; a 'fine politician' and 'religious man', with the 'smile of Belias'.

Fort Adrian. Near Hawkescliffe; where Mina Laury, and later, Louisa and Caroline Vernon are lodged.

Fortescue, Ernest. One of C.'s Twelves.

Foxley, Miss. Marian Hume's governess; tries to prevent her marriage to the Marquis of Douro.

Frederic. *See* Guelph.

Frederic's Town. In Stumpsland.

Frederick's Crag. Stands above the amphitheatre of the first African Olympic Games.

Freeling, Mr. Keeps a post office.

Freetown. Capital in Glasstown Valley; 150–200 miles from Glasstown; served by the mail coach from Verdopolis; on the River Niger.

Freetown Mercury. A mail coach.

Frenchland. An island; capital Paris.

Fringia. A grey monkey.

Gambia. River on which Glasstown situated.

Gazemba. Town and plain on banks of Calabar; 60 miles SE of Adrianopolis; where Zamorna reviews his troops before the battle of Eve(r)sham.

Genii. Chief Genii: Talli(i) – C., Branni(i) – B., Emmi(i) – E., and Anni(i) – Ae.; guardians and protectors of the Twelves; living in a remote mountainous region of Ashantee land.

Genii Inn. In Verdopolis; hosts – Talli(i), Branni(i), Emmi(i), Anni(i).

Genius of the Storm. Appears to C.'s Twelves after the building of Glasstown begun.

George Street. Leads to the Houses of Parliament in Verdopolis; where Rogue's Rebellion of 1831 begins.

Georgina. FitzGeorge's sister.

Gibbel (Gibble, Jibbel) Kumri. The dark Mountains of the Moon.

Gifford, Sir John. Chief judge in Glasstown; President of the Antiquarian Society; his home the old Kildenny Hall; Lady Emily Charlesworth's tutor.

Girnington Hall. General Thornton's residence and parkland.

Glasstown. Town built when Twelves Town destroyed; also the area in West Africa where the Young Men settle after their voyage from England on the *Invincible*; divided into four countries – Wellingtonsland (C.), Sneachiesland (B.), Parrysland (E.), Rossland (Ae.) – each having Glasstown as its capital. Great Glasstown is a separate area, with the same name for its capital, afterwards known as Verdopolis. (*See also* Twelves Town.)

Glasstown, battle of. 17 March 1831; taken over by Rogue; later retaken by the kings.

Glasstown Confederacy. The union of the four separate countries formed the Confederacy, with the addition of Monkey's and Stumps' islands, whose combined power was greater than that of any of the individual kings and by whose laws and orders they had to abide. It had its own house of parliament in Great Glasstown – later Verdopolis – which acted as a central government.

Glasstown Intelligencer. Newspaper.

Glasstown Moors. At end of Glasstown Valley – a 'ceaseless sea of heather' with moorcocks and poachers.

Globe. Newspaper.

Glory of Africa. Newspaper of Verdopolis.

Goat, Mr. Speaker of the Confederacy Parliament.

Goodman. A rascal who raises a rebellion against 'Little Branwell'.

Goody. One of the Young Men.

Gordon. Province.

Gordon, Baroness. *See* Wellington, Marchioness of.

Gordon, Edward Ernest. *See* Wellesley, Ernest Edward Gordon.

Gordon, Ernest FitzArthur. Mother Soffala beloved by Arthur Wellesley.

Gordon, George. Character in B.'s *And the Weary Are at Rest*.

Gordon, Julian. A friend of Charles Townshend; hanged William Rhodes.

Gordon, Miss. Whom Douro loves as a mere schoolboy.

Gordon Mountains. In the North.

Gordons, the. A 'dark malignant family'.

Graham, Ladies Sophia and Frances. 'Dark haired ladies with great brown eyes.'

Grand Canal. On its banks a series of nine palaces built by Zamorna.

Grand Inn. In Verdopolis.

Grand Provisional Directory. Government set up by Northangerland after the defeat and exile of Zamorna, with Richard Naughty (Naughten) as Lord Lieutenant.

Grantley. In Angria; scene of battle.

Gravey (Gravii), William Edward. One of the Twelves; King of Parrysland; Arch Primate of Verdopolis (E.'s soldier).

Great African Games. Held on 26 June 1832 and biennially.

Great Rebellion. Rogue's rising of 1832.

Great Tower. In Verdopolis.

Greenwood, Mr. Organist of St Michael's, Verdopolis; teaches music to Queen Mary, who floors him when he comments on her nose! (John Greenwood, Leeds organist.)

Gre(n)ville, Ellen. Wife of Warner Howard Warner.

Gre(n)ville, Colonel John Bramham. Wealthy millowner; chairman of the House of Representatives; shot by workmen on strike at the beginning of Great Rebellion.

Gre(n)ville, General. (Same person as above?); Mayor of Verdopolis, called out the Metropolitan Volunteers in Verdopolis 23 June 1836.

Greville, Lady Georgina. Northangerland's fair-haired mistress.

Greville's Wharf. In Verdopolis.

Grey, Catherine. Daughter of George Turner Grey; faithful follower of Zamorna; murdered after the battle of Edwardston.

Grey, George Turner. Owner of Ardsley Hall; throat cut after the battle of Edwardston.

Grey, Senora. Governess and tutor to Maria Enara.

Greygarach. High mountains in Sneachiesland.

Groby. Charles Wellesley's cat, brother to Muzzle.

Grog Bottle, The. A Glasstown newspaper.

Guadima (Guardina). River on which Verdopolis built.

Guelph, Frederic. Duke of York; Frederic Brunswick; one of B.'s Twelves; slain at the battle of Rosendale Hill (on the same date as the real Duke of York died) 'so as he could not be got alive' – because 'Stumps' is the same wooden soldier!

Guinea. Where C.'s Twelves land on 2 June 1770 at six o'clock in the morning; becomes Wellingtonsland.

Gulliver, Lemuel. A four-foot-high lean meagre being who nearly kills Charlie (Charles Wellesley), and bites Arthur, but escapes despite the fact that pistols are fired into both his ears.

Hafizeea. A 'pleasure house' in Shirez.

Haines, Mr. Writes for the Globe; MP for Freetown.

Halford, Sir H. Surgeon in Glasstown.

Hall of Justice. Built in Verdopolis.

Hall of Science and Arts. Built in Verdopolis.

Hamilton, Edwin. Architect; dyke-builder; author of *Petus and Aria*, a tragedy.

Hardings. One-armed; prepares army estimates for the Duke of Wellington.

Harland, Marquis of. 'Dark and sullen'; MP in Verdopolis.

Harriet. Caroline's sister. (*See also* O'Connor *and* Castlereagh.)

Hart, Lily. Plays the harp and sings; nurses, then marries in secret, John Sneaky; becomes Marchioness of Fidena; son – John Augustus Sneaky.

Hart, Mrs. Lily's mother; lives at Elm Grove Villa; dies 1831–2.

Hartford, Amelia. Lord Hartford's daughter whom Rogue abducts.

Hartford Hall, Wood and Vale. In Zamorna; Lord Hartford's property, won from him in gambling by Rogue.

Hartford, Lord Edward. Colonel in the Angrian army; has a distorting scar on his forehead (cf. Scroven); fights with Zamorna over Mina Laury; 'a sort of Angrian Greatheart'.

Hasleden, Mr. Edward Sydney's guardian.

Haslingden. A fortified town near Fidena; battle there during Rogue's 1832 rebellion.

Hastings, Elizabeth. Henry's sister; companion to Jane Moore; rejects Sir William Percy's plea she become his mistress.

Hastings, Henry. Son of a farmer; goes to Harrow; captain in the Infantry; cashiered, 19 March 1839, for his shooting of his superior officer and his part in the plot against Zamorna; transferred as a private soldier to troops under the command of Colonel Nicholas Balcastro; 'author' of *The Campaign of the Calabar, Sound the Loud Trumpet* and *Welcome Heroes*, amongst others (poet and narrator of many of B.'s stories).

Hawkescliffe. Forest-girt mansion where 'country plainness' is kept, half way between Angria and the foot of the Sydenham Hills; Zamorna's country residence, where he and Mary Henrietta roam when they are in love; where Caroline Vernon kept by her guardian, Zamorna.

Hawkins, Major. A charioteer in the African Olympic Games; a 'hero of turf and ring'.

Hay Man. C.'s character in *Our Fellows*.

Heart of Angria. Adrianopolis newspaper.

Helen, Lady. Of Beresford; FitzGeorge's sister; mother of Rogue.

Hill, General. Duke of Wellington's companion. (1st Viscount Hill served in the Peninsular War.)

Hobbins, Mr. Auctioneer.
Holy Trinity. Adrianopolis Cathedral.
Howard. 'A miserable little village, buried in dreary moors and moss-hags and marshes'; in Angria. (Haworth.)
Howard, Sir Marmaduke. Politician who keeps sheep.
Howards, the. Supporters of Zamorna.
Hume, Sir Alexander. Duke of Bad(r)y.
Hume, Lady Frances Millicent. Lives in a castle in Humeshire; dies when her daughter Marian age 14; great friend of Lady Percy.
Hume, (Florence) Marian. First wife of Zamorna; mother of Julius, Marquis of Almeida; as a child, betrothed to Henry Percy; dies of lingering consumption.
Hunter. Ae.'s character in *Our Fellows*.
Hunter, Eliza. Actress; prima donna of the Queen's Theatre; Segovia's rival; Northangerland's mistress.
Hyla (Hyle, Hylle). 'Vast and stormy lake.'
Hyla, Bishop of. Attends Mary Henrietta's deathbed.

Ierne. Daughter of Zamorna and Mary Henrietta.
Indi(r)ce. River on banks of which Wellington's palace situated.
Inez, Emily. Duchess of Valdecella, wife of Ernest Julius Mornington Wellesley.
Inglazen. Was tossed in a blanket by the 'Rare Lads'; asthmatic.
Inn, the Grand. In Glasstown.
Insurrection, the. Rogue's rising in 1831.
Invincible. A ship of 74 guns that, leaving England 5 February 1770, took the Young Men to Africa.
Ishington. In Angria.
Island Fleet. Set up 100 guns on Citadel Hill, Parliament Square and St Michael's on 25 June 1836.
Island of Dreams. *See* Dreams.
Irving, Mrs. Mary Henrietta in disguise.

Jack. King, leader of the negroes.
Jerry. *See* MacTerrorglen.
Jhonson. Lord Hartford's river.
Jibbel Kumri. *See* Gibbel Kumri.
John. *See* Sneaky, John.
Johnson's Hotel. In Verdopolis.
Jones, Lieutenant. Visitor at Hartford Hall.
Jordan Hall. A place of horror for Harriet.
Jordan, John. Earl of Jordan, Bedouin leader; a 'jaded idler'.
Julia. *See* Wellesley, Julia.
Julia Place. General Thornton's residence in Adrianopolis.
Julius. *See* Almeida, Marquis of.
Julius, Archduke. Son of Emperor – haughty and proud.
Juno. Zamorna's dog which catches a bat.
Justice, Hall of. In Verdopolis.

Kairail Fish. Creature described by B.
K(C)ashna, Quamina. Old king of the Ashantees; dies 1779, age 90.

Kashna, Quashia. Sai Tootoo's son; adopted by Wellington and brought up with his children; becomes leader of the Ashantees; murders Zamorna's son; a sullen black ingrate.

Kashna, Sai Tootoo. Quamina's son; headstrong and rebellious; killed at the battle of Coomassie.

Kasibec (Kasbec). Snowy region where the Genii hold court.

Keswick. Served by the Verdopolitan coach. (Town in Lake District.)

Kildenny Hall. 16th century building owned by Sir John Gifford.

Killala. Mountain.

King, Robert Patrick. Moneylender.

Kings, the Four. i.e. Kings of the Twelves – Wellington (C.), Sneaky (B.), Parry (E.), Ross (Ae.)

Kirkham. A wood.

Kirkwall, John. Baron; Angrian MP of Meadow Bank; tutor to Zamorna's eldest son; m. Jane Moore's sister.

Krista, Caroline. Flaxen-haired child living with Colonel and Mrs Grenville.

Lalande, Madame. The 'dark lady in white'; Northangerland's mistress.

Lapis, Mr. Jeweller.

Laury, Edward (Ned). Father of Mina; forester on Wellington's estates.

Laury, Mina. Ned's raven-haired daughter; born on the same day as, and bought up with, Zamorna; companion to his wife, Marian; nurse to his children; established by Zamorna, first at Fort Adrian, then at the Lodge of Rivaulx, Hawkescliff; meets the exiled Zamorna at Marseilles; helps restore him to his kingdom; Hartford and Zamorna duel over her; becomes Zamorna's mistress.

Leaf, John. Capt./General; referred to as 'our Thucydides'; sent to fetch one of the Twelves to help England against Napoleon; fights the Ashantee rebels; on one occasion wears a pink wig!

Le Brun. Painter of Angria, great for the 'passions'.

Leg, Capt. Publisher in Twemy's Glasstown.

Le Grand. Publisher in Glasstown.

Lelande, Madame. *See* Lalande, Madame.

Leslie, Mr. Lord St Clair in disguise.

Leyden. Scene of Zamorna's victory after his return from exile.

Lill. Kitten of the young Charles Wellesley.

Lindsay. Politician; High Chancellor; 'grim, gaunt, ghastly Scotchman'.

Lisle. *See* De Lisle.

Lismore Vale. In West, visited by Marquis of Douro as a boy.

Little King (and Queens). i.e. B. (and his sisters); the Little King was 'more evil brownie than a legitimate fairy'.

Loango. Where Zamorna camps; scene of battle. (District in S. Africa.)

Locksley, William. Doctor/surgeon.

Lode. Newspaper.

Lofty, Edward. Earl of Westwood and Arundel.

Lofty, Lord Frederic Macara. Leader with Montmorency of the Republicans; 'Hill o' the Mac'; 'a dashing young nobleman' said to be addicted to opium.

Lofty Square. In Verdopolis.

Lonsdale, Augusta. A 'pretty pleasant girl'.

Loo. Battle of, in which Boaster defeats Goodman.

Lorraine. Battle of, in which Goodman defeats Boaster.
Louisada, Don John. Grandfather of Zenobia.
Louise, Marie. Napoleon's wife.
Lowood. Dark gloomy wood.
Luckyman, Colonel. Trader lucky in his accumulation of wealth.
Lucy. Operated on by Ryder.
Ludlow. Scene of battle.

Macadin. Merchant.
Macara. *See* Lofty, Frederic.
Mackenzie. Supports Rogue in his Rebellion.
Macombirch. MP in Angria.
MacTerrorglen. J.J.H. de Bruce Maclarrin; head of the northern forces against Zamorna.
Maimoune. Guardian of Frederic, Duke of York. (Fairy in *The Arabian Nights*.)
Manfred the Magician. Brother to Crashey.
Marcella, Hermione. Wife of Archduke Julius.
March town. Town with a castle beyond the Great Red River.
Maria. Beloved of Lord Albert; elder sister of Julia Wellesley; the Lady of Edwardston.
Maria. *See* Segravia, Maria di.
Marian. *See* Hume, Marian.
Marina. Daughter of Sir Alured Angus (in *Albion and Marina*).
Markham, Sydney. Colonel; shot by Northangerland; steals Louisa Dance's slipper.
Marmont. French general.
Mary Henrietta. *See* Percy, Mary Henrietta.
Massena. French general supporting Northangerland.
Massinger Hall. Four miles from Zamorna.
Maxwells, the. Senior, and junior (William); Zamorna's servants.
Medina. Sheik; leader of the mercenaries.
Meerza. Chief royal physician in Persia.
Melton, Lady Celia. Friend of Julia Wellesley.
Mermaid. Ship on which Henry Percy sails.
Messenger. Evening newspaper.
Milner, General. Cavalry commander.
Mina. *See* Laury, Mina.
Ministerial Square. In Adrianopolis.
Mirabeau, Hector. *See* Montmorency.
Mitchell, Charles. Methodist class leader.
Monkey (Moncay). A middy; one of B.'s Twelves.
Monkey's Island. 300 miles from Glasstown; where Northangerland goes after the Revolution.
Monsieur Who-lives-and-dies. Innkeeper in France.
Mons Isle. Near Glasstown; described in *Young Men's Magazine*.
Monthly Intelligencer. One of B.'s magazines.
Montmorency, Hector Matthias Mirabeau. Rogue's familiar; Republican leader.
Montmorency, Miss. Lady Castlereagh's sister.

Moore, George. Jane's father; owns a boat called *The Lady Jane*; a magistrate.

Moore, Jane. Youngest daughter of George; known as the Rose of Zamorna; attends Lord Hartford's ball; 'handsome easy-conditioned creature'.

Morley. Minister in the Angrian government; a pedant and a bore; 'the slow-worm of the serpents'.

Mornington. Wellington's residence in the hills of Ellibank; poem in C.'s *Mina Laury*, dated 'Mornington: 1829'.

Mornington, Earl of. Title of the Duke of Wellington.

Mornington, Edward. Emperor Adrian's son; handsome, wild and wicked.

Morton. Woman with thick ankles.

Morven. Snowy mountain in the North.

Mountains of the Moon. Gibbel Kumri; beyond the Dahomey plain in the Genii country.

Mournly Crag. Where Arundel's ladylove lives.

Mowbray. Watering place and spa.

Mowbray, Bay of. North of Verdopolis.

Mowbray, Countess of. At Marian's tea party.

Mule Man. Commander of Goodman's troops.

Mulready, Dennis. Irish boy; knows all about ghosts and fairies.

Murat, Judge. Napoleon's brother; Mayor of the City of Paris; supports Northangerland.

Murray (Murry, Moray). On Wellington's staff.

Murza Messieo. Persian poet.

Musselburgh. MP in Verdopolis.

Muzzle. Charles Wellesley's cat; Groby's brother.

Napoleon. Buonaparte; B.'s soldier.

Naughten, Richard. Leader of the People's or Destructive Party; made Lord Lieutenant by Northangerland after the Revolution.

Naughty, Old Young Man. Giant, frightened by Lemuel Gulliver.

Naughty, Young Man. Cold, brutal follower of Northangerland with a cottage on the Great Glasstown Moors; in the Provisional Government's war department.

Nawhalgerii. Mountain in India.

Nevada. Calling place for the Verdopolitan coach.

Nevada Mountains. Where the River Ardrah flows.

Ney, Marshal. French general; supporter of Northangerland.

Nicholson, Patrick. Flautist.

Niger. River flowing beside the Guadima.

Nigrilis. Area in the Glasstown Confederacy.

Norkel Street. Street of fine shops in Verdopolis.

Northangerland. Province of Angria; 200 by 270 miles; capital Pequena; pop. 376,000; Lord Lieutenant, Earl of Northangerland.

Northangerland Arms. Verdopolitan pub.

Northangerland, Earl of. *See* Percy, Alexander.

Northangerland House. Northangerland's home.

Northern Hotel. In Sneachie's Glasstown.

Northwood Park. King of Sneachiesland's country home; 20 miles from Verdopolis.

Nowrhene. River; boundary of Angria.

O'Callaghan. A character in C.'s *Adventure in Ireland*.
O'Connor, Arthur. Colonel; leader of the Revolutionaries; fails in his duties, and tries unsuccessfully to shoot himself rather than be hanged.
O'Connor, Harriet. *Née* Percy; the 'flower of Senegambia'; buried in Fidena's Minster.
O'Don(n)ell, Henry. A nobleman who seeks for happiness; also called Captain Tarry-not-at-home.
O'Don(n)ell, Marcus. One of C.'s Twelves.
Olympia. Angrian river where Zamorna situated.
Olympic Games. Or the Great African Games; first held in the Olympian Hall, 4 June 1814; celebrated 23 March 1831, the end of Northangerland's insurrection, with an audience of 5–6 million, an orchestra of 10,000.
Opera House. In Verdopolis; above the Theatre.
Oriental Mail. Goes to Adrianopolis.
Orleans, Lord. Ellrington's son; Zenobia's brother.
Oxeye. Cloud off New Guinea, which heralds a storm.

Palm Grove House. Northangerland's place of exile in Stumpsland.
Parry, Arthur. Son of King William Edward of Parrysland; the 'most daring'; at age 16 a midshipman; 'rose through his own ability'.
Parry, Emily, Lady. Wife of William Parry.
Parry, William Edward. Marquis of Ardrah; one of B.'s Twelves; king of Parrysland; E.'s soldier, 'brave, sailor-like, but a little too fond of subterfuge'. (Sir W.E. Parry, 1790–1855, Arctic explorer.)
Parrysland. E.'s country in Africa.
Peel. Mr Secretary; friend of the Duke of Wellington.
Pelham, Sir Robert Weaver. Once engaged to Mary Henrietta; minister in the Home Office of Verdopolis.
Pendle Farm. Pendleton; at the foot of the Warner Hills, where Henry Hastings brought up.
Pepin. Louisa Vernon's spaniel.
Pequena. Capital of Northangerland.
Percy. As family – all fair or auburn haired, with fine foreheads and small correct figures (in contrast to the Wellesleys).
Percy, Alexander Augustus. b. December 1792; son of Lady Helen Beresford and Edward Percy; Lady Augusta Romana di Segovia is attracted to and marries him (1812); his father angry, sending him to the Philosophers' Isle, where he forms the Society of Atheistic Republicans; taken to trial and fined £100,000 or banishment to Ascension Isle; Lady Segovia's friends find the money, he takes his exams and joins Lady Segovia; plots his father's murder and, when Lady Segovia wants him to refuse to pay his fine, hers also; distracted by her death, broken by huge debts, becomes bitter and melancholic; in 1814 m. Mary (Henrietta) Wharton; 3 sons – Henry, Edward and William, whom he orders S'Death to dispose of, but S'Death saves Edward and William; also one daughter – Mary Henrietta; wife dies of consumption; heartbroken, he leads a dissipated life, gambling, drinking and cheating at cards; involved in the March 1831 and the 1832 rebellions; after the battle of Haslingden, is captured, executed by a

firing squad, but brought back to life again; returns as the handsome Colonel Alexander Augustus Percy; abducts Lady Emily Charlesworth, trying, unsuccessfully, to get rid of her fiancé, Lord St Clair, by getting him arraigned for treason; is imprisoned for treachery; released, he elopes with Harriet Montmorency, later forsaking her; spends many years wandering the world in his boat *The Rover*, as bandit, pirate, etc; seizes the Lady Zenobia Ellrington and her father from their ship, abruptly woos and marries her; returns to Verdopolis, entering politics as Leader of the Movement against the establishment and upper classes; produces bill to abolish the two Houses of Government and make the four kingdoms into one nation with a president; sets up his own provisional Government, dissolving the House of Commons; becomes great friends with Arthur Wellesley (Zamorna), the Marquis of Douro; helps him to become King of Angria (1834); becomes his Prime Minister – an alliance sealed by the marriage of his daughter, Mary Henrietta, to Zamorna; leads a Revolution (1836) against Zamorna; defeats him in battle at Edwardston, but saves his life by sending him safely into exile in *The Rover*; on Zamorna's successful attempt to regain his country, Percy allowed his life, provided he lives quietly as a private individual; grows more abrasive and irritable the older he gets. Variously known as Rogue, Percy, Ellrington, Northangerland; his mistresses include – Harriet, Lady Georgina Greville, Lady St James, Louisa Dance (Vernon), Miss Delph, Madame Lalande.

Percy, Cecil(l)ia. *See* Cecil(l)ia.

Percy, Mr (Lord) Edward. Alexander Percy's father; marries Lady Helen of the Beresford family; said to have murdered the Earl of Mornington.

Percy, Edward. Unpleasant, rejected eldest son of Northangerland; given at birth to S'Death to be destroyed but saved by him; a destitute and wicked childhood; later sets up with his brother in the wool trade; saves the Marquis of Fidena's life; founds Edwardston, where owns a new mill; becomes MP, Lord Viscount Percy, rising to post of Secretary of Trade in Angria; duels with the Marquis of Ardrah; m. Maria Sneaky in June 1834; haughty, handsome, cruel, dishonest, with a coarse mind.

Percy, Harriet. *See* O'Connor.

Percy, Lady Helen. Northangerland's mother; Lady Hume's friend.

Percy, Henry. Northangerland's son; drowned at Northangerland's command off Otaheite, South Sea Islands; as child betrothed to Marian Hume.

Percy, Lady Maria. *Née* Sneaky, Maria (q.v.).

Percy, Lady Mary. Northangerland's first wife; mother of Henry, Edward, William and Mary Henrietta; soft-tempered, sweet, kindly; benign to all, but never gay; her thoughts tinged with religious melancholy.

Percy, Mary Henrietta. Northangerland's daughter; reared by her Grandmother on the family estate; Zamorna's second wife; Marchioness of Douro, Duchess of Zamorna, Queen and Empress of Angria; rejected by Zamorna whom she loves passionately when Northangerland begins his revolution; sent to Alnwick, where B. allows her to die, C. lets her linger on in decline.

Percy, William. Capt.; rejected younger son of Northangerland; m. Cecilia, daughter of the Earl of Seymour; purchased Elm Grove; becomes Sir William, Lieutenant General who tracks down Henry Hastings, and unsuccessfully woos Hastings' sister, Elizabeth, to be his mistress; grows to hate his elder brother Edward who dominates him; plays flute; 'thin, pallid and taciturn'.

Percy Hall. On estate bought, 1792, by Lord Edward Percy; family home of Percys.

Petus and Aria. A tragedy by Edwin Hamilton, put on at the Theatre Royal, Verdopolis in which Mrs Siddons performs.

Philomel. A nightingale kept by Lord Charles Wellesley.

Philosophers' Island. Island 600 miles off coast where there is a college/university where philosophers and other learned men teach the children of noblemen.

Philosophers' Society. A secret society with Crashey as president.

Pighills, the. Family of Arundel.

Pigtail. French confederate of Scheckleton; cattle thief; champion of the French; 7–9ft. high and very ugly; arrested for selling 'white bread' (a mould of arsenic and oil of vitriol) and 'Prussian butter' (Prussic acid made up to look like butter); gets 'lost' under the mantelpiece for two weeks, found when Emperor Napoleon and his party are spring-cleaning; goes in a balloon to the sun; picks up stray children to sell to the mills or for torture for public entertainment.

Plume and Sabre. Hotel in Adrianopolis.

Poetaster, The. Play in which Young Soult satirized.

Ponte Corre, Jean. Leader of the Faction du Manège.

Porteous, Dr. Primate of Northangerland.

Pratee. Nickname for Flanagan.

Prettyman, Mr. Bought Daitura Arbora.

Price, Mr. Manager of the Theatre Royal, Verdopolis.

Provisional Government. Set up by Rogue, 18 March 1831, after the battle of Great Glasstown.

Quamina. *See* Kashna, Quamina.

Quashia. *See* Kashna, Quashia.

Quatre Deinne. Glasstown newspaper.

Quaxima Square. Where Gifford, Love-dust and other Antiquarians live.

Quays, the. Harbour of Verdopolis.

Queen's Theatre. In Verdopolis.

Rad, Tom, John and William. Tom and John, brothers – William the son of John; inhabitants of Howard.

Ramsay. Black scullion.

Rare Lads. Supporters of Northangerland in his revolution; local ruffians; tossed English visitors in a blanket.

Ras Michael. Abyssinian king from whom Quashia seeks help.

Ratten. Character in *Tales of the Islanders*.

Ravenswood. *See* Wellesley, Ernest FitzArthur.

Ravenswood, Alexander. Twin son of Emperor Adrian, who hates his twin, Adrian; keeps 'repulsive' company.

Rebellion, the. Rising by Northangerland in 1832.

Red Cross Knight. (In poem of that name by C.) John Gifford.

Red River, the Great. Rises in Robbers Hill, flows eastward into Bloody Lake; 352 miles long.

Reform Ministry, the. Ended 27 June 1836 when Northangerland took over.

Reformer, The. Newspaper.

Regina. Scene of battle between the Rebels under Capt. O'Connor and the Royal Armies.

Rendezvous. Square in Zamorna.

Revolution, the Great. Uprising of Northangerland against Zamorna on 26 June 1836; leads to the defeat and exile of Zamorna.

Rhodes, Mrs. William's wife.

Rhodes, William. Of Orchard Gate; opponent of Methodism; stupid country gentleman; hanged by Julian Gordon.

Richton, Lord. *See* Flower, John.

Rising Sun. Wayside inn.

Rivaulx, Cross of. A half-obliterated crucifix, sculptured on an obelisk in the Lodge garden near Hawkescliffe. (Name of village and Abbey in Yorkshire.)

Rogue, Alexander. *See* Percy, Alexander.

Rollrogthunderasqueakbotherboriemies. The organ built by Patrick Wiggins in Howard's Cathedral.

Ros(s)endale, Marquis of. *See* Sneaky, John Augustus.

Ros(s)endale Hill. In Sneachiesland; where Frederic Guelph was slain.

Ros(s)endale Town. Once had 500,000 inhabitants and ruled over all Southern Africa; after battle in November 1779, becomes a desolate place of tigers and owls.

Rosier, Eugene. Zamorna's French valet; a torturer at Solyman Palace.

Roslyn (Roslin). Supporter of Zamorna; son and heir of Lord St Clair; bounds 'like a deer from the mountains'.

Ross, Edward Tut. Son of John Ross; the 'most open'.

Ross, John, Lieutenant. One of B.'s Twelves; Ae.'s soldier; 'frank, open, honest, of a bravery approaching madness'. (Sir John Ross, 1777–1856, Arctic explorer.)

Rosses Town. In Rossesland.

Rossi, Signor di. Italian fiddler; duels with Northangerland over Augusta di Segovia.

Roswal. Zamorna's favourite stag-hound.

Rothesay, Felix de. One of C.'s Twelves.

Rotunda. An apartment house in Verdopolis; a meeting-place for the celebrated.

Rover. The (Red); Northangerland's boat.

Rowley, Hannah. Servant/housekeeper.

Royal George. Arthur Wellesley's ship, in which, 1 January 1783, leaves the land of the Twelves to help the English against the French.

Rundell, Mr. Minister of the church.

Sahala. River where Quashia found.

Sai Quarenqua. Eldest of 10 brothers, leads the natives of Acrofcroomb against the Twelves.

Sai Tootoo. *See* Kashna, Sai Tootoo.

St Abdiel. Church in Adrianopolis.

St Augustine's. Scene of Zamorna's coronation.

St Clair, Lord Ronald (Roland?). Of Clan Aldyon in the Brannii Hills, with a castle on Elimbos; about to marry Lady Emily Charlesworth when Northangerland abducts her.

St Cloud. Near Fidena.

St Cyprian. Church in Adrianopolis.
St George's. Street in Glasstown.
St James. Northangerland's mistress; of 'easy' character.
St Michael's. Cathedral in Glasstown; houses memorial to Frederic, Duke of York.
Salamanca Place. Residence of the Duke of Strathelleraye in *Albion and Marina*.
Saldanha. Green plain behind Zamorna's palace.
Sanderson, Mr. Who does not speak again!
Scar Chapel. One of earliest churches in Zamorna.
Scarlet Banner. Inn in Verdopolis.
Scavanger, Dick. One of Rogue's gang, living in a pigsty.
Sche(c)kleton (Sceleton, Skeleton), Monsieur. Helps Pigtail in his business – selling stray children and bodysnatching.
Scott, Adam. One of the correspondents in *Letters from an Englishman*.
Scroven, Tom. An 8ft. sinister scar-faced man, friend of Naughty; a poacher.
Scrub, Cornet. A 'conceited monkey', has his brains blown out by B., then turns into Branni(i).
S'Death, Robert Patrick. Alias King; Rogue's partner and servant; uncle of Patrick Benjamin Wiggins; saves William and Edward Percy as babies from death; lives at Jordan Villa, Senegambia; meets a violent death by poison; has magical connections with Chief Genius Branni.
Seaforth, Mr. Clerk.
Seaton, Timothy. In wool trade with Edward Percy.
Segovia, Augusta di. Northangerland's mistress with an 'Italian eye'.
Segravia, Maria di. Northangerland's mistress; mother of William Etty.
Se(i)ne-Gambia. On Angria's eastern borders. (Senegambia.)
Selateran, Lady. Elderly lady at Lord Selby's ball.
Selby, Lord and Lady. Elderly Major General and his wife; a ball held at their residence in Sulorac Street.
Selden Hall/House. Northangerland's home in Rossesland.
Senate, Grand General. Senate of all the Glasstown countries; first meets 18 March 1833, with Crashey on the throne.
Senegal. River on which Fateconda sited.
Seringapatan. Helps Wellington find his son, Arthur, when stolen by the fairies.
Seymour, Charles. Emperor Adrian's son.
Seymour, Countess of. *See* Wellesley, Lady Isabella.
Seymour, Earl of. Zamorna's uncle.
Seymour, Mr John. Alias of John Sneaky.
Seymours, the. Seymour girls – Eliza (plays the piano), Georgiana (plays the guitar; Northangerland's mistress), Cecilia, Agnes, Catherine, Helen.
Shaver. Northangerland's valet; torturer in Solyman Palace.
Skeleton, Monsieur. *See* Sche(c)kleton.
Sherwood, Mrs. Housekeeper to Marian Hume.
Shiraz. Persian city visited by Douro and Young Soult on a magic camel.
Silden. River flowing into the Great Red River.
Silden. Verdopolitan mail coach stops there.
Simpson. Clergyman of the Verdopolitan circuit; (same?) holds Ernest Edward Gordon Wellesley while Quashia murders him.
Skeleton. *See* Sche(c)kleton, Monsieur.

Sneachiesland (Sneakeysland). B.'s country in Africa.

Sneaky (Sneakie, Sneachie), Alexander. One of B.'s Twelves; King of Sneachiesland; 'ingenious, artful, deceitful, but courageous'.

Sneaky (Alexander), Wilkin. Son of Alexander Sneaky.

Sneaky, Edith. Alexander's eldest daughter; marries the Earl of Arundel.

Sneaky, John, 1st Duke of Fidena. Prince John, son of Alexander; m. Lily Hart – (John) Augustus their son; leader of the Constitutionalists; 'all good and wise'.

Sneaky, John Augustus, 2nd Duke of Fidena. b. at Elm Grove Villa, 1828; son of John, 1st Duke; Marquis of Rossendale; m. Ierne.

Sneaky, Lady Maria. Youngest daughter of Alexander; marriage with Arthur Parry arranged but prefers Edward Percy; loves Zamorna; has 'black eyes and raven hair', 'born to grandeur'.

Sneaky, William. John's brother – 'the gayest'.

Sneaky's Glasstown ale. The local brew.

Sneaky's Mail. Mail coach.

Snow, Sergeant. Publisher in Ross's Glasstown.

Sod. Place near Leyden.

Soffala. Stungaron's sister; deserted wife/mistress of Douro; buried in the desert; had a deformed son – a dwarf.

Solyman Palace. Palace with dungeons.

Soult, Young. Alphonse, Duke of Dalmatia; 'poet' of Angria (i.e. B.); his 'apparel torn; his shoes often slipshod and his stockings full of holes'; his expression 'wild and haggard, and generally he is eternally twisting his mouth to one side or another'; 'devilish but humane and good hearted'; possessed of 'true genius'; C. recognizes his 'beginnings are small' but believes 'his end will be great'. (Soult fought the Duke of Wellington; later ambassador at Queen Victoria's coronation.)

Spalding Hill. Across the Great Red River; army assembly point.

Spectator. Newspaper.

Spectre, the. Magics Napoleon to Marie Louise's ball.

Spinning Jenny. Coaching inn in Zamorna.

Stancliffes, the. Family of Arundel.

Standon, Cecilia. Beautiful young lady whom Capt. Bud admires and whom his wife kills by magic; plays a harp.

Stanhope, Dr. The Primate; christens Zamorna's twin sons.

Stanley, Augustus. Son of Emperor Adrian; 'most refined and deceitful'.

Stannidge. Supporter of Zamorna.

Staveley. Near Zamorna.

Steatons (Steightons), the. Family of Arundel; Timothy joins Edward and William Percy's wool business.

Stephens, W. Clergyman.

Stewart. Family name of Lord Castlereagh.

Stewart, Francis. One of C.'s Twelves.

Sting and Stretch. Charles Warner's ferrets.

Stongo. Capt. Bud's 'cherub' – a 'squawking brat'.

Strafford, Earl of. Edward Sydney, supporter of Northangerland.

Strand, the. In Adrianopolis.

Strathaye. Where, in a reverie, Charles and Arthur Wellesley live.

Strathelleraye. 'A sweet pastoral village' in south of England.

Strathelleraye, Duke and Duchess of. The parents of Albion in *Albion and Marina* (i.e. Duke and Duchess of Wellington).

Strathfieldsaye. In Vision Island; where three old Washerwomen live.

Stuart, Frederic. Earl of Stuartville, Viscount Castlereagh.

Stuart, Lady. Has oiled and curled locks.

Stuartville Road. In Zamorna.

Stumps, Frederic. A middy; one of B.'s Twelves who died on Ascension Island, but comes alive again as King Frederic (Guelph).

Stumps' Isle (Island, Isles). Hilly island off Africa, where Northangerland exiled; where 'round, rosy-faced, curly-pated, straight-legged, one-shoed beings live', 'eating melons and rice pudding' for which they 'roared incessantly'.

Stungaron. Quashia's brother whom Emperor Adrian beheads.

Sun of Angria. Evening newspaper.

Sunnart Lake. Where Lady Victorine comes from.

Sydenham. Hilly province in Angria.

Sydney, Edward G. Hero of *The Foundling*; goes to Eton and Oxford; marries and divorces Lady Julia Wellesley; story of his background as the unknown son of Guelph later denied; taken up by Pigtail and Skeleton in Verdopolis.

Sydney, John. William's eldest son.

Sydney, Lady Julia. *See* Wellesley, Julia.

Sydney, William. MP for Southwood; supports Northangerland.

Sylvester, Bob. Pugnacious and loquacious blacksmith; Republican supporter.

Tagus, Marquis of. *See* Albion. (River in Portugal crossed by Wellington in the Peninsular War.)

Talli(i) (Taley). One of the Genii; Arthur Wellesley's protector – i.e. C.

Tcherkash. Visited by the Old Man in *Ernest Alembert*.

Temple, Annabel. Zamorna's housekeeper.

Tennant. Zamorna's chaplain.

Tenterden, Mr. Village gentleman.

Theatre Royal. Beneath the Opera House in Verdopolis.

Thorncliffe. Where Patrick Benjamin Wiggins born.

Thornton, Edith. General Thornton's sister.

Thorton, Lady Julia. *See* Wellesley, Julia.

Thornton, Sir William. Field Marshal.

Thornton, General Sir Wilson. (Same as above?) Guardian of young Lord Charles Wellesley; owner of Girnington Hall and Thornton Hotel; m. Lady Julia Wellesley; a Yorkshire man in speech; an 'honest, honest man'.

Thurston, Marian. Character in B.'s *And the Weary Are at Rest*.

Thurston, Tom. Douro's servant – a 'Rare Lad'.

Thurston, William. Husband of Marian.

Tornado. Percy's horse.

Tower of All Nations. Which 'cleft clouds, tempests and lightenings at its base' and 'sought acquaintance with the skies'; where Crashey lived.

Townshend, Charles. i.e. Lord Charles Wellesley – renounces his family, becomes Charles Townshend; 'author' of *Julia, Mina Laury*, etc.; selfish, arrogant, but always curious with a wry cynical sense of humour; great friend of Sir William Percy.

Tracky, E. One of B.'s Twelves.

Traquair (Tragnarin), Ronald. One of C.'s Twelves.

Tree, Capt. Printer's devil, becomes a compositor, then author of 'snivelling rhymes and snivelling tales'; 'author' of many stories – incl. *The Characters of Celebrated Men, The Foundling*; does not always see eye to eye with Charles Townshend.

Tree, Sergeant. Publisher, printer and bookseller of Glasstown.

Trott. Name for Ross.

Tunstall, Sir Henry. A wanderer who returns to find his home and family destroyed.

Twelves, the. Originally B.'s toy soldiers; become the discoverers, explorers and settlers of Ashantee, forming the Glasstown Confederacy; the original Twelves chosen were: C.'s – Marcus O'Donell, Ferdinand Cortez (Corky), Felix de Rothesay, Eugene Cameron, Harold FitzGeorge, Henry Clinton, Francis Stewart, Ronald Traquair, Ernest Fortescue, Gustavus Donaley, Frederic Brunswick, Arthur Wellesley; B.'s – Butter Crashey (age 140); Alexander Cheeky, surgeon, age 20; Arthur Wellesley, trumpeter, age 12; William Edward Parry, trumpeter, age 15; Alexander Sneaky, sailor, age 17; John Ross, lieutenant, age 16; William Bravey, sailor, age 27; Edward Gravey, sailor, age 17; Frederic Guelph, sailor, age 27; Stumps (died 18 May 1770) age 12; Monkey, age 11; Tracky, age 10; Crackey, age 5 – these last four were middies. The First Twelves later became the House of Lords in Glasstown; a Second Twelves became the House of Commons; four of them – Arthur Wellesley, Sneaky, Parry and Ross became kings of their countries – Wellingtonsland, Sneachiesland, Parrysland and Ross(es)land.

Twelves Street. Leads to Parliament Square.

Twelves Town. Burnt down at the time of Duke of York's death; replaced by Glasstown. (*See also* Glasstown, Verdopolis.)

Twemy. Nickname for the Duke of Wellington.

Univers. Newspaper.

U.T. 'Us Two' – Marquis of Douro and Lord Charles Wellesley (i.e. C. and B.).

Valdecella, Duchess of. *See* Inez, Emily.

Valdecella, Duke of. *See* Wellesley, Ernest Julius Mornington.

Valence, Jean de. Swiss artist living in the Alps with his wife Louise, and child Alexandre.

Van Haalen. Dutch Governor of Ascension Island.

Verdopolis. Capital of the Glasstown Confederacy – first called Glasstown, then Verreopolis, then Verdopolis; on the river Guadima; centre for government, 'high life' and commerce; 'a splendid city rising with such graceful hautiness from the green realm of Neptune' with walls, battlements, a cathedral, the domed Bravey's hotel, the Great Tower and many fine streets, with fine shops. Here Pigtail and Scheckleton performed their tortures as sideshows. (*See also* Glasstown, Twelves Town.)

Verdopolitan Confederacy. *See* Glasstown Confederacy.

Verdopolitan Intelligencer. Newspaper.

Vernet. Painter of Angria, 'great in painting animals'.

Vernon, Anna. Embraces Arthur O'Connor.

Vernon, Caroline. Northangerland's and Louisa Vernon's (Dance's) daughter;

later Zamorna's ward, then his mistress; abducted by Zamorna, 7 December
1839.

Vernon, George. Friend of Northangerland; marries Louisa Dance.

Vernon, Louisa. *Née* Dance. Formerly opera singer and ballet dancer; flattered by
Vernon but becomes Northangerland's mistress; crawls back to marry Vernon
when he deserts her.

Verreopolis. Earlier name for Verdopolis.

Victorine, Lady Helen. Zamorna's mistress; dies giving birth to Edward Ernest
Gordon Wellesley.

Vision Island. *See* Dreams, Island of.

Waiting Boy. Later Ross; Ae.'s soldier.

Wareham, Lord. Supports Zamorna.

Warner. Angrian province.

Warner, Caroline. Warner Howard Warner's sister.

Warner, Charles. John Howard Warner's friend (brother?).

Warner, Dr. Primate of Angria.

Warner, Henry. Brother of Warner Howard Warner, a disreputable clergyman
reprimanded for keeping bad company.

Warner, Mrs. Rufus' young wife.

Warner, Sir Richard. Zamorna's physician.

Warner, Rufus. Guides Ernest Alembert to Fairyland.

Warner, Vincent James. Warner Howard's youngest brother.

Warner, Warner Howard. Barrister; head of Clan Agars, Howards and Warners;
Chancellor of the Exchequer for Zamorna; Lord Lieutenant of Angria; Fellow of
St Michael's; MP for the Philosophers' Isle; succeeds Northangerland as
Zamorna's prime minister; m. Ellen Greville; residences – Warner Hall, Warner
Hotel (Verdopolis), Howard House (Adrianopolis), Woodhouse Cliffe (near
Freetown); an honest man whose advice often rejected by Zamorna; credited
with the gift of second sight.

Warner Hills. Where Zamorna withdraws after Northangerland defeats him.

Washerwomen. Three old women (fairies?) employed by Wellington, who
disappear.

Waterloo Palace. Wellesley family home.

Wellesley. The family – all dark-haired, dark-eyed, in contrast to the fair Percys.

Wellesley. The 16 noble ladies around Zamorna – Julia, Amelia, Sophia, Arabella,
Harriet, Emily, Marcia, Madeleine, Zouey, Jessica, Olivia, Margaret,
Geraldine, Augusta, Rosamund, Adela.

Wellesley, (Prince) Adrian. Son of Emperor Adrian, Alexander Ravenswood's
twin; friend to men of letters and science.

Wellesley, Alexander Ravenswood. Son of Emperor Adrian, Adrian's twin.

Wellesley, Arthur. Trumpeter of the Twelves; later the Duke of Wellington;
father of Arthur Augustus and Lord Charles; adoptive father of Quashia;
protector of Edward Sydney; protected by the Geni, Talli (C.).

Wellesley, Arthur Augustus Adrian. b. 1812/13; Wellington's eldest son;
Marquis of Douro and Alderwood; Earl of Evesham and Baron Leyden;
becomes Duke of Zamorna; King of Angria; eventually Emperor Adrian; m. (1)
Marian Hume, one son, Julius, Marquis of Almeida; (2) Lady Mary Henrietta
(Northangerland's daughter); 6 sons – Archduke Frederic Julius and Alexander

(twins), Augustus Stanley, Charles Seymour, Edward Mornington and little Arthur, and a daughter, Ierne; mistresses include Rosamund Wellesley, Lady Helen Victorine, Mina Laury, Caroline Vernon. Loved by Lady Zenobia Ellrington who tries to prevent his marriage to Marian Hume by trickery and magic. Awarded territory, Angria – taken from parts of the other provinces of the Confederacy – for his fighting on behalf of the Glasstown Confederacy against the Ashantee, Napoleon and the French; there builds his capital, Adrianopolis, which he later destroys to prevent it falling into the hands of Northangerland's Revolutionaries; goes into exile; returns, helped by Warner Howard Warner and Mina Laury; retakes his kingdom, demoting Northangerland to the status of private individual (*see* Percy, Alexander). As Douro is 'tall and slender', with a slightly 'Roman nose', 'dark auburn hair' and of 'mild and human disposition'; as Zamorna becomes more flamboyant – 'impetuous and stormy pride, diving and soaring enthusiasm, war and poetry, are kindling their fires in all his veins and his wild blood boils from his heart'; he suffers paroxysms and fits; his relationship with Northangerland the pivot of many juvenile stories.

Wellesley, Lord Charles Albert Florian. Twin brother to Arthur; when presented to the public he leans too far out of the window and falls, seemingly to his death; at first an ugly meddling imp called Charlie (with a drink named after him); later a 'lively elegant' man with a 'strong and handsome' countenance; as Charles Townshend, the author of several works including *The Green Dwarf, Corner Dishes, The Spell, My Angria and the Angrians* (C.).

Wellesley, Edward, Marquis of. Wellington's brother; Lady Julia's father.

Wellesley, Edward Ernest Gordon. Baron Gordon, Lord of Avondale; son of Zamorna and Lady Helen Victorine; b. at Alderwood, when mother dies; a 'dark malignant thing'; murdered by Quashia putting burning rods through his eyes into his brain.

Wellesley, Frederick. Marquis of Arno; Zamorna and Mary's son; twin to Julius.

Wellesley, Ierne. Emperor Adrian and Mary's daughter.

Wellesley, Isabella, Lady. Countess of Mornington; Zamorna's aunt; m. Earl of Seymour – six beautiful daughters.

Wellesley, Julia, Lady. Zamorna's cousin; later Princess; m. (1) Edward Sydney; (2) General Thornton; a 'big bouncing girl' with raven curls; plays the guitar.

Wellesley, Julius, Archduke. Zamorna and Mary's son; Frederick's twin; haughty and disdainful.

Wellesley, Mary Henrietta. *See* Percy, Mary Henrietta.

Wellesley, Rosamund. Committed suicide for love of her cousin, Zamorna; 'Resurgam' written on her tomb.

Wellesley House. Zamorna's house in Verdopolis.

Wellington, Duke of. *See* Wellesley, Arthur.

Wellington, Marchioness of. Baroness Gordon, wife of the Duke.

Wellingtonsland. C.'s country in Africa – Senegambia.

Wentworth, Charles. Lofty's private secretary; visits Verdopolis.

Werner, Rufus. Ernest Alembert's fairy visitor.

Western Iris. Mail coach.

Western Street. In Verdopolis.

Westfield Tavern. Where Orient Mail stops.

Westwood. Town on the Niger; scene of fierce battle.

Wharton, the Hon. George. MP for Ardashire.

Wharton, Mary (Henrietta). Daughter of Lord George Wharton; m. Alexander Percy; dies of consumption. (*See* Percy, Alexander.)

Wheelhouse, Dr. The holy doctor.

White Lion. Hotel in Ardsley.

Widdops. *Widdops Hundredth* written for Weslyan Chapel meetings.

Wiggins, the. Family – Patrick Benjamin, Charlotte, Emily and Anne; C.'s caricature pictures of the Brontë family – Patrick is 'slightly built man attired in a black coat and raven grey trousers, his hat placed neatly at the back of his head revealing a bush of carroty hair so arranged that at the side it projects like two spread hands, a pair of spectacles placed across a prominent Roman nose, black neckerchief adjusted with no great attention to detail'; the others – described by Patrick Wiggins (B.) – are 'miserable creatures not worth talking about'; Charlotte 'a broad dumpy thing whose head does not come higher than my elbow'; Emily 'lean and scant with a face almost the size of a penny'; Anne 'nothing, absolutely nothing'.

Wilson, Jem. Gardener at Selden House.

Wilson, Mr. Born and brought up in Ross Town; steals money; becomes commercial traveller for the House of Macandlier and Jamieson in Stumpsland.

Wind, Colonel. Publisher in Parry's Glasstown.

Windlass, Sergeant. Glasstown printer and bookseller.

Wolverton, Talbot. Rogue's champion.

Wood, Mr. Manager of Queen's Theatre, Verdopolis.

Woodchurch Hall. Where Harriet sits recalling the past.

W.T. 'We Two', i.e. C. and B.

York, Duke of. *See* Guelph, Frederic.

York Place. In Verdopolis.

Young Men's Intelligencer. Verdopolitan magazine.

Young Men's Magazine. Great Glasstown Magazine; written first by B., then taken over by C.

Young Men's Tongue. Local language of Ashantee land (made by B. holding his nose tightly and speaking rapidly).

Young, Major St John. A gambler whose wife leaves him for Lord Caversham.

Young, Mrs. St John's wife; they have two children – a beautiful daughter and a son, who are deliberately separated from their mother.

Zamorna. Province of Angria; 170 by 112 miles; on the Olympian river with a fine suspension bridge; capital Zamorna; pop. 1,986,000; Lord Lieutenant – Viscount Castlereagh. (Town on River Douro in Spain.)

Zamorna, Duchess of. *See* Percy, Mary Henrietta.

Zamorna, Duke of. *See* Wellesley, Arthur Augustus Adrian.

Zamorna Telegraph. Angrian newspaper.

Zenobia. *See* Ellrington, Zenobia.

Zephyr Valley. Where Great African Games held.

Zorayda. Spanish lady – (1) wife of Frederic, Duke of York and mother of Edward Sydney; (2) daughter of Sir William Etty and Julia his wife; becomes Maid of Honour to Princess Ierne; marries Prince Adrian.

Gondal

Sources

Gondal is the world Emily and Anne created, as Charlotte and Branwell created Glasstown, but there are nothing like as many manuscripts dealing with it. In 1849/50, when Charlotte was preparing the reissue of *Wuthering Heights* and *Agnes Grey*, under the auspices of Smith, Elder and Co., she went through the papers of Emily and Anne that had been left when they died. She records in her letters of the time the great effect this had on her – she found it impossible to work at them in the evening because it led to sleepless nights, and, in the end, it caused a return of her nervous depression, affecting her own writing. How many of these prose manuscripts were then left, or whether Emily and Anne both cleared out their papers before they died, there is no evidence to tell. At least some of the poems were still in existence, for Charlotte chooses new ones to put into the 1850 edition of *Wuthering Heights* and *Agnes Grey*.

That so much of Charlotte's and Branwell's prose juvenilia should still be extant today and none of Emily's or Anne's suggests a deliberate act of destruction rather than the wayward one of time. Possibly when Charlotte had sorted out Emily's and Anne's papers, and used what she wanted of the poetry (altering it and adding to it as she thought fit, usually to its detriment), she then disposed of the rest including the prose stories, keeping only some books of copied-up poems for any further publication that might be called for. To modern ears this may sound like an act of treachery, even vandalism, but if Charlotte did do it, she probably did it from the best of motives. Emily and Anne were gone and their private papers were written for their eyes alone and would be of no interest to others. The only remaining references to Gondal, except for lists of names and places, are in the 'diary papers' which Emily and Anne produced jointly for the years 1834 and 1837 and separately for 1841 and 1845, and these are brief and tantalizing. Even as late as 1845, when Emily was twenty-seven and Anne twenty-five, these two sisters are still 'playing at' Gondal, as in earlier days all four Brontë children had 'played at' Glasstown.

Any story of Gondal, therefore, has to be re-created from the occasional list of characters and places, the few references in the diary papers and the poems; often the reconstruction of the saga is the result, more than anything else, of imaginative guesswork.

The Lists

The fullest lists are given by Anne. One is in her additions to Goldsmith's *Geography*, a book the children used, where the names of the various kingdoms of the two islands – Gondal and Gaaldine – are given. Both the other lists contain the names of characters, written out in two columns, the men's names on the left, the women's on the right. Some names are common to both lists, some have been erased and replaced with others, the relationships (if being opposite another person betokens a relationship) vary. There is no date to either of these lists, so whether they were written out by Anne as a reference source when she was writing a particular story, or whether just as a general record of the changes in the names and relationships of characters, we do not know. Emily's one reference plan has its own kind of code, with numbers and initials – R.N. and G.N., for example – which might, as has been suggested, mean Roman Nose or Greek Nose, but which, equally, might not!

The Diary Papers

Making anything constructive from the references in the 'diary' papers is a similar straw-catching business. In the earliest paper extant, 1834, we find it recorded that the Gondals are exploring the interior of Gaaldine (although, of course, 1834, is not necessarily the Gondal date for this event). From this, all one can with safety conclude is that, by 1834 at the latest, Emily and Anne were involved in their own make-believe world. In fact, it is about this time that Charlotte and Branwell are engaged in the founding of Angria as a kingdom for Zamorna – so it seems a suitable time, as new territories are being allocated, for Emily and Anne to 'go independent' as it were. In the 1837 paper Emily reveals she is engaged on a life of Augustus (not, as in some references, Augusta) Almeda, and that the Emperors and Empresses of Gondal and Gaaldine are preparing to leave Gaaldine for a coronation in Gondal on 12 July – whose we do not know, but it seems as though it should be Augustus's. Emily also adds news from Glasstown – Northangerland is at present in Monkey's Isle and Zamorna is at Eversham (sic). This suggests that the divorce between Glasstown and Gondal is not, as yet, total. By 1841, when Emily and Anne prepare separate papers, Emily records that 'the Gondalians' are in a threatening state, and that all the Princes and Princesses are at the Palace of Instruction, adding that she has a great many books on hand and so has just made a 'regularity paper' and 'means verb sap to do great things'. Anne, writing her paper in Scarborough, records that she is engaged in writing the fourth volume of Solala Vernon's life. Both of these references suggest that the juvenilia prose writings of Emily and Anne may well have been quite prolific and that by this time they are writing as eagerly as their older brother and sister.

By 1845 Anne, after her years as a governess at Thorp Green, is at home, and she and Emily can open and read the 1841 papers, and write the current ones together. Whether they ever did open these 1845 ones in July 1848 – an event to which both papers look forward – before they died, there is no record to tell. In 1845 both write about the journey they made – the first by themselves – to York and Keighley and how they 'were' Ronald Macglin, Henry Angora, Juliet Augusteena, Rosabella and others, escaping from the Palaces of Instruction to join the Royalists who are being hounded by the victorious Republicans. Emily adds that she herself is occupied on a work on the First Wars and Anne on articles on this and a book by Henry Sophona, adding that as long as the 'rascals' 'delight' them, as they do at present, they 'intend sticking firm by them'. Anne, however, is not quite so positive in her remarks. She and Emily are, she notes, still engaged in writing the Gondal Chronicles begun three-and-a-half years earlier; Emily is writing the Emperor Julius's life (presumably he was engaged in the First Wars) and, Anne discloses, is also writing poetry – Anne wonders what it is about. She records that the Republicans are uppermost, but that the Royalists are still not quite overcome, and the young sovereigns, with their brothers and sisters, are still in the Palace of Instruction; that the members of the Unique Society who were wrecked on a desert island about Christmas 1844 are still there, not having been 'played at much'. She adds, 'the Gondals are not in first-rate playing condition. Will they improve?' It has been deduced from this comment that Anne was no longer really interested in the Gondal world. Her experiences at Thorp Green, on her own testimony in this paper, had not been altogether pleasant and it is suggested she has little patience now with the 'web of childhood'. However, as she specifically states 'playing condition' it may be that it was the acting out of Gondal adventures, such as that engaged upon in her and Emily's excursion to York, that she had outgrown and perhaps found embarrassing. Certainly a race across the moors, as fugitives from some imaginary enemy, can hardly be said to be the kind of behaviour expected from young Victorian ladies in their mid-twenties!

The Poems

The third source of information – the poems – contains isolated incidents in the Gondal history, rather than any chronological narrative of it. Of Emily's poetry there are extant, besides the poems that were published in 1846, two manuscript volumes (from 1837 to 1846), as well as many separate pages of poems in an unrevised or rejected condition; of Anne's, a series of 'fair copy' books spanning the years 1836 to 1849. There is no cut-off date in these poems (as there is in the prose juvenilia of Charlotte and Branwell), for Anne continues writing poetry throughout her life, and Emily is still revising hers in May 1848. Not all of the poems are concerned with Gondal affairs. In this section only the Gondal poems (as far as they can be established) are dealt with. (For an evaluation of the 1846 volume of *Poems* by Currer, Ellis and Acton Bell *see* Poems 1846.)

Anne's Poems

The separation between 'personal' and Gondal poetry is fairly clear as far as Anne is concerned. There are a total of about twenty poems that are definitely Gondal, nine dated as written between 1836 and January 1840, one in January 1841, one in November 1843, one in February and one in December 1844, two in September and one in October 1845 and, finally, in 1846, two in July, one in August and one in September. The first group of nine poems is concerned with Alexander (Hybernia?) and Zenobia, who pledge their love to each other when young, re-meeting two years later at an appointed place, and with Alexandrina Zenobia (daughter of Alexander and Zenobia?), who, we learn, was once imprisoned, who either is Lady Alzerno or steals from her the love of her lord, and who has a child Flora, whose father deserts and forgets her. In the other poems various names occur – Marina Sabia, Olivia Vernon, Hespera Caverndel, Alexander Hybernia, and initials, A.H., E.Z., for example. Alexander himself is in prison in April 1826 and rejected by his beloved. The 1845–6 group of poems are all concerned with Z(erona) Z. and A.E., (Alexander?), who seems to have been imprisoned for Zerona's sake. One poem is about the childhood relationship of E.Z. with a younger boy, his companion, whom he later destroys for the sake of his country. Although these disconnected names and themes of love, treachery, desertion, patriotism, echo those of Glasstown there is insufficient material for any cohesive story to be drawn from them.

Emily's Poems

With Emily's poems problems arise, in the first place, as to what is Gondal and what is 'personal'. Indeed one critic – Fannie Ratchford – has fitted all Emily's poems into the Gondal story, although at times, it must be admitted, with some difficulty. There is, however, one clear indication of a dividing line, given by Emily herself. In February 1844, when she decided to copy out the poems she had written to date into two books – both of which are extant – she inscribed one, 'Emily Jane Brontë. Transcribed February 1844. Gondal Poems', and elaborated this with a pattern of scroll flourishes. On the other she merely wrote 'E.J.B. Transcribed February 1844'. This suggests that she was here making her own distinction between her Gondal and her 'personal' poetry.

Charlotte herself tells us the story of how she discovered Emily's poetry – 'One day, in the autumn of 1845, I accidentally lighted on a ms. volume of verse in my sister Emily's handwriting. Of course, I was not surprised, knowing that she could and did write verse; I looked it over...' Emily was not amused at Charlotte's action. It took Charlotte 'hours to reconcile her to the discovery I had made and days to persuade her that such poems merited publication'. The result was the volume of *Poems*, 1846, by Currer, Ellis and Acton Bell.

Charlotte's initial accident led her to break an unspoken law of privacy – in the Brontë household, certainly. It was only in late summer 1845 that Anne herself, always closer to Emily than Charlotte was, became aware that Emily was writing poetry, and wondered what it was about. (Did she pass that knowledge on to Charlotte?) The 'ms. volume' that Charlotte lighted on, and then read, must have been Emily's 'E.J.B.' manuscript, for there can be little doubt that if Charlotte had stumbled on and read the 'Gondal' one, the 'personal' one would not have been forthcoming. The degree of Emily's anger is surely shown in the fact that, as far as we know, after the autumn of 1845 (a time when she was writing a fair amount of poetry) she wrote only two more poems, and one of those is unfinished. Perhaps as a kind of determined gesture against Charlotte's 'treachery', she decided to write no more. Perhaps she chose to destroy anything she wrote subsequently, although this seems hardly likely, and one feels that if she had chosen to destroy some, she would have destroyed them all, including the transcribed books. Some may, of course, have been destroyed by Charlotte when she cleared out Emily's and Anne's papers.

Whatever the solution may be, it is in Emily's poetry, in the transcribed volume (February 1844) of Gondal Poems, that the fullest and clearest picture of Gondal and Gaaldine is given. At first, up to about April/May 1844 when she must have been copying the poems out, the chronological order of composition is abandoned in favour of poems grouped together according to subject matter. Some other poems, not transcribed, which are clearly Gondal (names or initials given in the title, or references in the text) have been taken into consideration, as well as the transcribed MS itself, in the following description of the world of Gondal.

The World of Gondal

Gondal is an island in the North Pacific, divided into four parts, Gondal, Angora, Alcona and Exina. Of these, Angora is in the northern part of the island, and Exina in the south. The island's capital is Regina. Gaaldine is a large island in the South Pacific, divided into six parts – Alexand(r)ia, Almedore, Elseradon, Zalon, Ula, each governed by a sovereign, and Zedora, a large province, governed by a Viceroy. The northern island has a similar landscape and climate to that of the Yorkshire moorland districts – heather, heath, fern, bluebells, bright brief July sunshine, cold winter winds and snows. Gaaldine, however, has a tropical vegetation and climate – palms, cedars, constant bright blue skies and hot suns. Nothing is known of Gaaldine until after the creation of Gondal, for it is the Gondals who 'discover the interior of Gaaldine'.

The two characters that dominate the first groups of poems are A.G.A. – Augusta Geraldine Alme(i)da, and J.B., Julius Brenzaida. One can be comparatively sure of what happened to these two during their lives, but not altogether of the order in which the events took place.

A.G.A. As a child A.G.A. is brought up with a girl, Angelica, as her companion. In the same household is a dark boy, Amadeus, with whom Angelica falls in love, but A.G.A steals his love away from her, eventually discarding him, and seeing that both he and Angelica are sent into exile, where they live a life of crime, waiting a suitable time for their revenge. A.G.A.'s second love is Lord Alexander of Elbe. He is either her husband or her constant lover, and dies in her arms on the shores of Lake Elmor, remembering his distant sunny southern home. After his death A.G.A. is imprisoned in a dungeon in the Northern College, on the wall of which she writes a lament for him, which she dates September 1826. Her next affair is with the fair-haired, blue-eyed Alfred Sidonia, Lord Aspi(e)n. Since she is referred to as Sidonia's deity, and her picture hangs in his ancestral home beside his, it looks as though she becomes his wife. On the other side of his portrait, is a painting of his fair-haired daughter whom he neglects for love of A.G.A. The tone often suggests that A.G.A. is looked upon as an interloper, with whom Sidonia is infatuated, and that his people dislike her. Sidonia dies in England, where his remains lie – but his ghost returns to haunt Aspin Castle, his ancestral home. Then A.G.A. has a brief affair with a guitar player, Fernando de Samara, who is different in temperament from the usual inhabitants of Gondal. He is brought up at Areon Hall in Exina and pledges his love to the daughter of the family there, but he breaks that vow for A.G.A.'s sake. She enjoys his attentions and gives him a miniature of herself, but then she grows tired of him and he is sent to a dungeon in the Gaaldine Caves, where he writes a passionate paean of hate against his deceiver –

> Go, load my memory with shame;
> Speak but to curse my hated name;
> My tortured limbs in dungeons bind,
> And spare my life, to kill my mind.

He manages to escape and, after looking at her miniature, decides to take his own life –

> Do I not see thee now? Thy black resplendent hair;
> Thy glory-beaming brow, and smile, how heavenly fair!
> Thine eyes are turned away – those eyes I would not see;
> Their dark, thin deadly ray, would more than madden me.

> There go, Deceiver, go! My hand is streaming wet;
> My heart's blood flows to bring the blessing – to forget!
> Oh could that lost heart give back, back again to thine
> One tenth part of the pain that clouds my dark decline!

He listens to the wind from Gondal –

> I do not need thy breath to cool my death-cold brow;
> But go to that far land, where she is shining now;
> Tell her my latest wish, tell her my dreary doom;
> Say that MY pangs are past, but HERS are yet to come.

> And yet for all her hate, each parting glance would tell
> A stronger passion breathed, burned, in this last farewell.
> Unconquered in my soul the Tyrant rules me still;
> *Life* bows to my control, but *Love* I cannot kill.

Fernando de Samara has the heart of a Heathcliff.

The last poem about A.G.A. tells of her death. The story falls into three parts – the planning of the murder, the killing of her two companions and of A.G.A. herself, and finally the discovery of her body. In the first part, Angelica tells her companion, Douglas, how

A.G.A. stole her lover's affection and then discarded him. She persuades Douglas to help her get her revenge, and she, in return, as Douglas has always loved her, will give herself to him. The scene then moves to another part of the moor, later in the day. There Surry, A.G.A.'s lady-in-waiting, and Lord Lesley, her escort, have been killed, Surry dying in Lord Lesley's arms, and he so weak that he dies before he can warn A.G.A. Douglas then lies in wait for A.G.A. above a little waterfall where she comes to drink –

> She turns – she meets the Murderer's gaze;
> Her own is scorched with a sudden blaze –
> The blood streams down her brow,
> The blood streams through her coal-black hair –
> She strikes it off with little care;
> She scarcely feels it flow;
> For she has marked and known him too,
> And his own heart's ensanguined dew
> Must slake her vengeance now!

She struggles with her murderer, wounding him as he kills her, and then

> The stream in silence sang once more;
> And, on its green banks, bathed in gore
> Augusta lay alone.

She and her escort are found by Lord Eldred, who sends his followers after Douglas, while he remains with A.G.A.'s corpse, thinking of her past, which was so full of promise, and the nonfulfilment of that promise:

> Cold as the earth, unweeting now
> Of love, or joy, or mortal woe.
> For what thou wert I would not grieve
> But much for what thou wert to be –
> That life so stormy and so brief,
> That death has wronged us more than thee –

Julius Brenzaida. This character combines a martial with an amorous career. In 1825 he is in prison, for, while there, in the customary manner of Emily's and Anne's characters, he writes a poem on the wall of his dungeon, which he dates. It gives us some idea as to why he is there. He is evidently a person of noble birth, and he and others were setting sail for the southern countries when, for some reason, his love and faithfulness to Rosina caused him to be left behind in prison, to think over his 'crime'. It seems probable that he marries Rosina, or at least becomes her constant lover, and that through her ambitious drive, he takes over Angora, makes conquests in Almedore (the name given him in one poem), takes Zalona by siege, and makes a pact with Gerald of Exina for peace and unity. He is, however, foresworn, overthrowing Gerald and his followers, and eventually making himself emperor. An opponent, Gleneden, tells of a dream he has whilst he is in prison, in which he sees Julius being murdered at the height of his power. This dream comes true, for having left Rosina behind ill with a fever, he sets out on a campaign and is stabbed in a marble hall in the midst of his guards and counsellors. The references Angelica makes (in the poem about the death of A.G.A.) to a murder in which she and her lover Amadeus are involved, and in which Amadeus, in killing the tyrant, is himself killed, suggests that it may well be Amadeus who murders Julius as an act of revenge.

Two affairs of Julius's are recorded in the poems – one with Rosina and one with a woman called Geraldine. Whether this Geraldine is A.G.A. is never clear – certainly she has raven black hair and fine eyes (both hallmarks of A.G.A.), but she lacks A.G.A's fiery spirit. This Geraldine does not trust J.B., so he discards her for one who has more faith in him; she solicits his help when she is left with a child by him, but her appeal seems to be in vain. Rosina, on the other hand, is his true faithful follower, in anguish when (after she has recovered from her illness) she hears of his death, and still remembering him fifteen years later.

Both A.G.A. and Julius Brenzaida are mourned after death by faithful friends or lovers. E.W. provides two laments for A.G.A., the first of which was once thought to be Emily's lament for her dead brother:

> How few of all the hearts that loved
> Are grieving for thee now!
> And why should mine, tonight be moved
> With such a sense of woe.

The second has a delicate singing quality, akin to Shakespeare's 'Fear no more the heat of the sun' with which it shares a similar rhythm and rhyme scheme:

> The linnet in the rocky dells,
> The moor-lark in the air,
> The bee among the heather-bells
> That hide my lady fair;
> The wild deer browse above her breast;
> The wild birds raise their brood;
> And they, her smiles of love caressed,
> Have left her solitude.

. . .

> Blow, west wind, by the lonely mound,
> And murmur, summer streams,
> There is no need of other sound
> To soothe my lady's dreams.

Rosina's lament for the dead Julius Brenzaida, fifteen years after his death, is the well-known 'Cold in the earth and the deep snow piled above thee'. The soft, effacing power of the passage of time, and the singing tones of E.W.'s lament for A.G.A. are not present here, and yet, although it is by comparison hard and direct in its approach, it still has that haunting quality of music that all Emily's poems have – part of which comes from the repetition of particular, often fairly common, words:

> Cold in the earth, and the deep snow piled above thee!
> Far, far removed, cold in the dreary grave!
> Have I forgot, my Only Love to love thee,
> Severed at last by Time's all-wearing wave?
> . . .
> Cold in the earth, and fifteen wild Decembers
> From those brown hills have melted in to spring –
> Faithful indeed is the spirit that remembers
> After such years of change and suffering.

The poems after 11 March 1844 in the Gondal manuscript retell old themes and develop some new ones, but never with the cohesion that the earlier groups of poems have. Many of the new themes are about children – suggesting that the interest, once A.G.A. and J.B. are dead, lies with the younger generation. One of them concerns a dark unwanted boy – A.E.:

> Never has a blue streak
> Cleft the clouds since morn,
> Never has his grim fate
> Smiled since he was born.

He is taken under the wing of a golden-haired girl – R.C.:

> . . . with sun bright hair,
> And sea blue, sea deep eyes;
> I, the image of light and gladness,
> Saw and pitied that mournful boy,
> And I swore to take his gloomy sadness,
> And give to him my beaming joy.

And, as a result,

> Guardian angel, he lacks no longer;
> Evil fortune he needs not fear;
> Fate is strong, but Love is stronger;
> And more unsleeping than angel's care.

The feelings R.C. has towards A.E. reflect both Cathy's towards Heathcliff and Catherine's towards Linton in the later *Wuthering Heights*. The antithesis between dark and fair, which is a part both of this poem and of *Wuthering Heights*, is present in another poem of Emily's written in May 1842 – about H.A. and A.S. (possibly the children of Alfred Sidonia and A.G.A.):

> In the same place, when Nature wore
> The same celestial glow
> I'm sure I've seen those forms before
> But many springs ago;
>
> And only *he* had locks of light,
> And *she* had raven hair,
> While now his curls are dark as night
> And hers as morning fair.

It is amongst these later Gondal poems that Emily gives a clear description of some kind of trance that comes upon A.G. Rochelle, but which was also, surely, an experience of Emily herself:

> A messenger of Hope comes every night to me,
> And offers, for short life, eternal liberty.
>
> He comes with western winds, with evening's wandering airs,
> With that clear dusk of heaven that brings the thickest stars;
> Winds take a pensive tone, and stars a tender fire,
> And visions rise and change which kill me with desire –
>
> But first a hush of peace, a soundless calm descends;
> The struggle of distress and fierce impatience ends;
> Mute music soothes my breast, unuttered harmony
> That I could never dream till earth was lost to me.

From these last poems of Emily's, with their many different names and initials, none of which seem to link up definitely with any other, one senses that there is some kind of civil war going on, which separates lovers, either through the necessity of one having to go away to fight and possibly being killed, or through each belonging to an opposing side – the Romeos and Juliets of Gondal, in fact. The last poem she wrote, dated 14 September 1846, which she started to revise in May 1848, refers to civil war conditions – where the speaker of the poems comments:

> When kindred strive – God help the weak!

and he tells how he drew his sword

> to free
> One race, beneath two standards, fighting
> For Loyalty and Liberty –

There is fierce pity in Emily's description of a child victim:

> a ragged child
> With wasted cheeks and ringlets wild,
> A shape of fear and misery,
> Raised up her helpless hands to me
> And begged her father's face to see.

This child is only saved by her father disclosing, as he is dying, where he has hidden his gold. Then the victor, to placate his own conscience, adopts the orphan, but

> She was full of anguish wild
> And hated me like we hate hell
> And weary with her savage woe
> One moonless night I let her go.

On the whole, however, without A.G.A. and J.B., it seems the 'centre cannot hold', and only when the poems are outstanding as poems, rather than for the tale they tell, do they attract attention.

It is the whole atmosphere of Emily's poetry – not just the themes, the characters or the situations she deals with, but the related sounds of the words, the rhythms behind them, as well as the kinds of words themselves – that is redolent of *Wuthering Heights*. In both poetry and novel (in the words of Charlotte about Emily's character), 'the extremes of vigour and simplicity seemed to meet'. If one adds to that the kind of delicate, often muted, music, that makes so much of her poetry memorable and fills the last paragraph of *Wuthering Heights* – 'I lingered round them, under that benign sky; watched the moths fluttering among the heath and harebells, listened to the soft wind breathing through the grass, and wondered how any one could ever imagine unquiet slumbers for the sleepers in that quiet earth' – then there can hardly be any doubt that the writer of each is one and the same person.

Glossary to Gondal
A glossary of the main references

A.A.A. Boy, doomed to misery.

A.E. A child of sorrow, linked with R.C., a child of joy.

A.G.A. *See* Alme(i)da, Augusta Geraldine.

A.H. Laments for his mother.

A.W. Z. Zerona's beloved; in prison because of her, which he endures for her sake.

Abrantez, Isabella. Opposite John Mertleheath and Alexander. (Ae.'s list.)

Aeron. Hall and forest connected with Fernando de Samara and Alcona.

Alcona. Dying, age 24, while waiting for someone who may never return.

Alcona, R. *See* Rosina.

Alexander, Lord. Of Elbe, from the soft southern parkland of Eden; dies in A.G.A.'s arms in exile on the shore of Lake Elnor.

Alexander. (Same as above?) Boy of 14 who arranges to meet Zenobia, age 13, in Araby in two years' time, by the little spring in Exina's woods; Zenobia keeps her promise, waiting until he arrives; in April 1826 Alexander is in a dungeon in the Southern Palace of Instruction pining for one who no longer cares for him, his spirit flying off to meet his Maria in snow-covered glades.

Alexander. Opposite Isabella Abrantez. (Ae.'s list.)

Alexander, D. (Ae.'s list.)

Alexandria. Kingdom of Gaaldine.

Alexandria. Child left on the snowy mountainside, unblessed, unbefriended.

Alfred. *See* Sidonia.

Alme(i)da, Augusta Geraldine. E.'s heroine, brought up with Angelica; watches from a dungeon of the Palace of Instruction the snow falling; in love with Alexander Lord Elbe, Alfred Sidonia, and Fernando de Samara who kills himself for her love; steals Angelica's lover Amadeus from her, then rejects him; is finally killed on Elmor's hillside by Angelica and Douglas; is found by Lord Eldred, who also seems to love her; has coal-black hair, a kind of wild savage beauty, ruthless, determined to get her own way, cost what it may.

Almedore. Kingdom in Gaaldine.

Almedore. Name given to King Julius Brenzaida.

Alzerno, Cornelia. Escaping Royalist; opposite Henry Sophona. (Ae.'s list.)

Alzerno, Flora. Opposite Eustace. (Ae.'s list.)

Alzerno's Hall. Where Lady Eliza of Alzerno awaits her lord; A.Z. (Zenobia?) tells her he must be dead – for only A.Z. knows he died with his head on her knees, his dark eyes on her.

Amadeus. Beloved by Angelica, seduced by A.G.A.; sent into exile with Angelica; he and she commit a murder together; although dead, he is not forgotten by Angelica.

Angelica. Brought up with A.G.A.; loves Amadeus; sent into exile with him; both commit a murder; she and Douglas kill A.G.A.

Angora. Kingdom of Gondal – snowy; Julius Brenzaida's country, where his crimson flags fly.

Angora, Henry. One of the escaping Royalists E. and Ae. 'play' at.

Angora, Julius. Has a great victory, with his crimson standards flying over Exina's green ones; known also as Almedore.

Angora, Lucia. Opposite Gerald. (Ae.'s list.)

Araby. Where Alexander and Zenobia meet and part.

Arthur (Exina?). Brother of R. Gleneden, who by his death purchased peace.

Aspin Castle. On the shores of Aspin Lake, and near Beckden's/Rockden's woods; Alfred Sidonia's home.

At – Julia. (Ae.'s list; crossed out.)

Augusta. *See* Alme(i)da.

Augusteena, Catharina T.G. (Ae.'s list.)

Augusteena, Juliet. One of the escaping Royalists whom E. and Ae. 'play' at.

Blanche. Singer of lullaby to A.A., a dark-haired baby; they cross the lake of Elderno together; once favoured in courts, becomes like a gipsy, forgotten through no fault of her own.

Brenzaida, Julius. Conquered Almedore in Gaaldine, with the fall of Zalona, when Exina was defeated; at the height of victory, while in the act of being crowned or making a false pact with Gerald of Exina, is murdered in a marble hall; buried in Angora; has two loves – Rosina who mourns at his grave 15 years after his death, and Geraldine, who scorns him, but bears his child, with his eyes; is put into a dungeon in the Southern College for Rosina's sake in 1825.

Campbell, Una. Opposite Gerald Exina. (Ae.'s list.)

Caverndel, Hespera. Remembers the warm home where warm hands and hearts banished her despair.

Claudia. Exiled, but her spirit goes to her own country; her Monarch is dead, but he lives for ever in her heart.

Clifford, Halbert. Opposite Eliza Hybernia. (Ae.'s list.)

College. Two – the Southern and the Northern, both having dungeons, as well as being places of instruction (cf. Glasstown – Philosophers' Isle).

D.G.C. Urges J.A. that they should love while they can, later they will destroy each other because of their fathers' wars.

Desmond. Place where R. Gleneden mourns for Arthur's death.

Douglas. Escapes from those who hunt him after he has killed their sovereign; topples a tree on top of them.

Douglas, Helen. Opposite Gerald F. (Ae.'s list.)

Douglas, M. Admits to E.R. Gleneden that he/she will be known publicly as a traitor and perjuror.

E.G. *See* Gleneden, E.G.

E.W. One of few who laments A.G.A. long after she is dead.

Eagle, Harriet. (Ae.'s list.)

Eden. A golden, fair, blue-skied place.

Edmund. Companion of R. Gleneden.

Egremont, Eliza and Julian. Escaping Royalists whom E. and Ae. 'play' at.

Elbe Hall. Remembered by the dying Lord of Elbe; later in ruins.

Elbe Hill and Lake. Near Lord Elbe's home.

Elderno, Lake. Lake which Blanche and A.A. cross; where Fernando de Samara and A.G.A. meet and he sings for her.

Eldred, Lord. He and his men find A.G.A. after she has been murdered.

Eliza. The Lady of Alzerno Hall, whose lover Alexandrina Zenobia steals.
Elm(n?)or Hill. Where A.G.A dies.
Elnor, Lake. Where Lord Elbe murdered.
Elseraden. Kingdom in Gaaldine.
Esmaldan, Rosabella. One of the escaping Royalists, whom E. and Ae. 'play' at.
Eustace. Opposite Flora Alzerno. (Ae.'s list.)
Exina. Kingdom in Gondal; has green standards.
Exina, Arthur. Opposite Alexandrina Zenobia Hybernia (Ae.'s list.); Marcius
    cannot sleep because Arthur is in the dungeons.
Exina, Gerald. Opposite Una Campbell (Ae.'s list); formerly opposite Isabella
    Senland, but crossed out; as Gerald – a Gondal monarch; makes a pact with King
    Julius; his subjects rebel against their overlords, gaining their freedom, though it
    means for him merely a few years of captivity and then death.

Fernando. *See* Samara, Fernando de.
First Wars. E. writing about them. Diary, 1845.
Fitzaphnold, Cordelia. One of the escaping Royalists Ae. and E. 'play' at.
Fitzher (Fitzhorch?). Opposite Eustace Sophona. (Ae.'s list.)
Flora (?Alzerno). Child of Florian; 'dared the main' a second time, as did two
    years before, going to Ula.
Florian. Beloved by Alexandrina Zenobia; has a child, Flora.

Gaaldine. Large island in the South Pacific, divided into six kingdoms –
    Alexand(r)ia, Almedore, Elseraden, Ula, Zelona, Zedora; 12 July 1837, the
    Emperors and Empresses depart from there to go to Gondal for a coronation;
    has prison caves where Fernando de Samara incarcerated, and from where he
    writes to A.G.A.
Gaul. When returning from Gaul the Unique Society is wrecked on a desert
    island.
Geralda, Lady. Her father and her mother dead; her brother far away; determines
    to leave her home in the mountains to search for happiness.
Geraldine S. Julius Brenzaida in love with her, writes songs to her, waits for her
    by moonlight on the moors, but, at the command of others, she breaks her
    vows to him; he determines to forget her, returning to those who love him
    truly; has raven black eyes and brows and lips of 'rosy charm'; is seen later in a
    lonely cave, talking to her baby who has Brenzaida's eyes.
Gleneden. A captive in prison, dreams of killing the tyrant who has taken
    Gondal's liberty; waking he wonders how long he has been asleep and if it was
    really a dream.
Gleneden, E. Asks his lover Mary R. to keep her tryst with him now her
    guardians are asleep.
Gleneden, E.R. m. Douglas; addresses her thoughts to him, before she commits
    her act of treachery.
Gleneden, R. Through his brother Arthur's death, he and others were able to
    return to Desmond; in another poem (possibly concerning R. Gleneden) he tells
    of his homecoming to Zedora and Ula, with Mary and Flora who remember
    being taken captive years before.
Gobelrin. Glen where Douglas drops a tree on his pursuers.
Goldsmith. The writer of the *Grammar of General Geography* where Ae. inserted

the following list of places – Alexandria, Almedore, Elseraden, kingdoms in Gaaldine; Gaaldine, a large island in the S. Pacific; Gondal, a large island in the N. Pacific; Regina, the capital of Gondal; Ula, Zalona, kingdoms in Gaaldine governed by four sovereigns; Zedora, a large province in Gaaldine governed by a Viceroy.

Gondal. Remote island in the North Pacific, with at least four kingdoms – Gondal, Angora, Alcona, Exina – the capital Regina; in 1837 the Emperors and Empresses of Gondal and Gaaldine are preparing to leave Gaaldine for Gondal for a coronation on 12 July; in 1841 the Gondalians are in a threatening state, with all the princes and princesses of the Royalty at the Palace of Instruction; in 1845 the Gondal Chronicles, begun three and a half years before, still not completed. It is often the contrast between the spare wild moorland Gondal and the softer warmer blue-skied Gaaldine, that brings out the best qualities in E.'s poetry – its uncluttered freedom and a haunting directness.

Gondal Chronicles. Begun *c*. January 1842, still not completed by July 1845.

Greecia. A 'classic plain' where Alexander and Zenobia meet.

H.A. His hair dark, where his father's had been fair; his meeting with A.S. (whose hair is fair, whereas her mother's was black) reminds the speaker of the poem of the past when a 'fair' man dies and is mourned by a 'black haired' woman (A.G.A. and Alfred Sidonia?).

H.G. Is incarcerated in a dungeon, having been saved from 'deadlier thrall'.

Hybernia, Alexander. Tired of his book work, so sends his spirit to waken Maria, his beloved, to walk across the snow with him.

Hybernia, Alexandria Zenobia. (Ae.'s list.)

Hybernia, Edward. Opposite Xirilla Senland. (Ae.'s list.)

Hybernia, Eliza. Opposite Halbert Clifford. (Ae.'s list.)

I.M. Ierne's father.

Ierne G. Her father, remembering the dead whom he has loved, is assured by Ierne his daughter that he and the dead will re-meet in heaven, that they are better off there; at some time is in prison.

J.A. D.G.C. urges her/him to love now, because later they will be foes, one Royalist, the other Republican.

Julian, M. Julian visits A.G. Rochelle in her dungeon, growing to love and pity her.

Julius. The Emperor; E. writing his life in 1845. (*See* Brenzaida.)

Lesley, Lord. Dies with Surry, whom he loves, when A.G.A. is murdered.

Lesley, Roderic. (Same as above?) Dies fighting for his monarch.

M.A. Writes on the Northern College dungeon wall that he would suffer and weep rather than those younger than him should.

M.A.A. (Same as above?) Laments his life is spent in gloom.

M.G. Writes, for the Unique Society, a poem asking who would want to be in Gondal with its snow and gloom if he has known the sweetness of Ula and Eden; yet for those sailing away from the southern ports even the snowflakes of Gondal will be welcome.

M.R. *See* Mary.

Macalgin, Ronald. One of the escaping Royalists that E. and Ae. 'play' at.

MacRay, Archibald. Opposite Isidora Montara. (Ae.'s list.)

Marcius. A fragment written by Arthur Ex(ina?) to Marcius. (*See also* Exina, Arthur.)

Mary. She and Flora are about to brave crossing the main for a second time, this time returning home, not going into captivity; possibly the Mary (R.?), beloved by E. Gleneden, who waits for her to keep her tryst when her Guardians are asleep.

Mertleheath, John. Opposite Lucia MacElgin (erased); opposite Angora (erased); finally opposite Isabella Abrantez. (Ae.'s list.)

Monkey's Isle. Northangerland there in June 1837.

Montara, Isidora. Opposite Archibald MacRay. (Ae.'s list.)

Navarre, Catherine. One of the escaping Royalists E. and Ae. 'play' at.

Northangerland. In Monkey's Isle in 1837.

Northern College. *See* Colleges.

Orlando. In prison and then freed by his friends, his foes all dead.

Palace of Instruction. Has dungeons where the prisoners write poems on the walls.

R.C. And A.E. – one a melancholy unsmiling boy, the other a child of delight who, taking pity on the mournful boy, becomes his 'Guardian angel'.

Regina. The towered capital of Gondal; at some time, is overthrown.

Rochelle, A.G. A fair-haired girl; Julian M.'s playmate; her parents dead; is put in prison and tended by Julian; describes to him her 'visions' – when the 'invisible dawns', her 'outward sense' goes and her 'inward essence feels', and how she suffers appalling 'agony' when, afterwards, the 'ear begins to hear' and the 'eye begins to see', and her soul is once more aware of the 'chains' of the flesh.

Rockden. Where the trees wave near Aspin Castle.

Rosina. The cause of J.B. (Brenzaida?) being in prison; has haughty ways and falcon's eyes; a despot queen and ambitious; unable to accompany J.B. when he leaves for battle, as she is suffering from the wild deliriums of fever; her reason restored, learns that J.B. has lost the battle, been treacherously murdered in the palace, and is now buried in the lonely northern mountains; speaks the fine lament over his grave – 'Cold in the earth – and the deep snow piled above thee'.

Sabia, Marina. Is in a dungeon, weeping for her little boy; dreaming of him and his father.

St Albert, Adolphus. (Ae.'s list.)

Samara, Fernando de. Parts from his beloved, in a glade in Aeron, to cross the sea; in the Gaaldine Caves prison bemoans the treachery and cruelty of her who has left him there to torture and despair; wishes that the hell he is experiencing should wring her spirit too; finally kills himself to escape despair and to win forgetfulness, affirming that although his 'pangs' are passed, 'Hers' are yet to come (cf. Heathcliff).

Senland, Isabella. Opposite Gerald Exina, erased. (Ae.'s list.)
Senland, Xirilla. Opposite Edward Hybernia. (Ae.'s list.)
Sidonia, Lord Alfred. Of Aspin Castle; seems to have left his ancestral home and family (a fair-haired daughter) for love of A.G.A. – he is A.G.A.'s 'golden June', with his blue eyes and fair hair; perhaps father to A.S. and G.S., whose mother's place A.G.A. took. The dark/fair pattern is used in *W.H.*
Sophona, Eustace. Of Exina; opposite Rosalind Fitzher(?). (Ae.'s list.)
Sophona, Henry. Of Exina; opposite Cornelia Alzerno. (Ae.'s list.)
Southern College. *See* Colleges.
Standards. Exina's are sea-green; Brenzaida's crimson.
Surry. Dies with Lord Lesley, when A.G.A. is murdered.

Tyndarum. A town which is besieged and conquered.

U.S. The Unique Society, shipwrecked on a desert island returning from Gaul.
Ula. Kingdom in Gaaldine.
Unique Society. *See* U.S.

Vernon, Albert. Erased in one list, opposite Emily Vernon in the other. (Ae.'s lists.)
Vernon, Emily. Opposite Albert Vernon (erased). (Ae.'s list.)
Vernon, Olivia. Likes playing simple airs; keeps her feelings to herself.
Vernon, Solala. In 1841 Ae. is writing the 4th vol. of her life. (*See also* Glossary to Glasstown.)

Werna. Lake.

Z. Remembers his boyhood, with a younger boy as friend; they become foes and Z. slays him for his country's good.
Za(e)lona. Capital of a kingdom in Gaaldine, with white steeples, besieged and taken.
Zamorna. In 1837, is at Eversham (sic).
Zedora. Gaaldine coastal kingdom, governed by a Viceroy, where possibly Brenzaida and Geraldine were lovers.
Zelona. *See* Zalona.
Zenobia. A fair young girl, age 13, makes a promise to meet Alexander again in Exina; nearly given him up as lost when, on her 15th birthday, he arrives.
Zenobia, Alexandrina. Is in a dungeon, where the North wind brings her news of the land of her birth; dreams of (?)Alexander, whom she longs to hold in her arms; is either herself the Lady of Alzerno who waits for her Lord's return or has stolen the love of that Lord from the Lady of Alzerno; has a child, Flora, with blue eyes, whose father no longer loves her, has forgotten her, though she will always remember him.
Zerona Z. He/she will not break his/her vow despite a mother's reproachful eye and a father's scowl.

III The Published Works

Poems 1846

The first published work of the Brontë sisters appeared in 1846, and was a slim volume of their poetry printed under the pseudonyms of Currer (Charlotte), Ellis (Emily) and Acton (Anne) Bell.

Its appearance seems to have been encouraged by Charlotte's discovery, which may or may not have been accidental, of a manuscript of Emily's poems – much to Emily's angry dismay – which prompted Charlotte to write to a London publisher. Whether she did this because she recognized the quality of Emily's poems or whether the publishing bug had infected her, is not known – it is unlikely that Emily and Anne were keen on publication. There is no doubt that Charlotte took the lead and wrote, under the name Currer Bell, to Aylott and Jones on 28 January 1846 asking if they would publish a collection of poems in one volume, and saying that if they did not want to publish at their own risk perhaps they would undertake it on the authors' account.

They replied by return of post that they would print at the authors' expense and Charlotte accepted the offer immediately. She wrote to them a number of times in the next few weeks with details of what she required – upon which matter she was very clear. She originally estimated for a volume of 200 to 250 pages, but by 16 February 1846 she had told Aylott and Jones that the manuscript would be thinner than she had expected. In fact it was a good deal thinner, and this raises the question of whether Charlotte's original estimate was simply faulty (though this would have been somewhat uncharacteristic) or whether Emily or Anne or both had put their feet down and excised a number of poems which Charlotte had originally scheduled for publication – this seems a more likely explanation.

There were nineteen poems by Currer and twenty-one each by Ellis and Acton, Charlotte having fewer poems, but most of hers are longer than any of her sisters'. There were, eventually, 165 pages of text. The sisters used the middle name of Patrick Brontë's new curate, Arthur Bell Nicholls, for the pseudonymic surname.

It was not a particularly well-executed piece of publishing, being on poor paper and containing an errata slip. Charlotte advanced £31.10s.0d. to the publisher on 3 March 1846. This went towards a final sum of at least £36. The printing cost £23.15s.9d., the paper £12.2s.6d., and the initial advertising £2. The money apparently came from a legacy of Aunt Elizabeth Branwell who had died in 1842.

Charlotte posted the manuscript on 6 February, and proof-sheets became available in the second week of March. Review copies were sent to eleven periodicals and three newspapers, and the book was on sale by the end of May at 4s. (Charlotte had wanted the price to be 5s.). One thousand copies were printed and on 7 September 1848 the publishers Smith, Elder and Co. purchased the remaining stock (a sad 961 unsold, unbound copies). The *Athenaeum* and *Critic* both gave favourable reviews, and Charlotte eventually received £24.0s.0d. against her initial outlay.

More often than not the first published works of writers who eventually rise to the top give some kind of clue to the eminence that is to come later. In the case of the Brontës they chose (or, more probably, Charlotte chose) to publish their first work as a threesome. But neither in a corporate nor an individual sense does it give much inkling of the quality that was to be achieved in their following works.

The volume contains much that is boring, undistinguished, derivative and unattractive. Occasional individual contributions mitigate this general judgement to an extent, but do not fundamentally change it – this first Brontë volume does not augur well. Emily's contributions have flashes of imaginative lightning as words and thoughts fuse; in Anne's there is a cool and lyrical reflectiveness; but Charlotte's work is unrelentingly bad and an ironic proof that her only poetry can be found in the prose of her novels.

Sir Walter Scott, the most popular poet, Lord Byron, the most popular Romantic poet, the ballad metre, the most popular poetic form, and the Gothic poem and story, both great stirrers of the senses, were the progenitors of the Brontës' poetry. There is virtually nothing to suggest that they read much of the chief products of the best-known Romantic and late-Romantic poets except Byron. The influences on them were few and suggestive of reading dominated by *Blackwood's* and the more readily available and acceptable contemporary periodicals in the Keighley Mechanics' Institute.

The poetry is, therefore, very limited in technical scope and, amazingly, the Brontës give no evidence of having deeply considered poetry, except as a convenient and emotive outlet for heartfelt notions and feelings. That wrestling with form, technique and the resources of language which is always characteristic of the natural poet to whom the writing of poetry is an absolute necessity, is nowhere apparent in Charlotte's verse. In her letters there is not one word to suggest that she had ever thought of poetry as more than an acceptable way of expressing 'elevated' notions emotionally though, ironically, she took a very serious view of it, and sent her poems to Southey, the Poet Laureate, for his comments. He was kind and succinct – 'write poetry for its own sake; not in a spirit of emulation', were his most telling words.

For Emily and Anne the writing of poetry seems to have been much closer to being a necessary act than for Charlotte. At times Emily seems to have found it the only way of communicating with or attempting to body forth 'a world elsewhere'. And for all the limited technical resources at her disposal the intensity of her need to remain in touch with that world makes her artlessness into a virtue.

Anne wrote poetry at first perhaps because her brother and her sisters did. Left to herself she might not have written anything, but played an instrument, and played it well and been satisfied. But she seems to have been, at first, a willing literary familiar to her sisters and produced an innocent, precise and often sweetly lyrical body of utterly minor, charming verse.

Charlotte's subject matter seems to be labouredly 'chosen' rather than inevitably 'achieved'. 'Pilate's Wife's Dream', is the title of one of her poems, and it does nothing to disabuse the reader of the opinion that it merely occurred to Charlotte rather than enforced itself upon her. Again 'Mementoes' brings to mind those set subjects for school poetry competitions and it lives up to nothing else but this description of it. 'The Wife's Will' is a typical melodramatic/sentimental Victorian ballad/morality, utterly bereft of conviction:

> 'Tis thy own hearth thou sitt'st beside,
> After long absence – wandering wide;
> 'Tis thy own wife reads in thine eyes,
> A promise clear of stormless skies,
> For faith and true love light the rays,
> Which shine responsive to her gaze.

'The Wood' is an awkward, set-piece narrative into which sententious moralizing has been laboriously placed:

> Refreshed, erelong, with rustic fare,
> We'll seek a couch of dreamless ease;
> Courage will guard thy heart from fear,
> And love give mine divinest peace.

The Victorian version of the ballad figures large in Charlotte's contributions, a conspicuous number of which make great play with Christian names used with trembling emotiveness – like 'Frances' and 'Gilbert' – very reminiscent of the later minor followers of Wordsworth and Browning. She seems incapable of rising above what, to us, would seem the cheap Christmas or birthday card level of versifying. She is much given to gross sentimentality and sententiousness. 'Life' begins:

Life, believe, is not a dream
So dark as sages say;
Oft a little morning rain
Foretells a pleasant day.

Sometimes there are clouds of gloom,
But these are transient all;
If the shower will make the roses bloom,
O why lament its fall?

The poem printed next to it is Ellis's 'Hope'. It is not by any means one of Emily's best, but by comparison with Charlotte's contrived sentiment it has a sense of emotional integrity and inevitability:

False she was, and unrelenting;
When my last joys strewed the ground,
Even Sorrow saw, repenting,
Those sad relics scattered round;

Hope, whose whisper would have given
Balm to all my frenzied pain,
Stretched her wings, and soared to heaven,
Went, and ne'er returned again.

It is an expense of spirit to devote much time to Charlotte's versifying: it inexorably signals its own deficiencies, and no more certainly than in its clichés – 'deepening glow', 'youthful brow', 'crystals bright', 'deep blue sky', 'light footsteps', 'clustering flowers', 'absorbing task', 'serious light', 'unfinished line', 'tearful gleam', 'clouded mass', 'faintly trace': all these occur in the space of six stanzas in one of her poems. The cliché is the last refuge of the writer who is in the throes of manufacture, not creation; and it is with clichés, not original images, that Charlotte assembles her verses. But, to be fair to Charlotte, she never considered her poetry to be of anything like the quality of Emily's, and described it with some accuracy as 'crude and rhapsodical'.

The most immediately realized difference in quality between Emily's and Charlotte's work is that which distinguishes a profitless prolixity from a telling economy. Emily's lines are what is left after excrescences have been removed – and, importantly, one has the impression that the operation is very much under conscious control. The verse is, at its best, pared clean of sentimentality, and seems charged with the kind of nervous strength you associate with lean athleticism.

Even when she is not writing at her best Emily manages to convey a sense of a reticent, almost parsimonious force:

> And, in the red fire's cheerful glow,
> I think of deep glens, blocked with snow;
> I dream of moor, and misty hill,
> Where evening closes dark and chill;
> For, lone, among the mountains cold,
> Lie those that I have loved of old.
> And my heart aches, in hopeless pain
> Exhausted with repinings vain,
> That I shall greet them ne'er again.

It may be protested that, like Charlotte, Emily was well acquainted with cliché and it is true that in this first volume there is plenty of evidence to support this. But, as the stanza above surely confirms (without attaining a particularly high altitude of competence) Emily's terseness has the effect of overriding the banalities of the clichés, so that they become part of an acceptable whole rather than isolated, unrelated embarrassments.

And when Emily, as she so often does, moves only an unexpected step away from cliché – for she is rarely adventurous in her verbal encounters – and combines her well-developed sense of sound with the images of her bleakly piercing eyes, she takes the reader into an entirely higher order of poetic creativity than Charlotte was ever able to reach:

> Cold in the earth – and the deep snow piled above thee,
> Far, far removed, cold in the dreary grave!
>
> . . .
>
> Cold in the earth – and fifteen wild Decembers,
> From those brown hills, have melted into spring.

And she is capable of effects that require a verbal subtlety and originality completely beyond Charlotte's range:

> The birds that now so blithely sing,
> Through deserts, frozen dry,
> Poor spectres of the perished spring,
> In famished troops, will fly.
>
> I was at peace, and drank your beams
> As they were life to me;
> And revelled in my changeful dreams,
> Like petrel on the sea.

The choice of 'petrel', alone, transmutes what would have been ordinary felicitous versifying into inevitable-seeming poetry.

Emily's sensitivity to the sound-values of words has been generally underestimated. Her ability to create vowel-music prompts the rather obvious recollection that she was regarded as the most musical of the family, and an accomplished piano-player. Perhaps such cross-fertilization is possible, but yea or nay, Emily's ears heard behind and beyond mere noise:

> Leaves, upon Time's branch, were growing brightly,
> Full of sap, and full of silver dew;
> Birds beneath its shelter gathered nightly;
> Daily round its flowers the wild bees flew.
>
> . . .
>
> And, behold! with tenfold increase blessing,
> Spring adorned the beauty-burdened spray;
> Wind and rain and fervent heat, caressing,
> Lavished glory on that second May!

Her sureness with sound sometimes deserts her with rhythm. Emily seems uncertain at times in initiating and maintaining a rhythmic structure in a poem: she falls back on conventional ballad metres derived probably from Scott and, like Charlotte, even falters with a fair copy in front of her!

But just as she was able to override cliché so Emily is often able to triumph over her uneasy grasp of metrics and rhythm, and a rough lyrical justice is achieved:

> How beautiful the earth is still,
> To thee – how full of happiness!
> How little fraught with real ill,
> Or unreal phantoms of distress!
> How spring can bring thee glory, yet,
> And summer win thee to forget
> December's sullen time!
> Why dost thou hold the treasure fast,
> Of youth's delight, when youth is past,
> And thou art near thy prime?

She achieves it because she allows passion access and to hell with the rules, while Charlotte is always on the look-out to control it, cool it, channel it. Emily gives immediate credence to the truth of her feelings, Charlotte is always subjecting them to the scrutiny and manipulation of her moral beliefs. They both have passion – but the one allows it house-room, the other requires it to wipe its feet before entering.

The content of Emily's poetry is discussed elsewhere, but what she communicates, be it personal or Gondal, private reflection or a more nearly public comment, always exhibits one characteristic which further distinguishes it from Anne's and Charlotte's. It is a poetry which gives the most potent sense of being spoken urgently and specially to you, to me, the reader. Reading it you have a strong impression of a voice and, moreover, of a presence standing near to you, at your side:

> And though I've said that conscience lies,
> And Time should Fate condemn;
> Still, sad Repentance clouds my eyes,
> And makes me yield to them.

> Then art thou glad to seek repose?
> Art glad to leave the sea,
> And anchor all thy weary woes
> In calm Eternity.

Whatever impression Emily as a person may have given of wishing to avoid company, her poetry seeks out a listener. It does not buttonhole or cajole, it simply demands attention because it seems so intent on speaking a truth. More often than not it succeeds, with unexpected felicity.

But it is not unexpected felicity alone that arrests your attention. Quite apart from the poems that sing you into close listening or the ballads that seem to carry the urgent voice of a narrator at your elbow, Emily's work is suffused with a dramatic quality.

The word 'dramatic' is slippery in definition but its implications for Emily's poetry are clear. First, her poetry earns the description because it is 'active'. For all its rhetoric and rhapsody Charlotte's verse is curiously lumbering, constantly near a kind of stasis; Anne's, though it flows with natural ease, does not have those surprising stops and starts and jerks, Emily's counterpointing of short staccato phrases with longer verbal episodes, which produces a constant impression of movement. Secondly, for all Charlotte's use of Christian names and her ballad-like preoccupation with human activities, and for all Anne's concern with the simplicities of the human heart, you do not get the sense, as you do in Emily, of dramatic (that is unexpected, tense, sometimes nervous) confrontations either between human beings or opposing points of view or even contrary areas of feeling.

In short, Emily's poetry is vivified by a verbal and human structure which never ceases to give the impression of movement from point to point, and hence, an impression of a restless search. Through her poetry Emily sought herself and her destination, and part of its drama is that death forced her to call off the search.

One of Anne's best poems is 'A Reminiscence', which begins:

> Yes, thou art gone! and never more
> Thy sunny smile shall gladden me;
> But I may pass the old church door,
> And pace the floor that covers thee,

May stand upon that cold, damp stone,
And think that, frozen, lies below
The lightest heart that I have known,
The kindest I shall ever know.

It has something of Emily's skill with vowel-music, something of her economy and of her ability to isolate a word (in this case 'frozen') to give it maximum power. But Emily rarely had its sweetly flowing ease, nor its curious 'innocence'.

Anne's poetry is an image of herself or, at least, what we know of her – with a dignified simplicity of its own. It is prevented from being naive and banal by putting its sentiments under very tight control – Anne's poems do not slop over the side of the basin as do Charlotte's. Neither is it given to the sudden, unexpected, and therefore dramatic image, like Emily's. It has no vices whatsoever, and all its virtues are those of an imagination that never tries to do more than it is capable of, never seems to be emulating the great and well known, never attempting to do more than set down what it is true and meet to set down.

Her moods do not have a great range; her passion, if she possessed it, does not enter her poetry as it does Emily's and, unlike Charlotte, she has no time for rhetorical or Gothic flourish. Her skills were best suited to the precise but limited demands made by hymns (*see* Family Portraits, Anne Brontë) which call for precision rather than subtlety of metre, plain rather than sophisticated statement of theme, and outright melody rather than delicate cadence. All Anne's best poems tend to the condition of hymns:

Oh, weep not, love! each tear that springs
In those dear eyes of thine,
To me a keener suffering brings,
Than if they flowed from mine.

And do not droop! however drear
The fate awaiting thee;
For *my* sake combat pain and care,
And cherish life for me.

It is Emily's and Anne's poems that make the volume readable. There is a certain irony in that it was their unpoetic sister who initiated its publication.

Charlotte Brontë

Jane Eyre (1847)

Commentary

Jane Eyre is a great novel which appeals to several levels of comprehension and appreciation. Its greatest attraction is its superb narrative which, while it does not have the complicated time-scales that overlap and enrich the story of *Wuthering Heights*, is full of unexpected incident and character, and of drama, pathos and passion. The narrative runs the gamut of emotional experience for the reader and compounds it with mystery, with the possibility and actuality of violence, and with the tenderness of love.

Moreover, the characters of *Jane Eyre* are not created in one single mode. Some are naturalistic, some are fantastic, even bizarre. And because of this mixture the novel seems, particularly to the undemanding reader, typically 'romantic'. On the one hand are the larger-than-life attributes of Rochester, and St John Rivers, on the other, the steady ordinariness of the Rivers sisters.

This mixing of natural and non-natural is not confined to the major characters. Other characters and situations, like Mr Brocklehurst and Lowood School partake of both – the school seems at one and the same time part of a grotesque nightmare and yet, doubtless for many of Charlotte's original readers, only too true; Brocklehurst, looming like some monster in a bad dream, must have activated the memories of some of those same readers and recalled a forgotten and unlamented tyrant of their own schooldays.

What we call 'romantic' in fiction always depends, to some extent, on a tension, an imbalance, between what 'is' and what 'seems'. Romantic fiction depends for its effects on the difference between what the reader recognizes as 'real' and what his imagination accepts as fiction. The first induces a necessary sense of actuality, the second encourages a desire to escape from the ordinary beaten ways of existence. This duality is embodied and exploited by the countless purveyors of popular romance. *Jane Eyre* employs the mode in a number of ways and helped to create what became, in a much debased form, the romantic-novel industry. But the story of Jane is an archetypal 'romantic' novel, for it is not only dominated by the subject of love but of love beset to the end by near-impossible obstacles. The very meaning of love is hedged around by one vicissitude after another.

For the majority of readers, *Jane Eyre*'s major 'romantic' appeal lay and still lies in its heroine, who is placed in a succession of situations which bare her vulnerability – physical, mental, spiritual, emotional and moral – and in its hero. Rochester is physically powerful, magnetic in personality, capable of a wide range of responses to his environment and those who inhabit it. He can, in turn, display a firmness of will which seems only a short step away from cruelty, and a tenderness which at times veers towards sentimentality.

Rochester and Jane are swept along by, and only partly able to withstand, a current of happenings which seems, for the greater part of the story, to be taking them further and further away from one another. For the greater part, too, it is Jane who suffers most. She is a victim of the traditional 'romantic' glosses on the story of love confounded – deprivation of physical security with little likelihood of a happy ending; powerful opposition from 'the other woman' to the success of the heroine's quest for love, with apparently all the advantages (particularly in beauty and wealth) being on the opposition's side; a brooding suspicion that the hero may be guilty of duplicity. This is coupled with what seems to be an intention to possess the vulnerable girl without benefit of clergy! The presence of these characteristics in *Jane Eyre* prompted the shocked outrage of some of its first critics and many of its original readers.

The miasma of vulnerability and deprivation which envelops the heroine is matched by an atmosphere which the hero seems to transport with him wherever he goes. It has two murky constituents. The first is a dark past which threatens to engulf the present and render even more difficult the hero and heroine's desire to declare their love. The second is the supernatural or the apparently supernatural. This is not a prerequisite of the modern popular romantic novel – it may be counted a bonus, perhaps – but it plays an important part in *Jane Eyre*. It comes to the forefront of the action from time to time to create a point of emphasis, as in the red-room episode and on the various occasions on which the maniacal presence of Rochester's wife looms large: 'The night – its silence – its rest, was rent in twain by a savage, a sharp, a shrilly sound that ran from end to end of Thornfield Hall.'

Conventional romantic novels of love are essentially optimistic because they are expected to, and almost invariably do, conclude with the achievement of a much-frustrated union of hero and heroine. But they achieve the sunlight only after a prolonged sojourn in the darkness of despair, anger, danger even. The final happy outcome is the greater because of the encircling gloom out of which it has leapt. The ending of *Jane Eyre* is, to a superficial eye, 'happy', but in fact constitutes one of a few exceptions to the generalization that it is an archetypal romantic novel. Jane and Rochester are united, but despite this and the final hint of his physical restoration, it is the hulk of a man that she marries. The happiness they both experience is complex, because it is demonstrably mixed with its own opposite – quite unlike the simple QED of the conventional romantic novel.

Suffering, anger, deprivation, doubt, scepticism, and moral qualms and questions have (so *Jane Eyre* seems to be implying) made of their union a bond whose spiritual strength is at least as great as its physical and emotional power. The novel's concluding pages have a gravity which is precisely the quality that most contributes to ensuring the superiority of this novel over those conventional romantic versions its influence helped to spawn:

> I will keep the law given by God; sanctioned by man. . . Laws and principles are not for times when there is no temptation: they are for such moments as this, when body and soul rise in mutiny against their rigour; stringent are they; inviolate they shall be. . .

The diminutive governess, Jane, is the very centre of the novel. Arguably, her presence penetrates more comprehensively than does that of any of Charlotte's other heroines. So strong is it that some readers confidently assume that the novel is Charlotte's autobiography. Certainly, much that Jane experiences and, indeed, much in the way she reacts, she shares with Charlotte, but it is the autobiography not of Charlotte but of the first person narrator – Jane herself – and we should accept it as such. Indeed, pound for pound, so to say, there is as much imagined fiction in the novel as there is of recalled actuality: there is nothing that is known about Charlotte's life that would suggest, for example, that the St John Rivers episode is anything but a brilliantly conceived fiction.

Jane's adventures are, in themselves, as fascinating and exciting as could be desired by the most demanding reader. But she is not simply a character in the accepted sense (that is, she is not just an impersonation of life). Jane also 'stands for' or, to put it perhaps more formalistically than Charlotte would have liked, is 'symbolic' of certain points of view, visions even, and attitudes. Many of her stances or postures are really stands in prepared positions – that is, Jane is used by Charlotte to embody certain principles, notions, beliefs which she (Charlotte) wishes to exploit or explore – the status of governesses, for example:

> 'You should hear Mamma on the chapter of governesses. Mary and I have had, I should think, a dozen at least in our day; half of them

detestable and the rest ridiculous.' . . . 'My dearest, don't mention governesses; the word makes me nervous.'

Little exercise of the reader's imagination or intellect is required to see the young Jane as representative of, stand-in for, all children robbed of their birthright – not merely dispossessed of material possessions, but, in a way, more pertinently, of love and affection.

This kind of delegation happens in *Villette*, too, but it seems more formally conceived in *Jane Eyre*, perhaps because the Reeds, to whose mercy Jane has been left, are so obviously the enemies of, the dispossessors of, love and affection and, as it turns out, also of material birthright.

In the awful context of Lowood School Jane begins to find an unexpected amelioration, but this, in itself, has its source in two minor characters who themselves 'stand for' something. What they offer is not a simple physical amelioration (though that is involved) but a restorative from a deeper source. Miss Temple is the embodiment of Christian loving kindness, and Helen Burns of a complete faith in God's mercy. In Helen, particularly, there is something unearthly. She is almost explicitly presented as an 'agent' of another order or reality (God's reality) rather than as a naturalistic character. There is something saintly about her, and if, as is probable, she is to an extent based on Charlotte's sister, Maria, then Maria must have been a remarkable child.

Jane suffers, both in Lowood and at the hands of the Reeds, one vicissitude after another, but gradually she seems to reach a stage where there is at least a likelihood of physical amelioration of her state – God does not completely desert his children. The appointment as governess to Rochester's household and, later, the possibility (if only fugitive at first) of marriage to Rochester are evidence enough. But the world steps in again and the reader is presented with another, somewhat different, 'symbolic' Jane – and a more complicated one.

She comes now to stand for the Governess class, whose welfare occupied a significant part of Charlotte's mind and conscience. In *Shirley* and *Villette*, as well as in *Jane Eyre*, Charlotte's fierce championing of the governess sometimes assumes the aspect of a crusade. From being vulnerable child Jane has become exploited governess and Charlotte uses her for propaganda, though the propaganda is less direct than in *Shirley*, on behalf of a whole professional class.

But Jane's symbolic role does not end even with this. Her refusal to marry Rochester on his terms is based on moral principles and precepts which are embedded in her nature and which, however much pain they cause her, she cannot abandon. She becomes, in effect, a spokeswoman for God's law and a reluctant condemner of man's flouting of it. It would be wrong for Jane to marry or live illicitly with Rochester not merely because it violates man's edicts but because it flies in the face of God's own prohibition.

So Jane creates an atmosphere of anguished irony about herself. That very amelioration which she seeks and which is represented by Rochester's offer has to be rejected – and however right her decision it inexorably puts her back into the trap, into the position of vulnerability from which she seemed so near to escaping:

> I was experiencing an ordeal: a hand of fiery iron grasped my vitals: full of struggle, blackness, burning! Not a human being that ever lived could wish to be loved better than I was loved; and him who thus loved me I absolutely worshipped: and I must renounce love and idol.

The irony and the anguish are the more fierce and poignant because however much, at this stage in the novel, Jane seems to be presented in symbolic terms, Charlotte never forgets that she is also Jane Eyre, a young woman, a character with human passions and emotions. Jane suffers not only because she obeys God's law but also because she is a woman – and needs that which she feels she has to deny herself.

All her instincts cry out for her to accept Rochester, all her moral precepts answer No!, and she is forced to say, 'I will keep the law given by God, sanctioned by man.' It is almost as if God has now taken over from the world the task of testing Jane and is applying a more direct pressure.

Some critics and readers have complained (and many did at the time of the novel's appearance) about some of the sensational episodes of the novel – and the criticisms range from accusations of unhealthy emphasis (in the deathchamber of Mr Reed) to incredibility (the strained coincidence of Jane's fainting at the very door of her unknown relatives). But such episodes, while they certainly play their part in increasing the tension of the reader's nerves, must not be taken on this level alone.

In Mr Reed's 'red room' Jane stares into eternity – for the first time a child learns of death; her apparently fortuitous arrival at the Rivers's doorstep is a signal, as it were, that Jane is to be tested yet again, and at least as severely as in the matter of her love for Rochester.

> Not his ascendancy alone, however, held me in thrall at present – of late it had been easy enough for me to look sad: a cankering evil sat at my heart and drained my happiness at its source – the evil of suspense.

Rivers's proposal that she should accompany him as a 'working' wife in an 'arranged' marriage on missionary work in Africa sends her into near-despair. It is her utter reliance on God alone, her complete fidelity to his laws, that keeps her from insanity.

The fact that Rivers is a religious man of God does not prevent Jane from following through her decision to reject his proposal. He is pure-living, conscientious, zealous, but for her he lacks what she calls 'consolatory gentleness'. What Rivers in fact lacks is the capacity to love – in contrast with Rochester who lacks the moral strength to prevent his love from violating God's law. There is a kind of irony in the fact that Jane rejects the one because he has no love and the other because, in a sense, he has too much.

In both cases Jane's emotional being is placed under a huge strain, but in both cases it is not only her feelings that are involved. A further irony is introduced by Charlotte in her insistent reminder to us, through her heroine's words, that another element of Jane's being is equally heavily involved – her own highly developed conception of reason is at work. In the case of Rochester reason wins its battle with passion (much against Jane's feelings), and the encounter ends in the correct moral victory. In the case of St John Rivers reason (much to Jane's relief) loses the battle with passion, despite the fact that it would be 'rational' to accept what he offers – security, friendship, the Lord's work, a 'good' life – particularly in Jane's present dependent and vulnerable position. This time, it is passion, the active, urgent voice of love itself, that urges the only right course for Jane:

> The feeling was not like an electric shock, but it was quite as sharp, as strange, as startling: it acted on my senses as if their utmost activity hitherto had been but torpor, from which they were now summoned and forced to wake. They rose expectant: eye and ear waited while the flesh quivered on my bones.

The unarguable indication that it is misleading to interpret this novel only on a naturalistic level is plainly proven by the manner in which Jane's wavering state of mind and feelings about Rivers's proposal is resolved. It is expressed by Charlotte as being of a supernatural order:

> I sincerely, deeply, fervently longed to do what was right; and only that. 'Shew me – shew me the path!' I entreated of Heaven. I was excited more than I had ever been; and whether what followed was the effect of excitement, the reader shall judge.

She hears the voice of Rochester calling her, and she responds in a way that makes it clear that for Jane, at least, it is God that brings this voice to her:

> I seemed to penetrate very near a Mighty Spirit; and my soul rushed
> out in gratitude at His feet.

God's amelioration which, long ago, came through Helen Burns and
Miss Temple, seems once more to hand.

Some readers have regarded *Jane Eyre* as a religious novel because
it is the record of the fidelity of a young woman to the inexorable laws
of God as she sees them. Even more, in her adherence to duty, to order,
and her fidelity to what is expected of her it might be said that Jane
demonstrates Christian principles in practice.

This may be so, but it is very doubtful whether Charlotte
consciously wrote with any thought to 'religious' themes. There is no
sanctimonious piety about Jane although it must be admitted that, at
times, her self-abnegation, her capacity to put herself in the worst
possible light, her relentless moral probity, can irritate the reader. By
comparison with Lucy Snowe, however, Jane is intellectually and
emotionally permissive at times. She can be verbally artful, wily –
without in any way losing grace, or face or favour, but sufficiently to
cause the severe straightness of the lines of her character to soften and
flutter just a little. For all her symbolic status in the novel she remains a
young woman suffering the pangs and pleasures of being in love.

The love interest and the depth of moral and emotional penetration
of *Jane Eyre* are themselves sufficient to qualify it as a fine novel, but
what increases its status to greatness is the immensely rich context into
which the story of Jane is placed. She is not placed in isolation, any
more than is Cathy in *Wuthering Heights* – a whole world envelops her.

Charlotte, like Emily, was extremely sensitive to both natural and
man-created background. Her powers of observation were such that
her short-sightedness was no liability. Indeed her ears were sensitive
organs, very alert to the sounds of voices in particular. There is no
more sharply realized scene of a human gathering even in Jane Austen
than Charlotte's depiction of Rochester's party. The voices' every
nuance is caught:

> A joyous stir was now audible in the hall: gentlemen's deep tones and
> ladies [sic] silvery accents blent harmoniously together, and dis-
> tinguishable above all, though not loud, was the sonorous voice of
> the master of Thornfield Hall.

She catches mood from what she hears:

> Then light steps ascended the stairs; and there was a tripping through
> the gallery, and soft cheerful laughs, and opening and closing doors,
> and, for a time, a hush.

But it is what Charlotte sees, and, despite her affliction, sees so clearly - for her mind's eye constantly fed her misty physical eyes – which always tempts her satirical spirit. She will never allow the slightest frailty which comes from a flaw in character, to escape her. The Dowager Lady Ingram becomes a victim:

> Most people would have termed her a splendid woman of her age: and so she was, no doubt, physically speaking; but then there was an expression of almost insupportable haughtiness in her bearing and countenance. She had Roman features and a double chin, disappearing into a throat like a pillar: these features appeared to me not only inflated and darkened, but even furrowed with pride; and the chin was sustained by the same principle, in a position of almost preternatural erectness.

Indeed, Charlotte does not merely describe, rather one might say that she finds, first of all, the character-principle behind the appearance, and works from that.

This, too, is characteristic of her descriptions and evocations of natural landscape – she discovers the 'mood' or the 'principle' which lies behind a particular natural scene or landscape before she commits herself to describing it. But there is a difference: whereas it is men and women who create the moods and atmosphere of artificial settings, in the natural world it is nature alone which governs mankind's state of mind and feelings:

> I touched the heath: it was dry, and yet warm with the heat of the summer day. I looked at the sky; it was pure: a kindly star twinkled just above the chasm ridge. The dew fell, but with propitious softness; no breeze whispered. Nature seemed to me benign and good; I thought she loved me, outcast as I was. . . To-night, at least, I would be her guest, as I was her child. . .

Indeed, where Emily may be said to be a part of nature, so much did she identify herself with it, Charlotte was in a very real sense its child, content to be guided by it, pleased when it seemed pleased, depressed when it seemed angry. Charlotte is much more opulent than Emily in her descriptions of nature. While they lack the dramatic terseness of Emily's, they have an amazingly sensuous quality which itself surprises:

> And now vegetation matured with vigour; Lowood shook loose its tresses; it became all green, all flowers; its great elm, ash, and oak skeletons were restored to majestic life; woodland plants sprang up profusely in its recesses; unnumbered varieties of moss filled its hollows, and it made a strange ground-sunshine out of the wealth of its wild primrose plants: I have seen their pale gold gleam in overshadowed spots like scatterings of the sweetest lustre.'

A good deal of the best of Charlotte is in *Jane Eyre*. Her feelings about governesses are not obtrusive; her moral severity is tempered by her recognition of the validity of passion; her satirical and ironic spirit is under super control, and her feeling for words at its most sensitive; she never allows moral attitude and narrative to trip each other over; and the larger excesses of her imagination are disciplined in those parts of the novel in which the fantastic or quasi-supernatural appear.

Anne Brontë's prose style is nearer to seeming unified and 'worked on' than either Emily's or Charlotte's. It is neat and pointilliste, carefully tucked in at foot, head and sides to present a tidy symmetry to the world. Charlotte's style (or more to the point her styles) is, by comparison, a sprawl, tending always to the untidy. You can gather it up in the expectation that you have it all, only to find bits and pieces spilling out.

Charlotte's writing in *Jane Eyre* well supports the proposition that style reflects its creator, for, if there is one certainty about her personality, it is that the parts viewed coolly and separately never quite add up to a unified whole, and there are always unexpected aspects which are either left over or appear as if from nowhere.

Jane Austen, George Eliot, Virginia Woolf, Iris Murdoch are immediately recognizable by the specific individuality of their writing, but Charlotte is not. What immediately distinguishes Charlotte is not how she expresses herself, but what she expresses. At times her style seems to be merely on duty, gravely deferential to the rules and regulations acquired from reading her father's serious periodical literature, his small but portentous library and, indeed, listening to his sermons:

> I returned to my book – Bewick's *History of British Birds*: the letter-press thereof I cared little for, generally speaking; and yet there were certain introductory pages that, child as I was, I could not pass quite as a blank. They were those which treat of the haunts of sea-fowl; of 'the solitary rocks and promontories' by them inhabited; of the coast of Norway, studded with isles from it southern extremity, the Lindeness, or Naze, to the North Cape . . .

This kind of writing betrays a mixed and somewhat inchoate literary source. But this is not the only style offered. Charlotte's approach can change unexpectedly, sometimes incongruously, sometimes dramatically, so that in the end we find we have been beguiled by a forceful variety. The general effect of its unexpectedness is to bring the narrator, her location and character, closer to the reader and so actualize what otherwise seems remote and over-bland. Such writing as this barely engages us:

Hitherto, while gathering up the discourse of Mr Brocklehurst and Miss Temple, I had not, at the same time, neglected precautions to procure my personal safety, which I thought would be effected, if I could only elude observation.

But it actually acquires a kind of glow when it is seen in the light of such a sequitur as this – when Jane in trying to elude observation drops and breaks her slate, which brings Mr Brocklehurst's immediate attention, and he calls for the child who broke her slate to come forward:

Of my own accord, I could not have stirred: I was paralysed; but the two great girls who sat on each side of me set me on my legs and pushed me towards the dread judge, and then Miss Temple gently assisted me to his very feet, and I caught her whispered counsel –

'Don't be afraid, Jane, I saw it was an accident; you shall not be punished.'

The kind whisper went to my heart like a dagger.

All the heterogeneous elements that go to make up Charlotte's style have a common factor – dramatic potency. It sometimes appears in short passages of astonishing vividness – as if the scene described were happening right in front of us:

A splendid Midsummer shone over England: skies so pure, suns so radiant as were then seen in long succession, seldom favour, even singly, our wave-girt land. It was as if a band of Italian days had come from the South, like a flock of glorious passenger birds, and lighted to rest them on the cliffs of Albion. The hay was all got in; the fields round Thornfield were green and shorn; the roads white and baked; the trees were in their dark prime; hedge and wood, full-leaved and deeply tinted, contrasted well with the sunny hue of the cleared meadows between.

Sometimes it fuses character and location to produce a feeling of sensuous tension, as if the seasons of the human heart were at the mercy of nature's fickle changes:

Jane Eyre, who had been an ardent expectant woman – almost a bride – was a cold solitary girl again: her life was pale; her prospects were desolate. A Christmas frost had come at midsummer; a white December storm had whirled over June; ice glazed the ripe apples, drifts crushed the blowing roses; on hayfield and cornfield lay a frozen shroud; lanes which last night blushed full of flowers, today were pathless with untrodden snow ...

This same dramatic quality often vivifies 'set-pieces' which otherwise would remain static, so that the nuances and tensions of the action seem to move within the confines of even short phrases and sentences:

> I had not intended to love him; the reader knows I had wrought hard
> to extirpate from my soul the germs of love there detected; and now,
> at the first renewed view of him, they spontaneously revived, green
> and strong! He made me love him without looking at me.

And it finds its way into the dialogue in the novel, giving a sense of
immediate, active conversation. In fact the success which has attended
the translation of *Jane Eyre* into stage and film versions is partly
accounted for by the amount of naturally dramatic, naturally speakable,
dialogue it contains.

Perhaps the best confirmation that Charlotte possessed a highly
developed dramatic imagination lies in the significantly large number
of changes of tense in *Jane Eyre*, and, even more significant than the
number, the particular moments when she chooses to change from the
past to the present tense. Often it occurs at the beginning of chapters –
as for example Chapter 31. The previous chapter ends:

> In a week Mr Rivers and Hannah repaired to the parsonage:
> and so the old grange was abandoned,

and Chapter 31 begins:

> My home then – when I at last find a home – is a cottage; a little room
> with whitewashed walls and a sanded floor . . .

No clear-cut stylish unity emerges, then, from *Jane Eyre*, rather
the reader is able to experience the astonishing effects of what might be
called inspired improvisation. It is this, given shape, credibility,
intimacy and activity by the dramatic cast of her imagination that so
distinguishes this novel from the run-of-the-mill romantic stories,
entitling it to take its place with the greatest fiction of the nineteenth
century.

Synopsis

Jane Eyre, an orphan, lives with her uncle and aunt, the Reeds, and
their children – Eliza, John and Georgiana – at Gateshead Hall. After
Mr Reed dies, her aunt treats Jane harshly, once locking her in the 'red
room', where Mr Reed had died, when Janes hits out at the overfed,
obese John, for bullying her. Her fear results in a kind of fit. Bessie, the
servant who alone shows her kindness, nurses her. She is sent to
Lowood Orphan Asylum, the director of which – the pious hypocrite,
Mr Brocklehurst – is led to believe she is a wayward liar, needing stern
discipline. There she is befriended by Helen Burns, whose stoicism,
honesty, complete faith and kindliness, far from exempting her from
punishment for untidiness – her one fault – seem to incite it, especially

from one cruel teacher, Miss Scatcherd. Helen dies of consumption, but Jane, with the help of the kindly Miss Temple, survives. An investigation into the school's poor condition leads to some improvements, and Jane, a promising pupil, stays on as a teacher until Miss Temple leaves to get married. She advertises for a position as governess and is engaged by a Mrs Fairfax of Thornfield Hall, near Millcote. Before Jane leaves Lowood, Bessie, now married, visits Jane telling her that a Mr Eyre, who she thinks is Jane's uncle, had called at the Reeds' on his way to Madeira on business seven years ago and asked for Jane.

On arriving at Thornfield, Jane learns that her employer is a Mr Edward Rochester, Mrs Fairfax being the housekeeper. She is to be governess to Rochester's ward, Adèle Varens. Being shown around the fine house, Jane hears a loud mirthless laugh from behind a closed door, which Mrs Fairfax explains as that of Grace Poole, a servant. Out walking, Jane offers help to a rider who has fallen as his horse slipped on some ice. On her return, being summoned to her employer, Mr Rochester's, presence, she recognizes him as the rider. He is as impressed by her quiet honesty and intelligence as she is by his dark mystery, deepened by his information that Adèle is the illegitimate daughter of a French opera dancer, who claimed Adèle to be his child, though Rochester does not believe this.

As time goes on, and Jane and Rochester get to know each other better, he tells her the story of Céline Varens, and gradually Jane finds 'his face the object she likes best'. One night, woken up by a strange laugh, Jane finds smoke pouring from Mr Rochester's bedroom. She throws water on him and on the fire. He encourages her to believe Grace Poole probably caused the fire, asking her not to mention it.

Rochester leaves to visit neighbours, the Eshtons, where amongst the guests will be the beautiful, raven-haired, Honourable Blanche Ingram. As a result Jane makes herself discard her foolish notions, drawing a portrait of herself entitled 'Portrait of a Governess disconnected, poor and plain'. Rochester returns with Blanche and others, whom Jane, escorting Adèle to the drawing-room, meets and observes. The lively house-party continues with charades and fancy dress, with Jane growing increasingly sure that although she loves Mr Rochester, he will marry Blanche.

One day when Mr Rochester is away on business, a Mr Mason arrives from the West Indies, where he once knew Mr Rochester, and a gipsy calls to read the palms of all in the house including Jane, with whom she discusses love and Mr Rochester. Analysing Jane's character, the gipsy changes, and is revealed as Mr Rochester himself in disguise. Between him and Jane grows a deep affection. At night Jane is woken by Rochester to help Mr Mason who has been stabbed, by

Grace Poole it seems, and who is taken hurriedly from the house. Rochester tells Jane that to help cure his restless wanderings he intends to marry, and asks her if she thinks Blanche Ingram would regenerate him.

Jane learns that John Reed is dead and her aunt ill. Given permission to visit her, Jane tells Rochester that as he is about to marry, she presumes Adèle will be going to school, so she will seek another post. He assures her he will find her one. Mrs Reed gives Jane a letter, which arrived three years previously for her, from her uncle in Madeira, saying he wishes to make Jane his heir. Mrs Reed had told him Jane was dead. After Mrs Reed's death, Jane, returning to Thornfield, meets Mr Rochester and confesses to him her joy at being home and her love for Thornfield. Rochester, declaring he could never love Blanche Ingram, asks Jane to be his wife. She accepts with great happiness. During that night in a wild storm the great chestnut tree in the garden is split by lightning. Jane writes to tell her uncle of her engagement. During the next month, Jane avoids meeting Rochester's urgent feelings by teasing him. However, a nameless apprehension builds up in Jane, intensified by nightmares and one real event when, two nights before her wedding, she wakes to find a strange creature trying on her wedding veil, then tearing it in two.

The wedding service begins, only to be interrupted by Mr Mason and a solicitor declaring that Rochester is already married, with a wife living at Thornfield. Rochester takes Jane to see the hideous mad woman, Bertha Mason, his wife, who is locked up on the third floor of the house, attended by Grace Poole. He explains that as the poor second son, he had been forced by his father into a marriage with the wealthy Bertha Mason, despite the fact that her brother and his own father knew there was madness in the family. It emerges that Jane's letter to her uncle in Madeira had arrived when Mr Mason was there and he had come to prevent the bigamous marriage. Jane, desolate, leaves Thornfield secretly at night, refusing to stay on despite Rochester's plea that his was no true marriage, and that he needs and loves Jane.

She takes a coach to Whitcross, a two days' journey, and eventually, tired, desperately hungry, and on the verge of collapse, she is taken in by the Rivers family of Marsh End (or Moor House – both names are used). Mr St John Rivers and his two sisters, Diana and Mary, care for Jane. St John gets her a post as a teacher in a school financed by an heiress, Miss Rosamund Oliver, who loves St John, but whom he feels is not a suitable mate for his chosen career – missionary work abroad.

Eventually St John, discovering Jane's true name, tells her advertisements have appeared in the papers asking for news of her as her uncle's heiress. She finds out that her uncle was also the Rivers's uncle, and that they are cousins. Jane insists on sharing the fortune – which might originally have been left to the Rivers – equally with each of them, hoping St John will settle in England and marry Rosamund. He, however, is adamant, and Rosamund becomes engaged to a Mr Granby. Then St John asks Jane to marry him, as 'helpmeet and fellow labourer'. His moral arguments are almost as persuasive as Rochester's emotional ones, but Jane, about to agree, hears Rochester's voice calling her name. She hurries to Thornfield Hall, finding it burned to the ground in a fire caused by Bertha, in which she plunged to her death. In his attempt to save her Rochester has lost his sight and the use of a hand. Jane finds him at Ferndean, a nearby country house he owns, and there they declare their love and – 'Reader, I married him'. Rochester recovers sufficient sight to see his firstborn, and Diana and Mary Rivers marry happily, while St John, unmarried still, dies in the service of his God in India.

Characters

Abbot, Martha. Mrs Reed's lady's maid at Gateshead Hall.
Barbara. Servant at Lowood School.
Bates, Mr. Doctor who treats Helen Burns.
Briggs, Mr. London solicitor to Richard Mason.
Brocklehurst, Augusta. Robert Brocklehurst's second daughter.
Brocklehurst, Broughton. Youngest child of Robert Brocklehurst.
Brocklehurst, Miss. Eldest daughter of the Brocklehursts.
Brocklehurst, Mrs. Wife of Robert Brocklehurst. An extravagant, self-indulgent woman.
Brocklehurst, Naomi. Robert Brocklehurst's mother.
Brocklehurst, Robert. Founder and Inspector of Lowood School. (Rev. Carus Wilson.)
Brocklehurst, Theodore. One of Robert Brocklehurst's sons.
Burns, Helen. Thirteen-year-old pupil who dies at Lowood. Jane's friend. (Maria Brontë.)
Carlo. St John Rivers's dog.
Carter, Mr. Surgeon who shares Rochester's secret about the identity of the madwoman, Rochester's wife.
Clara. Rochester's mistress, after Céline Varens and Giacinta respectively.
Dent, Colonel. A soldier who attends Rochester's house-party.
Dent, Mrs. Colonel Dent's wife. Friend of Jane.
Elliott, Jane. Name assumed by Jane Eyre for disguise when she enters Moor House, Morton.
Eshton, Amy. Eldest Eshton daughter.
Eshton, Louisa. An Eshton daughter.
Eshton, Mr. District magistrate, living at the Leas, ten miles from Millcote, near Thornfield Hall.
Eshton, Mrs. A good-natured handsome woman: Mr Eshton's wife.

Eyre, Jane. *Née* Reed. Jane Eyre's dead mother. Sister of Mr Reed of Gateshead Hall.

Eyre, Jane. Eponymous heroine of the novel. Daughter of a clergyman, she was orphaned and left in the charge of her uncle, then, after his death, her aunt, Mrs Reed.

Eyre, John. Jane's uncle. A wine-merchant in Funchal, Madeira.

Fairfax, Alice. Clergyman's widow who acts as housekeeper at Thornfield Hall.

Fitzjames, Capt. Navy captain who marries Diana Rivers.

Frédéric, Madame. Looks after Adèle Varens after Céline abandons the child.

Garrett, Mary. Pupil at Jane Eyre's school at Morton.

Giacinta. Succeeds Céline Varens as Rochester's mistress.

Granby, Mr. Grandson and heir to Sir Frederic Granby. Marries Rosamund Oliver.

Granby, Sir Frederic. Grandfather of Mr Granby.

Green, John. Clerk at Hay Church, near Thornfield Hall.

Grey, Mrs. Former governess to Blanche and Mary Ingram.

Gryce, Miss. Teacher at Lowood. A constant snorer.

Hannah. Elderly servant at Moor House.

Harden, Mrs. Housekeeper at Lowood School. A hard woman.

Ingram, the Dowager Baroness. Mother of the Hon. Blanche and Mary Ingram.

Ingram, the Honourable Blanche. Elder daughter of Baroness Ingram. A beautiful girl.

Ingram, Mary. Younger daughter of Baroness Ingram. A plain girl.

Ingram, Theodore. Son of the Baroness Ingram. Apathetic.

John. Servant/coachman at Ferndean Manor. Husband of Mary.

John. Footman at Thornfield.

Johnstone, Agnes and Catherine. Pupils at Brocklehurst's school at Lowood.

Joubert, Madame. Former governess of Blanche and Mary Ingram.

Leah. Housemaid at Thornfield.

Leaven, Bobbie. Son of Bessie and Robert Leaven.

Leaven, Jane. Daughter of Robert and Bessie Leaven (*née* Lee).

Leaven, Robert. Coachman to Mrs Reed at Gateshead Hall. Marries Bessie Lee.

Lee, Bessie. Mrs Reed's children's nurse. Becomes Mrs Leaven.

Lloyd, Mr. An apothecary employed by Mrs Reed.

Lynn, Sir George. Guest at Rochester's house-party. MP for Millcote.

Lynn, Lady. Wife of Sir George Lynn. Fat and forty.

Lynn, Henry and Frederick. Sons of Sir George Lynn. Described as 'dashing sparks'.

Mary. Cook at Ferndean Manor. Wife of John.

Mason, Bertha Antoinetta. Rochester's mad wife. Daughter of Jonas and Antoinetta Mason. Born in West Indies.

Mason, Jonas. West Indian planter/merchant, father of Richard and Bertha Mason and an idiot younger son.

Mason, Richard. Bertha Mason's brother, who interrupts Jane's and Rochester's wedding.

Mesrour. Rochester's horse.

Miles, Mr. John Reed's schoolmaster.

Miller, Miss. Assistant teacher at Lowood School.

Mope, Madam. John Reed's name for Jane Eyre.

Nasmyth, Rev. Mr. Maria Temple's husband.

O'Gall, Mrs Dionysius. Rochester teases Jane, when she believes he is to marry Blanche Ingram, that she might gain a post as governess to Mrs O'Gall's five children of Bitternut Lodge, Connaught, Ireland.

Oliver, Mr. Needle manufacturer of Vale Hall, Morton. Kindly friend of Jane Eyre.

Oliver, Rosamund. Daughter and heiress of Mr Oliver.

Pierrot, Madame. Teaches French at Lowood School.

Pilot. Rochester's dog.

Poole. Son of Grace Poole.

Poole, Grace. Servant at Thornfield, and keeper of the mad Mrs Rochester.

Reed, Eliza. Mrs Reed's daughter. Becomes a nun.

Reed, Georgiana. Mrs Reed's daughter. Spoilt and indolent.

Reed, John. Mrs Reed's son. A feckless, cruel, unhealthy young glutton.

Reed, Mr. Mrs Reed's husband, brother of Jane Eyre's mother.

Reed, Mrs Sarah. *Née* Gibson. John, Eliza and Georgiana's mother. Aunt by marriage of Jane Eyre.

Rivers, Diana and Mary. St John Rivers's sisters. Governesses in the South of England. Diana marries a naval captain, Mary a clergyman.

Rivers, St John Eyre. Vicar of Morton, who eventually discovers he and Jane are related. (Henry Nussey.)

Rochester, Edward Fairfax. Younger son of a county family, trapped into marriage with the mad Bertha Mason. Eventually marries Jane Eyre.

Rochester, 'Old Man'. Father of Edward Fairfax Rochester.

Rochester, Rowland. Elder brother of Edward Rochester.

Sam. Rochester's footman.

Sarah. Housemaid at the Reeds', Gateshead Hall.

Scatcherd, Miss. Teacher at Lowood School. (Miss Andrews.)

Severn, Julia. Pupil at Lowood. Her mass of curls is cut off at the order of Brocklehurst.

Smith, Miss. Teacher at Lowood.

Sophie. French maid and nurse to Adèle Varens.

Temple, Maria. Headmistress and superintendent of Lowood School. (Miss Evans.)

Varens, Adèle. Daughter of French opera-dancer, Céline Varens – once beloved of Rochester.

Varens, Céline. Mother of Adèle Varens.

Vere, Lord Edward. Georgiana Reed plans to elope with this young buck.

Vining, Mr. Theodore, Lord Ingram's former tutor who is dismissed for falling in love with Miss Wilson, the governess.

Wharton, Rev. Mr. A clergyman who marries Mary Rivers.

Wilson, Mary Ann. Pupil at Lowood and companion of Jane in the fever epidemic there.

Wilson, Miss. Hon. Blanche and Mary Ingram's former governess.

Wood, Alice. When Jane becomes schoolmistress of Morton this little orphan acts as her handmaid.

Wood, Rev. Mr. Clergyman who conducts the interrupted marriage service of Jane and Rochester.

Places

Bridewell. Hospital in Blackfriars, London, once used as a workhouse, then a house of correction. Most of it was demolished in 1864.

Brocklebridge Church. The pupils from Lowood School attend this church. Mr Brocklehurst officiates. (Tunstall, Cowan Bridge.)

Cairngorm. Peak of Cairngorm mountains in northern Scotland. Here presumably refers to colour – dark brown – of rock crystal.

Deepden. Helen Burns's home in Northumberland.

Eshton's Place, Mr. i.e. Eshton Hall, five miles from Skipton.

Ferndean Manor. A building on one of Rochester's farms to which he goes after Thornfield is destroyed. (Wycoller.)

Gateshead Hall. Mrs Reed's residence and Jane's temporary home. (Stonegappe, Skipton.)

Hay. A village near the gates of Thornfield Hall, 'half lost in trees'. Jane first meets Rochester in Hay Lane. (Wath, Norton Conyers.)

L——. ?Leeds. Large town between Gateshead Hall and Lowood School.

Lisle. Or Lille in France. Madame Pierrot, teacher of French at Lowood, came from there, and Eliza Reed was 'walled up alive' in a French convent there.

Lowood School. School attended by Jane Eyre. (Cowan Bridge.)

Lowton. The nearest town to Lowood School. (Kirkby Lonsdale.)

Millcote. Described as 'a large manufacturing town on the banks of the A——'. (Leeds.)

Moor House. Or Marsh End, the home of the Rivers family; a few miles from Morton. (North Lees, Hathersage, Moorseats.)

Morton. The village where Jane finds shelter after leaving Thornfield. (Hathersage.)

S——. A town described as twenty miles from Marsh End. (Sheffield.)

Thornfield Hall. Mr Rochester's residence, six miles from Millcote. (Birstall, Norton Conyers.)

Whitcross. A stone pillar surmounted with four arms which stands at a crossroads ten miles from the nearest town. Jane Eyre alights here from the coach after almost two days' travelling from near Thornfield Hall. (Moscar Cross.)

Shirley (1849)

Commentary

This novel, the fourth Charlotte wrote, has a number of characteristics which mark it off from both *Jane Eyre* and *Villette*. It does not, for example, have a single hero and/or heroine – the reader's attention is spread almost equally between Shirley, Caroline, Robert and Louis. It avoids concentration on a main theme, indeed, at times, it seems to lurch uncertainly from one subject to another, as if seeking a centre.

Essentially, there are two main themes which gradually emerge from the complicated narrative. The first one is what it has become popular to call 'sociological' – a singularly graceless replacement for 'documentary'. *Shirley* has an important place in that category of nineteenth-century fiction which either contains or is completely concerned with important social movements, events and upheavals. The 'documentary' novel is a literary camera employed to try and capture images of life as it is experienced in actuality, not as it is restructured by the imagination. *Shirley* is to a large extent concerned with depicting the human problems resulting from England's change from agrarian to industrial society. It is a retrospective documentary about events (1811–12) which occurred a few years before Charlotte's birth. Like Emily's *Wuthering Heights* (which is set thirty years before its author's birth) it is accurate in detail and indeed gives every appearance of being a contemporaneous account.

Both Emily and Charlotte, like the rest of the family, had a large appetite for contemporary events, which was whetted and satisfied by the opportunities Patrick Brontë provided for them to read both newspapers and periodicals. It was therefore no particular chore for them to use the events of their own day, or the day before, as material in their novels. Even the highly imaginatively charged worlds of Angria and Gondal drew many of their events and incidents and episodes, their heroes and heroines, from the same source – the today and yesterday of the Brontës' own lives. The 'naturalness', the ease, with which the material is used suggests that to Charlotte, as to Emily, the day before yesterday must have been a familiar.

But Charlotte still 'researched' for this book in a way she never did for her others. She read the back numbers of the *Leeds Mercury* for the period 1812–14 and, of course, assembled both her memory and her father's accounts of the militant activities of groups of Luddites in the Leeds/Bradford area. In particular Patrick Brontë could have revealed for her the attack on Rawfolds Mill not far from his incumbency of Hartshead in 1812, and she knew the country district near Roe Head School where the attack was organized. For the human dimensions of such events she could have had no better source than the kind of firm opinion and direct knowledge which circulated with passionate freedom in the home of her friends, the Taylor family, at the Red House, Gomersal.

Charlotte's accuracy is remarkable, and from the novel it is possible to reconstruct the historical context in which its narrative is so firmly set. In 1811/12 the war with Napoleon was still some way from its close, and England was feeling the economic consequences perhaps rather more than the military. To a degree England's ills were self-inflicted – the famous Orders in Council of the British government which, by blockade, were intended to deny essential supplies to

Napoleon's Europe, had the effect of restricting England's own trading capacity, and the manufacturing industries suffered greatly.

From the human point of view, the effects of the war were compounded first, by the weather – a bad harvest resulted in a shortage of food in a number of areas – and, second, by Britain's very genius for invention. The war increased unemployment, but the replacement of human labour by machines (particularly in the textile industries of the north) really created it.

In this atmosphere the Luddite movement was spawned in Nottingham and spread to the West Riding of Yorkshire. The Luddites were deprived and disaffected artisans, and the movement was a spontaneous attempt to ameliorate conditions which were rapidly worsening; but that spontaneity equally rapidly became organized, and specific grievances came to be subsumed beneath larger and wider socio-political notions. The growth of Trade Unions, the hardening of class antagonism, the development of working-class power and the foreshadowings of socialism owe much to these northern events which Charlotte so assiduously observed and recorded.

A modern left-wing politician or sociologist would almost certainly conclude that Charlotte failed to record the extent of the deprivation which led to Ludditism, or the cruelty and suffering which accompanied authority's fierce response – 12,000 troops were used to quell it. But this would be to condemn on grounds which do not apply. She could only have known of very local happenings; she had no access to the ubiquitous, comprehensive and rapid newscasting of our media; she was, after all, writing a novel not a tract – it would be as unfair to condemn her for exercising her right as a novelist to select as it would be to arraign Shakespeare for not showing us the 'other side' of Wat Tyler's rebellion in *Henry VI*.

If there is reason to question Charlotte's treatment of her documentary material it rests in the circumstances of her upbringing and her class. She naturally accepted the establishment explanation that the Luddites were dupes – naive, sincere men, incited by agitators with particular axes to grind. Again it was her inherited political Tory stance which, in the novel, prompted her to dismiss as shabbily self-interested the attempts of a section of the parliamentary opposition to sue for peace with Napoleon in order to ameliorate the economic situation in England.

Charlotte, like Shakespeare, was establishment in outlook and belief. Like him, she abhorred any kind of shift which would produce a profound change in the social pattern. But also, like him, she celebrates the individual human being, even of the lowliest kind, and his right to challenge the system if it is unjust, unfair or cruel. There is a striking similarity between his stance, and Charlotte's in *Shirley* in which, for all her conditioned Tory commitment to the status quo of her society, there is equal access given to her humanistic assertion of the right of the individual to challenge the system. To Charlotte and Shakespeare the cry of pain or the gasp of pleasure of the single individual is of far greater consequence than political movements and economic theories and practices. Their theme is humankind not population graphs. They offer no solutions to the cruelties, injustices, deprivations which they see, any more than they offer explanations for the far less frequent kindnesses, virtues, happinesses which they observe.

The true context of Charlotte's vision is best expressed by William Yorke's gardener –

> Human natur', taking it i' th' lump, is naught but selfishness. It is but excessive few; it is but just an exception here and there, now and then, sich as ye two young 'uns and me, that being in a different sphere, can understand t'one, t'other, and be friends wi'out slavishness o' one hand, or pride o' t'other.

But if she observed the Luddites without involvement, she experienced the world of the governess with total involvement. Intimacy concentrates the mind wonderfully, and there is a fierce, almost angry, proselytizing concentration of mental and emotional power in Charlotte's references (which are many) to the plight of governesses, which is quite different from the objective humanity with which she sees the Luddites.

It is inaccurate to confine Charlotte's concern within the phrase 'the governess theme', as most critics do; for Charlotte sees the plight of this huge employment class as part of a larger problem. Those who become governesses are almost invariably single young women, and although the rigours which often accompany their work rouses Charlotte's vehemence, it is the conditioning of single females for such work that deepens her concern:

> Look at the numerous families of girls in this neighbourhood: the Armitages, the Birtwhistles, the Sykes. The brothers of these girls are every one in business or in professions; they have something to do: their sisters have no earthly employment, but household work and sewing; no earthly pleasure, but an unprofitable visiting; and no hope, in all their life to come, of anything better. This stagnant state of things makes them decline in health: they are never well; and their minds and views shrink to wondrous narrowness. The great wish – the sole aim of every one of them is to be married, but the majority will never marry: they will die as they now live. They scheme, they plot, they dress to ensnare husbands. The gentlemen turn them into ridicule: they don't want them; they hold them very cheap: they say –

I have heard them say it with sneering laughs many a time – the matrimonial market is overstocked. Fathers say so likewise, and are angry with their daughters when they observe their manoeuvres: they order them to stay at home. What do they expect them to do at home? If you ask, – they would answer, sew and cook. They expect them to do this, and this only, contentedly, regularly, uncomplainingly all their lives long, as if they had no germs of faculties for anything else: a doctrine as reasonable to hold, as it would be that the fathers have no faculties but for eating what their daughters cook, or for wearing what they sew.

And if ever anyone doubted that the plight of governesses was part of a larger social reality the words of the character Mrs Hardiman to Mrs Pryor (who was her children's governess) starkly, almost shockingly, remove the doubts:

> We need the imprudences, extravagances, mistakes, and crimes of a certain number of fathers to sow the seed from which we reap the harvest of governesses. We shall ever prefer to place those immediately about our offspring who have been born and bred with somewhat of the same refinement as ourselves.

A great deal of Charlotte's personality is explained by her experience of being a governess and by her ruthlessly clear understanding of what that could mean. Her suspicion of people, her wariness in company, her silence, her penetrating observation, her occasional accesses of verbal cruelty, her satire, her intermittent sourness and, indeed, her obsession with the need for a love-affair to be based as much on unbreakable moral laws as on emotional and intellectual attraction – all these were either engendered, or exacerbated by her experience of a society which largely regarded governesses in the way described by Mrs Pryor:

> It was my lot to enter a family of considerable pretensions to good birth and mental superiority, and the members of which also believed that 'on them was perceptible' an unusual endowment of the 'Christian graces': that all their hearts were regenerate, and their spirits in a peculiar state of discipline. I was early given to understand, that 'as I was not their equal', so I could not expect 'to have their sympathy'. It was in no sort concealed from me that I was held a 'burden and a restraint in society'. The gentlemen, I found, regarded me as a 'tabooed woman', to whom 'they were interdicted from granting the usual privileges of the sex', and yet who 'annoyed them by frequently crossing their path'. The ladies too made it plain that they thought me 'a bore'. The servants, it was signified, 'detested me': *why*, I could never clearly comprehend. My pupils, I was told, 'however much they might love me, and how deep soever

the interest I might take in them, could not be my friends'. It was intimated, that I must 'live alone, and never transgress the invisible but rigid line which established the difference between me and my employers'. My life in this house was sedentary, solitary, constrained, joyless, toilsome. The dreadful crushing of the animal spirits, the ever prevailing sense of friendlessness and homelessness consequent on this state of things, began erelong to produce mortal effects on my constitution – I sickened. The lady of the house told me coolly I was the victim of 'wounded vanity'.

Charlotte told her publishers while writing the novel that she did not want to get involved again in the 'governess' theme and, certainly, it does not dominate; but she did not completely avoid it. The two heroines are not directly concerned with it, but it exists as a leit-motif, and comes to the surface in a number of almost vehemently urgent passages, and through the character of Mrs Pryor. *Shirley* is even more explicit than *Jane Eyre* in its passionate condemnation of the way in which the honourable profession of governess becomes so often a trap in which deprivation of freedom and psychological humiliation torture the sensibilities, the flesh and the spirit. In *Jane Eyre* the 'governess' theme is one element in the developing personality and destiny of Jane herself, in *Shirley* it appears more as a social problem.

The other theme of *Shirley* is that involving the quartet of young men and women. Shirley and Caroline, Robert and Louis are enveloped in this second and 'romantic' theme of the novel. The reader becomes preoccupied in wondering who will get whom, or whether anyone will achieve anyone! There is a great deal of concentration – arguably too much – on the state of mind, particularly of the heroines, and some might think there is a morbid emphasis on states of bodily health. Irritation in the reader might well be replaced by sympathy in the reflection that Emily was desperately ill during the time this novel was being written, and that she died when it was half-completed. The terrible grief that afflicted Charlotte could not be subsumed in art. The first chapter (number 24) she was able to write after some months following Emily's death unequivocally reflects her grief, and it may well be that the concentration on states of physical ill-being are themselves an emblem of what Emily suffered and Charlotte observed.

Indeed, the uneasy disposition of themes that has been noticed may have been the result of a disturbance in Charlotte's imagination inflicted by Emily's death. Certain it is that however much critical comment may try to present a tidy collection of themes, the actuality confounds it. The 'second theme' – which, for convenience' sake, can be designated 'romantic' – is invaded, sometimes puzzlingly and apparently fortuitously, by the force of the sociological realities of theme one. The intensely personal relationships between the four lovers often suddenly give place to considerations which have their source far outside the dictates of human hearts and heads. Considerations about class, money, status, power, authority, economic survival, incontinently dislocate the structure of romantic love that Charlotte is building. There is no reason in theory why this should not deepen, subtilize and enrich our experience of these people's lives, but, in practice, the effect is of a sudden wrenching of the narrative without convincing reason and motivation. In Charlotte's mind connections may well have existed between the documentary actualities of the real world and the romantic realities of her fictional world, but these connections are hardly ever easily perceptible to the reader. What emerges from *Shirley* is not what Charlotte probably intended – a combining of naturalism and imagination – but a restless unpredictable movement from one to the other.

It is important also to realize that Charlotte had taken to heart a number of adverse comments from critics whose opinion she took seriously, which deprecated the excessive 'fantasy' of her novels, and enjoined her to abandon imaginative excess in favour of stern realism. But this was tantamount to asking her to tear out her heart in order the better to display her intellect.

Shirley was perhaps an attempt to meet her critics head on. With typical strength of will she was determined not to abandon the dictates of her imagination so much as to try and relate them to the real world. With the odds represented by Branwell's then Emily's death, quite apart from the force of her imagination, stacked against her, she failed in the most difficult act of fusion any artist is likely to meet, but the failure is comparative.

There is much in *Shirley* to respect, and even more to please. The two heroines themselves are, if only relatively, much more pleasing in the simple sense of possessing more of the milder than the abrasive qualities of Jane Eyre and Lucy Snowe. Neither is prim, neither is prissy, neither is so obsessed by the moral context of actions, and neither has the lingering aura of self-pity which often irritates in the more celebrated heroines. Both are good-looking. They love for love's sake and while they are not by any means lacking in emotional self-indulgence there is a freer outline to their personalities. No effort of the imagination could place Jane and Lucy alongside Shirley – here, for instance:

> She stood quietly near the window, looking at the grand cedar on her lawn, watching a bird on one of its lower boughs. Presently she began to chirrup to the bird: soon her chirrup grew clearer: erelong she was whistling; the whistle struck into a tune, and very sweetly and deftly it was executed.

'My dear!' expostulated Mrs Pryor.

'Was I whistling?' said Shirley; 'I forgot. I beg your pardon, ma'am. I had resolved to take care not to whistle before you.'

'But, Miss Keeldar, where did you learn to whistle? You must have got the habit since you came down into Yorkshire. I never knew you guilty of it before.'

'Oh, I learned to whistle a long while ago.'

'Who taught you?'

'No-one: I took it up by listening. . .'

Shirley's and Caroline's male counterparts, Louis and Robert, are both demonstrably created in more human terms than either Rochester or Paul Emmanuel – who, particularly Rochester, seem at times to be more an assembly of sensational attributes than completely credible human entities. Robert Moore may well irritate us by his prevarications about public and private responsibilities, and Louis may exasperate us with what seems an occasional dithering of the spirit, but both are indubitably naturalistic and credible. This does not make them more interesting than Rochester and M. Paul but it contributes much to the novel's sharp thrusts towards actuality, and perhaps the more certainly enables the two men to engage our sympathies.

Perhaps, indeed, the word 'romantic' is too mild in its associations accurately to encompass the ambiguous personality of Robert Moore. He is far from being entirely attractive – indeed there is a sense in which we might feel that Caroline Helstone is too good for him. He allows the acquisition of profit to override the demands of love; he admits he was prepared to sacrifice Caroline for gain; he tells us that he proposed to Shirley to safeguard his business interests. Yet he displays goodness of heart, understanding of his employees' dilemmas and, although there is a strong element of artifice in it, he undergoes a kind of conversion to make him realize his love for Caroline and the necessity to give the personal life at least equal weight with the public. Robert Moore was perhaps meant to be the main link between the 'documentary' and the fictive bands of the novel. He fails to be so largely because his character is presented to us too much in fits and starts: it lacks a centre from which the personality can flow.

His counterpart, Louis, enters the novel at a very late stage, so late as to have almost the status of an afterthought, the more so since there is a deal in his character that is over-bland, cutting no kind of dash in the reader's mind:

As to Louis Moore himself, he had the air of a man used to this life, and who had made up his mind to bear it for a time. His faculties seemed walled up in him, and were unmurmuring in their captivity. He never laughed; he seldom smiled; he was uncomplaining. He

fulfilled the round of his duties scrupulously. His pupil loved him; he
ask nothing more than civility from the rest of the world. It even
appeared that he would accept nothing more: in that abode at least;
for when his cousin Caroline made gentle overtures of friendship, he
did not encourage them; he rather avoided than sought her. One
living thing alone, besides his pale, crippled scholar, he fondled in the
house, and that was the ruffianly Tartar; who, sullen and impractic-
able to others, acquired a singular partiality for him: a partiality so
marked that sometimes, when Moore, summoned to a meal, entered
the room and sat down unwelcomed, Tartar would rise from his lair
at Shirley's feet, and betake himself to the taciturn tutor. Once – but
once – she noticed the desertion; and holding out her white hand, and
speaking softly, tried to coax him back. Tartar looked, slavered, and
sighed, as his manner was, but yet disregarded the invitation, and
coolly settled himself on his haunches at Louis Moore's side. That
gentleman drew the dog's big, black-muzzled head on to his knee,
patted him, and smiled one little smile to himself.

The characterization of the novel is within certain limits conspicuously well achieved. The methods adopted are no more various than in
Jane Eyre and *Villette*, but there is often a greater assurance, a finer sense
of aptness, in the details chosen. Charlotte excels in quick sketches (a
kind of instant portraiture) such as that of the anguished child who sees
the greedy curates eating his favourite food. It is spice-cake and it
'vanished like a vision, and was no more found'. Charlotte then does
her lightning sketch:

> Its elegy was chanted in the kitchen by Abraham, Mrs Gale's son and
> heir, a youth of six summers; he had reckoned upon the reversion
> thereof, and when his mother brought down the empty platter, he
> lifted up his voice and wept sore.

But she is equally effective in slightly more ample vignettes, which
gave the impression of a summing-up of character rather than (as in the
case of the sketch of Master Abraham) an interim report:

> In stalked that lady [Mrs Sykes], a tall bilious gentlewoman, who
> made an ample and not altogether insincere profession of piety, and
> was greatly given to hospitality towards the clergy; in sailed her three
> daughters, a showy trio, being all three well grown, and more or less
> handsome.

And in her full-length portraits the instant assessment of sketching, the slower but equally economical brushwork of the vignette,
combine with a whole apparatus of feeling and moral judgement to
produce what always has a relentless clarity and truth. This more
studied method triumphs in the depiction of the three curates who
dominate Chapter 1, and of Mr Yorke:

A Yorkshire gentleman he was par excellence, in every point. About fifty-five years old, but looking at first sight still older, for his hair was silver white. His forehead was broad, not high; his face fresh and hale; the harshness of the north was seen in his features, as it was heard in his voice; every trait was thoroughly English, not a Norman line anywhere; it was an inelegant, unclassic, unaristocratic mould of visage. Fine people would perhaps have called it vulgar; sensible people would have termed it characteristic; shrewd people would have delighted in it for the pith, sagacity, intelligence – the rude, yet real originality marked in every lineament, latent in every furrow. But it was an indocile, a scornful, and a sarcastic face; the face of a man difficult to lead, and impossible to drive. His stature was rather tall, and he was well-made and wiry, and had a stately integrity of port; there was not a suspicion of the clown about him anywhere.

The portraits of the curates show similar control – with an added element of mocking satire, condemned by her critics but which Charlotte resolutely refused to expunge. She showed fine artistic judgement in this, for these portraits are comic masterpieces which enliven the novel and, because the comedy involved is satirical, in fact further its documentary intentions.

In her letters, quite apart from her novels, Charlotte has a large gallery of young minor clerics. Her memory of those who came to her father's church, to the parsonage, and those she met elsewhere, not least in Ellen Nussey's home, was precise and relentless. Charlotte seems not to have been over-fond of curates as a race, for she spices her memory with a gleeful spirit of mockery (the nearest she ever got to outright laughter in her novels) and, quite often, dismissive contempt. It is true that one, at least, of her trio in *Shirley* redeems his early disposition to unpleasant fatuity by turning out to be a model husband and shepherd of his flock, but, curiously, he is more convincing in his chrysalis stage – when he acquires wings it's all too contrived.

There is no other cohesive group in Charlotte's novels which stands out as her curates do. The lash of her tongue curls around many of her characters, but nowhere else is it so assiduous in seeking out its victims as with these reverend gentlemen. Yet, reader, she married one, in the end, and there is very little about the Rev. Nicholls that suggests that he was in any way much different from others she had, in the past, so frequently castigated. He was bigoted, narrow, peremptory, dutifully kind and dull.

Perhaps throughout her adult life, as the daughter of a man of the cloth, she instinctively knew that she was destined to marry, *faute de mieux*, one of the seemingly endless procession of curates her father's profession invited to his door, and perhaps she purged her distaste for them by her satirical portraits:

Of late years, I say, an abundant shower of curates has fallen upon the north of England: but in eighteen-hundred-eleven-twelve that affluent rain had not descended: curates were scarce then: there was no Pastoral Aid – no Additional Curate's Society to stretch a helping hand to worn-out old rectors and incumbents, and give them the wherewithal to pay a vigorous young colleague from Oxford or Cambridge.

The novel stands or falls in the reader's estimate according to how much the documentary material is acceptable. For the right kind of reader this material is fascinating, rich and important; for others it may be boring, irritating, irrelevant. They might well turn to the characters of Shirley and Caroline to find satisfaction. They are created with zest and a kind of imaginative athleticism; they both in their different ways have strong personalities without having sacrificed femininity. Dare one even suggest that Caroline is an idealized self-portrait, a what-might-have-been Charlotte, strong, brave, extrovert, intelligent, imaginative, long-suffering, cheerful and, above all, physically attractive? If Shirley is Emily then is Caroline Charlotte? Lucy Snowe and Jane Eyre possess so many of the physical and non-physical characteristics of Charlotte that one feels drawn to the fanciful proposition that having portrayed herself 'straight' twice, she eventually could not resist creating the other Charlotte – the familiar of her imagination.

Synopsis

As three curates, the bigoted Mr Donne, the ineffectual Mr Sweeting and the boisterous Irish Mr Malone, are at supper the Rev. Helstone calls to ask that, if any of them carry firearms, they go to Hollow's Mill, rented by Robert Gerard Moore, where trouble is expected as a result of the imminent arrival of new equipment there which will cut down the labour force. Malone, who carries a pistol, goes, and while waiting for the equipment to arrive he and Moore talk of marriage (Malone wishes to make a match with advantageous connections), the country's economic problems and the disaffection of the workers.

Moore's mother was Flemish, a Gerard, and his mill is even more vulnerable, the owner being part foreign. The carts arrive empty, with a note saying that the machines have been smashed and that Moore's employees, who were driving the carts, are bound hand and foot on Stilbro' Moor. Moore rings the alarm bell and helpers arrive, including Helstone. They find one of the employees wounded. Mr Yorke, a Yorkshireman of authority and decided opinions, another millowner, has already found the employees and takes them home. Mr Yorke is one of the most influential men in the area, well travelled, educated, respected, who had once loved Mary Cave. She eventually married Rev. Helstone and is said to have died of a broken heart. Yorke is now married to a formidable, tactless woman and has a large family – Rose, Jessie, Matthew, Mark, Martin and a baby. Moore lives at Hollow's Mill Cottage with his sister, Hortense, who speaks little English and teaches Caroline, Helstone's niece, French. Caroline, a distant cousin of the Moores, has never known her mother and when her father died she came as a child to live with his brother, Rev. Helstone, who is her guardian. Mr Moore is suggesting Hortense consult Caroline about English dress when Caroline arrives and Moore, reluctantly having to leave for work, suggests Caroline dines with Hortense and they will read together in the evening. Caroline gladly agrees and, after a pleasant evening, Moore escorts her home. She realizes she loves him and believes he loves her.

The next day, after Helstone has spoken disparagingly of marriage, Malone and then Mrs Sykes and her three daughters call. Caroline reluctantly asks them, and the two other curates who call, to tea. After a long tea-time and a tedious musical evening Caroline slips out of the house, meeting Moore, who is about to call to tell them he knows the identity of one of the attackers. As he leaves, after talking with Caroline, he kisses her three times.

A warrant is issued for the arrest of the Rev. Moses Barraclough, a dissenting preacher and one of the leaders of the anti-Moore faction. After heading a group to confront Moore to tell him to go back to Belgium, Barraclough is apprehended at gun point. Moore, asked to give the men more time to accept the changes, refuses, blaming the situation on the government. He visits the Yorke family in their comfortable home, where they try to draw him out about marriage.

Winter passes and spring comes. The uneasy atmosphere in the area still continues. Helstone, denouncing Moore as a Jacobin, tells Caroline not to go to the Moores' again. Caroline, having found Moore's attitude to her ambiguous and uncertain, agrees and goes to visit the grimly tidy Miss Mann and the plain Miss Ainsley, two elderly ladies. Miss Ainsley's involvement in helping the poor opens Caroline's eyes, making her determine to do something for those in her own neighbourhood. One evening out walking she sees Moore and Yorke together and, upset by Moore's presence, next morning suggests she finds a position elsewhere as a governess. However, her uncle takes her to visit the wealthy Shirley Keeldar, who lives at Fieldhead. Caroline takes an instant liking to Mrs Pryor, Shirley's former governess and now her companion. Shirley and Caroline become firm friends and Mrs Pryor, calling at the rectory one day, becomes agitated by some pictures on the wall there, which she questions Caroline about.

Caroline, who still walks out in the evening hoping to meet Moore, sees him one evening talking quietly to Shirley – about business, though Caroline does not know this. Calling at Fieldhead one day, where Shirley is asking Caroline to go on holiday with her, Moore meets Caroline and escorts her home, asking her, as Hortense misses her, to call on them again. Caroline confides to her maid, Fanny, that she is sure Moore will marry Shirley.

After Shirley's offer to help Caroline with the poor in the district, a meeting is called which the three curates attend, and Donne, behaving badly, is asked by Shirley to leave. Moore, through the offices of mutual friends, is reconciled with Helstone. During one night, after the Whitsuntide feast when Shirley is staying at the rectory, Hollow's Mill is attacked and Caroline has to be dissuaded from going to help Moore. The next day the wounded Moore goes over to Fieldhead, there meeting Yorke who is arguing with Shirley over the local troubles. Yorke asks Shirley when she is going to marry Robert Moore.

Shirley's and Caroline's holiday has to be cancelled because of the arrival to stay of the Sympson family. Caroline, taking tea with Hortense, is upset by the tactless Mr Yorke, but finds Rose and Jessie on her side. Robert Moore, whose engagement to Shirley, Hortense implies, is about to be announced, arrives with his taciturn brother, Louis, once tutor to Shirley, now tutor to the Sympson children. Caroline, becoming ill, is nursed by Mrs Pryor who notices a locket, containing a lock of a man's hair, which Caroline refuses to be parted from. Recovering, Caroline learns Mrs Pryor is her mother whose real name is Agnes Helstone and who left her husband because of their unhappy marriage. Mother and daughter become inseparable. Shirley becomes friends with her young cousin, Henry Sympson, who with Caroline finds an old school book of Shirley's from the time Louis Moore tutored her. Shirley angrily refuses both the offer from Mr Wynne, a local notable, that she marry his son, Samuel, and three other offers of marriage, including that of Sir Philip Nunnely, who affects to be a poet and takes Shirley on moonlight walks, intoning his poetry to her.

After Louis Moore recovers from an illness he, Henry and Shirley spend many happy hours together in the school room talking. Then Shirley, becoming ill herself, makes her will, leaving her property to Henry and her money to Caroline. Henry, informing Louis of this, blurts out that he loves her and will change his name to Keeldar. Shirley, having been bitten by Samuel's dog, who is believed to be mad, and having cauterized herself with a hot iron, asks Louis, should she have hydrophobia, to get her sufficient laudanum to put her out of her misery.

Robert Moore, who is in London, returns and tells Yorke he did propose to Shirley but her rejection made him decide never to propose to any woman again unless he truly loved her. Shirley, asked by the Sympsons what her marriage intentions are, declares she will marry the Duke of Wellington!

As the Sympsons prepare to leave, Robert is wounded in an assassination attempt and taken to the Yorkes', where Mrs Yorke tends to him. Martin Yorke, on his way home from school, meets the veiled Caroline, who asks after Robert. Martin tells her he is recovering and agrees to let her know how he gets on. Next day, having got the nurse out of the way, he takes Caroline in to see Robert. Robert improves, goes home and asks Caroline to spend the evening with him, when they talk of love and marriage, only to be interrupted by Hortense. Louis Moore, having decided to leave tutoring, tells Shirley of his love for her and she acknowledges she loves him, much to the annoyance of Uncle Sympson.

The story ends with a general tidying up of affairs – Mr Sweeting marries; Malone is dismissed and disappears; Donne marries a sweet, sensible girl who amends his manners and temper; Moore's business picks up, Caroline accepts his proposal of marriage, and he promises to set up a Sunday School and make his mill an example for its humane and just treatment of its workers; finally, on the same day, Shirley marries Louis and Caroline marries Robert.

Characters

Ainsley, Mary Ann. Old maid of Briarfield.
Armitage, Miss. One of six daughters of Mr Armitage.
Armitage, Mr. Millowner, sympathetic to workers.
Barraclough, Moses. A 'joined Methodist' (i.e. converted), and a preacher.
Ben. Son of William and Grace Farren.
Birtwhistle, Miss. One of the Birtwhistle family who attend the parish Whitsuntide tea.
Birtwhistle, Mrs. Miss Birtwhistle's mother.
Booth, James. Gardener at Fieldhead.
Boultby, Dr Thomas. Rector of Whinbury. (Rev. William Morgan.)
Boultby, Grace. Either (1) Dr Boultby's wife or (2) his daughter, as identified in the novel.
Broadbent, Dr. Speaker at Bible Society meeting in Nunnely.
Cary. Diminutive of Caroline.
Cave, Mary. Once loved by Hiram Yorke, but married Helstone, and died after five years.
Deb. Deborah, Hiram Yorke's servant.
Doad o'Bills. Character who finds freedom in the Methodist Chapel.
Donne, Joseph. Curate of Whinbury. Self-indulgent, arrogant, but eventually reformed by marriage.

Dora, Miss. *See* Sykes, the Misses.

Eliza. Rev. Helstone's cook.

Fanny. Rev. Helstone's servant.

Farren, Grace. William Farren's wife.

Farren, William. One of deputation attempting to persuade Robert to ameliorate working conditions.

Gale, Abraham. John Gale's son.

Gale, John. A smalltime clothier, landlord to Mr Donne.

Gale, Mrs. John Gale's wife. Long-suffering of the curates.

Gerard, Constantine. The Moore brothers' maternal grandfather.

Gerard, Hortense. Mother of Robert and Louis Moore.

Gill, Mrs. Shirley Keeldar's housekeeper at Fieldhead.

Grame, Mr. Sir Philip Nunnely's steward.

Graves, Mr. Also spelt 'Greaves'. Assistant to Drs MacTurk snr and jnr.

Grey, Caroline. Mrs Pryor's maiden name.

Hall, Cyril. Vicar of Nunnely. (Rev. William Margetson Heald.)

Hall, Margaret. Sister of Rev. Cyril Hall. (Harriet Heald.)

Hall, Mr Pearson. Shirley's family solicitor.

Hardman, Miss. A lady of snobbish pretensions.

Hardman, Mrs. Mrs Pryor's early employer.

Hartley, Michael. Drunk and mentally disturbed weaver who shoots Robert Moore.

Helstone, Agnes. Real name of Mrs Pryor.

Helstone, Caroline. Shares status of chief character with Shirley. Shy, introspective ward of her uncle, Rector Helstone. (Idealized self-portrait? Ellen Nussey?)

Helstone, James. Mrs Pryor's husband, Caroline's father. Died when she was eight.

Helstone, Mrs James. *See* Pryor, Mrs.

Helstone, Mrs Matthewson. *See* Cave, Mary.

Helstone, Rev. Matthewson. Rector of Briarfield, Caroline's uncle. (Rev. Hammond Robertson.)

Hogg, Mrs. Rev. Malone's landlady.

Horsfall, Mrs Zillah. Nurse who tends Robert Moore after the shooting.

John. Shirley's servant.

John-of-Mally's-of-Hannah's-of-Deb's. One of three suitors of Sarah, Hortense Moore's servant.

Keeldar, Charles Cave. Shirley's father; dies in her girlhood.

Keeldar, Henry Shirley. *See* Sympson, Henry (Harry).

Keeldar, Shirley. Eponymous heroine of the novel. A young, attractive heiress. (Emily Brontë.)

Langweilig, Mr. A German Moravian minister who discourses at Nunnely's Bible Society meeting.

Lina. Affectionate derivative of Caroline.

Macarthey, Mr. Malone's successor as curate of Briarfield.

MacTurk, the Drs. Father and son medicos. (Dr MacTurk.)

Malone, Peter Augustus. Greedy, noisy and opinionated Irish curate of Briarfield. (Rev. J.W. Smith.)

Mann, Miss. An old maid; acquaintance of Caroline's.

Moore, Gerard. Dead father of Hortense, Louis, Robert.

Moore, Hortense. Robert and Louis Moore's elder sister and the former's housekeeper. Tutor to Caroline Helstone.

Moore, Louis Gerard. Hortense and Robert's brother. Becomes tutor to Henry Sympson; teaches Shirley French, and marries her.

Moore, Robert Gerard. Cloth manufacturer at Hollow's Mill. Caroline Helstone's cousin and her eventual husband. (William Cartwright.)

Murgatroyd, Fred. Loyal employee of Robert Moore.

Noah o'Tim's. One of the leaders of the workers' deputation to Robert Moore.

Nunnely, Lady. Sir Philip's mother.

Nunnely, the Misses. Characterless sisters of Sir Philip.

Nunnely, Sir Monckton. Sir Philip Nunnely's late father.

Nunnely, Sir Philip. Owner of Nunnely Priory, infatuated with Shirley.

Pearson, Anne. Daughter of millowner; name linked with Robert Moore's.

Pearson, Kate. Apparently Mr Pearson's daughter.

Pearson, Mr. Millowner who is shot at.

Pearson, Susan. Apparently Mr Pearson's daughter.

Phoebe. Pointer bitch of Sam Wynne's.

Pighills, Jeremiah. Employee of Robert Moore's, alleged to be Sarah's sweetheart.

Pryor, Mrs. Real name, Agnes Helstone, *née* Grey. Caroline Helstone's mother. (Margaret Wooler.)

Ramdsen, Mrs. Resident of Briarfield who orders children's socks from Caroline's 'Jew Basket' (*see* Glossary to the Novels).

Ramsden, Timothy. Corn-factor of Royd Mill.

Rile, Dr. Caroline's doctor.

Roakes, Mr. Millowner.

Rouse, Mrs. Parishioner of Briarfield, and contributor to 'Jew Basket' (*see* Glossary to the Novels).

Ryde, Colonel. Officer in charge of the Briarfield District military which helps defence of Hollow's Mill against workers' attack.

Sarah. Servant to Robert and Hortense Moore.

Scott, Harry. Joe Scott's son, employed by Robert Moore.

Scott, Joe. Moore's mill supervisor.

Sugden. Police constable who arrests the agitator-preacher, Barraclough.

Sumner, Mr. Schoolmaster at Briarfield Grammar School.

Supplehough. Dissenting (Baptist) preacher.

Sweeting, David. Curate of Nunnely. Marries Dora Sykes. (Rev. James Chesterton Bradley.)

Sykes. Worker at Robert Moore's mill.

Sykes, Christopher. Wealthy millowner.

Sykes, John. Son of Christopher Sykes.

Sykes, the Misses. Six exist, four actually appear and are named: Harriet, Dora, Hannah and Mary.

Sykes, Mrs. Christopher Sykes's wife. Pious and 'bilious'.

Sympson, Henry (Harry). Only son of the Sympsons. Shirley's favourite cousin.

Sympson, the Misses. Mr and Mrs Sympson's daughters – Isabella and Gertrude.

Sympson, Mr. Shirley's uncle. Pious, nervous, respectable.

Sympson, Mrs. Wife of Mr Sympson. A bigot.
Tartar. Shirley's dog. Half-mastiff, half-bulldog.
Tom. Mr Helstone's assistant.
'Troubler, the'. At one point Shirley refers to Robert Moore by this description.
Whipp, Mrs. Sweeting's landlady.
Wynne, the Misses. Unnamed (one fair, one dark) daughters of Mr Wynne.
Wynne, Mr. Magistrate of Briarfield.
Wynne, Samuel Fawthrop. Wynne the magistrate's son.
Yorke, Hester. Wife of Hiram. Given to hysterics.
Yorke, Hiram. Blunt, much-travelled Yorkshire landowner. (Joshua Taylor.)
Yorke, Jessie. Younger daughter of Yorke family. Her father's favourite, she died young. (Martha Taylor.)
Yorke, Mark. Middle son of Hiram Yorke. (John Taylor.)
York, Martin. Younger son of Hiram Yorke. (Joseph Taylor.)
Yorke, Matthew. Yorke's eldest son. (Joshua Taylor, jnr.)
Yorke, Rose. Daughter of Hiram Yorke. (Mary Taylor.)
Zoë. Shirley's mare.

Places

Aire. Yorkshire river on which the city of Leeds stands and which gives its name to the famous dale and the famous breed of dog.
Badajos. After capturing this town the Duke of Wellington advanced to win the decisive battle of Salamanca (q.v.) in the Spanish Peninsular War.
Bilberry Moss. Apparently part of country near Stilbro'.
Botany Bay. On New South Wales coast immediately south of Sydney, discovered 1770 by Capt. Cook.
Briarfield. Parish where most of the action of *Shirley* happens. (Birstall.)
Briarfield Church. Parish church in *Shirley*. (Birstall.)
Briarfield Rectory. Home of Caroline Helstone and her uncle. (Birstall.)
Calder. Four rivers bear this name in England. Charlotte is probably referring to that which rises near Burnley and joins the River Aire near Castleford.
Cliff-bridge. There was a bridge of this name near the lodging house where Anne Brontë died. (Scarborough.)
Connaught. Western province of Eire, bounded by Atlantic to west and Ulster to north.
De Walden. Variant for Walden (Hall), seat of the Wynne family.
Ecclefigg. Hamlet in the parish of Whinbury.
Fieldhead. The home of Shirley Keeldar. (Oakwell Hall.)
Fitful-Head. *See* Stromoe.
George, the. Inn at Stilbro'. (George Inn, Bradford.)
Hollow's Mill. Located in a valley near Fieldhead, it belongs to Shirley. (Hunsworth.)
Milldean. Near Whinbury. Village to which Supplehough, the dissenting preacher, goes to preach.
Nunnely. (Hartshead; Kirklees Park; Kirklees Hall.)
Nunnely Common. (Hartshead Common.)
Nunnely Wood. (Nunwood, near Hartshead.)
Pampeluna. Captured by Wellington in Spanish Peninsular War.

Redhouse Inn. (At Gomersal.)

Royd-lane. Narrow lane leading to Nunnely Common. A common West Yorkshire street-name.

Rushedge. Described as 'sullen', it is an area of scrubland near Robert Moore's home. (Liversedge.)

St Sebastian. Captured by Wellington in Spanish Peninsular War.

Salamanca. Decisive battle in Peninsular War on 22 July 1812 which made final English victory in Spain inevitable.

Scheldt. River flowing from France through the Low Countries to the North Sea.

Shetland. Knowledge of the Shetland Isles was derived by Charlotte from Walter Scott's novel, *The Pirate* (1825).

Stilbro'. Market town with barracks. (Leeds; Huddersfield.)

Stromoe. One of a number of references to the islands lying north of the British Isles which Charlotte obtained from Sir Walter Scott's novel, *The Pirate* (1825).

Suderoe. *See* Stromoe.

Sympson Grove. In '——shire', a southern county, and presumably the home of the Sympson family.

Vittoria. Spanish battle, 21 June 1813, in which Wellington defeated Napoleon.

Walden Hall. Seat of the Wynne family.

Whinbury. A focal point for events in *Shirley*. Market town. (Dewsbury.)

Wormwood Wells. A famous spa. (Harrogate.)

Zahara. Sahara.

Villette (1853)

Commentary

Villette is regarded by many critics and readers as Charlotte's best novel. George Eliot wrote privately that she had 'only just returned to a sense of the real world about me, for I have been reading *Villette*, a still more wonderful book than *Jane Eyre*. There is something almost preternatural in its power.'

That is a very categorical statement about a work which is far less well known than *Jane Eyre* and probably less read than *Shirley* – with which it is, however, often very favourably compared, being regarded as excellently constructed by contrast with *Shirley*'s sprawling architecture.

Many people, too, accept it as Charlotte's most autobiographical novel, telling the story of her anguished love affair with Heger at the Brussels pensionnat to which she went with Emily, and of her life as a governess/teacher at the school. There can be no doubt of its closeness to many of Charlotte's experiences in Brussels, and it is easy to believe that its account of Lucy Snowe's on/off love affair comes close to the bone of actuality. But we must remember that there is no evidence which would enable us to know how close to what really happened are the events and inner feelings described in the novel; neither do we know enough about M. and Madame Heger to assume that they are portrayed with more or less truth.

One further important point of curiosity should be noted. It is that when we consider that Lucy Snowe occupies at least as prominent a place in this novel as Jane Eyre does in the earlier one – and that is saying a very great deal – it is surprising that its title is what it is. Even more curious – why *Villette* which, as a pseudonym for Brussels, is an insult? It suggests a mean little place. Did Charlotte hate it to designate it thus? Were the eventually unhappy associations of Brussels with Heger guiding her pen?

No answers are possible, but it is certainly reasonable to claim that the novel's strong aura of actuality, perhaps even its overall unity, derived from Charlotte's experiences in Brussels. However close to or far from the truth of those experiences the novel might be, it is about a governess/teacher and about her love affair with a senior teacher in the school – in other words, it could be the account of Charlotte's own life there.

But this impression of unity might well have an artistic rather than a geographical source. Charlotte had already worked over the same material in her novel *The Professor*. It was judged an artistic failure, but perhaps she was too near to its autobiographical sources; her experience of writing it may well have enabled her to distance herself to produce the greater, more integrated *Villette*.

Apart from this she had already had the gruelling experience of writing and publishing two major novels – a process which concentrates the mind wonderfully. She had, too, taken to heart a good deal of the criticism urged against her, particularly that which deplored her 'romantic' tendency to avoid hard realism and to indulge in fantasy. This criticism was first heard, of course, of the more sensational portions of *Jane Eyre*; *Shirley*, which followed, was in part intended to be an embodied rebuttal, but her critics were not easily mollified. *Villette* was, as certainly as *Shirley*, written with the strictures still ringing in her head – though curiously, as its readers will have noted, it contains, in one or two of its episodes, material at least the equal of those in *Jane Eyre* which were deemed over-romanticized. (See Contemporary Comments.)

Still, the experience of writing *Shirley* had undoubtedly honed Charlotte's pen more accurately to fit the task of reconciling and combining 'realism' and 'romanticism'. She is more successful in allowing equal status to both her sharp ability to observe and her limitless access of imaginative power.

Villette, however, has weaknesses, one of which is arguably the most serious to be found in all Charlotte's major work. The episodes in which a supposed spectral nun walks through the confines of the pensionnat can be judged a conspicuous failure in artistic judgement. As they occur they reply on Gothic fantasy and receive from the modern reader that heightened frisson of emotional expectation mixed with amusement that exaggerated Gothic usually inspires. But their explanation renders them not only ridiculous but quite superfluous. There was no reason whatsoever why they should have been allowed into the novel; they render no service to it.

Apart from this, it takes a patient taste to accept the somewhat overdone character of Paul Emmanuel. At times he is very near to being grotesque, a caricature:

> I used to think, as I sat looking at M. Paul, while he was knitting his brow or protruding his lip over some exercise of mine, which had not as many faults as he wished (for he liked me to commit faults: a knot of blunders was sweet to him as a cluster of nuts. . .)

He could be a figure out of the heightened world of Angria. We have to remember that, despite her ambitions to be more realistic, Charlotte's adhesion to her childhood universe still had force.

Several other characters and incidents (notably the Priest and Madame Walravens) have this patina of slight grotesquerie. Charlotte was a long way from ridding herself of that disposition to use overheated parts of her imagination, for which she had been so frequently taken to task. Paul Emmanuel's devotion to his dead fiancée becomes emotionally embarrassing. Judiciously employed it could have given a poignant aura to his character, but there is far too much of it, and it palls.

On the other hand the realistic parts of the novel are superbly done, particularly those which depict life in the school. They ring true, and, indeed, smell true – you can almost scent the distinctive school aroma in your nostrils. Even more are they true in their psychological effects – the sense of how difficult it is for the teachers/governesses to escape from the prison of the classroom and pupils; and in their visual detail – how well we get to know this pensionnat, its big and little rooms, the desks, their occupants, and that strange, forbidden walkway of its garden which is half a prisoner's prescribed exercise walk and half an escape-way, the *allée défendue*.

Some critics have commented on the picture of Brussels as convincing in its detail and accuracy. But what is remarkable is that, while it does have a vivid authenticity, this has in fact been achieved with, really, a minimum of material. Lucy Snowe has a quite parsimonious experience of the city; there is nothing comprehensive in her knowledge of it. This is, of course, true to Emily's and Charlotte's knowledge also, for they seem to have ventured out but rarely and quite unadventurously. One critic has written of *Villette*'s depictions of theatres, parks, art galleries, public buildings, and so on, but Charlotte actually describes only one representative of each. She pluralizes only in her mention of churches. (It would, in any case, be typical of Charlotte – and, we may guess, of Emily – to memorialize one single experience with such intensity that it would appear to have been encountered more frequently than it actually was.)

One characteristic of the novel considerably aids the impression of its authenticity with regard to place. It is the extensive use of French words and phrases, and with great naturalness. Not every reader will be happy, for obvious reasons, with those many pages of *Villette* dotted with Gallic patois, idiom and allusion – for them a glossary is invaluable – but the initiated will realize the amazing extent to which Charlotte had absorbed the culture of a country she knew virtually only through the activities of a school.

Her mind had widened also to accommodate a greater versatility of characterization than before. *Villette* contains far more characters than any other of her novels: a whole galaxy of pupils, who are given a sharp individuality by Charlotte's keen observation. Her satirical spirit was absolutely suited to quick sketches of young adolescents, few if any of whom she seems to have liked. The collection of middle-range characters (that is in terms of their importance in the process of the novel) – Madame Walravens, the Brettons, and Ginevra Fanshawe – are vividly and skilfully portrayed, particularly the last who could have come out overdone. The fact that she was as frivolous as she was beautiful means that Charlotte abhorred her, but, even though she did, she preserved her imaginative discipline and refrained from caricature. Ginevra is a very credible young thing, and so is Madame Beck – a cold, ruthless woman, always set on getting what she wants and the more dangerous because she pursues her aims with great practicality and an appearance of friendship.

Dr John Graham Bretton is one of Charlotte's typically ambiguous portraits of a male. Like Robert Moore in *Shirley* he is full of charm and kindness, but is equally full of unpredictability – his emotional reactions to a situation are always in doubt, and, therefore, so is his judgement of the people who are closest to him. He is not an altogether attractive character; there is a flaw in him (as in most of Charlotte's men), a failure of resoluteness in judgement, and a disposition to let his emotions lead him by the nose.

It is tacitly accepted that Paul Emmanuel is a portrait of Heger, but there is no proof of it or, if it is, of its accuracy. M. Paul is charming, easily exacerbated; he is fond of wielding authority, he is shrewd. He is full of contradictions and Lucy is attracted to him like a moth to a flame. The image is perhaps apter than it seems, for there is an aura of fatality around their relationship. Lucy's peace of mind is constantly disturbed by his sometimes inexplicable behaviour, he gives every impression of hoarding a secret grief or torment – and we finally realize that this is indeed the case. And though his disappearance at the end is ambiguous, death is probably the reason. The love Lucy and M. Paul generate is only streaked with light and it has an elegiac conclusion.

We do not, however, see Paul Emmanuel only through the eyes of Lucy Snowe. Sometimes we see him, so to speak, straight. This double dimension to the character certainly increases its depth, and the use of the objective method as well as the subjective one of presentation enables Charlotte to introduce humour to what otherwise might have been a cheerless and irascible creation. In the event, although Paul Emmanuel sometimes seems on the point of going off (as character) into some fantastic orbit, as Charlotte's romanticism works on him, there is always the strong gravitational pull of natural behaviour which she exerts to draw him back from suprahuman flights:

> He took my hand in one of his, with the other he put back my bonnet; he looked into my face, his luminous smile went out, his lips expressed something almost like the wordless language of a mother who finds a child greatly and unexpectedly changed, broken with illness or worn out by want.

The triumph of *Villette* as a novel is Charlotte's depiction of Lucy. She is in a number of ways an unlikeable young lady. She is not without priggishness, self-indulgence, and a certain morbidity of spirit and, perhaps, she seems less physically brave and emotionally tough than Jane Eyre. But there is no way in which the narrative of her experience fails to grip and hold our attention and no sense in which we disbelieve in her as a credible being.

On the contrary many readers find a great deal of mitigation for the less attractive parts of her character in accepting the proposition that Charlotte was embodying in Lucy a study of neurosis, of mental breakdown. There is much in the novel to support this. The build-up of Lucy's progress towards spiritual loneliness, at times in circum-stances of literal physical loneliness, is relentless and carefully achieved. It is done with such a deliberation that it is impossible not to believe that Charlotte intends to lead us to the experience of what loneliness is and what it can do. The love Lucy bears for John Bretton is unrequited – even more, its existence is treated almost flippantly by him; her relationship with Paul Emmanuel occasions more distress and anxiety than happiness. The culmination of this destitution of the spirit and draining of the emotions is almost symbolic in its implications, even though it is terribly realistic in its impact – Lucy's isolation with the idiot child throughout the long hot summer:

> My heart almost died within me: miserable longings strained its chords. How long were the September days! How silent, how lifeless! How vast and void seemed the desolate premises! How gloomy the forsaken gardens – grey now with the dust of a town summer departed.

The effects on Lucy's mind and spirit are reflected in areas of hallucinatory description. Indeed the accusations of Gothic overwriting to which reference has been made could be countered by suggesting that the descriptions of the visitations of the strange nun are less ridiculous than an awful emblem of Lucy's growing disordered state. Similarly, the account of Lucy's wild rush to the park festival can be taken as not so much over-sensational as a very precise evocation of mental disorder:

> I knew my route, yet it seemed as if I was hindered from pursuing it direct: now a sight, and now a sound, called me aside, luring me down this alley and down that. Already I saw the thick-planted trees which framed this tremulous and rippled glass, when, choiring out of a glade to the right, broke such a sound as I thought might be heard if Heaven were to open – . . .

Jane Eyre makes almost a virtue of emotional and spiritual isolation, constantly using it to steel her moral resolve; Lucy Snowe almost becomes a victim of it. But it is at the point where she seems most likely to succumb that some hint of amelioration appears.

If *Villette* is a triumphant study of mental breakdown, it is also a remarkable embodiment of a return to equilibrium. This is not easily achieved (one could never imagine a Brontë depicting anything that was easily achieved!) Lucy has to learn simply not to want what she cannot receive – the most difficult lesson for any human being. She has to learn, too, absolutely to accept what the truth of her situation is, and that kind of acceptance involves a fight within the spirit; it is not a silent, still, matter.

It is surely not accidental that there should be such frequent references to Bunyan's *Pilgrim's Progress* in the middle and latter stages of this novel, and in particular to Christian's fight with the Giant Despair. Lucy emerges from her battle chastened but in a state of relative quietude.

And, at this point, an irony begins to enter the novel. As her wanting of Bretton diminishes and dies her realization of the possibility of a love relationship with Paul Emmanuel grows. The irony is that it grows, begins to flower, and is recognized by both only to be stopped, suddenly, by Paul Emmanuel's departure.

There is an analogy with *King Lear*, in the nature of the inner struggle and the irony of the resolution of *Villette*. Both protagonists, Lucy and Lear, achieve a kind of dignified equilibrium after a period of storm within; in the case of Lear his love for Cordelia is restored, in the case of Lucy she discovers a love. But they both lose what they have gained, in Lear's case almost at the moment of attainment, and in Lucy's very near to it.

But *Villette* is positive in its conclusion, *King Lear* is ambiguous. Lear dies, and we do not know how far Shakespeare intends us to interpret his story as an affirmation of the value of human existence or as a bitter comment on it. In Lucy's case she loses her love but we sense, surely, that Charlotte intends us to be left with the proposition that life must be faced if truth is to be found, and peace of mind and soul is to be assured.

Charlotte learned that lesson somewhere – perhaps after her life in Brussels with Heger. If we are considering how much this novel derives from Charlotte's own experience, it is as well to record that in it there is an account of a spiritual turmoil which, we know from her letters, Charlotte herself experienced. Simply expressed it was brought about by her reflections on her religious faith and observance. She had, at one time, found her curiosity about that religion which lay at the extreme end of the spectrum from her own – Roman Catholicism - too strong to deny. But it was not simple curiosity that had led her when she was living in Brussels to go to the Cathedral of Ste Gudule. In a letter to Emily from Brussels in September 1843 she said that she went in and 'I really did confess. A real confession.' What, indeed, had prompted her to do this was a terrible access of depression and loneliness when she had been left alone in the Heger pensionnat during the school holidays. The confession was a flirtation with peril, a salve to curiosity and (though she might never have admitted it) an attempt to find a balm to a hurt spirit.

The case for this novel's close attachment to Charlotte's own experience is very strong but not completely watertight. Areas of it with no affiliations to actuality may well have been created inside that fertile imagination.

What, however, is undeniable is the quality of writing in the novel. There is an easy versatility of moods, therefore of stylistic emphases and modes, which suggests a confidence in her abilities she had not before shown with such sureness. Her description of romantic love is beautifully balanced in its sentiment and its detail:

> Once more I see that moment – I see the snow-twilight stealing through the window over which the curtain was not dropped, for I designed to watch him ride up the white walk; I see and feel the soft firelight warming me, playing on my silk dress, and fitfully showing me my own young figure in a glass. I see the moon of a calm winter night float full, clear, and cold, over the inky mass of shrubbery, and the silvered turf of my grounds. I wait, with some impatience in my pulse, but no doubt in my breast.

Only rarely in her published novels, though much more commonly in her Angrian stories, did Charlotte allow herself so much sensuousness.

Her ability at thumbnail sketching is even more economically brilliant than in *Shirley*. Her eyes in *Villette* not only missed nothing, they selected with a ruthless efficiency:

> So trim her waist, her cap, her dress – I wondered how they had all been manufactured. Her speech had an accent which in its mincing glibness seemed to rebuke mine as by authority.

And a scornful one:

> ... her liking and disliking, her love and hate, were mere cobweb and gossamer; but she had one thing about her that seemed strong and durable enough, and that was – her selfishness.

Or a viciously pitying one:

> The sight of a piece of gold would bring into her eyes a green glisten, singular to witness. She once, as a mark of high favour, took me upstairs, and, opening a secret door, showed me a hoard – a mass of coarse, large coin – about fifteen guineas, in five-franc pieces. She loved this hoard as a bird loves its eggs. These were her savings. She would come and talk to me about them with an infatuated and persevering dotage, strange to behold in a person not yet twenty-five.

The identification of self with nature which was noted in *Jane Eyre* is not completely in abeyance in *Villette* – 'Twilight was falling and I deemed its influence pitiful' – but has largely given place to a greater largesse of natural description, with more emphasis on its sensuous effects than its spiritual relationship with human moods and attributes:

> The morning broke calm as summer, with singing of birds in the garden, and a light dew-mist that promised heat. We all said it would be warm, and we all felt pleasure in folding away heavy garments, and in assuming the attire suiting a sunny season.

Everything about *Villette* bespeaks the accomplished professional writer. Charlotte was at the top of her powers when she wrote it. If it is as autobiographical as many believe it to be then her achievement is compounded, for it is probably the most difficult task any writer can attempt – to tell one's own story while preserving that sense of imaginative balance, discipline, and above all, selectivity, by which, alone, a work of art is achieved.

Synopsis

Lucy Snowe, an orphan, visits her godmother, Mrs Mary Bretton, where she meets Paulina (Polly) Home (whose mother has recently died) who is staying with the Brettons, and the handsome auburn-haired John Graham, Mrs Bretton's sixteen-year-old son, whom Polly adores.

For a great part of the next eight years Lucy acts as companion to the stern irascible Miss Marchmont, an elderly cripple. One February night, Lucy hears wailing outside her window, and at the same time Miss Marchmont dies. Lucy is left alone in London. On impulse she crosses the channel to Boue-Marine, meeting on board Miss Ginevra Fanshawe, a perky, attractive but not over-intelligent girl who, at the instigation of her godfather, the Comte de Bassompierre, is en route to Madame Beck's school in Villette. Ginevra tells Lucy that Madame Beck needs an English governess. Lucy makes her way to Villette, and helped by a mysterious Englishman finds herself outside the Pensionnat des Demoiselles, where Madame Beck offers her a post as governess to her children. M. Paul Emmanuel, a teacher at the school, intervenes, however, judging Lucy to be worth more, and she is offered a teaching post instead. Lucy quickly learns French, as well as the good and bad points of Madame Beck herself – on the one side, her care of her pupils' physical needs; on the other, the espionage system by which she gets her pupils to spy on each other for her. She renews her acquaintance with Ginevra who is interested in nothing but music, singing, dancing, the mysterious man who is wooing her, and the dandy, Colonel de Hamal, who attracts her. When Madame Beck's daughter breaks an arm, Dr John is called in and Lucy realizes he is not only Ginevra's mystery man, but also the man who helped her when she first arrived in Villette. Lucy takes part in the school play directed by Paul Emmanuel, when de Hamal is pointed out to her.

In the summer vacation Lucy remains at the school looking after a deformed pupil, and when the pupil leaves, Lucy is alone. She spends her time exploring Brussels and growing increasingly unhappy, until one day she is drawn to a Catholic church. She enters the confessional where the priest realizes she is ill. She collapses on the way out and the priest leaves her in the care of a doctor who takes her to his home, where Lucy recognizes his mother as Mrs Bretton, and the doctor – Dr John – as the grown-up John Graham Bretton. Staying with them, she upsets Dr John by trying to find out his involvement with Ginevra, but his infatuation for the girl takes a severe blow because of her discourteous behaviour towards Mrs Bretton, whom she meets at the theatre. On the same evening Paul Emmanuel expresses disapproval of Lucy's pink dress.

On her return to the Pensionnat, Lucy puts an unopened letter from Dr John in a locked casket to read later. That night, having read the kindly letter, she is terrified by the apparition of a nun. The letter disappears, but Dr John is on hand to pacify her. His friendly letters continue. One night at a theatre they attend, a fire breaks out and a young girl is hurt, whom Dr John attends. She turns out to be Polly and the old affectionate relationship between them is renewed.

After discovering Madame Beck has been reading her letters, Lucy decides to bury them in a jar in the garden, when the nun appears again. Paul Emmanuel makes sarcastic remarks about her visits to her friends, but Lucy finds herself attracted to his odd mixture of gallantry and gaucherie, sensibility and sourness, anger and affection. After seeing him and Madame Beck conferring together, Lucy is sent to an old cantankerous woman, Madame Walravens, once supported by Paul Emmanuel. He was engaged to her grand-daughter who died in a convent. Lucy reveals to him that she knows of this and they resolve to be friends.

De Bassompierre gives permission, at Lucy's request, for Dr John and Polly to be married. Paul Emmanuel sends Lucy a note saying he must see her before he leaves on an unexpected visit to the West Indies on Madame Walravens' behalf. Madame Beck gives her a drugged drink, lest Paul Emmanuel might entangle himself with her, but it makes her more wakeful. Wandering into the Park where there is a festival, she see Paul Emmanuel, Madame Beck, Madame Walravens, Père Silas (to whom she had made confession) and a young girl together. Learning Paul Emmanuel has postponed his journey, Lucy naturally believes the young girl is in some way connected with this. She realizes she herself is in love with Paul Emmanuel. Returning to bed, she discovers the nun's habit on her bed and learns that Ginevra has eloped with de Hamal who had been using the nun's disguise to meet her secretly.

Paul Emmanuel visits Lucy, rebuking and dismissing the interfering Madame Beck. He arranges for Lucy to have charge of a school during his absence, and before he leaves they declare their love for each other. Lucy is a successful head of the school and the novel ends on a note of uncertainty with reports of storms and shipwrecks likely to affect Paul Emmanuel on his return home.

Characters

A—— and Z——, Messieurs. A—— is a French Academician. Z—— is a gracious, quiet, learned Frenchman. They both dine at Mr Home de Bassompierre's.

Agnes. Ill-tempered servant of Madame Walravens.

Aigredoux, Madame. Paulina Home's former schoolmistress.

Angélique. Pupil at Madame Beck's.

Barrett, Mrs. Once Lucy's nurse. Housekeeper to Mrs Leigh.

Bassompierre, M. de. Formerly Mr Home. Father of Paulina.

Beck, Desirée. Madame Beck's unpleasant eldest child.

Beck, Fifine. Madame Beck's pleasant second child.

Beck, Georgette. Madame Beck's affectionate youngest child.

Beck, Marie Modeste. *Née* Kint. Directs the school in Rue Fossette, Villette, to which Lucy Snowe goes as teacher. (Madame Heger.)

Boissec and Rochemort, Messieurs. A couple (one dark, one fair) of pedantic, sceptical mockers on Madame Beck's staff.

Braun, Anna. Middle-aged German who teaches Lucy Snowe and Paulina Home.

Bretton, Dr. Deceased husband of Lucy's godmother.

Bretton, John Graham. Young English doctor to the Pensionnat of Madame Beck. The son of Lucy Snowe's godmother. Marries Paulina Home de Bassompierre. (George Murray Smith.)

Bretton, Mrs Louisa. Godmother to Lucy Snowe. Widow of a physician. Resides first in Bretton, then at La Terrasse, Villette. Mother of Dr John Bretton. (Mrs George Smith.)

Broc, Marie. Deformed cretin pupil at Madame Beck's.

Candace. Paulina Home's doll.

Charles. Lucy's uncle.

Charlotte. Younger sister of stewardess of cross-channel ferry.

Cholmondeley, Mrs. Ginevra Fanshawe's chaperone.

Coralie. Pupil at Madame Beck's school.

Davies, Augusta. Ginevra Fanshawe's sister, married to a man who looks much older than her.

Davies, Mr. Augusta Fanshawe's husband.

Digby, Dr. Headmaster of John Bretton's school.

Dindonneau, Duc de, Prince of Labassecour. The title means 'young turkey-fowl'. The owner is a small boy who accompanies his parents (King and Queen of Labassecour) to a concert also attended by Lucy Snowe.

Dolores. Catalan pupil at Madame Beck's.

Dorlodot, Madame la Baronne de. Colonel Comte de Hamal's aunt.

Emmanuel, Josef. Paul Emmanuel's half-brother.

Emmanuel, Paul Carl David. Professor in his kinswoman's, Madame Beck's, school. He and Lucy Snowe exhibit a strong mutual attraction. (M. Heger.)

Fanshawe, Capt. Ginevra's father. An officer on half pay.

Fanshawe, Ginevra. Niece of de Bassompierre. Pupil at Madame Beck's Pensionnat. Flits by moonlight with the Comte de Hamal.

Frank. Miss Marchmont's lover, killed in riding accident shortly before their marriage.

Goton. Flemish cook at Madame Beck's.

Gustave. Nephew of Comte de Hamal who attends the school next door to Madame Beck's.

Hamal, Colonel Comte Alfred de. Elopes with, and marries, Ginevra Fanshawe.

Hamal, Alfred Fanshawe de Bassompierre de. Son of Colonel Comte de Hamal.

Harriet (Hurst), Mrs. First, nursemaid to Paulina Home; later her maid.

Home, Mrs Ginevra. Wife of Mr Home, afterwards Comte de Bassompierre. Mother of 'the little Countess'.

Isabelle. Outspoken pupil at Madame Beck's.

Isidore. Name given by Ginevra Fanshawe to her suitor, John Bretton, because she believes his own name to be unromantic.

Jones, Mr. Keeper of bookstore in Paternoster Row, London.

Justine-Marie. The dead fiancée of Paul Emmanuel who, when separated from her family, became a nun. Though dead, her character is used as an influence on others.

Kint, Madame. Madame Beck's mother.

Kint, Victor. Madame Beck's brother.

Labassecour, King of. A melancholy man of fifty. (King Leopold I of the Belgians.)

Labassecour, Queen of. Mild, thoughtful, graceful, kind, loving, elegant. (Louise, Queen of the Belgians.)

La Malle, Mlle. Pupil at Madame Beck's school.

Leigh, Charles. Young son of former schoolfellow of Lucy's.

Leigh, Mrs. Schoolfellow of Lucy Snowe, subsequently mistress of mansion employing Mrs Barrett as housekeeper.

Louison. Servant of Paulina Home de Bassompierre.

Lucien. Character in school play at Madame Beck's, acted by Lucy Snowe.

Manon. Flemish-speaking servant of Paulina Home de Bassompierre.

Marchmont, Miss Maria. Crippled old lady. Lucy acts as her companion.

Marchmont, Mr. Miss Marchmont's heir and cousin.

Martha. Mrs Bretton's servant.

Mathilde. Pupil at Madame Beck's.

Matou, Rosine. Portress at Madame Beck's.

Matthieu. Servant to M. de Bassompierre.

Melcy, Blanche de. Aristocratic pupil at Madame Beck's school.

Minnie. Name given to Lucy Snowe by Georgette Beck.

Miret. Bookseller to Madame Beck's school. Becomes Lucy's landlord and sends his three daughters to her rented school.

Mühler, Heinrich. Young, fair-headed German merchant engaged to Justine-Marie Sauveur.

Paul Carlos. Carlos – a diminutive of Carl – Paul Emmanuel's middle name.

Père Silas. Seventy-year-old Jesuit priest to whom Lucy Snowe 'confesses'. Former tutor to Paul Emmanuel.

Pillule, Dr. Madame Beck's family surgeon, but his absence during an accident enables Dr John Bretton to acquire his position as physician to the Pensionnat.

Polly. Shortened form of Paulina, daughter of Bassompierre.)

Rochemort, M. *See* Boissec.

Ruth. Miss Marchmont's servant.
St Pierre, Zélie de. Teacher at Madame Beck's. (Mlle Blanche.)
Sara, Lady. English peer's daughter; accompanies Ginevra to the concert.
Sauveur, Justine-Marie. God-daughter of Paul Emmanuel; niece of Justine-Marie, his dead fiancée. Engaged to Heinrich Mühler.
Snowe Lucy. Heroine of *Villette*. The novel is largely an account of her life in a school in Brussels, and is probably based on Charlotte's own experiences in the Pensionnat Heger.
Staas, M. le Chevalier. A Villette citizen who attends the Athenée prize-giving.
Svini, Madame. French version of Sweeney. She is superseded as a nursery governess to Madame Beck's children by Lucy Snowe.
Thomas. Miss Marchmont's servant.
Trinette. Maid ('bonne') to Madame Beck's children.
Turner, Miss. English teacher at Madame Beck's.
Vanderkelkov, Louise. Pupil at Madame Beck's whose part in a vaudeville fête is taken by Lucy because of illness.
Vashti. A celebrated actress.
Virginie. Pupil at Madame Beck's.
Walravens, Madame Magliore. Grandmother of Justine-Marie Walravens.
Warren. Mrs Bretton's servant.
Watsons, the. Affluent travellers across the channel; one of the family, a beautiful girl, is married to an old man.
Wilmot. Lucy's uncle.
Wilson, Mr. English master at Madame Beck's school.

Places

Basse-Ville. Lower part of a city; the unfashionable area.
Bois l'Etang. The wood in which Lucy and Dr Bretton ride together. (Palais Royale.)
Boue-Marine. The French port (with a fictional name) to which Lucy Snowe sails.
Bretton. Ancient town, home of Lucy Snowe's godmother, Mrs Bretton. (Bridlington; York; Leeds.)
Cornhill. Former site of City of London corn market; a street running from near Mansion House into Leadenhall Street.
Faubourg Clotilde, numéro 7. Location of the school found by Paul Emmanuel for Lucy Snowe and of which she becomes Directrice.
Grande Place. Open area in front of the Hôtel de Ville in Brussels.
Haute-Ville. Palatial residential and park area of Brussels.
Hôtel Crécy. Where Paulina and her father stay. (Hôtel Cluysenaar, later Hôtel Mengelle.)
La Terrasse. The Bretton's home outside Villette. (Château de Koekeberg.)
Labassecour. Fictional name for Belgium.
Paternoster Row. London Street near St Paul's, associated with bookselling. In the Middle Ages rosaries (paternosters) were made and sold there.
Porte de Crécy. (Porte de Namur.)
Rue de Mages. Home of Madame Walravens at number 3.
Rue St Jean. Referred to in Ginevra's letter to Lucy in which she tells of her elopement.

St Jean Baptiste. (Ste Gudule.)
Strand. Broad street running from Trafalgar Square to join Fleet Street at
Aldwych.
Temple Gardens. Gardens attached to the Inns of Court (e.g. Fountains, Gray's
inn) famous for training of barristers, and situated between river Thames and
Fleet Street.
Villette. Charlotte's name for Brussels.
West End, the. Leisure and entertainment area of London which Charlotte found
inferior to the City in providing her with a sense of deep excitement.

The Professor (1857)

Commentary

It is not clear when Charlotte began writing what many regard as her
most unsuccessful novel, but by April 1846 it was completed. Nine
publishers rejected it, but the last gave Charlotte sufficient encouragement to persuade her to continue writing. The result of this was *Jane
Eyre*.

The lesser work, then, was partly responsible for the genesis of the
greater one, and, in its turn, *Jane Eyre*'s success aided the eventual
appearance of *The Professor*. W.S. Williams, publisher's reader for
Smith, Elder and Co., urged Charlotte to try and re-make *The Professor*
in three-volume form, but it was not until early 1851 that Charlotte
declared it to be ready. Still it was delayed, however, to such an extent
that Charlotte never saw it published.

It eventually appeared in 1857 after it had undergone what can only
be described as a process of interference by Charlotte's husband, Arthur
Nicholls. His excisions and changes were motivated by principles
which had little to do with artistic realities, but more with current
moral susceptibilities.

The Professor, then, had a not altogether happy launching. To an
extent it may be said to have come into the world 'scarce half made up'.
Charlotte herself had doubts about it:

> I found the beginning very feeble, the whole narrative deficient in
> incident and in general attractiveness. Yet the middle and latter
> portion of the work, all that relates to Brussels, the Belgian School,
> etc., is as good as I can write: it contains more pith, more substance,
> more reality, in my judgement, than much of 'Jane Eyre'.

So she obviously entertained some admiration as well. She said that she
wanted to produce something 'soft, grave and true'. Not all, by any

means of its critics and reviewers would agree that this is what she achieved, but some, a minority, have the opinion that it is a far better piece of work than it has ever been allowed to be and that its virtues conform very closely to Charlotte's ambition for it.

It is unfortunate that its background is very similar indeed to that of *Villette*, for this has persuaded some commentators to assume that her writing of it was a trial run for the later, more mature novel. As with *Villette*, so many of its incidents are close to Charlotte's own experiences. Crimsworth's meeting with Frances Henri in the Protestant cemetery is based on Charlotte's visit to the grave of Martha Taylor. Crimsworth's sojourn at the pensionnat of Rue d'Isabelle derives from Charlotte's memory of Heger's school. The master/pupil relationship of Crimsworth and Frances echoes strongly the Heger/Charlotte relationship.

But, as usual, it is necessary to be cautious in assessing the 'natural' sources of a work of art. While Brussels, and Charlotte's experiences there, are undoubtedly a potent source, the citizens and locations of Charlotte's own imagination are of equal status in the creation of the novel.

For example, contrary to a superficial conclusion, M. Pelet is very probably not a direct portrait of M. Heger. The fictional character is very much a sensualist – Heger was not; Pelet was volatile – Heger was unpredictable; Pelet was morally permissive – Heger was a conformist: Madame Heger saw to that!

We must not forget that Angria still lurked inside Charlotte's imagination. The character of Pelet has much more in common with the flamboyant, eccentric, larger-than-life men of Angrian society than with the bourgeois of early nineteenth-century Brussels. And, to a lesser degree, Mlle Reuter is Angrian – particularly in her coquetry, her craftiness, her disposition to hunt and ensnare the male animal.

But it is less easy to see Frances Henri as anything other than yet another version of Charlotte herself. Frances is perhaps not so much Charlotte as she saw herself as Charlotte as she desired to be – loved (above all), the directrice of a school, praised by a superior (who should be a man). Frances Henri is an emblem of Charlotte's modest hopes for herself and the novel is very near to the centre of Charlotte's preoccupations. Not only is it, in a sense, a mirror of her experiences in Brussels, it also reflects some of those subjects which stirred her mind and conscience.

The Professor is written, too, with perhaps an over-conscious addiction to a principle Charlotte had decided should govern her creative work. All her life she was haunted, as an artist, by the fear that she might overwrite, might be found guilty of excess of one kind or another. In particular she yearned to be regarded as a realist, devoid of extremes – 'soft, grave and true'. She was never so explicit about this ambition with respect to her other novels as she was about *The Professor*.

And she studiously attempted to put this into practice: the school is depicted with a sure sense of actuality, the character of Frances, though it sometimes edges towards sentimentality, never loses decorum. She is the 'personification of discretion and forethought, of diligence and perseverance, of self-denial and self-control'. She has as much passion as Jane Eyre and as many moral scruples as Jane and Lucy Snowe, but she differs from them in being altogether less a slave to her passions and emotions. In fact, the novel as a whole seems to shun over-excitement of any kind. It preserves an even tenor. Some people find it dull.

Sometimes the expression is elegiac in tone:

> Belgium! I repeat the word, now as I sit alone near midnight. It stirs
> my world of the past like a summons to resurrection; the graves
> unclose, the dead are raised...

Sometimes (as when she writes of the condition of womankind) it has a kind of sad firmness which lacks her customary sharp satiric bite:

> Monsieur, if a wife's nature loathes that of the man she is wedded to,
> marriage must be slavery. Against slavery all right thinkers revolt,
> and though torture be the price of resistance, torture must be
> dared...

And sometimes (as when she writes of the Catholic church which she professes to abhor while remaining strangely fascinated by its outward show and its power) she writes with barely concealed venom: she attributes all the unpleasant characteristics of the girl pupils in the Belgian school of the novel to the influence of the Roman Catholic Church:

> I am not a bigot in matters of theology but I suspect the root of this
> precocious impurity, so obvious, so general in popish countries, is to
> be found in the discipline, if not the doctrines of the Church of
> Rome.

But in no other novel does Charlotte come so close to explicit sexuality in her descriptions of the growth of a love relationship. One senses the physical very near the surface of *Jane Eyre*, but in *The Professor* its presence is plain:

> ... she passed before me to stir the fire, which did not want stirring;
> she lifted and put down the little ornaments on the mantelpiece; her

dress waved within a yard of me; slight, straight, and elegant, she stood erect on the hearth.

There are impulses we can control; but there are others which control us, because they attain us with a tiger leap, and are our masters ere we have seen them.

The Professor needs to be read in a certain mood if the best of it is to be tasted. It asks for complete relaxation from the reader, for its own style is relaxed – certainly by comparison with the sudden tensions of *Jane Eyre* and *Villette*. There is even a certain languidness in Charlotte's descriptive passages:

Not only the winds, but the very fitful, wandering airs, were that afternoon, as by common consent, all fallen asleep in their various quarters.

Sometimes, too, that acuteness of observation, so characteristic of Charlotte in her major work, has a softer edge. Indeed, artistically the most remarkable feature of this novel is its comparative closeness in tone to the novels of her young sister, Anne. It is, to a degree, untypical of Charlotte.

Synopsis

William Crimsworth, writing to his friend Charles whom he has not seen for many years, tells how he has refused his uncle's offer to help him become a clergyman, and is now with his brother, Edward, a manufacturer who is married to a rich millowner's daughter, and that he is living at Crimsworth Hall. We are then introduced to Edward (whom William finds autocratic and disagreeable), who offers William a menial post, at the same time putting an employee, Timothy Steighton, to keep an eye on him. At a ball at Crimsworth Hall, William meets Yorke Hunsden, a blunt but kindly businessman, who advises him to leave his brother's firm. Edward accuses William of disloyalty and William resigns his post. On Hunsden's advice, he goes to Brussels to take up teaching. Introduced to M. Pelet, he takes a teaching post at his boys' school, where the window of his room overlooks the garden of the girls' school next door. The headmistress, Mlle Zoraïde Reuter, a domineering coquettish woman, offers him a part-time post in the girls' school. She is very attentive to him, and although not his type, he finds her interesting. He overhears Pelet and Mlle Reuter discussing their wedding arrangements, and is very disturbed to hear Pelet assure her that William is in love with her.

The next day a new pupil, Mlle Henri, arrives, whose full name he discovers is Frances Evans Henri. Intrigued, he resolves to find out more about her background. Her mother was English, her father a Swiss pastor; her only surviving relative is her Aunt Julienne; she hopes to go to England to teach French. He finds himself drawn to her despite Mlle Reuter's disparaging comments – that her connections are obscure, her resources scanty, and her health uncertain. Soon after this Frances is absent. Mlle Reuter denies dismissing her, but cannot give William her address. William resigns from Mlle Reuter's employment.

One day he sees Frances in the Protestant Cemetery tending the grave of her now dead aunt. He discovers Mlle Reuter had dismissed her and that Frances is now employed lace-mending. Meanwhile the relationship between William and Pelet fluctuates, Pelet at one time telling William about his past. In summer, as preparations are made for Pelet's marriage to Mlle Reuter, William, realizing he cannot stay under such circumstances, tenders his resignation. Frances's prospects improve with the offer of a teaching post, and William is distraught at the thought that if he had not resigned they could have got married on their joint incomes. He decides to ask Mr Vandenhuten, whose son he had once saved from drowning, for help. Hunsden arrives in Brussels with news of the sale of Crimsworth Hall, when Edward's business failed – though he is successful again now. Hunsden manages to get back for William the picture of his mother that was in the Hall. Eventually William gets a post as English Professor at a college in Brussels. Apprehensively he goes to see Frances, impulsively embracing her. They declare their love and marry. Hunsden, seeing William with Frances, mistakes her for Mlle Reuter whom he believes William loves. However William takes him to see Frances, and he is quite won over by her, leaving for England believing William to be a lucky man indeed.

Characters

Blemont, Caroline de. A pupil at Mlle Reuter's pensionnat. A girl of coarse sensuality.

Brown. Unpleasant acquaintance of William Crimsworth.

Brown, Mr. Gossipy, meticulous old gentleman who finds William Crimsworth a teaching post at Pelet's school.

Catherine, Lady. Young Irish baroness; pupil at Mrs William Crimsworth's school. Generous, clever.

Charles. Boyhood friend of William Crimsworth to whom William relates, by letter, the story of his early life.

Crimsworth, Edward. William's eldest brother. Employs William as clerk, wrongly accuses him of fomenting false rumour and drives him out.

Crimsworth, Mr. Shrewd businessman, Crimsworth's uncle, who rears William until the age of nine then blackmails the Seacombes into paying for his Eton education.

Crimsworth, Mrs. Edward's wife, elegant, red-haired, materialistic. Ill-treated by Edward.

Crimsworth, Victor. Son of William and Frances Evans Henri. A serious, strong-willed boy.

Crimsworth, Wilhelmina. Name that William Crimsworth suggests Hunsden has given Frances Henri.

Crimsworth, William. The Professor of the novel, youngest son of unsuccessful businessman and aristocratic wife. Driven out by his brother he makes a career in Belgium.

D——, Mrs. Directress of the first English school in Brussels. Accepts Frances Henri as a teacher after her dismissal by Mlle Reuter.

Dorlodot, de, La Petite. Small pupil at Mlle Reuter's.

Dronsart, Adèle. Belgian pupil at Mlle Reuter's. Vicious, deceitful and envious.

Eccles. Acquaintance of William Crimsworth.

Eulalie. Big blonde pupil at Mlle Reuter's; sits in front row.

G——, Georgiana. Sister of Julia G——.

G——, Julia. Daughter of English baronet, pupil at Frances Crimsworth's (*née* Henri's) boarding school established in England.

Henri, Frances Evans. Daughter of Swiss father, English mother. Lace-mender who earns money to pursue education and become a teacher. Marries William Crimsworth after several vicissitudes.

Henri, Julienne. Frances Evans Henri's aunt, at whose grave William Crimsworth discovers Frances after her departure from Mlle Reuter's.

Hortense. Fat, graceless, vivacious occupant of front row in William Crimsworth's class.

Hunsden, Hunsden Yorke. Slightly eccentric successful millowner who befriends William Crimsworth.

Jack. Edward Crimsworth's vicious horse.

King, Mrs. William Crimsworth lodges at her house while working for his brother.

Kint and Vandam. Two well-meaning, stupid Flemish ushers (i.e. monitors) at Pelet's school.

Koslow, Aurelia. Russo-German pupil at Mlle Reuter's.

Ledru, Léonie. Pupil at Mlle Reuter's. Small, bright, emaciated and short on conscience.

Ledru, M. Fifty-year-old music master at Mlle Reuter's.

'Lucia'. Raven-haired Italian beauty whose head painted on a miniature is shown to Crimsworth by Hunsden.

Lupton, Mrs. Fat, turbanned guest at Edward Crimsworth's ball. Mother of Sarah Martha.

Lupton, Sarah Martha. At Edward Crimsworth's ball, this well-built belle is flattered by Hunsden's flirtatiousness.

—— Mlle Mathilde de. Heiress of Belgian count, and pupil at Frances Crimsworth's (*née* Henri's) English boarding school.

Minnie. Servant employed by William Crimsworth after his marriage.

Müllenberg, Amélie. Pupil at Mlle Reuter's who, being both the oldest and most turbulent, is a torment to Frances Henri's attempts to teach.

'Ned'. Diminutive of Edward (Crimsworth).

Nicholl. Unpleasant acquaintance of William Crimsworth.

Path, Louise. The pleasantest of Mlle Reuter's pupils – but not altogether honest or well-mannered.

Pelagie, Mlle. French teacher at Mlle Reuter's, who was totally 'ordinary'.

Pelet, François. Employs William Crimsworth to teach English and Latin; engaged to Mlle Reuter.

Pelet, Madame. M. Pelet's mother, also his housekeeper. A happy, coarse-grained lady.

Reuter, Madame. Mlle Reuter's mother, and housekeeper. Fun-loving, bucolic.

Reuter, Zoraïde. Headmistress of girls' school. Employs William Crimsworth for extra lessons. Turns hot and cold in her relations with him, and eventually marries Pelet.

Rosalie. Portress at Mlle Reuter's.

Seacombe, the Hon. John. Crimsworth's mother's brother.

Seacombe, Sarah. One of Hon. John Seacombe's six daughters.

Smith. Unpleasant acquaintance of William Crimsworth.

Steighton, Timothy. Edward Crimsworth's sly chief clerk who spies on William Crimsworth.

Suzette, Mlle. A carbon copy of the ordinary Mlle Pelagie.

Sylvie. Pallid, unattractive pupil at Mlle Reuter's. Destined to be a nun.

Trista, Juanna. Gaunt-faced Belgo-Spanish pupil at Mlle Reuter's.

Tynedale, Lord. William Crimsworth's mother's brother who rejects her after a misalliance, leaving her destitute. Reluctantly finances Crimsworth's Eton education and offers him a rich church living.

Vandam, Monsieur. *See* Kint and Vandam.

Vandenhuten, Jean Baptiste. Pupil of Pelet rescued by William Crimsworth after falling out of a boat. His father advances Crimsworth's career in gratitude.

Vandenhuten, Victor. Jean Baptiste's father.

Vanderkelkov, Jules. Flemish pupil at M. Pelet's school.

Voss Brothers. German firm whose letters William Crimsworth translates as part of his work.

Waddy, Sam. At Edward Crimsworth's ball his attentions to a local belle are neatly cut out by Yorke Hunsden.

Wharton, Mrs. Englishwoman living in Brussels. Employs Frances Henri to mend lace and obtains her a post as French teacher; she has at least three daughters, one of whom is about to be married.

Yorke. A mastiff given by Hunsden to Victor Crimsworth.

Zénobie. Hunsden's version of Zoraïde – Mlle Reuter's name.

Zéphyrine, Mlle. French teacher at Mlle Reuter's.

Places

Crimsworth Hall. Home of Edward and Mrs Crimsworth, 4 miles from X——. (Crimsworth Dean; Hebden Bridge; Heaton Hall.)

Daisy Lane. House to which William and Frances Crimsworth and their son Victor retire after leaving Brussels. It is 30 miles from X——. (Nova Lane; Oakwell Hall; Birstall.)

Grovetown. The village 5 miles from X—— to which William Crimsworth walks after being dismissed by his brother. (Mirfield.)

Hunsden Wood. Below Daisy Lane – an Elizabethan mansion in a wooded valley.

Liège. Mr Brown suggests that William Crimsworth may find a job in trade there.

London. William Crimsworth stays there on his journey to Belgium and comments on St Paul's striking midnight and on his view of its dome seen from his inn window.

Louvain. Mr Brown suggests that William Crimsworth may find a job in a bookseller's there.

Rue Royale. One of Brussels' great streets admired by William Crimsworth. Runs almost due north/south to the Place Royale.

Rue d'Isabelle. A narrow back street, near to the statue of General Belliard in the Park at Brussels, where the pensionnat stands at which William Crimsworth teaches.

Seacombe, the living of. At Seacombe-cum-Scarfe; offered by his nobleman uncle to William Crimsworth.

Ste Gudule. Brussels cathedral.

X——. Edward Crimsworth's mill stands in this 'great town'. (Huddersfield.)

Emma – A Fragment (1860)

Commentary

At face value the marriage of Charlotte to the Rev. Arthur Nicholls could be represented as the greatest threat to her continuing to write. Charlotte herself wrote to Ellen Nussey in September 1854 that she should 'Take warning . . . the married woman can call but a very small portion of each day her own. Not that I complain of this sort of monotony as yet and I hope I never shall incline to regard it as a misfortune, but it certainly exists.' Her tongue is barely in her cheek. In the same letter she reports, with some amazement, that, 'Time is an article of which I once had a large stock always on hand; where it is all gone now it would be difficult to say, but my moments are very fully occupied.'

She focused a little more clearly on the matter in a group of letters in the autumn of 1854, where it is revealed that it is not so much a matter of where time has gone but who has used it:

> . . . my life is changed indeed, to be wanted continually, to be constantly called for and occupied seems so strange; yet it is a marvellously good thing. . . As far as my experience of matrimony goes, I think it tends to draw you out of and away from yourself.

And, focusing much more precisely:

> Not that I have been wearied or oppressed; but the fact is my time is not my own now; somebody else wants a good portion of it and

says, 'We must do so and so'. We *do* so and so, accordingly; and it generally seems the right thing.

Such remarks seem to cry out to the reader to read between the lines and, taken in conjunction with specific reference to Nicholls any disposition to see the tongue in the cheek gives place to an awareness of a sense of anxious irony:

> My own life is more occupied than it used to be. I have not so much time for thinking: I am obliged to be more practical, for my dear Arthur is very practical as well as a very punctual and methodical man. Every morning he is in the National School by nine o'clock; he gives the children religious instruction till half-past ten. Almost every afternoon he pays visits amongst the poor parishioners. Of course he often finds a little work for his wife to do, and I hope she is not sorry to help him. I believe it is not bad for me that his bent should be so wholly towards matters of life and active usefulness, so little inclined to the literary and contemplative.

The real danger to Charlotte was not that he would prevent her writing – to be fair to him there is not the slightest evidence to suggest this, though there can be little doubt that he would have been happier if she had given up. Charlotte needed writing as certainly as Emily needed the moors or Branwell his opium, and it would have taken more than Nicholls to have prevented her. More tangible barriers lay in Nicholls's profession, and in Charlotte's highly developed sense of duty.

It is too seldom realized that, when Charlotte married, she joined herself to a Victorian man of the cloth whose duties were all-enveloping and consuming of both time and energy. She should have known better than most what it would mean to become the wife of a pastor. His life and its works would become her life and her works. Her sense of duty and rightness would not have had it otherwise. But, if we may allow ourselves some reading between the lines of the letters of the early days of her married life, does not the question arise – had Charlotte thought right through the implications of being Nicholls's wife? It is over-subtle, perhaps, to believe that he was well aware that he had no need to raise specific barriers to her writing, that it would gradually have to recede behind his world and its works. It is, however, just possible that Charlotte had not even considered that the joining of her life to his did not only mean vast changes for her, but a total submergence of *all* her life in his.

In the light of these speculations there is a poignancy in Thackeray's introduction to the unfinished fragment of Charlotte's novel which was published (with Nicholls's permission) in *Cornhill Magazine*, 1860:

One evening, at the close of 1854, as Charlotte Nicholls sat with her husband by the fire, listening to the howling of the wind about the house, she suddenly said to her husband, 'If you had not been with me, I must have been writing now.' She then ran upstairs, and brought down, and read aloud, the beginning of a new tale. . .

This was *Emma* (which Charlotte began on 27 November 1853). Something rather sadly clandestine emerges from Thackeray's account, whose authenticity has the stamp of his having heard it from Nicholls himself.

Emma had been one of a large number of manuscripts which Nicholls (who inherited Charlotte's entire estate) handed over to Mrs Gaskell and Sir James Kay Shuttleworth when they visited the Rev. Brontë and Nicholls at Haworth in August 1856. In a letter to a friend in the following month, Mrs Gaskell describes one of the manuscripts:

> This fragment [only about 20 pages] was excessively interesting; a child left at a school by a rich flashy man, who pretended to be her father; the school mistress's deference to the rich child – her mysterious reserved character evidently painfully conscious of the imposition practised; the non-payment of the bills; the enquiry – no such person to be found, and just when the child implores mercy and confesses her complicity to the worldly and indignant school mistress the story stops – for ever -

Winifred Gérin in her biography of Charlotte Brontë declares that this 'hurried resumé' of the tale by Mrs Gaskell 'perfectly corresponds to *Emma*'. This is not so. In *Emma* the child neither implores mercy nor confesses her complicity. In fact one of the tantalizing features of the fragment is that it stops short of informing us what the child's function is. Mrs Gaskell's résumé may well refer to some other manuscript, and Gérin's conclusion is both unwarranted and misleading.

Nicholls's comment should allow us, perhaps, to think less dismissively of his critical perception than we might otherwise. He said: 'The critics will accuse you of repetition' – a far more precise notion of the story than Mrs Gaskell's or Miss Gérin's. Charlotte quickly responded that she would alter it – 'I always begin two or three times before I can please myself.'

The *Emma* manuscript was in pencil, of twenty 8vo pages. With it was a complete manuscript of *The Professor* and another fragment of a story called *Willie Ellin* (Ellin, it should be noted, is also the name of what appears to be intended as one of the chief characters of *Emma*).

Simply because we do not know how Charlotte proposed to continue the narrative and the characterization of these two chapters we may be beguiled into thinking that it has more intriguing possibilities than it really has or would have had. There is no way of resolving the difference between how far our own speculation excites us and what might have, in fact, happened. Nevertheless the two existing chapters do possess a certain set of characteristics which are interesting, and there is no doubt that at the end of these chapters we feel that we want to know what happens next. We never will know.

There is no sense of strain or tiredness whatsoever in the narrative, despite the fact that it was written at a time of some tension and activity in Charlotte's life, attendant on her marriage to Arthur Nicholls. On the contrary there is a clarity in the style and a sharpness in the delineation of character which suggests a mind happy in its task and keen to get on with it. Indeed, so great a sense of mental activity and control is present that one might conclude that Charlotte knew exactly where the narrative was going. There is no sense of her tentatively feeling forward and allowing the characters and the story to go where they will, taking the author with them, but rather an impression of a purposeful direction well mapped out.

Again, there is a very strong sense of narrative. It is important to recognize this despite the small amount of writing actually achieved. A story can be seen to be developing with great rapidity and, so far as we have it, the story is already beginning to hint, at least, of mystery, of depths of activity into which a fuller-developed novel might well have taken us.

There is, too, a strong appearance of that quality in Charlotte which critics have not only undervalued but under-considered. Admittedly it sometimes goes underground in her other novels but still, as in *Shirley*, manages to make its presence felt in the overall style of the novel. This is her satirical spirit. Both Miss Wilcox and Mr Ellin who dominate these first two chapters are presented to us in superbly sharp satirical colours. Charlotte's satire here derives from the source where she had always found it – her extraordinarily clear, deep observation of humankind. Her realism and her satire have been undervalued. They go in tandem, and this increases their potency. For example the description of Miss Wilcox's personality is a masterpiece of economical satire and although Mr Ellin is perhaps rather more subtly portrayed there are remarkable brush strokes which give a significant depth (even at this early stage of the novel) to his character.

It is apparent that Charlotte's favourite locale occupies, or seems to be going to occupy, a large space in the growth of *Emma*'s narrative – that is, a school setting. It would also seem that the unhappy girl who is left at the school is likely to become the novel's heroine – is her true name Emma? Indeed, the hints we have that she has been forsaken by someone who purported to be her father, and eventually rejected by the superficial but determined school mistress, Miss Wilcox, suggest that she may grow into yet another version of the governess heroine whom Fate has thrust into penury and dependence. If this is so, Mr Nicholls's fear of repetition could well have been only too pointed.

There is nothing in these two chapters to suggest that Charlotte is to explore a new area of experience, or even a customary one in a new way. But there is enough to tell us that she was in good creative fettle for writing whatever it was she had decided upon.

Synopsis (2 *chapters only completed*)

The story is told by Mrs Chalfont who lives near Fuchsia Lodge, a girls' school owned and directed by the Misses Wilcox. One day an apparently affluent gentleman, Conway Fitzgibbon, comes to enrol his daughter, Matilda, who is neither beautiful, clever, nor good-tempered, at the school. She is made a great fuss of, sharing Miss Wilcox's bedroom, and being paraded in her fine dresses, but she is unpopular and, so Mr Ellin (the local rector) thinks, unhappy. When he receives Miss Mabel Wilcox's urgent note saying the Post Office has returned undelivered her letter to Mr Fitzgibbon, he agrees to investigate, but can find nothing. When sent for, the girl, in great agitation, faints. Mr Ellin agrees to question her later when she is better.

(*Emma*, by Charlotte Brontë and Another Lady, was published by J.M. Dent and Sons in 1980 as a possible continuation and conclusion to this beginning.)

Emily Brontë

Wuthering Heights (1847)

Commentary

It would not be easy to specify the two outstandingly great poems of Western literature, nor indeed the two outstanding dramas – though both of them might well be by Shakespeare. A consensus might well clearly emerge, however, to name *War and Peace* and *Wuthering Heights* as conspicuously dominant even in a list of novels that contained the finest work of Austen, Dickens, Eliot, Mann, Balzac, Joyce.

Tolstoy's and Emily Brontë's novels stand apart and alone for a number of reasons, but pre-eminently because no other novels approach them in the richness of their embodiment of so many of the aspects of what we call human passion. Hatred, anger, love, lust, affection, revenge, envy, grief, frustration rise up before us like that long line of Banquo's heirs that haunt Macbeth.

Apart from this, both novels have a narrative which is as varied, devious and unexpected as the passions that are exposed. What happens and what is felt move together in a close and intense parallel.

Again – and this is a quality that Tolstoy and Emily share with Shakespeare – in these works the characters acquire a reality and an actuality for the reader that is in danger of annihilating the distinction between art and life. For all his Byronic/Gothic excesses Heathcliff exists, and steps out of the confines of fiction as easily as does Hamlet (who is equally built upon the interplay of excesses). And it is not accidental that so many readers of *Wuthering Heights* find themselves equating Emily herself with Cathy – her invention. It is as if the paucity of our knowledge of Emily's life and character can be quite naturally compensated for by our unconsciously accepting that Cathy *is* Emily.

In a way Emily's achievement is greater than Tolstoy's, for his epic pattern gives him, so to speak, far more potential material to create the illusion of fiction-become-life. Emily works essentially on a domestic scale, lacking Tolstoy's space and, moreover, leaving herself open to the distortions of exaggeration in exacting so much emotional force from so small a source.

In *Wuthering Heights* the writer's need to explore the depths of human passion and emotion has either forced or enabled her to avoid being over-concerned with the conventions of private and public morality. What people *are* to themselves (particularly Cathy and Heathcliff) is more important to Emily than whether they must be judged good or bad by normal standards. The decision is left to the reader whether or not to judge them on moral grounds, but the reader will find that if too much attention is paid to making judgements, more important considerations will be missed. Neither Cathy nor Heathcliff judge themselves, and any outraged judgements made about them by others (notably Nelly Dean, who has all the gossip's penchant for being both judge and jury) seem too slight to accommodate the case. To say that Heathcliff is evil, and that Cathy represents virtue corrupted and self-corrupted, explains and means nothing.

In this separating of the realities of her two main characters' souls from the moral environment in which they exist Emily has exploited one of the great themes, which only the greatest writers can develop without descending into either mawkishness or cheap sensationalism. Unlike the conclusion of the conventional romantic novel there is no resolution to the main theme in *Wuthering Heights* – the Cathy/Heathcliff syndrome is neither bounded by time nor intellectual barriers, and unlike the novel of sentiment there is no sop to ordinary emotions and sensibilities: there is as much ferocious cruelty, anguish and even morbidity (as when Heathcliff causes Cathy's coffin to be opened) in their relationship, as there is love. Indeed one of the most astonishing ironies of the book is that we cannot be at all sure that love *is* the theme until Cathy and Heathcliff are separated. The book, then, stands virtually alone by virtue also of the massive ambiguity of its main theme, which is pushed to the limits of credibility but ends by triumphantly asserting the quite unequivocal naked power of human love.

And it may be observed, as a last example of the qualities which give *Wuthering Heights* its status in the canon of Western novels, that it has that uncommon characteristic in its style of writing that we call 'inevitability'. Apart from Joseph's tortured dialect – and even here, the very distortions themselves seem to emblematize this most awful man – there is little or no sign of contrivance by the author in attaining this or that effect. Indeed, you have to dig deep in *Wuthering Heights* to find the various seams which together make up the structure. They are there, but well beneath the surface. There is, therefore, a sense of natural inevitability – not a word or phrase is superfluous; no other words or phrases, in whatever combination could be envisaged, would ever do.

Yet neither the style nor structure is smooth or bland. The style itself is rugged, at times almost crude or uncouth in its directness and bluntness, and its lyrical moments are only momentary, though astonishing therefore in their effect. It is tempting to believe the book was written in one huge push of the imagination, and as the result of an absolute necessity, except that evidence suggests quite the opposite.

Mankind is as hot for certainties with its art as with most other matters. Mankind cannot bear very much 'unreality' – it requires what it calls an 'explanation'. And, much to the chagrin of the majority of people, it seems to be one of the common characteristics of the greatest art to leave at least an area of mystery, of the inexplicable. Great art might, indeed, take us up to the frontiers of enlightenment, but no further. Perhaps it would cease to be art if it did, because, in the final analysis, it is the function of art to reveal not explicate.

Nevertheless, readers and critics demand answers. 'What is the meaning of *Hamlet*?' they ask, ignoring the possibility that Shakespeare neither knew nor intended us to know. 'What is the answer to Elgar's *Enigma*?' they cry, sidestepping the fact that enigma is at the very heart of its creation. And so with *Wuthering Heights*. Critical commentary, since its first publication, has displayed a variety of responses and explanations as bewildering as some of the commentators seem to have found the novel itself.

There are probably two reasons why the book has occasioned critical commotions. First, it is off-putting to many critics to find a writer who does not come down either against or on the side of her two major characters, in the moral sense. What the question amounts to is – 'What did Emily Brontë intend us to think of Cathy and Heathcliff's behaviour?' – but the silence is as profound as that which greets the question 'What did Shakespeare really expect us to think of Isabella's behaviour in *Measure for Measure*?'

Second, many critics are unnerved by a relationship which seems to be based on an almost violent clash of absolutely opposed emotional states – with anger as prominent as affection, recrimination as strong as reconciliation, mental cruelty as prominent as tender emotion – while notwithstanding, they are asked, in the end, to believe that love triumphs. Colossal irreconcilabilities united with absolute certainty are not calculated to quieten the critical mind. Indeed, the most that criticism can do is to describe what happens in *Wuthering Heights* and to place, so far as is possible, each event and occurrence and character in the pattern of the novel as it exists – not as the reader supposes it might, or ought to be.

This pattern is derived from three sources, the first being the contents of the Brontë children's world of childhood, the details of which are discussed elsewhere (*see* Juvenilia). All four children shared the imaginative world of the Glasstown Confederacy, which later became split into the two separate entities of the kingdom of Angria and the kingdom of Gondal. It was not, indeed, till about 1836 that Anne and Emily seem to have hived off from the other two, taking, so to speak, Gondal with them. An infinitely greater amount of Angrian material exists than of Gondal, but what does remain of the latter (in Emily's and Anne's poetry) suggests very convincingly that the characteristics of Angria were carried through into Gondal. There is a similar sense of larger-than-life characters of noble origin and epic personality – flamboyant and Byronic; great events always seem to be either happening or threatening to happen; much of the activity of the inhabitants has to do with love and love relationships, with hate and hate relationships – a tremendous access of passions of all kinds is released; a vivid, even sensational transgressing of public and private moral behaviour is common.

Angria and Gondal may have been separated by the disposition of Emily and Anne to become a duo, but their natures seem to have remained very similar – much that is in those natures has informed the writing of *Wuthering Heights* and, with a different emphasis, *Jane Eyre*.

The Cathy/Heathcliff relationship, which acquires the status less of two separate identities irresistibly drawn to one another, than of a fusion of two into one, is prefigured in Charlotte's juvenilia of 1835 onwards, particularly in the characters of Zamorna and Northangerland. Their relationship, like Cathy's and Heathcliff's, encompasses love, hate, anger and affection, but includes also honour, treachery, deceit and fidelity. They become, so to speak, one, in a fire of conflicting passions.

The utter devotion of Cathy to Heathcliff which, while it stops short of being abject is committed to the point of self-abnegation, is prefigured in the story of Zamorna and Mina Laury, who follows him into exile with a kind of slavish intensity of worship.

The anguished reactions of Heathcliff to Cathy's death are prefigured in Zamorna's reactions to his wife's death with amazing similarity of detail, not least when Zamorna looks 'amid driving sleet and rain' where she has gone, and sees her 'like an apparition beckon'.

Set against this background some elements of *Wuthering Heights* fall into place: spiritual kinship between lovers, for which they will break any law of conventional morality, without thought of transgression; the sense of inevitable attraction of one to another involving unhappiness, often resulting in mental and physical illness; the fear that even after death there will be no peace; the desire of the surviving lover to be haunted by his dead lover. These are common to *Wuthering Heights*, to Branwell's juvenile poetry, to Charlotte's Angrian stories and poems – they all derive from the same source, the common spinning-place of their imaginations.

The second source of *Wuthering Heights* is, of course, Emily's intensely personal imaginative world, perhaps an anguished one, whose existence finds most direct expression in her poetry. Deep in Emily's soul there seems to have been an aspiration for peace and quietude, and a knowledge that this could only be brought about by reconciling the apparently irreconcilable. Whilst this quest is described most directly in the poems, *Wuthering Heights* is, in its way, a profounder expression of it.

Emily's own personality, so far as we know it, was a mass of contradictions – an astonishing mixture of the physical and non-physical. Time and time again we come across references which suggest that at one minute she could be committed, even bustlingly, to the world's work, and the next minute seem utterly disengaged from corporeal existence. The peace and quiet she seems to have sought was a kind of heaven, but not the conventional Christian heaven. She does not appear to have rejected Christianity's God or its theology, but, on the evidence of her poetry and of *Wuthering Heights*, her heaven, her peace, was to be found on this earth, if anywhere – there was no guarantee (as her poetry indicates and as Cathy and Heathcliff confirm) of peace after death:

> '. . . Catherine, you know that I could as soon forget you, as my existence! Is it not sufficient for your infernal selfishness, that while you are at peace I shall writhe in the torments of hell?'
>
> 'I shall not be at peace,' moaned Catherine, recalled to a sense of physical weakness by the violent, unequal throbbing of her heart, which beat visibly and audibly under this excess of agitation. . . 'I'm not wishing you greater torment than I have, Heathcliff! I only wish us never to be parted – and should a word of mine distress you hereafter, think I feel the same distress underground. . .'

At face value the narrative of *Wuthering Heights* is unpleasant, being populated by a number of volatile and unpredictable characters capable of verbal, even physical, violence. The emotional atmosphere of the novel hardly ever relents from being forbidding and foreboding. Apart from this, one of its chief characters, Heathcliff, dedicates a good deal of his life and energy to breaking people, to taking his revenge on a family by taking away its birthright and by forcing it, particularly its female members, to be completely dependent on him. In some ways Heathcliff can be regarded as a villain determined to exact an eye for an eye and a tooth for a tooth. But even those he is determined to humiliate are, most of them, very far from enjoying our sympathies. We feel some pity for old Mr Earnshaw and for Linton but we do not find either Cathy senior or Catherine junior attractive, because they are self-indulgent, selfish, petulant – at times we perhaps feel that they deserve all they get. It is difficult to feel anything but contempt for the drunken sot, Hareton, whom Heathcliff does break, almost literally. So the narrative is certainly not the record of pure-white victims being persecuted by an out-and-out villain – though a terribly rough justice may be discerned behind the novel's often ferocious actions.

It is in the difference between Heathcliff's relationship with Cathy and with others that the deep heart and soul of this novel lies. She accepts his domination of her because she instinctively and naturally realizes that its motivation has a profounder significance than the mere acquisition of property. It is equally true that Heathcliff's way with Cathy is quite different from, and must therefore be judged differently from, his treatment of every other inhabitant of Thrushcross Grange and Wuthering Heights. To her as to them he is mentally cruel, often peremptory in manner and prone to anger and irrationality, but, inexorably, he finds himself in the same relationship to Cathy as she to him – he cannot live without her. He, like her, is a victim of a reality deeper in its effect and importance than the day-to-day satisfying of revenge, and slaking of pride, which is the daily diet of the disarranged world they live in. Cathy and Heathcliff are presented as participants in a reality well beyond the naturalistic narrative of the story. The surface narrative runs parallel to this deeper, secret narrative of which we only get hints – which is concerned with Cathy and Heathcliff alone. These hints explain nothing, but they give us glimpses by flashes of lightning of the contrary passions at work fusing these two people together in an indissoluble union.

The surface narrative, which tells the history of the Earnshaws and Lintons and the depredations wrought by Heathcliff on the even tenor of their ways, is a melodrama which owes a lot of its characteristics to the Gondal/Angria myths, to Emily's fertile imagination and, of course, to the popular Gothic and semi-Gothic novels whose influence was widespread. But the story of Heathcliff and Cathy seems to be reaching for the status of a poem whose full implications we will never understand but whose immense emotional force we can never forget.

We can only go so far in trying to specify the nature of Cathy and Heathcliff's relationship. It exists in a rhythm between acceptance and rejection. Every time their souls meet it is as if the impulse to separate is also there. Its positive and negative fields of love are expressed with equal emphasis. It is not a vaguely spiritual relationship but, in some ways, is sharply defined: for example, Heathcliff becomes very jealous when any other man pays attention to Cathy – he shows a very definable and normal human reaction; in Cathy's case, her feelings about him become very clear, particularly when he comes physically near her – she becomes agitated and is jealous for his presence, wanting it strictly for herself alone. When he is not there she is always looking for him – her possessiveness, like his, is strongly natural and human.

Their relationship is also characterized by a reckless disregard not only for the conventions of social behaviour but for other people's feelings and responses. Heathcliff does not care if Linton sees his obvious involvement with Cathy, and she is apparently oblivious to her husband's anguish at her emotional entanglement with Heathcliff. One of the criticisms registered against the novel was generated by their behaviour which, some critics felt, was emblematic of sexual licence. This, to the nineteenth century, was enough to condemn the book on the strongest possible grounds – an offence to public decency.

In fact, the physical characteristics of their relationship are not emphasized by Emily. The most specific, and repetitive, indication in the novel of a physical attraction is their expressed idea to be always next to one another. On the occasions when Heathcliff talks about after-life it is lying next to Cathy in the grave which represents for him the apotheosis of physical union.

Heathcliff feels the metaphysical aspects of their union as powerfully as Cathy does, but it is she who voices them the most strongly and frequently. Perhaps the most poignant and forceful expressions of this are her crying out that, in a sense, she *is* Heathcliff, and he *is* her. It is through Cathy that the sense of total unity, of total reconcilability of so much that seems irreconcilable is most apparent:

> ... he's more myself than I am. Whatever our souls are made of, his
> and mine are the same, and Linton's is as different as a moonbeam
> from lightning, or frost from fire.

The anguished quest of the two lovers for fusion seems to become more and more pagan in its implications as the novel progresses. In no sense is life after death related by these two to tranquillity in a Christian heaven or even eternal torment in a conventional hell. In fact there is nothing tranquil either in the present, nor will there be in the future, in this love, and as for torment – no supernatural agency can inflict on them more than they can inflict on themselves. Cathy it is, again, who voices the most telling account of what heaven is to her in her memorable description of what would happen if she did find herself in a conventional heaven:

> ... I was only going to say that heaven did not seem to be my home;
> and I broke my heart with weeping to come back to earth; and the

angels were so angry that they flung me out, into the middle of the heath on the top of Wuthering Heights; where I woke sobbing for joy.

This is both pagan and metaphysical in its implications. In its way, too, it poignantly unites the naturalistic and non-naturalistic areas of the novel.

These two areas are, of course, connected by a number of features. First, there is the inevitable connection ensured by the fact that Cathy is the mother of the young Catherine who comes to live in Wuthering Heights after her father's (Edgar Linton's) death and who is being forced to marry Heathcliff's weakling son, Linton. The connection is reinforced by Heathcliff's increasingly frequent seeing of Cathy in Catherine, and particularly in her eyes. He is more and more reminded of his own love for Cathy as he observes her with young Linton. The participants in the one, naturalistic, narrative, come to haunt, so to speak, a survivor of the other:

> The entire world is a dreadful collection of memoranda that she did exist, and that I have lost her! Well, Hareton's aspect was the ghost of my immortal love; of my wild endeavours to hold my right; my degradation, my pride, my happiness, and my anguish.

Second, the Bible-touting Joseph establishes another connection. He finds the world a place of misery and all men sinful. He has many inklings of the emotional forces generated both by Heathcliff alone, and by him and Cathy together. In a sense Joseph seems to inhabit a dark dead space between the everyday world and another beyond the material world. He is bigoted, surly, ill-disposed and dangerously spiteful, but he is, nevertheless, a link to remind us that Wuthering Heights is a place of unknown forces as well as familiar passions.

And, thirdly, there is the great connective presence of Nelly Dean. How cunningly Emily manages to have Nelly present at most of the important events of the novel. What is more it always seems right that she should be there. She is nurse, adviser, confessor, confidante, gossip and layer-out. And on those occasions when the demands of time and geography make Nelly's presence at an event quite impossible or incompatible, we still feel she is there; indeed, by letter or word of mouth all gets back to Nelly – then, from her, to Mr Lockwood and us. In fact, Lockwood's function is as a kind of feed to Nelly, goading her to her revelations, acting as our agent.

Nelly is at the centre of the action, and, as a character, she has been given two commissions by Emily. First, she functions as a kind of chorus/narrator. So ubiquitous is Nelly's knowledge and presence that she can be seen almost as the occupant of a spaceship who is observing simultaneously on the earth happenings which are taking place many miles apart. Nelly has what might be called the 'collecting' quality of a chorus – by which we feel that she has gathered all that needs to be known and that everything that we learn has been filtered through her quirkish sensibilities.

But Nelly, secondly, is a unique character because she has a kind of immunity to events. She shunts to and fro, she is berated, she is regarded as fair game when there is any question of attributing blame or fault. Yet there remains a sort of inviolability in her – nothing touches her beyond her skin, so to speak; her heart and soul stay her own.

This is not to say that she is, somehow, more of a convenient agent than human being. On the contrary, one of Emily's triumphs is to sustain Nelly as very much a creature of our world – as much as is Juliet's nurse. She can display curiosity, spite, affection, a predisposition to betray confidences, even a mite of cruelty (as when she burns Catherine's letters with a cat-and-mouse pleasure). Without her, this novel would, in fact, lose much of its relationship with a sense of actuality. If Nelly were not as Emily has created her there would be very little in the novel (and Lockwood is too paper-thin as a character to be considered) to naturalize the events and to give them a credible context.

To praise Nelly Dean as a creation is to admire, simultaneously, the third source of the novel's power – its superb structural pattern – for she, of course, is part of that. To a superficial view its construction is ungainly, but nothing could be further from the truth. Emily may well have been seven years in the writing of it. Whether she was or not, great care is obvious.

The narrative itself has an amazing symmetry, which can be demonstrated if the reader takes time to indicate the pedigree of the characters in diagrammatic form: what, in reading, is obscured can then be clearly seen. The architecture of the novel is perfectly symmetrical:

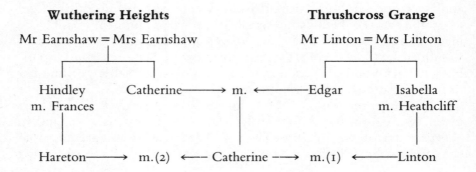

This gives a tremendous sense of inevitability and of recapitulation to the novel which tends to raise it above the merely naturalistic.

Again, there is great care taken in the manner of direct narrative to the reader. Few readers realize that for the major part of the book Lockwood is telling us what Nelly Dean told him, but sometimes what Nelly Dean told him that someone else (e.g. Isabella) told her! Only a tenth of the book is direct narrative by Lockwood.

Far from muddling the reader this technique gives a huge sense of human depth, of interest, and of a kind of urgent curiosity as one narrator is superimposed on another. In any case Emily has been meticulous in making sure that the reader can, at any time, check his bearings, so to say: she is exact in giving both direct and indirect information about dates, locations and the like. She uses intervals of time, ages of characters, the state of the moon, seasonal activities (e.g. grouse-shooting time) to establish signposts for the reader. Nelly Dean will even specify a day of the week when an event occurred. And the reader who wishes to draw a map of the location of the novel may easily do so – from details supplied there. For example, if you wish to go from Thrushcross Grange to Gimmerton the road branches to the left over the moor; it is marked by a stone pillar. Gimmerton lies to the east, Thrushcross Grange to the south-west, Wuthering Heights to the north, of this pillar. The distance from Wuthering Heights to Thrushcross Grange is four miles, and it takes half an hour from Thrushcross Grange to Gimmerton.

If all this were not sufficient evidence that *Wuthering Heights* is well-formed, deliberately designed, not an emanation of 'native woodnotes wild', the reader may care to examine perhaps the most impressive (certainly the most astonishing) evidence – the exactness of the novel's legal knowledge. A lawyer who, early this century, subjected to scrutiny the very complicated legal processes by which Heathcliff gained his property, involving both law of land and law of money and goods, found that Emily's knowledge was deep, and accurate; not only accurate but, amazingly, accurate *not* for the 1840s (when the novel was written) but for the time in which the events of the novel occur – i.e. 1771–1803. Emily must have engaged in very detailed research to achieve this tour-de-force.

No excuse is required for emphasizing these aspects of *Wuthering Heights* in view of the amount of critical opinion which insists on its being some kind of passionately inspired outburst done at a single sitting. It is time that criticism realized the conscious deliberation with which the novel was written – Emily was a professional, not a pixillated amateur.

Perhaps it is in the style that the least deliberation has been expended by Emily – though this is a mere impression and can never be confirmed. Indeed it may well be that a good deal of deliberation went into it so that eventually it turned out seemingly so natural, unforced and devoid of artifice.

It is an undistinguished style which lacks that kind of positive identity by which you immediately recognize Jane Austen or Virginia Woolf. It is, perhaps, hardly a style at all in the very strictest sense of the word, to mean that it bears the unmistakable handprint of its creator. There are times when it could be Charlotte, occasionally even Anne, and sometimes any nineteenth-century romantic writer.

Emily's literary background was scanty in scope but her mind and imagination were impressionable – capable of receiving and recalling at will that untidy orchestration of reflex, convention and deliberation which we call ordinary speech. What we have here is educated ordinary speech (except for the dialect), for there is in it an abundance of Latin-based words, and it suggests that Emily's ears had been closely attuned to, for example, her father's public utterances, or those of his professional colleagues and literate friends. It is, at base, the style of people who have grave things to say, and it is stiffened by that of the more respected and respectable periodicals which made it their mission to say everything with some gravity:

> The stolidity with which I received these instructions was, no doubt, rather exasperating, for they were delivered in perfect sincerity; but I believed a person who could plan the turning of her fits of passion to account, beforehand, might by exerting her will, manage to control herself tolerably even while under their influence; and I did not wish to 'frighten' her husband, as she said, and multiply his annoyances for the purpose of serving her selfishness.

When we remember that this is Nelly Dean speaking we may be even the more prepared to accept how natural this gravely neutral style was to Emily.

But it is a groundnote and, after the first chapter or so, it is less obtrusive. Indeed the change is distinct enough to have made some commentators reflect that it can be accounted for by dual authorship (Branwell's, to begin the novel). This may or may not be so – the evidence is inconclusive – but the truth still is that it remains the basic style, if subsumed.

What is mixed in it is, in the final analysis, more important, for it gives the novel its sense of contrasts in communications, and hence, its drama. This is a much less discursive kind of writing. It has what we habitually call Yorkshire bluntness in its directness and terseness, both in dialogue and description. It is to be distinguished absolutely from

Emily's use of dialect which is a very heady broth of actual dialect words, phonetic renderings of words Emily had never seen written down, and (so far as we can tell) words made up by Emily. The result is sometimes starkly effective, sometimes over-vocal in effect, and sometimes downright baffling. Indeed, Emily's dialect use veers between giving an impression of almost sensational authenticity and one of studied artifice.

But the worst effects of her dialect are overcome by, and its best effects made an ally of, her blunt direct mode. It vivifies its subject matter by the simple expedient of avoiding frills and fancies, and it is always sparse rather than flatulent. It seems reluctant to secede to any softer mode of expression and of mood, but it is always ready to create, by its contrast with the groundnote of urbane discursiveness, a tense dramatic moment:

> The following evening was very wet; indeed it poured down, till day-dawn; and, as I took my morning walk round the house, I observed the master's window swinging open, and the rain driving straight in.
>
> He cannot be in bed, I thought; those showers would drench him through! He must be either up, or out. But I'll make no more ado, I'll go boldly and look!
>
> Having succeeded in obtaining entrance with another key, I ran to unclose the panels, for the chamber was vacant; quickly pushing them aside, I peeped in. Mr Heathcliff was there – laid on his back. His eyes met mine so keen and fierce, I started; and then he seemed to smile.

Yet, when it does relax, the effect is the greater for its habitual unrelenting terseness – as if a shaft of sunlight, slightly guilty, had invaded the privacy of a crag:

> 'These are the earliest flowers at the Heights!' she exclaimed. 'They remind me of soft thaw winds, and warm sunshine, and nearly melted snow. Edgar, is there not a south wind, and is not the snow almost gone?'
>
> 'The snow is quite gone down here, darling,' replied her husband, 'and I see only two white spots on the whole range of moors. The sky is blue, and the larks are singing, and the becks and brooks are all brim full...'

Emily's style never has a melting mood, for it hardly ever allows much more than a fugitive relenting of its hold on the graver matters and modes of life. Yet it is never gloomy, never depressing in its effects, and it can often be sharp and peremptory, with a kind of sardonic humour. It is an ideal reflection of the novel itself, attempting to reconcile light and shade, as it tries to reconcile the positive and negative sides of Heathcliff and Cathy's relationship. Above all, it is a style that never seems to be trying to cajole the reader into the novel's world – it works imperceptibly and one becomes an inhabitant of Wuthering Heights with almost frightening ease.

Synopsis

In 1801 Mr Lockwood, the new tenant of Thrushcross Grange, visits his landlord, the gipsy-like Heathcliff of Wuthering Heights, but his reception is hardly welcoming. Intrigued he visits a second time, mistaking Catherine, Heathcliff's sullen daughter-in-law, for his wife, and meeting a wild oafish young man – Hareton Earnshaw. Forced by the weather to stay the night, he finds in the bedroom the name Catherine, linked with those of Earnshaw, Heathcliff, and Linton, scratched in the paintwork, and some books inscribed 'Catherine Earnshaw'. In the page spaces is recorded the cruel treatment of both Cathy and Heathcliff by Hindley, Cathy's brother. Lockwood has a nightmare and hearing a knocking at the window, smashes his hand through it to stop the branch outside tapping, but his fingers are grasped by a small frozen hand, and a childish face peers through the window. He tries to free himself by rubbing the wrist against the broken pane, and he hears a voice crying to be let in. Hearing Lockwood's horrified cries, Heathcliff arrives and Lockwood hears him calling for Cathy, his 'heart's darling'. Returning to Thrushcross Grange, Lockwood asks his housekeeper, Nelly Dean, about the inhabitants of Wuthering Heights. Nelly Dean takes over the story.

One day, some quarter of a century before, her master, Mr Earnshaw, on a journey to Liverpool, returns with a filthy black-haired waif – Heathcliff. Hindley resents him and his favoured treatment, but Cathy becomes very fond of him. Hindley is sent to college. Cathy grows into a wild attractive girl. She and Heathcliff are inseparable.

When Mr Earnshaw dies, Hindley returns with a young wife – Frances. Heathcliff is relegated to farm-labourer status, but he and Cathy remain close, spending their time together on the moors. Once, looking in at the windows of Thrushcross Grange, where the affluent, fair-haired Lintons live, they are set upon by Mr Linton's bulldog and, trying to escape, Cathy hurts her ankle. Heathcliff is dismissed, but Cathy is taken in, staying there for five weeks while her ankle mends. She returns to Wuthering Heights an elegant lady, who mocks Heathcliff's uncouth appearance. Heathcliff asks Nelly to tidy him up, which angers Hindley, making Heathcliff vow he will be revenged on him.

In 1778 Frances has a son, Hareton, and after her death from consumption Hindley begins drinking very heavily. Meanwhile Edgar Linton courts Cathy, who is elegant and haughty with him, though she reverts to her old wild primitive ways with Heathcliff. Hindley's condition deteriorates and he nearly kills Hareton, dropping him over the banisters. He is caught by Heathcliff who later regrets the missed opportunity for revenge. Overhearing Cathy tell Nelly she has agreed to marry Edgar Linton, for to marry Heathcliff now would degrade her, Heathcliff slips away too early to hear her add how much she loves him – for their souls are the same. Heathcliff disappears. Cathy after searching for him desperately in a storm, becomes ill, and is taken to Thrushcross Grange to convalesce. There Mr and Mrs Linton catch her fever and die. Three years later Cathy marries Edgar.

Heathcliff, no longer the rough ploughboy, returns to rent Wuthering Heights from Hindley. Cathy, delighted, relapses into her old familiar ways with him. Edgar, coldly civil, allows him to call, and Edgar's sister Isabella, falls in love with him. Cathy tells Heathcliff of Isabella's infatuation, and although Heathcliff despises Isabella, he is aware she is Edgar's heir. Meanwhile at Wuthering Heights he is encouraging Hindley to gamble his money and property away. After a quarrel with Edgar over Heathcliff, Cathy shuts herself in her room, becoming ill and delirious. Nelly, being sent for the doctor, finds Isabella's dog hanging by its neck from a hook in the garden. Isabella has eloped with Heathcliff. When they return to Wuthering Heights, Isabella writes asking to be reconciled with Edgar. Her misery at Wuthering Heights, not sure whether Heathcliff is man or devil, is shared by Hindley and the now-savage Hareton.

Nelly, fearful for Cathy's life, lets Heathcliff in to see her. He takes her in his arms in a passion of anger, grief and overwhelming love. Edgar returns, but Cathy refuses to let Heathcliff leave. Later that night she dies giving birth to a daughter, Catherine (the girl Lockwood has met at Wuthering Heights). Nelly tells the distraught Heathcliff, who has been waiting for news in the garden, and, when Edgar is absent for a couple of hours, Heathcliff slips in to where Cathy is lying in her coffin. He substitutes in her locket a curl of his own dark hair for a fair one of Edgar's, which Nelly later intertwines with one of Cathy's.

Heathcliff reverts to his old wild behaviour and, after a fight with Hindley, wounds Isabella with a knife. She escapes to London and gives birth to a fair-haired son, Linton.

Hindley dies, having mortgaged all his property to Heathcliff, so that now both Thrushcross Grange and Wuthering Heights are within Heathcliff's grasp. In the next twelve years Catherine grows up beautiful but spoilt. Isabella dies, begging Edgar to look after Linton, an ailing petulant child. He comes to Thrushcross Grange, but is claimed by Heathcliff, who insists he go to Wuthering Heights. Catherine, who has petted and fussed him, still meets him secretly and Heathcliff plans to marry them. Edgar objects, forbidding Catherine to go to the Heights, but, told by Heathcliff that Linton is dying, she agrees to visit him, and continues to do so clandestinely in the evenings, once meeting Hareton, whom she mocks, but who tries to impress her.

Whilst Edgar Linton is lying ill, Catherine and Nelly are lured to Wuthering Heights to the ailing Linton, where they are kept by force until Catherine agrees to marry Linton. Once married, she returns home to find her father dying. After Edgar's burial, Heathcliff tells Nelly how he has had Cathy's coffin opened to see her again, and has loosened the coffin's side panel, so that when he is buried next to her, they will be together again. He now feels at peace for the first time in eighteen years.

Catherine returns to Wuthering Heights to be with Linton, who dies, leaving everything to his father. After Linton's death, Hareton tries to become friends with Catherine.

Nelly, having brought the story up to date, is replaced again by Lockwood as narrator. When he visits Heathcliff to tell him he is giving up the tenancy of Thrushcross Grange, Catherine complains to him that Hareton has stolen her books. Treated with great contempt, Hareton slaps her face, thrusting the books on the fire.

In September 1802, on a visit to the area, Lockwood again goes to Wuthering Heights, where he finds Catherine teaching Hareton to read – they are now obviously in love. Heathcliff, horrified by Catherine's likeness to her mother, has told her to keep away from him – all he wants is to be reunited with Cathy in death. He retires to his room one night, and in the morning is found mysteriously dead, a mocking sneer on his face. He is buried as he directed, the sliding panel of his own coffin next to the loosened one of Cathy's. The ghosts of a man and a woman are seen frequently in the area. Lockwood, having learnt that Catherine and Hareton are to be married and to move to the Grange, returns home through the churchyard pausing to look at the three graves peaceful amongst the heath and harebells, under a benign sky.

Characters

Archer, Dame. Possibly a midwife – she first shows the newborn Hareton Earnshaw to his father.

Branderham, Rev. Jabez. Delivers a sermon called 'Seventy times Seven and the First of the Seventy-First' at Gimmerton Chapel.

Charlie. Catherine Linton's pointer dog.

Dean, Ellen (Nelly). Housekeeper at Thrushcross Grange, and part-narrator of the story.

Earnshaw, Catherine. Daughter of Mr Earnshaw snr. Marries Edgar Linton. Mother of young Catherine.

Earnshaw, Frances. Secretly married to Hindley after his father's death.

Earnshaw, Hareton (1). His name and the date 1550 are carved on Wuthering Heights which he may have built.

Earnshaw, Hareton (2). Son of Hindley and Frances. Marries his cousin, Catherine Linton.

Earnshaw, Heathcliff. A dead son of the Earnshaws from whom Heathcliff gets his name.

Earnshaw, Hindley. Catherine's brother, son of Mr Earnshaw snr.

Earnshaw, Mr. Catherine and Hindley's father, owner of Wuthering Heights and foster-father to Heathcliff.

Earnshaw, Mrs. Mr Earnshaw's wife. Dies two years after Heathcliff comes to live with her family.

Fanny. Isabella Linton's springer dog.

Gnasher. Guard dog at Wuthering Heights.

Green. Edgar Linton's lawyer.

Grimalkin. Lockwood's name for a cat at Wuthering Heights.

Heathcliff. A dirty foundling from the streets of Liverpool, found by Mr Earnshaw and given a home at Wuthering Heights. Becomes indissolubly involved with Catherine Earnshaw. Marries Isabella Linton.

Heathcliff, Linton. Son of Heathcliff and Isabella, born after his mother runs away.

Housekeeper. A woman of Gimmerton who keeps house at Wuthering Heights after Hindley's death.

Jenny. Old Mr Linton's servant at Thrushcross Grange.

John. Old Mr Linton's servant at Thrushcross Grange.

Joseph. Old servant at Wuthering Heights. A troublemaker.

Juno. Pointer bitch which attacks Lockwood.

Kenneth, Dr. Doctor who attends at Thrushcross Grange and Wuthering Heights.

Linton, Mrs Catherine. *See* Earnshaw, Catherine.

Linton, Catherine. Daughter of Edgar and Catherine Linton. She is forced into marriage with Heathcliff's son, Linton. After his death she falls in love with and eventually marries her cousin Hareton.

Linton, Edgar. Son of Mr Linton snr, of Thrushcross Grange. Married to Catherine Earnshaw.

Linton, Isabella. Edgar's sister. Elopes with Heathcliff, but after his ill-treatment, leaves him. Dies a few months after her son Linton is born.

Linton, Mr. Owner of Thrushcross Grange. Isabella and Edgar's father.

Linton, Mrs Mary. Edgar and Isabella's mother.

Lockwood, Mr. Tenant of Thrushcross Grange to whom Nelly Dean tells the story of the Earnshaws, the Lintons and Wuthering Heights.

Mary. Servant at Thrushcross Grange.

Michael. Groom at Thrushcross Grange.

Minny. Catherine Linton's pony.

Phoenix. Catherine Linton's dog.
Robert. Old Mr Linton's servant.
Skulker. Old Mr Linton's dog.
Throttler. Guard dog at Wuthering Heights.
Wolf. Guard dog at Wuthering Heights.
Zillah. Housekeeper at Wuthering Heights.

Places

Blackhorse Marsh. A treacherous bog near Gimmerton. (Stanbury.)
Fairy Cave. The magic cave that Hareton shows to Catherine. (Peniston Quarry.)
Gimmerton. Nearest village to Wuthering Heights and Thrushcross Grange.
Gimmerton Sough. Jabez Branderham preaches a 'Pious Discourse' in Gimmerton Sough chapel. (Chapel-le-Breer.)
Liverpool. Heathcliff is found there by Mr Earnshaw as an abandoned waif. The only location identified by its real name in *Wuthering Heights*.
Penistone (Penistow) Crags. A mile or so beyond Wuthering Heights, and four more from Thrushcross Grange. A favourite destination for Catherine Linton's youthful excursions. (Ponden Kirk.)
Thrushcross Grange. Home of the Linton family. Becomes Heathcliff's property by his devious and vengeful methods. Stands in a large park. (Ponden Hall.)
Wuthering Heights. Home of the Earnshaw family. Later becomes Heathcliff's property. Four miles from Thrushcross Grange. (High Sunderland Hall; Top Withins.)

Roe Head: sketch by Anne

Thorp Green: sketch by Branwell

Rydings, Ellen Nussey's home, today

The Red House, Mary Taylor's home, today

Ponden Hall today (Thrushcross Grange, *Wuthering Heights*)

Oakwell Hall today (Fieldhead, *Shirley*)

Haworth parsonage today

Haworth church and Sunday school today

Anne Brontë

Agnes Grey (1847)

Commentary

Anne Brontë had far more experience as a working governess than either Charlotte or Emily, and it was perhaps inevitable that she should turn her pen towards writing about what she recalled from her work at Blake Hall and Thorp Green.

The result of her recollections is charming. *Agnes Grey* engages any reader who is prepared to accept the unexceptional in style and manner, the unsensational in theme and narrative, and the unrelentingly honest in sentiment. Despite the moods of depression, malcontent and self-indulgence which the novel encompasses, it has a faint sweet smile on its face. Its underlying current is in the direction of a happy conclusion, not towards the moral stringencies of *Jane Eyre* or the massive, passionate force of *Wuthering Heights*. The novel has an easy, relaxed movement, with no complications – it does not come from the same imaginative source as do Charlotte's or Emily's.

The obvious question that it raises is whether Anne's quantitatively superior knowledge and experience of being a governess results in something superior to *Jane Eyre* or *Villette*. In a sense the question is perhaps superfluous because Anne was not in contention with Charlotte nor, more important, can her novel, as an entity, be compared with any of Charlotte's. Anne is a minor writer if we are pushed to comparisons with either of her sisters.

But Agnes Grey is a different kind of governess from either Lucy Snowe or Jane Eyre. For one thing she has the immense support of her family (as, we presume, Anne herself did); for another, we learn much more of the dreary day-to-day life of a governess from this novel than from Charlotte's work. Apart from these differences there is no relentless and painful search for an elusive love as there is in Charlotte's books. Agnes is shown undergoing the trials and tribulations of her profession, and love just sidles up, so to speak. There is no passion in this novel, so there is not much drama of either incident or character. Neither is there any burning fusion of emotion and morality as in Charlotte's heroines. Agnes follows her profession, she does her best, she suffers somewhat, and she is simply but deeply beloved of a young man of the cloth who appreciates her honesty and her humility and her kindness.

That is how the story develops, easily and, on the whole, convincingly and without any apparent attempt to force a moral. Yet it would be completely wrong to assume that Anne had no moral intentions, though perhaps another word would more accurately describe one of her chief motivations in writing – that word is 'instruction'. Anne was convinced that the novelist had a duty to instruct the reader.

In this case the subject of this educational process is quite plain – the reader is to be taught about the condition of work and the social status of governesses. To achieve this Anne totally avoids what may have been a temptation to lead the reader by the nose, jog his elbow or bellow in his ear about the deprivations of the governess class. What Anne reveals about the horrors of spoilt children, the self-indulgence of parents and their habitual failure to support their governesses in matters of discipline strikes one as unexaggerated and immaculately accurate. When Anne becomes quite explicit in her comments she does not lose control but employs irony with the surest touch and (a sharp testimony to her underrated skill) does not distort her characters.

And as she builds up an edifice of simple truth Anne takes time to carve a number of convincing character effigies. She lacks Charlotte's devastating cutting edge but makes up for that by an ability to chip away until she achieves and isolates characteristics which she must know will absolutely identify and tabulate the personality of the subject. The Bloomfields are particularly well cornered and placed. Mr Bloomfield inquires what is for dinner:

> 'Turkey and grouse,' was the concise reply.
> 'And what besides?'
> 'Fish.'
> 'What kind of fish?'
> 'I don't know.'
> '*You don't know?*' cried he, looking solemnly up from his plate, and suspending his knife and fork in astonishment.
> 'No, I told the cook to get some fish – I did not particularize what.'

Charlotte's satirical spirit lurks behind that, but Anne is equally capable of defining and embodying characters whom she actually seems to like – in this case quite contrary to Charlotte who is far more assured in depicting what displeases her. Mr Weston is described by Anne in a manner so unobtrusive that it is easy to underestimate not only the skill being employed but the comprehensive credibility of the portrait. He and Agnes meet in a rain shower:

'. . . an umbrella will do you no harm at any rate,' he replied, with a smile that showed he was not offended; as a man of worse temper or less penetration would have been at such a refusal of his aid. I could not deny the truth of his assertion, and so went with him to the carriage; he even offered me his hand on getting in: an unnecessary piece of civility, but I accepted that too, for fear of giving offence. One glance he gave, one little smile at parting – it was but for a moment; but therein I read, or thought I read, a meaning that kindled in my heart a brighter flame of hope than had ever yet arisen.

Anne's lightness of touch, irony, and ability to search out essentials are often as effective as Charlotte's more active, passionate and calculated technique. For example, although Charlotte's Irish curate, Malone (*Shirley*), perhaps lodges closer to the front of our memories than Anne's vicar, Mr Hatfield, one realizes, on reflection, that the latter is just as completely (and perhaps more credibly) exposed as a bad man of the cloth. Charlotte errs in the direction of overstating her case and advancing into caricature, but Anne relies on a quiet, relentless, ironically coloured realism.

So the reader is 'instructed' about governesses, about good and bad clergymen, and about the iniquities of doting and dotty parents. But there is a less formalized and fugitive kind of instruction also going on: it is to do with Anne herself.

If we keep in mind two aspects of Anne's life it is impossible not to be drawn towards reflecting that, in some ways, *Agnes Grey* is autobiographical in rather more than the obvious sense that it is clearly based on Anne's experiences as a governess.

The theme involving good and bad clergymen surely cannot but have its source in Anne's own experience of life in Haworth parsonage – not just as an observer of the motley men of the cloth who came there and worked there, but as an interested party. To express it bluntly one asks the question: Is Weston a portrait of poor doomed young Weightman the curate who seems to have captured Anne's heart? If he is then one can only marvel at the tact and control over her craft displayed by this young authoress fresh from her love affair and the death of her beloved. The portrait has its sentimental glosses and there is a suddenness in the happy dénouement, but Anne cannot be denied something she has never even been credited with – the ability to achieve a courageous credibility in her depiction of Agnes's and Weston's relationship.

The other, more elusive, shadow of actuality is the picture of Agnes's home life. Anne could not possibly have remembered her own mother, and Aunt Branwell, with her well-meant but chilly severity, was no more than a functional mother-surrogate. Again the blunt question arises: Is Anne's portrait of Agnes's mother a wish-fulfilment of her own lost mother? It is less important to gnaw at the question than to observe that the presence of Mrs Grey, representing stability, love and wise advice, is not only credibly maintained but suffuses the whole novel with a warmth, a sense of domestic security which does not exist in any other Brontë novel.

Anne's quiet achievement in this novel was not the result of a blind exercise of automatic writing, for it is full of effects of description and characterization that cannot be ascribed to accident. Everything of an artistic nature that Anne did – and we have the evidence of her drawing as well as her novels – has a precise architecture about it. It gives the impression of total naturalness, candour and sincerity. *Agnes Grey* is like a totally unexpected but absolutely inevitable slow, sad smile on the face of the moors outside Haworth parsonage.

Synopsis

Agnes Grey and her sister Mary, an accomplished artist, are the only two surviving children of Richard Grey, a poor clergyman, and his wife, who forfeited her dowry by going against her parents' wishes and marrying him. After some rash speculation Richard finds himself weighed down by debts. Mary seeks to help by suggesting selling some of her drawings, while Agnes decides to become a governess. She gets a post with the Bloomfields at Wellwood. Mrs Bloomfield is self-indulgent, Mr Bloomfield peevish, and the children are spoilt, unintelligent, disobedient and unruly. Agnes's only happy time is her Christmas break at home. The Bloomfield's grandmother sheds doubt on Agnes's competence and Agnes's only friend, the children's nurse, is dismissed. Uncle Robson, Mrs Bloomfield's brother, encourages Mary Ann to be affected, and Tom to be cruel to animals. At midsummer Agnes is dismissed and remains peaceably at home until she gets another post with the Murrays of Horton Lodge. There she sees little of the swearing, blaspheming Mr Murray, and is treated in an offhand manner by the party-going Mrs Murray. Only with Rosalie, one of the daughters, does a mutual respect develop – the other children, Matilda, John and Charles, are spoilt brats.

In the summer holidays, Agnes's sister marries Mr Richardson, a vicar, and on her return to Horton, Rosalie and Matilda vie with each other to tell her of Rosalie's coming-out ball and the new curate, Weston, who was present. Rosalie and Matilda amuse themselves by visiting the poor and aged of the parish, while Agnes visits Nancy Browne who tells her what a good friend and help Weston has been, unlike the vicar, Hatfield, whose main interests are with the rich and influential members of his parish. She begins to feel Weston's presence a comforting emblem of goodness and kindness, but after walking and talking with him she is teased by the Murray girls. Rosalie flirts with, but refuses to marry Hatfield, turning her attention to Weston and thereby upsetting Agnes. She and her sister seek to convince Weston that Agnes is more interested in reading than in churchgoing and Agnes in her unhappiness takes refuge in writing poetry. Then Agnes learns her father's health has deteriorated and she loses her little dog Snap.

Rosalie finally decides to marry the rich Sir Thomas Ashby, leaving Matilda to flirt with Weston, but Weston seems more drawn to Agnes and to be happy in her company. Receiving news that her father is dying, she arrives home to find him dead. Her mother wishes to start up a small school and Agnes agrees to join her. Her sad parting from Weston is cheered by his asking her if she would be happy to see him again.

After some time she has an invitation to go to stay with Rosalie, who is installed at Ashby Hall, with her child, to whom she wishes Agnes later to be governess. At Ashby Hall, Agnes learns that Rosalie is now regretting her marriage and detests her husband, and that Weston has left the area. Returning home and taking a walk on the beach, Agnes is accosted by her own excited Snap, followed by Weston, who has been looking for her. He is now Vicar of nearby F——. He visits Agnes and her mother frequently and, eventually, having got Mrs Grey's permission, asks Agnes to marry him. They marry and live frugally but happily with their three children.

Characters

Ashby, Lady, (The Elder). Mother of Sir Thomas.
Ashby, Sir Thomas. Disagreeable owner of Ashby Park, who marries Rosalie Murray.
Bligh, Mr. Mr Weston's predecessor as Mr Hatfield's curate at Horton.
Bloomfield, Fanny. Four-year-old unpleasant child of the Bloomfields.
Bloomfield, Harriet. Two-year-old fat child of the Bloomfields.
Bloomfield, Mary Ann. Six-year-old eldest daughter of the Bloomfields. Affected and stupid.
Bloomfield, Mr. Ill-tempered husband of Mrs Bloomfield and ill-mannered employer of Agnes Grey.
Bloomfield, Mrs. Blind to her children's faults, she undermines all Agnes's attempts to discipline them.
Bloomfield, Tom. Seven-year-old son of the Bloomfields – viciously unpleasant.
Brown. Bloomfield's servant.
Browne, Bill. Nancy's son.
Browne, Nancy. Elderly widow of Horton, befriended by Agnes Grey and helped by Weston.

F——, Lord. Nobleman much taken with Rosalie Murray, greatly to his wife's annoyance.

G——, Lord. Nobleman spurned by Rosalie Murray at her coming-out ball.

Green, Jane and Susan. Sisters to Mr Green, friends of Rosalie Murray.

Grey, Agnes. Eponymous heroine of the novel. Becomes governess, first to the Bloomfields, then to the Murrays. Falls in love with and marries Mr Weston, the curate.

Grey, Alice. Richard's wife. A capable friendly woman who, after his death, sets up a school with her daughter Agnes.

Grey, Aunt. Agnes's father's sister who recommends Agnes as governess to Mrs Bloomfield.

Grey, Mary. Artistically gifted elder sister of Agnes, who marries Mr Richardson, a clergyman.

Grey, Richard. Impecunious clergyman, father of Agnes and Mary. Dies when Agnes is away working as a governess.

Hatfield, Mr. Rector of Horton. A worldly sycophant who spurns the humble and cultivates the rich.

Higgins, Mr. Villager of Horton.

Hobson, Mr. Tradesman to whom Richard Grey owes money.

Holmes, Betty. Elderly pipe-smoking cottager of Horton.

Jackson, Mr. Tradesman owed money by Richard Grey.

Jackson, Thomas. Curmudgeonly elderly villager for whom Nancy Browne knits stockings as a gesture of reconciliation.

Joseph. Coachman/groom at Horton Lodge whose company Matilda Murray enjoys.

Meltham, Harry. Younger, impecunious son of Sir Hugh Meltham, who is fancied by, and flirts with, Rosalie Murray.

Meltham, Sir Hugh. Attends Rosalie Murray's coming-out ball with Lady Meltham.

Meltham, Mr. Sir Hugh's eldest son who lives in London.

Murray, Charles. Youngest, most unpleasant and most ineducable son of the Murrays.

Murray, John. Rough, tough, unteachable Murray child.

Murray, Matilda. Gawky, foul-mouthed, horse- and dog-loving younger daughter of the Murrays.

Murray, Mr. Gouty, stout, roistering country squire with fierce temper.

Murray, Mrs. Mr Murray's forty-year-old wife and Agnes's employer. Indulgent to herself and her children.

Murray, Rosalie. Physically attractive, vain elder daughter of the Murrays, who later develops a mutual affection for Agnes Grey and marries the rich, ugly, Sir Thomas Ashby.

Richardson, Mr. A decent, shrewd clergyman who marries Mary Grey.

Rogers, Hannah. Irascible Horton villager.

Sally. The Grey's family maid.

Smith, Mr. Haberdasher and grocer to whom Richard Grey owes money.

Somebody, Captain, and Lieutenant Something Else. Two army fops who escort the Green and Murray girls from church.

Weston, Edward. Sensible, devout, kindly curate to Hatfield at Horton. Marries Agnes Grey, after weathering the attentions of Rosalie Murray.

Williamson. Murray's servant.
Wilson, Sir Bradley. Attends Rosalie Murray's coming-out ball.
Wood, Mark. Dying labourer of Horton, acquaintance of Agnes. Called Jem by his wife.

Places

A——. Seaside resort where Agnes and her mother have a school. (Scarborough.)
Ashby Park. Home of Sir Thomas Ashby. A stately mansion in a spacious and beautiful park.
Horton Lodge. Agnes Grey journeys there by train and phaeton to take up the post of governess to the Murray family. (Thorp Green Hall.)
Moss Lane. Near Horton Lodge. A favourite meeting-place.
O——. Not far from Horton Lodge. An industrial town with a railway station. (York.)
Wellwood. Home of the Bloomfield family where Agnes first becomes a governess.

The Tenant of Wildfell Hall (1848)

Commentary

In recent years a special breed of novelists has been sighted and identified – young female liberationists. You need only be female, reasonably literate, young and militant about 'the state of woman' to be qualified apparently for inclusion in the hall of fame as soon as '*the* novel' appears from your confident but statutorily unmanicured hand. Most of what emerges from this application of minor talent to major activity has a kind of frantic inefficiency both of conception and execution, but the quality does not seem to matter so long as the fervour is there.

Anne Brontë's *The Tenant of Wildfell Hall* puts most of our contemporary female novel-writers to complete shame, but it has still not received its deserved acclaim as a novel that, in construction, style, clarity of theme, compares with the greatest that Emily and Charlotte wrote. Apart from this, it is as fearless and affirmative in its assumption and declaration of the independence of woman as any of Charlotte's, and is more clear-headed, shrewd and unsentimental about womankind than today's noisy proselytizers.

The Tenant of Wildfell Hall is, however, almost universally undervalued because, by accident of age, Anne was born under the existing shadows of Emily and Charlotte, because of her retiring temperament, and because death robbed her of the chance to build upon the outstanding promise of this novel. The greatest tragedy of a family who seemed to harbour it as a matter of course, might well be taken to be the clipping off, before full development, of Anne's life and work.

The Tenant of Wildfell Hall is a conspicuously better written, more ambitiously conceived novel than *Agnes Grey*, and the reason is not far to seek. Anne learnt quickly and thoroughly – her work shows how much she had benefited from reading *Wuthering Heights* and from speaking with Emily, her closest companion. Charlotte recognized Anne's powers of assimilation and, in a very revealing comment in her 'Biographical Notice of Ellis and Acton Bell', she takes us some distance into an understanding of what lay behind Anne's quick maturing:

> She had, in the course of her life, been called on to contemplate, near at hand, and for a long time, the terrible effects of talents misused and faculties abused. . .

Anne probably witnessed in her work as a governess (in which she had a lot of experience), and in the dreary pathos of Branwell's decline, the effects of excess on an individual – for that is the basic theme of *Wildfell Hall* – and the way in which moral turpitude can spread like a disease from an individual through family and friends and society. The novel is one more example of the ghastly truth that Branwell's life was fulfilled in its decay not in its achievement – the terrible irony of a bequest to his sisters' imagination which would be the last thing they would wish to receive.

It has been suggested that the novel has more specifically defined sources in Thomas Moore's biography of Byron with its episodes on gambling and dissipation, and in *Some Passages in the Life and Death of John, Earl of Rochester* – Rochester being the sensationally erotic poet of the eighteenth century, who gave his titular name to the hero of *Jane Eyre* and his given name – John – to an old roué in *Wildfell Hall*.

Anne was writing the novel during the summer of 1847 and it appeared in June 1848, just over twelve months before she died. The year 1847 is presumed to be that in which the narrative, which is related by the character Gilbert Markham, concludes. It is not a simply constructed story, and it bears much evidence of careful thought.

The preliminary chapters create the situation, and then – not unlike the intervention of Nelly Dean in *Wuthering Heights*, who gives us her memory's journal of how the present situation came about – we read Helen Graham's journal which she has given to Gilbert in an attempt to clear up the speculations which concern her, her widowhood, and her relationships.

The journal method creates no problem for the reader, for it is very skilfully deployed. For example, each year's events occupies a different amount of space, thus avoiding an impression of mechanical sameness, and giving variety of emphasis to different episodes. Moreover, Anne makes a neat balance between progressive narrative and dramatic event. The narrator's, Markham's, relationship with Helen ebbs and flows with a very satisfactory credibility, and the sickening climaxes of Huntingdon's drunken life are brought in at precisely the correct moments. One might almost say that there is a dapper control at work in the novel.

The greatest achievement, however, probably represents as much a triumph over personality as a mastery of artistic technique. It is the absence of sentimentality.

This may seem a negative virtue but, given Anne's personality, it would not have been in the least surprising if her book had besieged us with a kind of innocent sweetness of mood, character, plot and theme. The fact that it doesn't should alert us to the danger, first, of assuming that a novel, or any work of art, can be taken as a mirror of the artist's own personality and, second, of accounting Anne's equable, agreeable, bland, kindly temperament as lacking in will. She had a deep sense of the nature of good and evil and a relentless capacity for telling the truth, however distasteful, of any experience.

Wildfell Hall has a moral intention – as, in fact, did everything that Anne did or wrote. The novel presents five realities, each one of which amounts to a kind of warning to the unprepared, the innocent, the gullible.

They are – one: that man or woman is a fool who is dazzled by good looks. Shakespeare's words in *Macbeth* – 'there's no art to find the mind's construction in the face' – might well have been approved by Anne as a warning motto to Helen to beware the lures and traps of dashing and handsome Huntingdon. Two: if you transgress or sin, you must pay a price. The fate of Huntingdon and some of his dissolute friends is presented as inevitable, a QED of existence. Three: the sins of the fathers can be visited upon the sons. But in *Wildfell Hall* this belief contains, for Helen Graham, a dilemma which affects a good deal of her social activities. She believes her son can only be protected from the excessive drinking habits of her husband by denying him every and any opportunity to indulge. But the society around her, living, as most people do, in the spirit and practice of compromise, presents the attractive alternative of immunization from excess by controlled introduction to moderation. Anne's horrifying depiction of the physical end of excess leaves the reader in no doubt about where she stands – she had lived with Branwell.

Anne's most persistently expressed belief is her fourth – the ability to forgive is at once the most difficult and most potent virtue. She expresses it in strictly Christian terms, largely through the words and actions of her heroine, Helen, whose life with the profligate Huntingdon approaches martyrdom. But Helen also has to extend forgiveness to the man she comes to love – Gilbert. He wavers in his fidelity to her because of the gossiping of his neighbours, who themselves also require her forbearance.

The depiction of acts of forgiveness carries, always, the danger of being sentimental and of bestowing prissy quasi-sainthood on the one who does the forgiving. Anne avoids this, by the sheer simplicity of her expression of her faith in the power of forgiveness, and by the total lack of self-consciousness in the character of Helen.

She is by far the most attractive in personality of all the Brontë heroines. Her toughness of will and purpose do not have any of that slight aura of self-congratulation we find in Lucy Snowe and Jane Eyre. She has nothing either of the petulance of Catherine in *Wuthering Heights*. Her ability to forgive is not accompanied by bland forbearance, for she is capable of anger. Above all, she is perhaps the most obviously sexually alive of the Brontë heroines. Her delight in the sensuous aspects of love – in glances, touches, smiles, blushes, ardours – is never overwhelmed by any vast moral or spiritual theme. In fact, though she most certainly is a woman of the highest moral rectitude, we have the feeling that true passion means as much to her as strict codes of thought and action.

The fifth theme is one which broadens the implications of the book. Anne, like Charlotte, felt very keenly the state of Victorian womankind, the absence of so many of the privileges of action and speech enjoyed naturally by men. She expresses her awareness of this subtly and indirectly but with fine precision by showing the crass and cruel double standards which a society like Victorian England, demonstrated. Huntingdon 'offers' his wife as a chattel which he can dispose of to his friends, but not much later on he accuses her, quite falsely, of being unfaithful to him!

The abiding overall effect of the novel is to induce a feeling that the writer is one whose observations and emotional responses one can completely trust. One is never afraid, as with Charlotte, of what might be around the corner of the next paragraph or chapter. Anne doesn't embarrass with any kind of excess, like Rochester's disguise, or the nun, or with waves of sentiment that occasionally sweep across Charlotte's pages. She seems to know exactly where her novel is going, and, just as important, how far she can go in leading the reader.

Her eyes are as keen as Charlotte's for detail both of character and natural surroundings but she does not deploy, perhaps didn't possess, that satirical knife with which Charlotte dissected her victim once her senses had provided her with the required data. It is sober truth rather than sharp judgement that Anne is interested in:

My mother, as usual, was cheerful and chatty, full of activity and good-nature, and only faulty in being too anxious to make her guests happy, thereby forcing several of them to do what their soul abhorred, in the way of eating or drinking, sitting opposite the blazing fire, or talking when they would be silent.

But she is not, by any means, averse to making it quite clear where the character stands:

Mrs Wilson was more brilliant than ever, with her budgets of fresh news and old scandal, strung together with trivial questions and remarks, and oft-repeated observations, uttered apparently for the sole purpose of denying a moment's rest to her inexhaustible organs of speech.

Her feeling for place is very strongly developed. She shares with Charlotte and Emily the gift of being able to give location a personality. Just as Wuthering Heights and Thrushcross Grange gradually become dramatis personae in their own right, so do Wildfell Hall and Markham's farmhouse home:

... the castellated towers of laurel in the middle of the garden, the gigantic warrior that stood on one side of the gateway, and the lion that guarded the other, were sprouted into such fantastic shapes as resembled nothing either in heaven or earth, or in the waters under the earth; but, to my young imagination, they presented all of them a goblinish appearance, that harmonizes well with the ghostly legends and dark traditions our old nurse had told us respecting the haunted hall and its departed occupants.

Still, her descriptions of natural scenes are blander than her sisters' – indeed, when one looks at those unsurprising, meticulous vignettes from nature that she drew for exercise, one sees an exact visual counterpart for her verbal descriptions:

That day was rainy like its predecessor; but towards evening it began to clear up a little, and the next morning was fair and promising. I was out on the hill with the reapers. A light wind swept over the corn; and all nature laughed in the sunshine. The lark was rejoicing among the silvery floating clouds. The late rain had so sweetly freshened and cleared the air, and washed the sky, and left such glittering gems on branch and blade, that not even the farmers could have the heart to blame it.

Anne's chief strength lies, however, in the areas of truth to human nature and cunning manipulation of plot. We shall never know how much anguish it cost her to depict the dissolution of Huntingdon in the context of her experience of Branwell's death, but what is plain is the astonishing control and the refusal to lapse, as perhaps Charlotte might have done, into Gothic excess. Anne is relentless in her selection of detail, and spares nothing to achieve what she wants – as she tells us in the preface to the second edition – 'I wish to tell the truth, for truth always contains its own moral ...' On every page, she confirms this.

And, equally, she constantly confirms that her process of selection of detail is frequently related to a highly developed sense, but an economically used sense, of drama. She does not have to give best either to Emily or Charlotte in the depiction of any scene or incident which requires the provision of a well calculated climax:

> I said no more; but observing that he kept gazing towards the foot of the bed, I went and sat there, placing the light so as to shine full upon me, for I thought he might be dying, and I wanted him to know me. For a long time he lay silently looking upon me, first with a vacant stare, then with a fixed gaze of strange growing intensity. At last he startled me by suddenly raising himself on his elbow and demanding in a horrified whisper, with his eyes still fixed on me – 'Who is it?'
> 'It is Helen Huntingdon,' said I ...

The Tenant of Wildfell Hall is a lesser novel than the major ones of Charlotte and than *Wuthering Heights*, but that is not because it is demonstrably inferior, but because Anne is not attempting to scale the heights which her sisters achieved. Too many critics have unfavourably compared her novel with those of her sisters. There is hardly any other novel by anyone which can be compared with *Wuthering Heights*, and few other novelists achieved the passionate moral grandeur, rich characterization and thematic complexity of *Villette* and *Jane Eyre*.

One final reflection on this so underrated work is inevitable to anyone who admires it. Its theme – largely untouched by her sisters – is not only unique in that sense, but in another, very poignant one. Anne, the shy one, the last of the Brontës to be born, the latecomer to that strange family, was the only one of them to grasp firmly the one theme that had its roots deep in their family's life – wilful dissolution.

Synopsis

In autumn 1827 a twenty-four-year-old farmer, Gilbert Markham, is living with his gossipy mother, his sulky brother Fergus, and his pretty sister Rose at Linden-Car in ——shire. Nearby the tenant of Wildfell

Hall, the beautiful and mysterious Mrs Graham, lives with her son Arthur, whom Rose and her mother call on. Gilbert sees her in church, but his interest is in Eliza Millward, the youngest daughter of the vicar. Through saving Arthur from a fall, Gilbert gets to know Mrs Graham, who seems overprotective of her son, especially as far as alcohol is concerned. After several visits, during which Gilbert discovers Mrs Graham paints and has a painting of a handsome young man turned face to the wall, Gilbert finds he is attracted to her. One day he meets Mr Lawrence, whose family once occupied Wildfell Hall. He suggests Gilbert may have changed his mind about Mrs Graham. Gilbert's retort is to ask Mr Lawrence if he is in love with Mrs Graham, only to be told that Lawrence thought Gilbert was engaged to Miss Millward. As Gilbert's feelings for Mrs Graham grow, those for Eliza lessen. Village gossip suggests there is something unpleasant about Mrs Graham's past. Eliza suggests she is in love with Lawrence and that Arthur resembles him. Mrs Graham refuses to meet Gilbert except as a friend. When Gilbert asks Lawrence what all the mystery is about, Lawrence refuses to answer. On one visit, after telling Helen Graham of his feelings for her, he is told to leave. Hearing voices he delays and sees Mrs Graham come into the garden with a man she calls Frederick. His arm is about her waist and her head on his shoulder. Next day, out riding, the distraught Gilbert meets Lawrence who asks him why he is so quarrelsome. Angrily Gilbert attacks and wounds him with his whip. Later while in the fields with his reapers, Gilbert receives a message via Arthur that Mrs Markham wishes to see him. She sees him briefly and the next day he hurries over to Wildfell Hall, and, after an emotional scene, is given a journal to take away and read. It is the journal of Mrs Graham's life up to that point. It tells of her marriage, despite her family's warnings about his profligacy, to Mr Huntingdon, the son of her uncle's friend; how she hoped to reform him; how he turned out to be an unrepentant roué, spending his time with Lord Lowborough, Hattersley and other drinking and wenching companions; how her relationship with him deteriorates after Arthur's birth; how she discovers he is having an affair with Annabella (now Lady Lowborough); how, finally, the marriage breaks up as a result of Huntingdon's selfish behaviour, drinking and womanizing; how she decides to leave him but he discovers the plan and prevents it, and, as a result of his dissipation, becomes very ill; how her brother, Frederick Lawrence, coming to stay with her, helps her to escape with Arthur and her faithful servant, Rachel, to Wildfell Hall, leaving Huntingdon to search for her. Here the journal ends.

Gilbert hurries over to Wildfell Hall to ask forgiveness, declaring he will marry her when Huntingdon dies. She makes him promise not to return for six months, when she will let him know where she is. Gilbert apologizes to and makes friends with Frederick Lawrence, who gives him news of Mrs Graham who has gone to care for the dying Huntingdon. Then Eliza informs him that Mrs Graham is about to be married to a Mr Hargrave at Grassdale. Gilbert arrives there just in time to see a bridal party leave the church, but, to his great relief, the groom is Frederick, and his bride Esther Hargrave. Lawrence's letter to Gilbert about his marriage had gone astray. Eventually, discovering Helen Graham, now a widow, living with her aunt, Mrs Maxwell of Staningley, he seeks her out. They declare their love for each other and Helen agrees to marry him.

Characters

Benson. The Huntingdons' butler.

'Blatant, Mr'. Name given by Huntingdon to Mr Leighton, preacher at the church attended by Helen's aunt and uncle.

Boarham, Mr. Friend of Helen Huntingdon's aunt, who pay court to Helen.

Caroline. Lord Lowborough's fiancée.

F——, Lady. Married woman who intrigues with Arthur Huntingdon before his marriage.

'Graham', Arthur. *See* Huntingdon, Arthur.

'Graham', Helen. *See* Huntingdon, Helen.

Greaves, Mrs. Servant of Arthur Huntingdon.

Grimsby, Mr. Arthur Huntingdon's corrupt and despicable friend.

Halford. Gilbert Markham's confidant who marries Rose Markham.

Hargrave, Esther. Millicent's younger sister. Friend of Helen Huntingdon. Marries Frederick Lawrence, Helen's brother.

Hargrave, Millicent. Walter Hargrave's sister, Annabella Wilmot's cousin. Has a great affection for Helen Huntingdon. Marries Ralph Hattersley.

Hargrave, Mrs. Mother of Walter, Millicent, Esther.

Hargrave, Walter. Arthur Huntingdon's friend, brother of Millicent and Esther.

Hattersley, Helen. Daughter of Millicent and Ralph. Eventually marries Arthur Huntingdon jnr.

Hattersley, Millicent. *See* Hargrave, Millicent.

Hattersley, Ralph. Rich banker's son, acquaintance of Huntingdon. Begins as a coarse boor. Marries Millicent Hargrave.

Huntingdon, Arthur (1). Marries Helen Lawrence ('Mrs Graham'), and has an affair with Lady Lowborough. A charming, unreliable, drunken cad.

Huntingdon, Arthur (2). Young son of Arthur and Helen Huntingdon. Marries Helen Hattersley.

Huntingdon, Helen. *Née* Lawrence. Marries Arthur Huntingdon and takes the name of Graham as a disguise after leaving him. After his death marries Gilbert Markham.

Jacob. A casual labourer who happens to be in earshot when Eliza Millward tells Gilbert Markham that Helen Huntingdon is to be married.

John. Huntingdon's servant.

Lawrence, Frederick. Brother of Helen Huntingdon ('Mrs Graham'); squire of Lindenhope. Eventually marries Esther Hargrave.

Leighton, Mr. *See* 'Mr Blatant'.

Lowborough, Lord. Friend of Arthur Huntingdon. Married to, then divorced from, Annabella Wilmot. A profligate who later reforms.

Markham, Fergus. Gilbert's younger brother. Uncouth, superficial.

Markham, Gilbert. Elder son of gentleman farmer. Falls in love with and subsequently marries Helen 'Graham' (Huntingdon). Honest and generous.

Markham, Mr. Gilbert, Fergus and Rose Markham's father. A successful farmer.

Markham, Mrs. Gilbert, Fergus and Rose Markham's mother. A doting parent.

Markham, Rose. Gilbert Markham's sister. Marries Halford.

Maxwell, Mrs Peggy. Helen Huntingdon's aunt.

Millward, Eliza. Vicar of Lindenhope's mischief-making daughter.

Millward, Mary. Vicar of Lindenhope's daughter. Secretly becomes engaged to Richard Wilson whom, when he becomes curate of Lindenhope, she marries.

Millward, Rev. Michael. Vicar of Lindenhope.

Myers, Alice. Arthur Huntingdon's mistress who enters his home as his son's tutor.

Oldfield, Mr. Persistent suitor for the hand of Esther Hargrave.

Rachel. Lady's maid to Helen 'Graham' (Huntingdon).

Richard. Arthur Huntingdon's coachman.

Sarah. The Millwards' maid.

Thomas. The Maxwells' manservant.

Wilmot, Annabella. Mr Wilmot's niece. An heiress who marries Lord Lowborough for his title, and becomes Huntingdon's mistress. Finally elopes with a third man, is divorced by Lowborough and is reported to have died in penury and misery.

Wilmot, Mr. Helen Huntingdon's uncle's disgreeable friend.

Wilson, Jane. Ambitious lady of twenty-six. Has designs on Frederick Lawrence.

Wilson, Mrs. Widow of affluent farmer, mother of Robert, Richard, Jane.

Wilson, Richard. Younger son of Mrs Wilson. Eventually marries the vicar's elder daughter Mary, and succeeds him as Vicar of Lindenhope.

Wilson, Robert. Mrs Wilson's elder son.

Places

F———. Quiet seaside town which is visited by Helen 'Graham' (Huntingdon), her widowed aunt (Mrs Maxwell) and Esther Hargrave.

Fernley Manor, Cumberland. The false name given to her painting of Wildfell Hall by Helen Graham (Huntingdon).

Grassdale. Home of Helen and Arthur Huntingdon.

Grove, The. Home of the Hargrave family in Grassdale.

L———. Market town seven miles from Wildfell Hall.

Linden-Car. Name given to the home of Gilbert Markham, and to the surrounding countryside.

Lindenhope. Village near Wildfell Hall where Rev. Millward is vicar.

M———. The nearest coach stop for Grassdale Manor.

Ryecote Farm. Home of Robert Wilson.

Staningly Hall. Helen's home before her first marriage.

Wildfell Hall. Sometimes identified with Ponden Hall though the proximity to the sea of its immediate surroundings suggests the area south of the coastal town of Scarborough which Anne loved.

Woodford. Mr Lawrence's home in Lindenthorpe.

Glossary to the Novels

The material included in this section falls into the following categories:
(**1**) Unusual words, e.g. 'eleemosynary'. (**2**) Words which have changed their meaning, to a degree, from the nineteenth century to the present day, e.g. 'nervous'. (**3**) Words which have become archaic since the Brontës' time or were even, in one or two cases, archaic at the time, e.g. 'yclept', 'lameter'. (**4**) Slang words and idiomatic expressions – in many cases still having currency in the twentieth century – e.g. 'Nancy' (for an effeminate boy) and 'on-going'. Charlotte was particularly immune to inhibitions about the use of slang. (**5**) Dialect words – almost invariably West Yorkshire dialect. Some are no longer in use, others are, and yet others barely survive. In one or two cases even the most diligent inquiries have failed to elicit precise meanings and guesswork aided by context has been employed. Emily's 'Yorkshire' dialect in *Wuthering Heights* is, in many cases, her written approximation to what she heard, not what she had ever seen written down. It should be remembered that Charlotte altered a good deal of Emily's dialect to conform with what Charlotte believed was a more correct form. (**6**) Foreign words and phrases – almost invariably French and, expectedly, often from *Villette* and *The Professor*. It should not be surprising, however, to realize that *Shirley* also contains a considerable amount of French, when one recalls that Charlotte became a fluent speaker of, and writer in, that language. (**7**) Biblical and other references – literary, topographical etc. Charlotte's novels are full of biblical references, testifying to her intimate knowledge of the Authorized Version. (**8**) Topical references. The Brontës, particularly Emily and Charlotte, were deeply interested in all kinds of contemporary matters relating to politics, transport, fashion, science etc., etc. This is reflected in the great number of often quite fascinating references to now completely obsolete matters and objects – e.g. 'backboards', 'phaeton', 'lappets'.

Aaron, breastplate of SEE Exodus 28: 15–30
Aaron, three rods of SEE Exodus 28: 2–4
Abdiel Seraph who rebuked Satan (Milton, *Paradise Lost*)

Abel's offering SEE Genesis 4: 4, for Abel's offering to God of the firstlings of his flock
Abigail lady's maid
aboon above

Absalom, the locks of Absalom's hair weighed 5 pounds at its annual shearing; SEE 2 Samuel 14: 26

accost interference

accoutrements at Joan of Arc's trial 'accoutrements' (soldier's gear and equipment such as she had worn) were placed near her to persuade her to confess

acerb sharp

Achan, tent of Joshua commanded the children of Israel to stone Achan to death and burn and stone his children because he stole part of the spoils which accrued when Joshua sacked Jericho; SEE Joshua 7: 25

Additional Curate's Society founded by wine merchant in 1837 to provide aid, but especially to increase curate strength, to cater for growth and movement of population in Industrial Revolution

'Adonis of fifty' pejorative reference to the Prince Regent (later George IV) who devoted a good deal of his life to various kinds of dissipation

adytum secret chamber in ancient temples from which oracles were issued

Aeolus Zeus appointed him ruler of the winds

afore before

agait a'going

Agar Mt Sinai

agate afoot

agean against

agent representative

agrin grinning

agt out

Ahab/Micaiah Micaiah, son of Imla, foretold the fall of Ahab at Ramoth–Gilead; SEE 2 Chronicles 18

Ahasuerus, King biblical name of Artaxerxes, wealthy king of Persia, 6th century, bound to marry Esther

ahr our

aht out

Albion (cliffs of) Albion = England

aliment food, nourishment

allas, allus always

l'allée défendue forbidden path

Alnaschar dream SEE *Arabian Nights*; Alnaschar is a beggar who inherits riches with which he buys precious glass; he inadvertently destroys it while dreaming

alow ablaze

alpha and omega the beginning and end

Alpine Peri SEE Peri

Amaranth bloom imaginary unfading flower

Amazon's cap on the British Museum frieze the Amazons are shown wearing Phrygian caps

amused deluded

an even if

Anak, sons of ancient giants of Israel; SEE Deut. 9: 2

anent concerning, near to

aneurism abnormal dilation or enlargement of an artery

ange farouche fierce angel

Anglisé made into English

animated (with) overactive (as the result of)

answer, made the living made the living (i.e. the priest's parish) answer (i.e. suffice) for his needs

Antinomian describes sect or individual who believed Christians are exempted by grace from necessity to observe any moral law; derives from Cromwellian period, in England

Antwerp the French occupied Antwerp in 1792 – dangerously near the Channel ports

Anversois, an citizen of Antwerp

Aphrodite Greek form of Roman Venus, goddess of love and beauty

Apollo Belvedere Roman marble copy (modern hands) after a Greek statue, probably dating from *c.* 350 BC, in the Vatican Museum

Apollyon Greek form of Hebrew Abaddon; angel of the bottomless pit in Revelations 9:11, and appears in *Pilgrim's Progress*, where Christian conquers him

apostacy state of abandonment of one's faith

apostrophe rhetorical passage in a speech or statement

apple of his eye, the the pupil of his eye

approach bring nearer

aqua fortis early scientific, now popular, name of commercial nitric acid – a solvent and corrosive

Arabian Arabian bred horse

Arabian Tales The *Arabian Nights* to which Charlotte makes several references

armoire linen cupboard or closet

arn earn

(th') arrand arrant

aspiration sometimes used by C. to mean diatribe or flight of speech

Assumption, the Feast of the the reception of the Virgin Mary into heaven, with body free from corruption, celebrated by Roman Catholics on 15 August

'as well soon as syne' 'as well soon (i.e. now) as later' (Scots prov.)

as where wherever

'at that

at hend at hand

Athanasius, St the 4th-century creed (Athanasian) summarizing beliefs concerning the Trinity is attributed (without support) to him and is usually recited at communion service

Athenée derived from Athens – hence any seat of learning and wisdom (e.g. French literary academy)

Athenian message message summoning M. Paul to the Athenée

Atlas one of Hercules' twelve labours imposed by Hera was to fetch the golden apples; Atlas did this for him while Hercules temporarily held up the sky

attent delay

atween between

Aurora goddess of dawn

aw I

aw'll I'll

aw' noan I'm not

ax ask

ayont beyond

Azrael angel responsible for separating the soul from a dead body, in Mohammedan and Jewish mythology

azury blue, bluish: in *SH.*, Charlotte refers to 'azury snow', having noticed the bluish haze sometimes observable in intensely white colouring

Baal chief god of Phoenicians and Canaanites: Old Testament false god

Baal (of a Lord Wellington) any false god. Following his spectacular victories against the French and the equally spectacular honours poured on him, Wellington acquired the status of a god for many worshipping Englishmen

Babylonish furnace where Nebuchadnezzar tried to destroy Shadrach, Meschach and Abednego

Babylonish masons those who built the tower of Babel

back-boards young ladies wore them to encourage a straight back

bahn going

'baht without

bairnies little ones

balled clogged

balsam plant one-time popular annual garden plant – genus Impatiens

band cord, rope

bane cause of misery

banning cursing

Banshee supernatural being which announces sudden death in a house by shrieking and chanting mournfully under a window

barcarole gondolier's song

Barmecide ('s loaf) name given to Baghdad (*Arabian Nights*) princes, one of whom put empty dishes before his banquet-guests, pretending they were full; HENCE any illusory gift; ALSO 'Barmecide supper'.

barn child

barouche two-seater, four-wheeled, falling-top carriage

barren, the an area of barren land

barthens burdens

bas-bleu blue-stocking

basement a ledge over a basement window

bashaw SEE Pasha

basilisk fabulous reptile (cockatrice) whose gaze and breath were fatal

basin a cup without a handle

Basseterre chief town of Guadeloupe, largest of Caribbean Leeward Isles

baudet ignoramus

Bäuerinnen German peasant woman

be by

beamy shiny

beaten exhausted

beaten (out of that) beaten in that attempt

beaufet a niche, cupboard or sideboard for holding glass or china

beck brook with stony bed

bedizenings gaudy dressing-up

Bedreddin Hassan in *Arabian Nights* he is married to Shems-ed-din's daughter instead of a hunchback forced on her by her father; the happy conclusion involves magic performed by a friendly Djinn.

Beelzebub prince of evil

Béguines order of nuns founded 12th century by Le Bèghe, and best known in Holland and Germany

Bel Assyrio-Babylonian god

belangs belongs

beldame old hag

Belial spirit of evil personified – used by Milton as name for one of the fallen angels

belladonna tincture purple-coloured drug derived from Deadly Nightshade (genus Atropa B) sometimes used for cosmetics

bend-leather (heart) hard as tough leather

Benedict bachelor

Benefit of Clergy mediaeval clergy accused of a felony were exempt

from secular trial. Subsequently, after a first conviction the exemption no longer held. The practice was abolished in England in 1827

bénitier font

Béranger Pierre Jean de, 1780–1857; French poet, satirist and political writer

berceau trellissed arbour

Berenice beloved by Emperor Titus and heroine of Racine's play of the same name

Berlin wools fine dyed knitting wool

bésicles old-fashioned large spectacles with hinged nosepiece but no side pieces

bespoke reserved

bête fauve wild beast

bêtes de somme beasts of burden

Beth-el where Jacob experienced his vision; SEE Genesis 28: 11–22

Bethesda SEE John 5: 2–9

. . . better end, the . . . the better kind

Beulah, hills of Beulah = 'marriage' or 'married'; SEE Isaiah 62: 4

Bewick's History Thomas Bewick (1735–1828) produced *British Birds*, two vols, 1797–1804, noted for its magnificent illustrations

biggin building

black aviced black complexioned

blacklegs swindlers, not the modern usage associated with industrial strikes

blanc-bec young man without experience

block stone pillar acting as signpost

blond, the fair hair

blonde meshed lace of unbleached white or black silk

Bluebeard villainous and murderous protagonist of European stories who disposed of several wives

Boadicea, Queen Buddica, British monarch, AD 62

t'boards the doors

bogard ghost

Bohemian glass

bombazeen mixed worsted and silk

cloth, dyed black for mourning use

bonbonnière sweet-box

bonne female servant

bonnet grec smoking cap

bonny pickle, in a in a bad way

boobies and bedlamites phrase used by Huntingdon in *T. of W.H.* to describe some of the frequenters of gaming-houses

book-muslin muslin used for book covers and dress-making

Bossuet Jacques Bénigne Bossuet (1627–1704); famous French Catholic cleric, writer of sermons, histories, essays

bothom ut a bog-hoile bottom of a bog-hole

Bothwell, Earl of or James Hepburn, who murdered Darnley, and married Mary, Queen of Scots

Bothwell, Sergeant Character in Walter Scott's *Old Mortality*; a sergeant in army of John Grahame who took up arms against Scottish Covenanters (i.e. Protestants) in the late 17th century

bottines bootees, fastened on the side, or elasticated

Bottom comic victim of Puck's mischievousness in Shakespeare's *A Midsummer Night's Dream*

boudoir small, private, elegantly furnished lady's room

boudoir-oratoire small private chapel

bougie candle

bouilli, bouillon bouilli = boiled or stewed meat; bouillon = strong broth

bourne boundary

'bout without

bowstring used for garrotting

Brabantoises natives of Brabant, province of the Netherlands

brach bitch-hound

Brahma in Hindu religion, the divine reality which is manifested by the universe and human consciousness

brass money

bravely fine

braw brave

brazened brazen

brioche pastry

British gin gin became a cheap alcoholic drink in the 19th century – its use was widespread and much abused

Brobdignagian for Brobdingnagian: Swift's imaginary country (in *Gulliver's Travels*) where everything is on a gigantic scale

brocken broken

brodequins laced half-boots

brooch, paste brooch made of vitreous composition

brown study deep in thought

brown stuff frocks rough woollen frocks

brownie shaggy, kindly goblin of the North who engages in nocturnal housework

brusqueries rude behaviour

brusts bursts

buck raffish man-about-town

bucking-basket receptacle for clothes destined to be washed (bucked)

bud but

bugbear stories stories told to frighten children (i.e. about the bogeyman or bugaboo)

build up covering over

bullaces wild plum (or any fruit) trees

bure plain material

bureau office

Cabas flat two-handled basket

cabinet small room

Cachmire, un véritable a true Cashmir shawl

cadet of the house youngest son or brother of family

Cadmus mythological founder of Cadmea (later Thebes)

Caffre Bush term formerly used of Bantu tribe of Africa

cahnt (1) count; (2) 'mak noa cahnt' – take no account

Cain (-like) SEE Genesis 4: 12–16

callant a youth

Calvinistic doctrines among them are: (1) 'election' – God elects or chooses, by

his irrevocable authority, some
creatures for eternal salvation, and
rejects others; (2) 'reprobation' – the
state of being rejected by God; (3)
'predestination' – mankind's fate is
pre-ordained by God; C. expressed
doubts to E.N. about her own
position relative to God's will if
Calvin's doctrines were true

cambric fine white Flanders linen

camel-hair pencils fine paint brushes

Canaan paradise, land of promise

Candace title of Queens of Abyssinia in
Greek and Roman times

candle dip candle made by repeated
dipping of a wick into melted tallow

canker of the mind mental anguish of
great severity

can'le light candle light

cannie supernaturally wise

Canova's marbles Antonio Canova
(1757–1822); neo-classic sculptor,
famous for sculptures of
Buonaparte's family

cant humbug talk

cantlet a small amount

cant(y) lively

cap (1) (n.) night head-wear; (2) (v.) to
surpass

capped brought to a climax of absurdity

Carmelite order of friars (White Friars)
founded 1156; in 15th century
Carmelite Order of Nuns founded

carn can't

carré general purpose room

Carthage, ladies of noted for their beauty

caryatid female figure used as pillar

cas le appropriate, timely

Castaway, The William Cowper's
(1731–1800) poem

*Castlereagh, Robert Stewart,
Viscount* 1769–1822; unpopular
authoritarian Secretary for War and
the Colonies (1812–22)

castor a hat of beaver or rabbit fur

cat used as term of abuse

catalepsy temporary loss of sensation of
consciousness accompanied by body
rigidity

Catalonian distinctive region of north-
east Spain with strong sense of
cultural entity and its own dialect

Catholic or Methodist enthusiast two
religious revivals contested for public
notice in the late 18th/early 19th
centuries – John Wesley's Methodist
revival and an upsurge in Catholic
conversion

cawlf calf

ceiled roof-plastered

ceinture bleu céleste sky-blue sash

centipede from the Indies West Indian
centipedes are very poisonous

certy, my on my oath! (ejaculation)

Chaldeans natives of Chaldea credited
with occult powers; Chaldeans were
employed as Nebuchadnezzar's
soothsayers

*Chambers' Journal Chambers' Edinburgh
Journal* – famous weekly started in
1821 by William Chambers

cham'er chamber

chapeau vert tendre spring-green hat

chapman a purchaser

charity-schoolboy a pupil in a school for
the poor, supported by endowments
or gifts; used pejoratively in *V.*

charivari a great din intended to mock
the unpopular: literally 'cats'
concert'; used against widows who
had married a second time (SEE
Thomas Hardy's novels)

Charon the ferryman who conveys
dead souls across the river Styx
(q.v.)

chat de ma tante Julienne, le appellation
for unnamed cat left in Frances
Henri's care (*The Professor*)

chaussées roads, carriageways (Flemish)

cheeney china

chemises undergarments, normally short
sleeved

chemisette female undergarment

Chénier André Marie de, 1762–94;
French poet

chetive weakly

chicken in the pip diseased chicken

chiffonière ornamented cabinet for

storing clothing, with working top
childer children
'Child's Guide' a memory of Carus
  Wilson (Head of Cowan Bridge
  School) whose magazine *The Child's
  Friend* promised hell-fire for
  recalcitrant children
chimbley chimney
china-topped topped with porcelain
'chitty-faced creature' childish-faced
cholera-tint yellow
choucroute sauerkraut
Christian and Hopeful SEE John Bunyan's
  The Pilgrim's Progress (1768) –
  favourite reading of Charlotte's
chuck term of endearment, but
  occasionally used sardonically
churl Charlotte uses it in its original
  sense of a lowly rustic labourer
Churstmas Christmas
chuzzen chosen
Cicerone guide who understands and
  explains antiquities etc.
clear you too clear off, too
'Cleopatra' painted by Defiefve,
Belgian artist, and exhibited at the
Brussels 'Salon' while Charlotte was
there
cloes clothes
cloised closed
clomp clump, tread noisily
cloth, the removal of the order of release
  for a guest – when the cloth covering
  the tea-table is removed
cloth-dressers those who combed the
  cloth and raised a smooth map in the
  process of cloth manufacture
cloth-hall wool exchange
clothes-press oak-cupboard
cockatrice tiny poisonous monster; SEE
  basilisk
codger a roguish fellow
co-elevate of the same height as
colifichet de plus one more piece of
  frippery
collation light meal
collect the prayer appropriate to the
  particular day of the year
collyrium an eye-wash

cols brodés embroidered collars
comed come
comfits sweetmeats
comminations threatening denunciations
commissionaire a porter
compassionating showing compassion
concern, such a such a person
  (derogatory)
conclave private assembly
conformable conforming to
congeries accumulation
congfiters sweetmeats
consarned concerned
conscience SEE phrenology
conservatoire public school of music
  (e.g. Paris)
console small table fixed to wall by
  bracket
consoles brackets (often decorated) fixed
  to a wall which supported a table top
  or small figures, busts or vases
conventical of a convent
conventicle strictly a clandestine
  religious meeting, but used in 19th
  century to refer to any
  nonconformist gathering
conventual belonging to a convent
convive a table companion
coquelicot poppy
coquine slut
corbeille carved basket with sculptured
  flowers and fruits; in *SH.* – 'the full
  effect'
Corneille 1606–84; French classical
  tragedian
cornicing (1), fluting (2) and garlanding (3)
  (1) ornamental moulding just below
  a ceiling round a wall; (2) semi-
  cylindrical grooves in pillars; (3)
  plaster-moulded flower wreathes,
  leaves, etc. for ceiling decoration
coronel in *V.* – 'head of a bed'
Corsairs refers to Byron's *The Corsair*
  (1814)
cotch catch
cotelettes de mouton mutton cutlets
cottier originally an Irish tenant holding
  land as the highest bidder
countenance expression

courroucée enraged

courtesy curtsy

crack, a two-handed cracking a whip in a two-horse carriage

cracknels hard, brittle cake or biscuit

crahner's quest coroner's inquest; compare Shakespeare's usage in *Hamlet*, V, i

cranerie boldness

cranky shaky

crape thin transparent material of raw silk used for mourning and, occasionally, evening gowns

crater, cratur creature

craunch violent crunch

Creole, the antipodes of the West Indies

criminate incriminate

crimped pleated

crock (1) a sooty pot; (2) a pot (metal); (3) soot (occasionally)

Croesus 6th century BC fabulously rich King of Lydia

croisées casement windows

croquant crunching

crosspatch ill-natured person

crotchets fads

crow to pluck bone to pick

crutch forked rest for rider's leg in a side-saddle

cui bono? what good will come of it?

cuirass joined breast and back-plate

cuisinière cook

cumberer encumbrance

Cunegarde character from von Kleust's (1777–1811) play *Das Kätchen von Heilbronn* who is notoriously ugly but, by cunning, makes herself attractive

currently fluently

curtain, white day-beds were, in the Brontës' time, almost invariably surrounded by a curtain

curtain lecture reprimand given by wife to husband in bed; beds often had curtains in the early 19th century

cushet ring-dove or wood-pigeon

custen dahn cast down, depressed

Cuyp-like Aelbert Cuyp (1620–91); Dutch landscape painter

cyphering arithmetic

Dagon god of the Philistines, half man and half fish

dahn down

daht, aw I don't doubt

dames, des experienced women

Danaë imprisoned in a brazen tower by her father Acrisius because of a prophecy that she would bear a son who would kill him; Zeus visited her and Perseus was conceived – he killed Acrisius later, by accident

Daniel for story of lion's den SEE Daniel 6: 16–22

darnut dare not

darr dare

darr be laiking dare to be playing

daughterling little daughter

David SEE 2 Samuel 13–18

day-dawn dawn

dayspring on high SEE Luke 1: 78

Borgia, Lucrèce de 1480–1519; Duchess of Ferrara; legend attributes several murders by poison to her, but historical evidence is lacking

dead-thraw death-throe

deave break violently

debarrassed relieved, freed

dee die

deead dead

deed is there indeed there is

delf-case crockery cupboard; Delf ware was made in Delft in Holland and cheap copies were produced in England

Demas SEE Timothy 4: 10

demi-grisette working-class French girl employed as apprentice shop assistant or seamstress

demoiselles de magasins girl shop-assistants

den hollow

dentelles lace garments

denty dainty

determine into one to end up as one

devastate hunt

device motto

dew-vials drops of dew

diligence French stage-coach

dimity strong cotton fabric woven with raised figures or stripes; used for bedroom hangings

Diogenes Greek philosopher who lived in a tub to indicate contempt for life's amenities

discussed consumed

Dissenter Protestants who, after Restoration of Charles II, refused communion with Church of England; one who separates from the service and worship of any established church

distaff, spun off the exhausted, finished, like thread coming off a distaff (cleft stick used for winding wool)

Dives means rich man; SEE Vulgate version of story of Lazarus, Luke 16

Divine Right of Kings belief, whose sources lie deep in mediaeval theory and practice, in supernatural sanction (symbolized by annointing with holy oil at coronation) of monarch's status and rule; much cultivated by Tudor (SEE Shakespeare's history plays) and Stuart dynasties, and, as late as 19th century, proselytized by High Tory clergy

doddered (1) describes a tree which has lost its top branches; (2) a tree covered with parasitical vine

Dome, the of St Paul's Cathedral

door-stones doorstep

Doric, (native) broad or rustic dialect

doubt fear

douche shock

Douglas larder chaos, disorder

dowdyish shabbily dressed

down of suspicious (of)

downdraughts bankrupts

dragees almonds covered in sugar

drawing away passing away, dying

dree sadly tedious

dressing-shop shed where one of the processes in cloth manufacture took place

Dryad wood-nymph

dry-nurse medical nurse as opposed to a wet-nurse

dulcet-creams sweet creams

'duller-witted farmer' King George III – his favourite theme and occupation was agriculture

dunnock hedge-sparrow

dunnutt do not

E He

Earl of Huntingdon, ghost of Robert Fitzooth, Earl of Huntingdon, often identified as legendary Robin Hood

ébats happy promenading, pleasant diversions

éclat showy splendour

eea yes

een eyes

eft a small lizard

Egypt, frogs of for the account of the story of Moses, Aaron, Pharaoh and the plague of frogs SEE Exodus 8: 1–14

eht out

elate elated

eld old age

eleemosynary charitable

elf-bolts flint arrowheads, alleged by tradition to have been shot at cattle by fairies

elf-land and the shores of reality childhood and adulthood

Eli for God's judgement on the house of Eli SEE 1 Samuel 3: 12–14

Eliah eldest son of Jesse whose appearance and stature impressed Samuel but David, the shepherd boy, was preferred as king; SEE 1 Samuel 16: 6

Eliazar and Rebecca SEE Genesis 24

elves (1) mischievous diminutive spirits of wild and mountainous places; (2) any small living things

embonpoint ample and well-shaped

empressement animated display of cordiality

en grande tenue in full evening dress

en l'air flighty

en revanche in compensation

enah soon

Endymion mythological Greek
   shepherd, son of Aethlius, fathered
   50 daughters on Selene, the moon-
   goddess
enrhumée having a head-cold
Epicurean one devoted to refined
   pleasure of the senses; derived from
   Epicurus (Greek philosopher, 341–
   270 BC)
erst as before
Esau Jacob's twin; SEE Genesis 25
esprit-fort (an) one who puts himself
   above received opinions and maxims
estrade a raised level in a room
eulogist, partial not an impartial one
Eutychus SEE Acts 20: 9; young man of
   Troas, Asia Minor, who fell asleep
   by a window while St Paul preached,
   and dropped through it
evil genius one who exerts a powerful
   evil influence on another; SEE section
   on Glasstown Confederacy for
   explanation of the Brontës'
   childhood notion of themselves as
   'Genii'
exigéant difficult to please
exigeante, petite demanding little
   creature
externats day-scholars

faal, fahl ugly
fagging tiring work
fain desire to
fair as if just as if
fairishes fairies
faishion bring oneself to
false front wig or hairpiece for front of
   head, above forehead
fancy head a portrait of an imaginary
   person
fancy vignettes imaginary scenes
fand found
fane temple
faquin scoundrel
fashion (1) bring oneself to; (2) contrive
   to
Fatherland accents English accents
fatuitous fatuous
Faubourg reserved for most ancient

sections of towns and cities in France,
   particularly Paris
fauteuil armchair
'faux air' of some resemblance to
feard lest
feck quantity
Felix SEE Acts 24: 25 for the account of
   Paul's arraignment before Felix the
   governor of Caesarea
fell fierce
fellies fellows
felo de se suicide
Ferdinand King Ferdinand VII of Spain;
   despite being lackey of Napoleon,
   restored by popular demand to
   Spanish throne by British, 1814
festal festive
fettle (1) put in order; (2) complete,
   finish off; (3) kill
feuilleton bottom of newspaper page
   devoted to humour, criticism,
   fiction, etc.
fiacre horse-drawn cab for hire; first
   recorded rank outside hotel Saint-
   Fiacre, Paris, 1640
fiat (of fate) edict
figure chiffonée rumpled face
filleule god-daughter
finical finicky
fit feet
fix attach, win affections of
flag flagstone
flambeaux torchlights
flay, fley frighten
Flamand native of Flanders
Flanders veil veil of Flanders lace
flaysome terrible
fleyed frightened
flighted frightened
flirting flourishing
flit to leave
flitting moving out
fluting semi-cylindrical grooves in
   pillars
following the house doing household
   work
fooil fool
forgie forgive
forrard forward

fortin' fortune
fougue fury
fowks folks
t'fowld the fold (sheep)
frame (1) go quickly; (2) imagine, conjure up, invent
frames and shears among many mechanized devices introduced during Industrial Revolution; many claimed that they created unemployment and poverty; their introduction incited riots and demonstrations
freak of manner capricious manner
free sittings seats (usually to the rear) in a church, not designated for any specific occupant
fresh slightly under the influence of drink
frieze coarse wool cloth with nap
frogs of Egypt SEE Exodus 8: 1–15 for the account of the plague of frogs
front forehead
froo from
frough from
f'r out eee knaw for all you know
froward forward
fry bustle
fugleman leader
fuller's earth earthy aluminium silicate, containing water and very absorbent of grease; formerly commonly used as a skin powder, particularly for the feet
fun' found
Funchal capital of Madeira
furrin' foreign
furze gorse
fustian (1) coarse twilled cotton fabric; (2) an unnaturally pompous style

Galloway breed of short strong horse common to Galloway, West Scotland
gambado literally a horse's leap, but describes any fantastic movement or unusual escapade
gamboge reddish-yellow gum resin used as pigment

gang go
gangs banning goes cursing
gapingly with wide-open mouth
garlandry in *V.* – plaster-moulded wreaths, leaves etc., for ceiling decoration
gart way, manner
gasconading the Gascons (French provincials) are traditionally reputed to be boastful
gate to put a stop to
Gateh Gath
gaufrés waffles, honeycombs
gaumless witless
Gehenna Hell
generation, not wise in SEE Luke 16: 8
Genii SEE section on Juvenilia
Genii-elixir magic potion of a Djinn
Genius more frequently found in plural (Genii); equivalent to Arabian Djinns = spiritual beings, some good, some bad, who influence human affairs and people
gentianella species of gentian (esp. *Gentiana acaulis*) – plant bearing intensely blue flowers
gentle and simple all kinds and conditions of rank and class
German Moravian Moravian Brethren Church founded by John Hus in 1457; it regarded the scriptures as embodying exclusively the rules of faith and conduct
German gräfinnen German countess
getten got
gibbous literally 'humped'; used frequently to describe moon between half and full
Gideon, the army of SEE Judges 7: 16
gie give
giftie gift (source 'To a Louse' by Robert Burns)
gig-mill rotary cylinder, covered with wire teeth for raising the nap on cloth
Gilead, balm in the balm of Gilead was famous for healing and cosmetic properties; SEE Jeremiah 8: 22; 46: 11
girandoles branched candleholders

gird, sick a sick spasm

girn a laugh a toothy laugh

girned grinned

girt great: 'girt eedle seaght' = great idle sight

give over to stop, to finish

gladiator, the wound of the SEE Byron, *Childe Harold's Pilgrimage*, IV, 140

glebe-house abode made of earth, a grave

gleg sharp: 'gleg light' = bright light

glories Anglicization of 'glorias'; in *W.H.* used pejoratively – 'yah set up them glories tuh Sattan' = 'you begin with irreligious singing to worship Satan'

goan gone: 'goan aght' = gone out

gnarl snarl

goblin evil creature

gooid good

goûter midday meal

goûter un peu les plaisirs to enjoy oneself a bit

Gob scene of encounter between Saph (q.v.) and Sibbechai

government order for army-cloth government contracts were eagerly sought by northern cloth manufacturers, particularly during Napoleon's blockade of Continental ports which drastically reduced exports

t'grand 'sizes grand assizes

Grand Turk name given to Sultan or Emperor of Turkey

grat wept

grave-mould soil of a grave

greasehorn flatterer

Great Mogul Emperor of Delhi

Greatheart protector of Christian and his friends in *Pilgrim's Progress* (part II) by John Bunyan (1628–88)

Greek Fire inflammable mixture ignited to set fire to ships in battle; first used by the Greeks

grenier garret

grey mare stolid, powerful, colourless (used to describe overbearing wife)

gripe grip

gris de poussière dusty grey

grisette French working-class girl, habitually dressed in grey cloth

Grizzle Griselde, heroine of Chaucer's *The Clerk's Tale*, whose name became synonymous with patience, and reduced to the popular form of Grizzle

grogneuse female grumbler

gros-bonnets important people: big-wigs

grub-worm insect larva (e.g. caterpillar)

guelder-rose species of Viburnum, sometimes called 'snowball tree' because of its bunches of white flowers

guéridon round table

guess sort different kind

gulip iron pot for making porridge

guinea, colour of a guinea (£1.05) being gold, i.e. yellow

Guthrum d. AD 890; leader of Danes who fought against King Alfred

Gyges, ring of Plato describes how Gyges discovered the carcase of a man inside a brazen horse found in a chasm; on the corpse's finger was a brazen ring which, when Gyges wore it, rendered him invisible.

Gytrash a spectre in the form of a black dog, dragging a chain, or a black calf, or even a stone rolling

hae have

Hagar Egyptian bond-servant, handmaid of Sarah, in Abraham's household; SEE Genesis 16: 1–16

hagh, hah how

hahs(e) house

hahsiver howsoever (anyhow)

halcyon (weather) halcyon was a fabled bird (Greek/Roman) which built a floating nest on the sea in the winter for its progeny; it calmed wind and wave to achieve this

half-pay amount payable when military men were not on active service, but liable to call-up if war came

hankerchir handkerchief

happen perhaps

harried carried off

harsh set rough company

hauding holding

haught haughty

haulf half

hearthstun hearthstone

hearty in good condition

hebdomadal (customs) weekly

Hebe Roman Juventas, daughter of Zeus and Hera; goddess of youth who filled the cups of the gods

Heber SEE Jael

Hebrew ark (types of) ornamental veil covering the coffer (ark) containing the tables of Jewish law; SEE Exodus 36: 35, 37

hempseed used expletively – 'you hempseed' – in *SH.*

hend hand

Henry, Earl of Moreland The History of Moreland was recommended to Victorian readers by Charles Kingsley, and much read by Methodists

Hermon, Mount situated on Palestine border 35 miles from Damascus; constantly mentioned in Hebrew poetry

Hesperides, fruit of the golden apples given to Hera (Roman Juno) when she married Zeus (Jupiter); they were guarded (in a remote garden beyond the sea) by nymphs (Hesperides) and a fierce dragon (Ladon)

hetman head man, captain

Hibernicé made into Irish

hierophant an experienced priest

him as allas makes a third the Devil

hisseln himself

hodden coarse, undyed homespun woollen cloth

hoile, hoyle room, house

Holland apron linen fabric apron

Holland blouse unbleached or brown dyed coarse linen blouse; original Dutch material was fine linen

Holland pockets pockets made from linen

Hollands gin made in Holland

holld hold

holm meadow

hornbook rectangular wooden flat covered with parchment and protected by transparent horn; contained alphabet, Lord's Prayer, Roman numerals and other necessities for rudiments of education; it had a handle for holding and a small hole for string to attach it to pupil's waist

hor her

horse fit horse('s) feet

hotel town house

houri voluptuously beautiful woman; a nymph of the Mohammedan Paradise

House of Commons the foundations of the present parliament buildings were completed in 1840, in C.'s lifetime

howe depth: 'howe of the night' = 'middle of the night'

humour bad temper

Humphrey Davy's 'Last Days. . .' Sir Humphrey's *Consolations in Travel, or the Last Days of a Philosopher* published 1830; the Brontës (certainly Anne) probably borrowed a copy from the Mechanics' Institute Library, Keighley

Hungary, Conrad and Elizabeth of Conrad of Marburg (c. 1180–1233); member of Catholic Inquisition, responsible for converting heretics and torturing dissenters; also he was confessor to St Elizabeth (1207–31) daughter of King Andreas II, famous for her piety, generosity and self-mortification

hymeneal marital

Hymettus Greek mountain famous for its honey

hypochondria general gloomy feelings not, as in modern sense, confined to melancholy imaginings about one's own health

Ichabod name given to her child by
Phinehas on hearing of the Ark's
capture and of the death of Eli and his
sons (1 Samuel 4: 21); by association
– 'inglorious'

ichor ethereal fluid flowing in veins of
the gods

i'course, in course of course

idea, his my idea of him

ideal imaginary

Ignacia feminine form of Ignatius;
derived from Ignatius Loyola (1491–
1556), founder of the Jesuits

ignis fatuus or blue will o' the wisp; light
that appears and misleads travellers
over marshy grounds; result of
decomposition of vegetable and
animal material; sometimes called
Jack o'Lantern

ill childer bad children

imp (1) little child; (2) small devil; (3)
malevolent spirit

impalpable intangible

in propria persona in her own person

incarnate goblin evil spirit in human
shape

Incas highly civilized Peruvian Indians
whose civilization was destroyed by
the Spanish conquistadores under
Pizarro, 1533

incremation cremation

Indian plague cholera; it reached Britain
in 1831 and the epidemic lasted until
1837; a second epidemic began in
1847

Indian darling favourite Indian cigar

inductile inflexible

indurated hardened

inertion inertia

infantine infantile

'ing and holm meadow liable to flooding

ingrate ungrateful

innoxious harmless

interlocutrice French version of
interlocutress

intuh into

'invincible genius' Napoleon

irids irises

it passes me it baffles me

'Italian, The' The Italian, or the
Confessional of the Black Penitents –
one of Mrs Ann Radcliffe's (1764–
1825) most powerful novels of
terror, romance and mystery

iv'ry every

Jack-o'-Lanthorns will-o'-the-wisp

Jacob twin brother of Esau; son of Isaac
and Rebecca; SEE Genesis 25–29

Jacob at Peniel SEE Genesis 32: 24–30

Jacob's favoured son Joseph

Jacobin (1) French society of violent
revolutionaries; (2) anyone opposing
established government or
institutions by violent or factious
methods

jaconas probably 'jaconet', a thin cotton
fabric, between cambric and muslin,
used for dressmaking

Jael to Sisera Sisera, captain of the
Canaanite armies, is entertained by
Jael, wife of Heber, in her tent after
his defeat by the Israelites; she
hammers a tent-peg into his temple
while he sleeps; SEE Judges 4: 18–22

Jäger chorus either a German military or
hunting chorus

jargon chatter

Jean-Jacques' sensibility SEE Rousseau

Jehu Jehu drove his chariot furiously;
SEE 2 Kings 9: 20

Jericho, I wish you were at i.e. a long way
off

Jew Basket a collecting-basket for goods
to be sold – the proceeds to be used
towards converting the Jews

Job, as poor as to test his faith God
caused many sufferings for Job,
including poverty

Job's Leviathan for Job's invulnerability
SEE Job 41: 26

jocks jugs

'John Anderson, my jo, John' first line of
poem by Robert Burns;
jo = sweetheart

John Knox 1505–72; famous Scots
Protestant writer and preacher who
denounced Mary Stuart's

Catholicism

Jonah's Gourd God caused a gourd (large, fleshy fruit of a climbing plant) to grow fully in one night to provide Jonah with shade

Joseph (in the pit) SEE Genesis 37: 23–34

jours de sortie days for going out

Juggernaut Hindu idol annually dragged in procession in pyramidal cart 200 ft high; formerly, devotees frequently sacrificed themselves by falling between the carriage wheels

Juno, marble Queen of the Gods (Roman); innumerable sculptures of her were made

jupon sleeveless close-fitting jacket extending over hips

juron oath

justice-meeting country bench meeting of Justices of the Peace

J'y tiens I insist upon it

kaleidoscope invented (1817) by Sir David Brewster

keen, keening wailing lamentations over the dead

kennel gutter

Kim-kim-borazo Chimborazo – one of the highest mountains in the Andes; cf. poem 'Romance' by W.J. Turner

King's brows, foreign crown pressing Leopold I of Belgium (1790–1865) was elected to the throne following a revolution, but as former Prince of Saxe-Coburg was counted a foreigner

kirstened christened

kittle puzzlingly difficult

knaw know

La Fontaine, 'Le Chène et le Roseau' fable by Jean de la Fontaine (1621–95), French poet

laced thrashed

lack used intransitively as in 'a man in whom awe, imagination, and tenderness lack'

laiking playing, enjoying oneself

laith barn

Lamb's book of life, the the Lamb = Christ; SEE Revelations 21: 27

lameter cripple

lapis-lazuli aluminious mineral, vivid blue in colour

lappets pendants attached to ladies' hats

Lares ancient Roman household gods

lath thin weakling

lave leave

Lazarus, a new SEE John 11: 1–44

leads, the leaded roof

lean type bad type

leas, the SEE lees

lees, the high grazing for cattle

Leman, Lake Swiss lake with Geneva at its southern extremity

leprous memory, cleanse a for the story of Naaman whose leprosy was cured by immersion in the river Jordan SEE 2 Kings 5: 1–14

leveller originally member of 17th century party dedicated to religious and political equality; generally used to describe any dissident

Levi third son of Jacob by Leah

levin-brand lightning flash

Levites descendants of Levi; used ironically by C. to describe Donne, Sweeting and Marlowe

lick beat

lickspittle sycophant

lig, ligging lay, lying

Lightning, The stagecoaches were customarily given names

Ligue des Rats, La La Fontaine, *Dernière Fables* xxv, 22

likely right, suitable

likker more like(ly)

ling a coarse, larger form of heather

list slipper cloth slipper

loadened loaded

locataire lodger, tenant

Lodi, conqueror of Napoleon, who, in one of his earliest battles (1796) defeated the Austrians at Lodi Bridge in north Italy

loike like

looard lord

loon a mischievous fool

Lot's wife SEE Genesis 19: 26

loundering thrashing, beating

lourdauds awkward, maladroit

low glow

Lowlanders (of Scotland) Covenanters –
Scottish Presbyterians

lubberly clumsy

luckless bringing ill luck

Lucretia Tarquinius Collatinus' wife –
both dutiful and beautiful; raped by
Tarquinius Superbus; SEE Ovid's
Fasti ii, 741–6

lug (1) ear; (2) carry

lught light

lumber rubbishy tracts

lunettes spectacles

luscious honey the manna caused to fall
from the sky by the Lord on the
starving Israelites – it tasted like
'wafers made with honey'; SEE
Exodus 16: 31

lustre chandelier

lustre (cup of) glossy finish on china

lusus naturae freak of nature, anomaly

Lutheran one who follows the doctrines
of Martin Luther and his followers,
whose cardinal doctrine is that of
justification by faith alone

lymphatic frantic, over-emotional

Macedonia, him of for account of St
Paul's vision of the man of
Macedonia SEE Acts 16: 9

manège studied movements of limbs (as
in horse dressage)

marsh-phlegm condition caused by
inhalation of vapours released by a
marsh

mask face, head, appearance: 'exactly
one mask' = a perfect likeness

mast collective word for fruit of
chestnut, oak, beech; often food for
pigs

maun must

Mause, Headrigg character in Walter
Scott's *Old Mortality* (1816); a stout
defender of Protestantism (i.e. a
Covenanter)

maw my

maxillary pertaining to the jaw

méchant naughty

Medes and Persians SEE Esther 1: 19 and
Daniel 6: 8

Medusa mythological beautiful maiden
whose hair was turned to serpents
and her face so ravaged as to reduce
all who gazed on it to stone

meeterly reasonably, tolerably

Melancthon 16th century German
Protestant reformer

mélasse molasses

mells meddles

Men of Manchester Powerful group of
radical businessmen, led and inspired
by Richard Cobden and John Bright;
they advocated laissez-faire in
economics, non-intervention in
foreign affairs, and minimum
government interference in business;
as originators of the Anti-Corn Law
League they claimed responsibility
for Corn Law repeal in 1846

ménagères avares, des penny-pinching
housewives

mensful respectable

Meribah's waters the name given by
Jehovah to the waters released when
Moses struck the rock with his rod;
SEE Numbers 20: 13

Mädchens Klage, des 'The Maiden's
Lament' – ballad by Schiller (1759–
1805) set to music

madling young mad thing

maened frenzied woman, bacchante

magi-distillation potion made by the
magi, sages and holy men of Persia
(HENCE 'magic')

magian member of the magi – ancient
Persian caste noted for sorcery

Mahomet prophet Mohammed, *c.* 571–
632, founder of Islamic faith

maigre-day day of the week designated
by the church as meatless

maitresse d'auberge mistress (manageress)
of small hotel

mak' type: 'raight mak'' = the right
kind

maks no 'cahnt takes no account

malaria-haze yellow

malevola malevolent spirit

manchette lace edging on the collar of dress or chemise

manes nowt means nothing

manikin diminutive of 'man'

mantling covering

marble, toads buried in there were many fairy stories of toads being found embedded in tree trunks or solid stone

marcy mercy

mark to embroider an identifying mark on linen

Marmion Sir Walter Scott's novel, published 1808

marmot small monkey

Maroon Negro slaves originally found in forests of Dutch Guiana and West Indies

marred spoilt

Marseilles stiff cotton fabric, similar to piqué

merino soft wool material sometimes mixed with cotton

merino pelisse long cloak of merino

merlin small hawk (genus *Falco columbarius*) common on Yorkshire moors

Mérovée French form of Merovaeus, 5th century AD legendary founder of Merovingian (Frankish) royal dynasty

Mesrour executioner (his name means 'Happy') at Haroun al-Raschid's court in the *Arabian Nights*

mess portion of food

Messalina profligate wife of Roman Emperor Claudius

Methodist enthusiast SEE Catholic enthusiast

Methody, joined a paid-up member of Methodists – who required a weekly subscription

Mezentius tyrant ruler of Caere in Etruria; SEE Virgil, *Aeneid*, vii–x

mezzotint a method of engraving on steel or copper

miasma infection of the air, e.g. from putrefying bodies

midden-cock on pattens the traditional self-importance of the farmyard cock would be increased if he could be imagined wearing pattens – i.e. clogs

Milan and Berlin decrees 21 November 1806 (Berlin), 23 November and 17 December 1807 (Milan) – decrees increasing the severity of Napoleon's blockade of north German ports

Milesian Milesius, Spanish king whose sons allegedly conquered Ireland in 14th century

Milo, the fate of when Milo tried to uproot a tree it seized his hands and held him tightly; wild beasts devoured him; SEE Byron, *Ode to Napoleon Buonaparte*

mim (1) a mere expression, like 'mmm'; (2) demure

mimmest-looking demurest-looking

minauderies affectations

minching un' munching mincing and affected speech (as in Joseph's description of Lockwood in *W.H.*); but 'munching' does not have any particular meaning

minois chiffonné delicately attractive, without regular features

'minois mutin' roguish face

Minos legendary ruler of Crete who conquered Athens and demanded tribute of seven youths and seven maidens per year to be devoured by the Minotaur (half-man, half-bull)

mista'en mistaken

mitch, mich (1) much; (2) great – as in 'it'ule be mitch' = 'it'll be a great thing'

mither mother

mob-caps plain caps for women, tied under chin with broad band

mode black glossy silk

Moloch (1) a power which demands sacrifice of that held most dear; (2) god of the Ammonites who devoured human sacrifices in the Valley of Tophet

monomaniac self-obsessed

mony many

mools earth of a grave

moreen strong woollen, or cotton and woollen, cloth

Morton probably suggested by Hathersage where Charlotte spent three weeks in 1845 at Henry Nussey's vicarage as the guest of Ellen Nussey

Moses, rod of carried by Moses when he led Israelites to the Promised Land and endowed by Jehovah with miraculous powers; Charlotte wrongly ascribes the accomplishment of the parting of the waters to the rod's powers – in fact it was done by a stretching of Moses' hand

Mother Bunches a famous late 16th century London ale-wife, gossip and raconteur; various popular books of lore were named after her

mousseline-laine dress material of wool and cotton

moyens talents

mucky dirty

mud might

muh may

mumming play-acting

mun must

mun'nt, munnunt mustn't

murthering on him murdering him

mutism total silence

muttons subject under discussion

my view sight of me

mystic mysterious, puzzling

nab jutting-out hill or rock

nacarat bright orange-red colour

Nancy, Miss an effeminate young man

napkin, talent in a SEE Matthew 25: 14–30

nave, neive fist

near (1) niggardly; (2) close-fisted

Nebo ancient Sumerian god of writing and wisdom

Nebuchadnezzar King of Babylonia (605–562 BC); restorer of city of Babylon to magnificence and creator of a golden image for worship; SEE Daniel 2, 3.

Nebuchadnezzar's hottest furnace when Shadrach, Meschach and Abednego refused to worship Nebuchadnezzar's (q.v.) golden image they were cast into a fiery furnace, but an angel joined them and they were unharmed; SEE Daniel 3: 13–30

neck can often refer to women's upper breasts or shoulders

neckclothed wearing a cravat

neeght night

negro the colour of black

negus port or sherry with hot water, sweetened and spiced

Nemesis, fane of shrine of Nemesis, Greek goddess of retribution

neophyte a new convert

Nereides mythological Greek sea-nymphs

Nero Roman emperor (54–68 AD) of notorious excess

nerves sinews

nervous vigorous, strong

netting needles a popular female pastime was to make objects, especially purses, out of netting

nice discriminating

nicher snigger

niver shouldn't

nivir never

nip up pull up

no sich stuff no such thing

noah no

noan not

nobbut (1) no one, nothing, but; (2) only

nobbut wish only wish

nor – ne (nuh) – me not me

norther . . . nur neither . . . nor

Northern Streamer column of light shooting upward from horizon as part of Aurora Borealis

nowt nothing

nur him than him

nut o'ered not over

nuts expletive, as in American usage

oak-case box-bed

oblation literally the act of presenting bread and wine in the mass; hence 'sacrifice' or 'victim'

O'Connell, Daniel 1775–1847; MP, Irish Nationalist

odalisque concubine in Turkish Sultan's harem

Oedipus the Greek sphinx (SEE sphynx) set Oedipus a riddle which he solved: Q. what goes on four feet, on two feet, and three, But the more feet it goes on the weaker it be? A. a man

oe'red gone by

offald (1) good for nothing; (2) disreputable; (3) awful

Old Gentleman, the Satan

old October ale brewed in October 1708; it was commonly held in 18th century that ale should be brewed in October

on hands in hand

on town in fashionable circles

onding on snaw heavy with snow

on-going proceeding

'only lonely

onst once

ony any

opened on me started to speak to me

oppen t'pikes open the gates

oppugnant argumentative

or iver before

oratory small chapel

orderations orders; dispositions

Orders in Council Britain, after Napoleon blocked north German ports to her shipping (1 April 1806) and by successive treaties imposed severe burdens on her economy, introduced these Orders; they imposed taxes and controls on neutral European trade; their results were counter-productive, inciting financial and economic crises and social unrest which almost brought about Britain's collapse

Oread mountain-nymph

Orestes son of Agamemnon and Clytemnestra; with his sister, Electra, killed his mother and her lover Aegisthus in revenge for their murder of his father; pursued by Furies until pardoned by Athena; became King of Argos, Mycenae and Sparta; married Hermione

organs of acquisitiveness, adhesiveness, benevolence, comparison, ideality, veneration, wonder, etc SEE phrenology

orgueil de diable devil-like pride

orther (1) other; (2) either

ortherings orders

ot' of the

otto of roses attar of roses – perfume derived from rose petals

ourse Britannique British bear

ousel or ouzel; probably the ring–ouzel, a blackish thrush with broad white crescent on the throat, indigenous to moorland country; a sketch of an ouzel by Emily (dated 22 May 1829) is at Haworth Parsonage Museum

out-and-outer complete scoundrel

ouvrier artisan

ouvrière female manual worker

overdone overcome

overdrawn (tea) left overlong to brew

overlooker supervisor

overreach outdo

owd book the old book, i.e. the Bible

ower over

owt anything

packet-deck the deck of a vessel officially commissioned to carry letters, packets, despatches and passengers at fixed sailing times

pain bis brown bread

pale knock

pale t'quilp off cool off the pot (of porridge) by alternately taking out and replacing one ladleful

Palestine mediaeval crusades went there

paletôt loose cloak

'Pamela' Samuel Richardson's novel (1740)

panoply complete suit of armour

pantaloons garment of stockings and breeches in one piece

pantoufles slippers

papers in which pins and darning needles are stuck for storage

papillotes curl-papers

Parian relating to marble of Aegean island of Paros

t'parish literally 'the parish'; often refers to poor-relief payment which was the responsibility of parish government, but which was frequently spurned by the pride of many who were entitled to it

parrain godfather

parterre flower-bed

parure set of ornamental jewellery

pas de fée fairy footsteps

Pasha high-ranking Turkish officer, sometimes endowed by hearsay with romantic sensual characteristics

passenger-bird may have been the now-extinct North American wild pigeon – capable of flying long distances

pastille small piece of perfumed paste for burning as disinfectant or air-freshener

pâtes à la crème custard pies

patriarch, dying when Isaac was dying he asked Esau his son for venison; SEE Genesis 27: 3

patte de velours cat's paw with claws retracted – hence any soft, smooth treatment

patten-strings laces of high-heeled shoes

Paul, Vincent de 1576–1660; founder of Sisterhood of Charity and Paris Foundling Hospital

Paul and Silas's prison Silas was Paul's companion on his second missionary journey; SEE Acts 16: 25–6

pawsed his fit intuh ground his foot into

paynim heathen

peccant sinful

peignoir dressing-gown

pelisse three-quarter or ankle-length coat with cape

pendule small clock with pendulum mechanism

penetralium interior

Peninsular news news concerning the military campaigns on the Spanish Peninsula

pensionnaire boarder

pensionnat boarding-school

pent enclosed

Pentelicus Greek mountain famous for fine white marble

Penthesilea Amazon Queen

Perceval, Spencer 1762–1812; only British Prime Minister yet to be assassinated; victim of opponents of Orders in Council (q.v.)

Père la Chaise main Paris cemetery

Peri a legendary Persian fairy; also associated with imaginary beautiful female sprite descended from fallen angels and excluded from Paradise until the completion of a penance; later, name was applied to any beautiful girl

Peri-Banou in the *Arabian Nights* Ahmed meets this beautiful fairy, who has a magic tent

person physique

Peruvian bark bark of cinchona tree, highly celebrated for medicinal qualities

pet petulantly

petit maître coxcomb

petit verre small glass (i.e. of liquid refreshment)

Phaeton open four-wheeled carriage drawn by one or two horses

Pharamond legendary first king of the Franks

Pharisee and Publican SEE Luke 18: 10–14

philippic a declamation involving acrimonious invective; derives from Demosthenes' speech against Philip of Macedon

Phillis popular name for shepherdess or nymph in pastoral poetry

phrenology many references (beginning always with 'organ of...', as for example, 'organ of veneration') occur in C.'s novels; phrenologists believe that personal character is revealed by examining the shape of the skull; the skull's various parts were named according to the

characteristics associated with them –
e.g. 'organ of acquisitiveness';
George Smith took C. for a
phrenological examination to J.P.
Browne in 1851; his report is
astonishingly accurate, especially
since C. was unknown to him (SEE
Mrs Gaskell's *Life*, ii, 224–5); C.
probably read George Combe's
Elements of Phrenology (Edinburgh,
1828, 3rd edition)

phthisis pulmonary consumption

phylactery a good luck charm, but in
J.E. its original meaning is implied –
something attached to the person as a
reminder of the human obligation to
abide by the law

physician's almanack the annual
publication, containing prophecies
and general advice, entitled 'Old (*or*
Dr) Moore's Almanac'

physiognomist one who purports to tell
character from appearance, especially
facial; SEE ALSO phrenology

pie magpie

piece-hall where cloth is sold in lengths
(pieces)

piecing joining (broken threads)

pigeon's feathers in the pillows death is
delayed if the dying lie on a bed
containing pigeon's feathers,
according to Yorkshire folklore

piked aht froo' th' rubbidge picked out
from the rubbish

pikes turnstile gates

pillar, cloud and in the daytime a pillar of
cloud, at night of fire, guided the
Israelites in the flight from Egypt

pinchbeck watch cheap watch, because
made of gold-like alloy of copper and
zinc

pinched deprived (by hunger or cold)

pining starving

pip, in the diseased; SEE chicken in the
pip

piqued (herself) prided herself

pis-aller the worst that can happen

pistolets au beurre breakfast rolls and
butter

pitchers, lights in in his battle against the
Michans, Gideon divided his army
into three companies with each man
carrying a jar containing a torch, and
a trumpet; at a given signal the jars
were broken and the torches
exposed; SEE Judges 7: 15–20

Pitt, William 1759–1806; First Lord of
Treasury and Prime Minister during
revolutionary wars against France

Plain of Shinar SEE Shinar

plain-workwoman woman employed for
'plain' serving only

plat plot of ground

plate-closet crockery cupboard

plisky rage, temper

plotter (1) scramble through mud; (2)
mud

plucked to be failed in an examination

poignée handful

Polichinelle, the secret of Neapolitan
version of the English name 'Punch';
the phrase means 'what the whole
world knows'

pony-phaeton four-wheeled open
carriage drawn by two ponies

Pope Alexander the Sixth (Rodrigo
Borgia) 1492–1503; licentious,
avaricious, nepotistic, cruel; one of
worst Popes in history; father of
Cesare and Lucrezia Borgia;
employer of Michaelangelo and great
patron of art

porridge, these northern English and
Scots usage of collective plural

port demeanour

porte cochère carriage entrance

porter dark-brown malt liquor

portmanteau set of hooks for clothes-
hanging

pose puzzle

pour me donner une contenance to restore
my composure

pragmatical self-important

preachments preaching –
contemptuously applied

pregnant significant

press a clothes cupboard

'Prester John' cf. novel by John Buchan

(1875–1940)

pretercanine literally 'superdog'

preterhuman more than human

prie-dieu kneeling-desk for praying

prière du midi midday prayers

prière du soir evening prayers

Prince Ali's tube a magic tube possessed by a prince in the *Arabian Nights* story of 'Prince Ahmed and the Fairy Peri-Banou'

proclaimant proclaimer

Progressist one who believes that society progresses inevitably towards perfection

Promethean spark Prometheus, son of Japetus, a Titan; he made mankind from clay and stole fire from heaven

propaganda, the Catholic Cardinals' committee (Societas de Propaganda Fide) charged with supervision of foreign Catholic missions – hence any organized propagation of a doctrine

propping lit. propping up

prosing speaking boringly

proximate nearest

Pusey, Dr 1800–82; a leader of the Oxford (Tractarian) movement

Pylades uncle-by-marriage of Orestes (q.v.)

Pythian pertaining to Delphi and/or the priestess of Apollo; by association = 'inspired'

quadrille popular dance for four couples executing five figures

Quaker-dials refers to habitual grey colours favoured by Quakers

quean slut

Queen Charlotte, old George III's wife

quit lease

quiz (1) (n.) a mockable person; (2) (v.) make fun of

Rafaelle Raphael, the Renaissance painter

ragout strongly seasoned meat dish

ragweeds ragwort (*Senecio Jacobaea*) – coarse, yellow-head pasture weed

rahm room

rahnd round

raight (1) right; (2) very: 'raight dahn' = 'very down', i.e. 'a long way down'

'raised' wild-eyed, apprehensive look

rally rail at

ranny sharp, keen

Ranter's Chapel Ranters was name given to primitive Methodists who seceded from Wesleyan Methodism because of its alleged lack of fervour and zeal

rare and pleased unusually pleased

rarely extremely

'Rasselas' novel (1759) by Dr Johnson, in which a character voices similar opinions to Helen Burns about where true happiness is to be found

ratton rat

rayther rather

reaming foaming

reasky rancid

Rebecca SEE Genesis 24

receipt recipe

recherché peculiarly refined

red-coats British soldiers

redd up generally to tidy, specifically to 'do up' the hair

reflets satines satiny reflections

regale princely hospitality

Regent, Prince George, Prince of Wales (1762–1830) later King George IV – a prodigious roué

Rehoboam a priest's shovel-hat

remand countermand

remarked noticed

rencounter encounter

resuming putting on again

retreat asylum

retroussé turned up

revival religious movement whose meetings are characterized by mass fervour, sensational preaching and multiplicity of prayers; common feature in 18th and 19th century Methodism

rigs ridges of crop growth

rill a very small brook

Rimmon Assyrian god mentioned in Kings and made into a fallen angel in Milton's *Paradise Lost*

riots, the Luddite riots of 1812

riven torn

Rizzio, Mary Mary, Queen of Scots' second husband, Darnley, murdered her alleged lover, David Rizzio, a singer

road way, manner

roast make a joke of

robe de soie silk dress

Robin Hood's haunts Kirklees Park (the original of 'Nunn Wood') – said to be a haunt of Robin Hood

Romanists members of or adherents to the church of Rome

Rosinante Don Quixote's horse

rouleaux rolls

Rousseau Jean-Jacques Rousseau (1712–78); French political writer and philosopher; his novels and polemical works, often advocating abandonment of traditional 'restrictions' and the liberation of man's emotional responses, considerably influenced the 'Romantic' imagination

rout fuss

Rowe, Mrs Elizabeth 1674–1737; nonconformist religious poet and prose-writer; much admired by Dr Johnson

rubbidge rubbish

Rubens, Paul Peter 1577–1640; Flemish painter; noted, as Charlotte observes, for his portraits of ample women

Rubric, The instructions for conduct of service in Book of Common Prayer

rude savon harsh scolding (lit. rough soap)

rule the roast to be master of

rullers rulers

rume room

Runic lit. pertaining to the ancient Germanic alphabet, but used in *The Professor* to suggest secret symbols

rush bullrush (implying 'as thin as a . . .')

rush of a lass a weakling of a girl

rusty meat rancid ('reasky') meat

sabots wooden shoes (clogs)

sackless feeble, dispirited

sacque loose-fitting dress, with two box pleats hanging from shoulder to skirt top

sad sober

t'sahnd the sound

St John's locusts and honey SEE Matthew 3: 4

St Paul's (the great bell of) C., her father, B. and Ae. stayed at the Chapter Coffee House in the shadow of St Paul's Cathedral

St Pièrre, 'Fragments de l'Amazone' novel by Jacques-Henri Bernardin de Sainte-Pierre (1737–1814), best known for *Paul et Virginie*

St Simeon Stylites AD 390–459; an eccentric ascetic who spent 30 years on top of a pillar near Antioch

Saladin AD 1137–93; Sultan of Egypt ?1174; captor of Jerusalem and attacked by Richard I and his crusaders; SEE *The Talisman* (1823) by Walter Scott

salamander lizard-like creature allegedly capable of living in fire

sall stall

salon a room, often elegantly furnished, used for the reception of guests

salt fish and hard eggs reference to Catholic tradition of eating fish and plain food on Fridays

salut, hour of time to say farewell

sampler a collection of needlework patterns

Samuel, a new SEE 1 Samuel 1: 9–28

Samuel, the calling of God called upon Samuel in a vision to become his prophet; SEE 1 Samuel 1–8

sand-pillar, rough called stoops or stoups, they were old milestones of a kind well known to the Brontës

sap blockhead (as in modern American usage)

Saph descendant of the giants slain by Sibbechai (q.v.) at Gob (q.v.); SEE 2 Samuel 21: 18

sartin certain

sarve ye eht give you what (punishment) you deserve

sarved served

satrap of ancient Egypt a satrap was a provincial governor in ancient Persia

Sattan Satan

Saturn, Hyperion, Oceanus, Prometheus the first three were the children, the last, the grandchild of the Titans of Greek mythology – Uranus (Heaven) and Gaea (Earth)

Saul, sad as first king of Israel; became acutely melancholy when God withdrew his favour from him; SEE 1 Samuel 16: 23

Saul, stately as SEE 1 Samuel 9: 2

savant learned man

savoir-faire know-how

savon scolding

say see

scantling smattering

Schiller Johann Christoph Friedrich von (1759–1805); German poet and dramatist

schönes Mädchen pretty girls

sconce head

scouted treated with contempt

scrag neck

scratch, bring myself up to the slight variant on the usual term; 'the scratch' was made in the ground as a start-marker in a sporting contest

scroop spine of a book

scutter disturbance

seed saw

seeight sight

Semele Greek mythological daughter of Cadmus, mother of Dionysius; tricked into seeing her lover Zeus (Jove) in his godly splendour by Hera (Juno); his thunderbolts killed Semele but she later became an Olympian immortal

sempstress seamstress

seraglio harem

sesame-charm magic word which opens the cave in the story of Ali Baba and the Forty Thieves

seventy and seven times Jesus' answer when Peter asked how many times 'my brother shall sin against me, and I forgive him?'; SEE Matthew 18: 21–22

sharpish, I'm like to look I'm obliged to be on my guard

shaume shame

Sheltie Shetland pony

shepherd of Horeb Napoleon, identified as Moses, who tended his father-in-law's sheep on Mount Horeb; SEE Exodus 3: 1

Shinar, Plain of country of which Babylon was the capital and Nebuchadnezzar the king

shog jog along

shoo she

shoon shoes

shopkeepers, a nation of contemptuous phrase used by, but not originating from, Napoleon to describe the English

shopping being instructed while being employed

shovel hat shape of hat favoured by 19th century clergy

shut rid: 'get shut of' = 'get rid of'

Sibbechai the slayer of Saph (q.v.)

side aht set out

siding staff putting things away

Sidonia as chief character of *Sidonia von Bork, die Klosterhexe* by Johann Wilhelm Meinhold (1797–1851), German theologian; trans. (1843) as *Sidonia the Sorceress* by Lady Wilde

signet mark, imprint

Silas SEE Paul and Silas

sin' since

Sinai (Oreb) both names sometimes used to designate Mount Sinai in the Sinai peninsula

sine as when

Sirius the brightest fixed star; sometimes called the Dog Star

Sisera Canaanite who led an army against the Israelites and was killed by Jael; SEE Judges 4: 5

sizer (sizar) an undergraduate member of a Cambridge college who receives an allowance from the college; in the past the student undertook certain duties in exchange

skift shift, move

skurrying scurrying

slattenly slovenly

slide out of t'gait move out of the way

slip slight in form

small beer in thunder all beer can be adversely affected by thundery weather, but small (i.e. ordinary weak) is particularly prone to decay in bad atmospheric conditions

Smart, poor Christopher Smart (1722–71) English poet: author of *Song to David*

smoking steaming

snook pry

snoozled nuzzled

soa so

soart sort

Sodom ancient Dead Sea city, destroyed, like Gomorrah, by heavenly fire, for its wickedness

Solomon's virtuous woman the catalogue of the perfect woman's virtues as conceived by Solomon; SEE Proverbs 31: 10–31

songs unreligious music (pejorative)

sooin soon (easily)

soubrette coquettish female character (sometimes a servant) in a play

sough (1) a drain; (2) a murmuring sound, as of a light breeze

souliers de silence silent slippers

southern southerner

southernwood aromatic plant of S. Europe, akin to wormwood

sowl soul

spake tull speak to

spar bluejohn (?), violet fluorspar, found in Derbyshire

sperrit spirit

sphinx-riddle the sphinx legend

originated in Egypt, and concerned a monster with woman's breasts and lion's body (the famous Egyptian statue at Ghizeh is a male version)

sphynx of Greek mythology, not to be confused with the more famous Egyptian sphinx, which she strongly resembles; said to have human voice, lived near Thebes, and terrorized the inhabitants by setting riddles – failure to answer was met by swift devouring; Oedipus destroyed her

spice mixture

sponsers responses

spoonie an amorous oaf

spreed spread

springer springer spaniel

Staël, Madame de 1766–1817; French critic and novelist, who established a group of disaffected liberals, and was three times exiled by Napoleon

stale, staling steal, stealing

stalled tired of

Stamboul Istanbul

stark (1) stone dead; (2) rigid

starving shivering cold (often with an implication of hunger)

statuary sculptor

sternutation a sneeze

stickle for contend

stirred my corruption raised the devil in me

stirs disturbing events

stiver, not a not a whit

stock stiff wide band of leather or other material worn around neck

stock-fish cod and similar fish split and dried in the sun and unsalted

storied celebrated in legends, stories or history

strait straight

stretched went on with hurried effort

stuff (petticoat) material, often coarse, but, adjectivally, means woollen

stunner shock; no earlier recording of this usage is known

stylet slender pointed instrument (cf. stiletto)

Styx the river surrounding Hades

(Greek mythology) sometimes called Land of Shades

suall shall

subjoined added

sud should: 'sud uh taen tent' = 'should have taken care'

suld should

summut something

sun-dahn sunset

sup of drop of

surtout overcoat

surveillante overseer

suttee Hindu widow who immolates herself on her husband's funeral pyre

Sweeny's soothing syrup, Mrs whisky

swells, the uplands

swung to hanging from

syncope irregular heart-beat

syne since

t' the

taan taken

tabouret small seat, often without arms or back

tached taught

Tadmor or Palmyra (city of palms), built by Solomon in territory east of Syria

taen taken

taen tent taken care of

tailleuse tailoress

tak take

tak' tent take notice

taking plight

taking, such a such a state (or 'plight')

Talleyrand-Périgord Charles Morice de, Prince de Bene, 1754–1838; French statesman of outstanding intellect and political acumen

Tartar member of group of peoples including Turks, Cossacks – generally alleged in 19th century to be of both ferocious disposition and appearance

tartar-emetic compound of potassium, antimony, carbon, hydrogen, oxygen

tartine a slice of bread, with jam or butter

teed tied: 'teed wi' a bit o' band' = tied with a bond'

tent care

tenters machines for stretching cloth for setting or drying

Thalestris Queen of the Amazons

that road that way

theare there

theirsel'n themselves

thereanent concerning that

thibble smooth stick for stirring porridge or broth

thick-soled high-lows leather lace-up boots, reaching above ankle

thought bothered, a somewhat troubled

thrang busy

thrashing him to a mummy beating him senseless

thread-paper thin strips of paper for wrapping up skeins of thread

threap maintain stubbornly

throne, pale perhaps refers to Revelations 20: 11, which tells of the great white throne before which the judgement of the dead takes place

thunder-clap, sour in thunder is reputed to turn alcoholic beverages sour; SEE ALSO small beer

thur there

Timon SEE Shakespeare's *Timon of Athens* where the hero is so disillusioned by the ingratitude of mankind as to become a misanthropic recluse

tinkler tinker

tisane (ALSO ptisan) a nourishing decoction (e.g. barley-water) – sometimes of herbs

Titania Queen of the Fairies (SEE Shakespeare's *A Midsummer Night's Dream*)

toast-and-water water in which toast has been steeped – usually for invalids

Tophet a place of human sacrifice to false gods in the valley of Hinnom; SEE Jeremiah 7: 31–2; 19: 1–6

Tories originally supporters of Church and King, but, by 19th century, anyone who supported the establishment

traffic trade

train-oil oil derived from seals or whales, used for cleaning guns; from Dutch 'traan' = exuding matter; Anne Brontë referred to her medicine – cod liver oil and iron compound (to combat tuberculosis) as tasting like 'train-oil'

trenching on encroaching

tribe, stiff-necked the Lord used the phrase to Moses in criticism of the Israelites' refusal to adhere to all of his commandments; SEE Exodus 33: 3

tribune raised stage with pulpit

tripotage chore

tub a pulpit; nonconformist preachers were called tub-thumpers

tuckers frilly soft material tucked into dress necks

tuh to

tull't to it

tumbler, smoking the 19th century was much given to heated drinks – including alcohol

tum'le tumble

twal twelve o'clock

twelve tribes, the any 'chosen' people; originally described the twelve tribes of Israel descended from Jacob's twelve sons

two-three, a two or three

tyne lose

tympanums ear-drums

Tyrian purple (derived from dye formerly prepared at Tyre from shell fish)

ud, uld would

uf of

uh (1) have; (2) of

ull will

un' (1) one; (2) and

un air fin sly

un war and worse

unachieved unfinished, incomplete

underdrawn covered with boards or lath and plaster

Undine water sylph

unemulous no desire to imitate

unlikely (1) inconvenient; (2) unsuitable

upas tree Javanese tree, poisonous to animal and vegetable life

ut that, at, of

ut' of the

ut's that has

ut's soa up uh going who is so determined to go

'Vanity Fair' *Vanity Fair: Pen and Pencil Sketches of English Society* by William Makepeace Thackeray (1811–63); it first appeared serially January 1847– July 1848

Varens, the an unusual way of referring to a beautiful woman who is either famous or notorious

varra(y), varry very

Vashti Vashti, King Ahasuerus' wife disobeys her husband's command to display her beauty to some visiting princes; Esther replaces her as Queen; SEE Esther 1: 10 passim

vassalage domestic staff

veil, the torn SEE Mark 15: 38

veneration, organ of SEE phrenology

verdigris cupric acetate – the green coating on copper or brass

vestry-meeting parish (local government) meeting

'Vicar of Wakefield, The' written 1761–2, by Oliver Goldsmith (1730–74)

vicarial (1) pertaining to a vicar; (2) vicarious (rare)

victrix conquering woman

view, my the sight of me

volatile salts sal volatile

wah! why! (used expletively)

wake (1) watch; (2) guard; (3) wait up for

wake with, to to keep watch, sit up, with

wald would

war (1) was; (2) worse

war un war worse and worse

warks works

warld world

wassail-cup for drinking toasts on festival occasions

watchguard pocket-watch chain

watermen in the 19th century the Thames was still an everyday thoroughfare as in the preceding centuries; watermen could be hired for transportation by rowing boat both to sea-going vessels and destinations on the north and south bank

wearifu' wearisome

wearisome nowt tedious nonentity

welkin sky

wenting wanting

wer our

we're no war nor we're no worse than

werselen ourselves

we'se do we'll do (we're alright)

we'se hev we shall have

Wesley, John 1703–91; founder of Wesleyan Methodism, although he lived and died a priest of the Church of England; his religious doctrines lay great stress on personal conversion and the priesthood of all believers

wet 'tuh be ganging? will you be going?

whet what

whet are ye for? what do you want?

Whigs by 19th century, anyone who was not a Tory; inaccurately but persistently linked with supporters of reform, or non-establishment radicalism

whinstone hard, compact rock, e.g. basalt

whudder, wuther bluster (of wind)

wick (1) mischievously lively;

(2) week

wicket small gate or door

wildered distraught

will n't wash will not be accepted

willut will not

win reach

wind shower tears

wink at affect not to notice

wisht hush

wi't with it

Witch-of-Endor when Saul was forsaken by God, this witch called up the dead Samuel who then prophesied the death of Saul: SEE 1 Samuel 28

wollsome wholesome

womenites women (pejorative)

wool-comber separator of wool fibres preparatory to spinning

wor, wer were

work needlework

work-box for holding sewing or writing materials

worriting incessant worrying

wurseln ourselves

wuther Yorkshire dialect = windy, gusty (e.g. Wuthering)

yah you

yah'd as good you might as well

yah're a nowt you're a nothing

yate gate

yclept named

yill ale

yoak yoke

yon's that's

yourseln yourself

zone girdle

Contemporary Comments

Poems by Currer, Ellis and Acton Bell (1846)

Critic, 4 July 1846

No preface introduces these poems to the reader. Who are Currer, Ellis, and Acton Bell, we are nowhere informed. Whether the triumvirate have published in concert, or if their association be the work of an editor, viewing them as kindred spirits, is not recorded... Perhaps they desired that the poems should be tried and judged upon their own merits alone, apart from all extraneous circumstances, and if such was their intent, they have certainly displayed excellent taste in the selection of compositions that will endure the difficult ordeal.

Indeed, it is long since we have enjoyed a volume of such genuine poetry as this. Amid the heaps of trash and trumpery in the shape of verses, which lumber the table of the literary journalist, this small book of some 170 pages only has come like a ray of sunshine, gladdening the eye with present glory, and the heart with promise of bright hours in store. Here we have good, wholesome, refreshing, vigorous poetry – no sickly affectations, no namby-pamby, no tedious imitations of familiar strains, but original thoughts, expressed in the true language of poetry – not in its cant, as is the custom with mocking-bird poets... We see, for instance, here and there traces of an admirer of Wordsworth, and perhaps of Tennyson, but for the most part the three poets are themselves alone, they have chosen subjects that have freshness in them, and their handling is after a fashion of their own ... those whose hearts are chords strung by nature to sympathize with the beautiful and the true in the world without ... and their embodiments by the gifted among their fellow men, will recognize in the compositions of Currer, Ellis and Acton Bell, the presence of more genius than it was supposed this utilitarian age had devoted to the loftier exercises of the intellect.

Athenaeum, 4 July 1846

The second book on our list furnishes another example of a family in whom appears to run the instinct of song. It is shared, however, by the three brothers – as we suppose them to be – in very unequal proportions; requiring in the case of Acton Bell, the indulgences of affection ... and rising, in that of Ellis, into an inspiration, which may yet find an audience in the outer world. A fine quaint spirit has the latter, which may have things to speak that men will be glad to hear, – and an evident power of wing that may reach heights not here attempted.

W.A. Butler, *Dublin University Magazine*, October 1846

Of the triad of versemen, who style themselves 'Currer, Ellis and Acton Bell', we know nothing beyond the little volume in which, without preface or comment, they assume the grave simplicity of title, void of *proenomen* or *agnomen*... Whether ... there be indeed 'a man behind' each of these representative titles; or whether it be in truth but one master spirit ... – that has been pleased to project itself into three imaginary poets, – we are wholly unable to conjecture... The tone of all these little poems is certainly uniform; this, however, is no unpardonable offence, if they be, as in truth they are, uniform in a sort of Cowperian amiability and sweetness, no-wise unfragrant to our critical nostrils...

Spectator, 11 November 1848

The essence of poetry – that quality so difficult to define yet so easy to recognize – is rare in the volume. Of the formal and secondary properties there is a good deal. The poems have frequently much strength of thought and vigour of diction, with a manner which, though degenerating into manner*ism*, is very far removed from commonplace; while in the poorest 'stanzas', without a subject at all there is still a style which separates them from the effusions of poetasters... The novels of the Bells have stopped short of an excellence that seemed attainable, from ill-chosen subjects, alike singular and coarse. This defect is visible enough in the poems; but a greater cause of ill success is a disregard of the nature of poetical composition... Few persons who write down any sudden thoughts that strike them would dream of publishing them in prose; and wherefore in verse? A promising idea rises in the poet's mind, and he commits it to paper; but time is needed to test its value – careful labour to elicit its full proportion, and to clothe it in the most apt language; after all, it may be doomed to the flames, as falling short of necessary excellence. We suspect such kind of care has not been bestowed upon this volume: the indispensable arts of selection and of blotting are yet to be learned by the Bells...

Jane Eyre by Currer Bell (1847)

Unsigned review, 30 October 1847

Jane Eyre is a remarkable novel, in all respects very far indeed above the average of those which the literary journalist is doomed every season to peruse... It is a story of surpassing interest, riveting the attention from the very first chapter, and sustaining it by a copiousness of incident rare indeed in our modern English school of novelists... We can cordially recommend *Jane Eyre* to our readers, as a novel to be placed at the top of the list to be borrowed, and to the circulating library keeper, as one which he may safely order. It is sure to be in demand.

W.M. Thackeray, Letter to W.S. Williams, 23 October 1847

I wish you had not sent me *Jane Eyre*. It interested me so much that I have lost (or won if you like) a whole day in reading it at the busiest period with the printers I know waiting for copy. Who the author can be I can't guess, if a woman she knows her language better than most ladies do, or has had a 'classical' education. It is a fine book, though, the man and woman capital, the style very generous and upright so to speak... The plot of the story is one with which I am familiar. Some of the love passages made me cry, to the astonishment of John, who came in with the coals. St John the Missionary is a failure I think, but a good failure, there are parts excellent. I don't know why I tell you this but that I have been exceedingly moved and pleased by *Jane Eyre*. It is a woman's writing, but whose? Give my respects and thanks to the author, whose novel is the first English one (and the French are only romances now) that I've been able to read for many a day...

Spectator, 6 November 1847

The fiction belongs to that school where minute anatomy of the mind predominates over incidents; the last being made subordinate to description or the display of character...

A story which contains nothing beyond itself is a very narrow representation of human life. *Jane Eyre* is this, if we admit it to be true; but its truth is not probable in the principal incidents, and still less in the manner in which the characters influence the incidents so as to produce conduct. There is a low tone of behaviour (rather than of morality) in the book; and, what is worse than all, neither the heroine nor hero attracts sympathy. The reader cannot see anything lovable in Mr Rochester, nor why he should be so deeply in love with Jane Eyre; so that we have intense emotion without cause. The book, however, displays considerable skill in the plan, and great power, but rather shown in the writing than the matter; and this vigour sustains a species of interest to the last.

Era, 14 November 1847

We have no high life glorified, caricatured, or libelled; nor low life elevated to an enviable state of bliss; neither have we vice made charming. The story is, therefore, unlike all that we have read, with very few exceptions; and for power of thought and expression, we do not know its rival among modern productions... It is no woman's writing ... no woman *could have* penned the 'Autobiography of Jane Eyre'... The tale is one of the heart, and the working out of a moral through the natural affections; it is the victory of mind over matter; the mastery of reason over feeling, without unnatural sacrifices... There is a vigour in all he says, a power which fixes the reader's attention, and a charm about his 'style and diction' which fascinates while it edifies...

The apt, eloquent, elegant, and yet easy mode by which the writer engages you, is something altogether out of the common way... There is much to ponder over, rejoice over, and weep over, in its ably-written pages...

A.W. Fonblanque(?), *Examiner*, 27 November 1847

There can be no question but that *Jane Eyre* is a very clever book. Indeed it is a book of decided power. The thoughts are true, sound, and original; and the style, though rude and uncultivated here and there, is resolute, straightforward, and to the purpose... There are, it is true, in this autobiography (which though relating to a woman, we do not believe to have been written by a woman), struggles, and throes, and misgivings, but in the end, the honesty, kindness of heart, and perseverance of the heroine, are seen triumphant over every obstacle...

Whatever faults may be urged against the book, no one can assert that it is weak or vapid. It is anything but a fashionable novel... On the contrary, the heroine is cast amongst the thorns and brambles of life... The hero, if so he may be called, is (or becomes) middle-aged, mutilated, blind, stern, and wilful. The sentences are of simple English; and the only fragrance that we encounter is that of the common garden flower, or the odour of Mr Rochester's cigar.

G.H. Lewes, *Fraser's Magazine*, December 1847

... This, indeed, is a book after our own heart... The writer is evidently a woman, and, unless we are deceived, new in the world of literature. But, man or woman, young or old, be that as it may, no such book has gladdened our eyes for a long while. Almost all that we require in a novelist she has: perception of character, and power of delineating it; picturesqueness; passion; and knowledge of life. The story is not only of singular interest, naturally evolved, unflagging to the last, but it fastens itself upon your attention, and will not leave you. The book closed, the enchantment continues. . .

Reality – deep, significant – reality – is the great characteristic of the book. It is an autobiography, – not, perhaps, in the naked facts and circumstances, but in the actual suffering and experience. The form may be changed, and here and there some incidents invented; but the spirit remains such as it was. . .

When we see a young writer exhibiting such remarkable power as there is in *Jane Eyre*, it is natural that we should ask, Is this experience drawn from an abundant source, or is it only the artistic mastery over small materials? . . . Has the author seen much more and felt much more than what is here communicated? Then let new works continue to draw from that rich storehouse. Has the author led a quiet secluded life, uninvolved in the great vortex of the world, undisturbed by varied passions, untried by strange calamities? Then let new works be planned and executed with excessive circumspection; for, unless a novel be built out of real experience, it can have no real success. To have vitality, it must spring from vitality. All the craft in the circulating-library will not make that seem true which is not true – will not affect the reader after his curiosity is satisfied.

Christian Remembrancer, April 1848

Since the publication of *Grantley Manor*, no novel has created so much sensation as *Jane Eyre*. . . The name and sex of the writer are still a mystery. . . However, we, for our part, cannot doubt that the book is written by a female, and, as certain provincialisms indicate, by one from the North of England. . . However – throughout there is masculine power, breadth and shrewdness, combined with masculine hardness, coarseness, and freedom of expression. Slang is not rare. The humour is frequently produced by a use of Scripture, at which one is rather sorry to have smiled. The love-scenes glow with a fire as fierce as that of Sappho, and somewhat more fuliginous. . . If the authoress has not been, like her heroine, an oppressed orphan, a starved and bullied charity-school girl, and a despised and slighted governess (and the intensity of feeling which she shows in speaking of the wrongs of this last class seems to prove that they have been her own), at all events we fear she is one to whom the world has not been kind... Never was there a better hater... 'Unjust, unjust,' is the burden of every reflection upon the things and powers that be...

The plot is most extravagantly improbable, verging all along upon the supernatural, and at last running fairly into it...

... It is 'high life below stairs' with a vengeance; the fashionable world seen through the area railings, and drawn with the black end of the kitchen poker.

... She has depth and breadth of thought – she has something of that peculiar gift of genius, the faculty of discerning the wonderful in and through the commonplace – she has a painter's eye and hand – she has great satiric power, and a good fund of common sense... Let her take care that while she detects and exposes humbug in other minds, she does not suffer it to gain dominion in her own.

George Eliot, Letter to Charles Bray, 11 June 1848

I have read *Jane Eyre*, mon ami, and shall be glad to know what you admire in it. All self-sacrifice is good – but one could like it to be in a somewhat nobler cause than that of a diabolical law which chains a man body and soul to a putrefying carcase. However the book *is* interesting – only I wish the characters would talk a little less like the heroes and heroines of police reports.

Eugène Forçade, *Revue des Deux Mondes*, October 1848

But what I shall never cease to praise is the vigorous, healthy, moral spirit that informs every page of *Jane Eyre*. Whatever our novelists may say, this book proves once more that there are infinite resources for fiction in the depiction of the upright morals and straightforward events of real life and the simple and open development of the passions.

E.P. Whipple, *North American Review*, October 1848

The leading characteristic of the novel, however, and the secret of its charm, is the clear, distinct, decisive style of its representation of character, manners, and scenery; and this continually suggests a male mind. In the earlier chapters, there is little, perhaps, to break the impression that we are reading the autobiography of a powerful and peculiar female intellect; but when the admirable Mr Rochester appears, ... the profanity, brutality, and slang of the misanthropic profligate give their torpedo shocks to the nervous system...

... The authors of *Jane Eyre* ... have made the capital mistake of supposing that an artistic representation of character and manners is a literal imitation of individual life. The consequence is, that in dealing with vicious personages they confound vulgarity with truth, and awaken too often a feeling of unmitigated disgust.

E. Rigby (Lady Eastlake), *Quarterly Review*, December 1848

... *Jane Eyre* is the story of a child, an orphan, cast alone on the world and fighting a solitary battle. The account vibrates with a feeling which seems sometimes to bear the accent of a personal confession and it has that passion and animation which always inspire the beginner in the zest of a first work. But what especially charmed me was that the author has relied solely on the eloquence of the emotions depicted and has not for a moment thought of calling down a fiery judgement on society in a drama in which society nevertheless plays more or less the cruel and tyrannical role assigned to fate in the tragedies of antiquity.

... Jane Eyre is not one of those beautiful, smiling young ladies pursued by elegant suitors, idealized in the golden light of girlish dreams... The novelist has taken the bold step of making his hero and heroine decidedly ugly, allowing them to catch here and there as best they may under the influence of emotion, that chance beauty which we call the beauty of the devil... Nor have I any reproach to level at the characters in *Jane Eyre*: they are energetic and emphatic rather than delicate; but they are true, that of Jane especially, and every scene in the novel gives them in the smallest details a solidity which is full of life. But the plot, here is the weak side of the work. I cannot understand why the author of *Jane Eyre* could not have found a simpler action through which to develop her situation and characters; I cannot understand why she should have thought she needed to have such complicated and disjointed incidents, often improbably linked...

... Altogether the auto-biography of *Jane Eyre* is pre-eminently an anti-Christian composition. There is throughout it a murmuring against the comforts of the rich and against the privations of the poor, which, as far as each individual is concerned, is a murmuring against God's appointment – there is a proud and perpetual assertion of the rights of man, for which we find no authority either in God's word or in God's providence – there is that pervading tone of ungodly discontent which is at once the most prominent and the most subtle evil which the law and the pulpit, which all civilized society in fact has at the present day to contend with. We do not hesitate to say that the tone of mind and thought which has overthrown authority and violated every code human and divine abroad, and fostered Chartism and rebellion at home, is the same which has also written *Jane Eyre*...

Shirley by Currer Bell (1849)

Daily News, 31 October 1849

The story is in keeping with the scenes and the class in which it is laid. The adventures are simple, brief, and few: scarcely culled indeed, but almost carelessly taken from every-day life; a love story of the simplest, chequered by the very smallest of obstacles, and solved by the most awkward of devices. If the adventures are not the most stirring, the characters are not of the most striking. But what is striking is the sentiment. *Shirley* is the anatomy of the female heart. . .

The merit of the work lies in the variety, beauty, and truth of its female character. Not one of its men are genuine. There are no such men. There are no *Mr Helstones, Mr Yorkes*, or *Mr Moores*. . . Let Currer Bell get some one else to paint men, and himself do none but the female figures, or dissect at least none save female hearts.

A.W. Fonblanque, *Examiner*, 3 November 1849

The peculiar power which was so greatly admired in *Jane Eyre* is not absent from this book. Indeed it is repeated, if we may so speak of anything so admirable, with too close and vivid a resemblance. . . The expression of motive by means of dialogue is again indulged to such minute and tedious extremes, that what ought to be developments of character in the speaker become mere exercitations of will and intellect in the author. And finally the old theme of tutors and governesses is pushed here and there to the tiresome point. . .

While we thus freely indicate the defects of *Shirley*, let us at the same time express, what we very strongly feel, that the freshness and lively interest which the author has contrived to impart to a repetition of the same sort of figures, grouped in nearly the same social relations, as in her former work, is really wonderful. It is the proof of genius . . . the characters, imagery, and incidents are not impressed from without, but elaborated from within. They are the reflex of the writer's peculiar feelings and wishes. . . Keen, intellectual analysis is her forte. . .

Eugène Forçade, *Revue des Deux Mondes*, 15 November 1849

I said at the outset that the finest and most characteristic qualities of this book defied analysis. The drama, in fact . . . is made up of the thousand moral situations, the thousand infinitesimal feelings and sweet passions which slowly intertwine and grow out of the least incidents, the least contact between the characters in scenes of everyday life which are minutely etched. It must be understood that in literature of this type, the chief merit is the perfection of the detail, the fidelity with which the design is traced, the liveliness and variety of the style, the naturalness, fire, spirit and fantasy of the dialogue, in short a certain general grace which invites and retains the reader's attention in the familiar labyrinth through which he is led to the dénouement. Currer Bell possesses these qualities in a high degree. His language has the freshness, the unexpectedness, the mixture of poetic fervour and positive firmness, the richness and precision, the boldness and strength which make his inspiration so original. It is a style that cheers the mind like something fresh, alert and sane.

The Times, 7 December 1849

Shirley is very clever, as a matter of course. It could not be otherwise. . . The faculty of graphic description, the strong imagination, the fervid and masculine diction, the analytic skill, all remain visible as before, but are thrown away upon a structure that bears no likeness to actual life, and affords no satisfaction or pleasure to those who survey it. The story of *Shirley* may be told in a couple of pages, yet a more artificial and unnatural history cannot be conceived; and what is true of the plot is even more applicable to the dramatis personae. . .

. . . Indeed, the whole structure seems erected for the simple purpose of enabling these creatures of the author's brain – certainly not of our every-day world – to do nothing, but talk after the manner of such purely intellectual companions.

. . . *Shirley* is not a picture of real life; it is not a work that contains the elements of popularity, that will grapple with the heart of mankind and compel its homage. . . Millions understood her before – she may count by units those who will appreciate her now.

G.H. Lewes, *Edinburgh Review*, January 1850

Shirley is inferior to *Jane Eyre* in several important points. It is not quite so true; and it is not so fascinating. It does not so rivet the reader's attention, nor hurry him through all obstacles of improbability, with so keen a sympathy in its reality. It is even coarser in texture, too, and not unfrequently flippant; while the characters are almost all disagreeable, and exhibit intolerable rudeness of manner. . . There is no passionate link; nor is there any artistic fusion, or intergrowth, by which one part evolves itself from another. Hence its falling-off in interest, coherent movement, and life. . . The various scenes are gathered up into three volumes – they have not grown into a work. The characters often need a justification for their introduction; as in the case of the three Curates, who are offensive, uninstructive, and unamusing. That they are not inventions, however, we feel persuaded. For nothing but a strong sense of their reality could have seduced the authoress into such a mistake as admitting them at all. We are confident she has seen them, known them, despised them; and therefore she paints them! . . . they have no relation with the story, have no interest in themselves, and cannot be accepted as types of a class – for they are not Curates but boors. . .

Again we say that *Shirley* cannot be received as a work of art. It is not a picture; but a portfolio of random sketches for one or more pictures. The authoress never seems distinctly to have made up her mind as to what she was to do; whether to describe the habits and manners of Yorkshire and its social aspects in the days of King Lud, or to paint a character, or to tell a love story. All are by turns attempted and abandoned; and the book consequently moves slowly, and by starts – leaving behind it no distinct or satisfactory impression. . . Currer Bell has much yet to learn – and, especially, the discipline of her own tumultuous energies. She must learn also to sacrifice a little of her Yorkshire toughness to the demands of good taste: neither saturating her writings with such rudeness and offensive harshness, nor suffering her style to wander into such vulgarities as would be inexcusable – even in a man. No good critic will object to the homeliness of natural diction, or to the racy flavour of conversational idiom; but every one must object to such phrases as 'Miss Mary, getting up the steam in her turn, now asked,' . . . however, let us cordially praise the real freshness, vividness, and fidelity, with which most of the characters and scenes are depicted. . .

. . . her eye is quick, her hand certain. With a few brief vigorous touches the picture starts into distinctness. . .

The two heroes of the book, however, – for there are two – are not agreeable characters; nor are they felicitously drawn. They have both something sordid in their minds, and repulsive in their demeanour. . .

Villette by Currer Bell (1853)

Harriet Martineau, *Daily News*, 3 February 1853

In regard to interest, we think that this book will be pronounced inferior to *Jane Eyre* and superior to *Shirley*. . . But under all, through all, over all, is felt a drawback, of which we were anxious before, but which is terribly aggravated here – the book is almost intolerably painful. We are wont to say, when we read narratives which are made up of the external woes of life, such as may and do happen every day, but are never congregated in one experience – that the author has no right to make readers so miserable. . . With all her objectivity, 'Currer Bell' here afflicts us with an amount of subjective misery which we may fairly remonstrate against; and she allows us no respite – even while treating us with humour, with charming description and the presence of those whom she herself regards as the good and gay. In truth, there is scarcely anybody that is good – serenely and cheerfully good, and the gaiety has pain in it. An atmosphere of pain hangs about the whole, forbidding that repose which we hold to be essential to the true presentment of any large portion of life and experience. In this pervading pain, the book reminds us of Balzac and so it does in the prevalence of one tendency, or one idea, throughout the whole conception and action. All the female characters, in all their thoughts and lives, are full of one thing, or are regarded by the reader in the light of that one thought – love . . . so dominant is this idea – so incessant is the writer's tendency to describe the need of being loved, that the heroine, who tells her own story, leaves the reader at last under the uncomfortable impression of her having either entertained a double love, or allowed one to supersede another without notification of the transition. It is not thus in real life. There are substantial, heartfelt interests for women of all ages, and under ordinary circumstances, quite apart from love: there is an absence of introspection, an unconsciousness, a respose in women's lives – unless under peculiarly unfortunate circumstances – of which we find no admission in this book; and to the absence of it, may be attributed some of the criticism . . . whose reason and taste will reject the assumption that events and characters are to be regarded through the medium of one passion only.

. . . We have thought it right to indicate clearly the two faults in the book, which it is scarcely probable that anyone will deny. Abstractions made of these, all else is power, skill and interest. . . The humour which peeps out in the names . . . and so forth – is felt throughout, though there is not a touch of lightheartedness from end to end. . .

A striking peculiarity comes out in the third volume. . . 'Currer Bell' . . . goes out of her way to express a passionate hatred of Romanism. It is not the calm disapproval of a ritual religion, such as we should have expected from her, ensuing upon a presentment of her own better faith. . . We do not exactly see the moral necessity for this (there is no artistical necessity) and we are rather sorry for it, occurring as it does at a time when catholics and protestants hate each other quite sufficiently. . .

We cannot help looking forward still to other and higher gifts from this singular mind and powerful pen. When we . . . think what an accession there will be when the cheerfulness of health comes in with its bracing influence, we trust we have only to wait to have such a boon as

Jane Eyre gives us warranty to expect, and which 'Currer Bell' alone can give.

George Eliot, Letters to Mrs Bray, 1853

15 February
I am only just returned to a sense of the real world about me, for I have been reading *Villette*, a still more wonderful book than *Jane Eyre*. There is something almost preternatural in its power. . .

12 March
Villette – *Villette* – have you read it?

W.M. Thackeray, Letter to Lucy Baxter, 11 March 1853
So you are all reading *Villette* to one another – a pretty amusement to be sure – I wish I was hearing of you and a smokin of a cigar the while. The good of *Villette* in my opinion Miss is a very fine style; and a remarkably happy way (which few female authors possess) of carrying metaphor logically through to its conclusion. And it amuses me to read the author's naive confession of being in love with 2 men at the same time; and her readiness to fall in love at any time. The poor little woman of genius! the fiery little eager brave tremulous homely-faced creature! I can read a great deal of her life as I fancy in her book, and see that rather than have fame, rather than any other earthly good or mayhap heavenly one she wants some Tomkins or another to love her and be in love with. But you see she is a little bit of a creature without a pennyworth of good looks, thirty years old I should think, buried in the country, and eating up her own heart there, and no Tomkins will come. You girls with pretty faces and red boots (and what not) will get dozens of young fellows fluttering about you – whereas here is one a genius, a noble heart longing to mate itself and destined to wither away into old maidenhood with no chance to fulfil the burning desire.

W.M. Thackeray, Letter to Mrs Carmichael-Smith, 1853
Villette is rather vulgar – I don't make my *good* women ready to fall in love with two men at once, and Miss Brontë would be very angry with me and very fierce if I did.

W.M. Thackeray, Letter to Mrs Proctor, 1853
That's a plaguey book that *Villette*. How clever it is – and how I don't like the heroine.

Eugène Forçade, *Revue des Deux Mondes*, 15 March 1853

Currer Bell has chosen to place her novels in a middle-class setting, she seeks out the grey and arid realities of life, she traces the events in ill-shaped, mediocre, laborious existences; she is a middle-class writer... Currer Bell's manner is harsh, tormented, a little uncouth; the author of *Villette* is scrupulous as to details, though abrupt and fanciful in her arrangement of them; her narrative is full of abrupt transitions, the scenes of her drama are arranged with a skill disguised beneath a contempt for the conventional and the commonplace; and by the artful use of combination and contrast, this author is able to lend a strange and romantic colour to the most common occurrences of everyday life...

Currer Bell's sentences are wayward and broken; her language is, in the English phrase, more idiomatic, that is to say more Anglo-Saxon in its vocabulary and phraseology... Currer Bell has a mixture of restrained passion and irony, a kind of virile power; the struggles she delights in are those in which the individual, alone and thrown entirely on his own resources, has only his own inner strength to rely upon ... she preaches with Titanic pride the moral power of the human soul; her books contain vigour and originality, never tears; she surprises, she interests, but she does not soften us, she is protestant to the last fibre of her being...

It is the minutely depicted scenes that endow the characters with a living and piquant reality; it is the author's technique that enhances with a personal touch and with unexpected and original handling the most apparently common subjects. It is the fiery spirit of the mind and the pen, that bursts through the deliberately prosaic nature of the incidents and situations.

G.H. Lewes, *Westminster Review*, April 1853

It is a work of astonishing power and passion. From its pages there issues an influence of truth as healthful as a mountain breeze. Contempt of conventions in all things, in style, in thought, even in the art of story-telling, here visibly springs from the independent originality of a strong mind nurtured in solitude. As a novel, in the ordinary sense of the word, *Villette* has few claims; as a book, it is one which, having read, you will not easily forget... Much of the book seems to be brought in merely that the writer may express something which is in her mind; but at any rate she has something in her mind, and expresses it as no other can...

... indeed it is ... the utterance of an original mind... In it we read the actual thoughts and feelings of a strong, struggling soul; we hear the cry of pain from one who has loved passionately, and who has sorrowed sorely. . . There are, occasionally, touches approaching to the comic in *Villette*, but they spring mostly from fierce sarcasm, not from genial laughter.

Anne Mozley, *Christian Remembrancer*, April 1853

We have said that Currer Bell has found life not a home, but a school. . . She may, indeed, be considered the novelist of the school-room . . . because, as the scholastic world would seem to have been the main theatre of her experience . . . she chooses that others shall enter it with her. She will not condescend to shift the scene . . . what has interested her, she means shall interest them. . . Not that she wishes to represent life in the schoolroom as happy; far from it; but she shows us that life does not stagnate there in an eternal round of grammar and dictionary. . .

 . . . The consciousness of being undervalued, the longings for someone to care for her leading to some undignified results, the necessary self-reliance, the demure air, the intellect held in check, but indemnifying itself for the world's neglect and indifference by the secret indulgence of an arrow-like penetration. . .

The moral purpose of this work seems to be to demand for a certain class of minds a degree of sympathy not hitherto accorded to them . . . to express a character which finds itself unworthily represented by person and manner, conscious of power, equally and painfully conscious of certain drawbacks, which throw this superiority into shade and almost hopeless disadvantage. . . But in truth she draws a character unfit for this home which she yearns for. We want a woman at our hearth; and her impersonations are without the feminine element, infringers of modest restraints, despisers of bashful fears, self-reliant, contemptuous of prescriptive decorum; their own unaided reason, their individual opinion of right and wrong, discreet or imprudent, sole guides of conduct and rules of manners, – the whole hedge of immemorial scruple and habit broken down and trampled upon. We will sympathize with Lucy Snowe as being fatherless and penniless . . . but we cannot offer even the affections of our fancy . . . to her unscrupulous, and self-dependent intellect – to that whole habit of mind which, because it feels no reverence, can never inspire for itself that one important, we may say, indispensable element of man's true love.

Matthew Arnold, Letter to A.H. Clough, 1853

Hideous, undelightful, convulsed, constricted ... one of the most utterly disagreeable books I have ever read – and having seen her makes it more so. She is ... a fire without aliment – one of the most distressing barren sights one can witness.

Matthew Arnold, Letter to Mrs Forster, 14 April 1853

... the writer's mind contains nothing but hunger, rebellion, and rage, and therefore that is all she can, in fact, put into her book. No fine writing will hide this thoroughly, and it will be fatal to her in the long run.

The Professor by Currer Bell (published posthumously, 1857)

Elizabeth Gaskell, Letter to George Smith, 1 August 1856

I have not seen the 'Professor' as yet, you must remember, so perhaps all my alarm as to the subject of it may be idle and groundless; but I am afraid it relates to M. Heger, even more distinctly and exclusively than *Villette* does.

Elizabeth Gaskell, Letter to George Smith, 13 August 1856

I have read the *Professor*... I don't agree with Sir James [Kay Shuttleworth] that 'the publication of this book would add to her literary fame' – I think it inferior to all her published works – but I think it a very curious link in her literary history, as showing the *promise* of much that was afterwards realized. Altogether I decline taking any responsibility as to advising for or against its publication ... the decision as to that must entirely rest with Mr Nicholls.

Elizabeth Gaskell, Letter to Emily Shaen, 7–8 September 1856

... the MS of the Prof: was returned a fortnight ago... Would I edit it? (No! for several reasons.)

Elizabeth Gaskell, Letter to George Smith, October 1856

... The *Professor* is curious as indicating strong character and rare faculties on the part of the author; but not interesting as a story... But oh! I wish Mr Nicholls wd have altered more! ... For I would not, if I could help it, have another syllable that could be called coarse to be associated with her name...

I think that, – placing myself in the position of a reader – instead of a *writer* – of her life, – I should feel my knowledge of her incomplete without seeing the *Professor*. I suppose biographers always grow to fancy everything about their subject of importance, but I *really* think that such is the case about her; that leaving all authorship on one side, her character as a woman was unusual to the point of being unique. I never heard or read of anyone who was for an instant, or in any respect, to be compared to her. And everything she did, and every word she said and wrote bore the impress of this remarkable character. I as my own reader should not be satisfied after reading the Memoir – (of which I may speak plainly enough for so much of it will consist of extracts from her own letters,) if I did not read her first work, – looking upon it as a phsychological [sic] curiosity.

Wuthering Heights by Ellis Bell (1847)

Unidentified review, *c.* 1847

This is a work of great ability, and contains many chapters, to the production of which talent of no common order has contributed. At the same time, the materials which the author has placed at his own disposal have been but few. In the resources of his own mind, and in his own manifestly vivid perceptions of the peculiarities of character – in short, in his knowledge of human nature – has he found them all... It is not every day that so good a novel makes its appearance; and to give its contents in detail would be depriving many a reader of half the delight he would experience from the perusal of the work itself. To its pages we must refer him, then; there will he have ample opportunity of sympathizing, – if he has one touch of nature that 'makes the whole world kin' – with the feelings of childhood, youth, manhood, and age, and all the emotions and passions which agitate the restless bosom of humanity. May he derive from it the delight we have ourselves experienced, and be equally grateful to its author for the genuine pleasure he has afforded him.

Examiner, 8 January 1848

This is a strange book. It is not without evidences of considerable power: but, as a whole, it is wild, confused, disjointed and improbable... Heathcliff may be considered as the hero of the book, if hero there be. He is an incarnation of evil qualities; implacable hate, ingratitude, cruelty, falsehood, selfishness, and revenge ... and it is with difficulty that we can prevail upon ourselves to believe in the appearance of such a phenomenon, so near our own dwellings as the summit of a Lancashire or Yorkshire moor... We detest the affectation and effeminate frippery which is but too frequent in the modern novel, and willingly trust ourselves with an author who goes at once fearlessly into the moors and desolate places, for his heroes; but we must at the same time stipulate with him that he shall not drag into light all that he discovers, of coarse and loathsome, in his wanderings... It is the province of an artist to modify and in some cases refine what he beholds in the ordinary world.

Britannia, 15 January 1848

The uncultured freedom of native character presents more rugged aspects than we meet with in educated society. Its manners are not only more rough, but its passions are more violent... It is more subject to brutal instinct than to divine reason.

It is humanity in this wild state that the author of *Wuthering Heights* essays to depict... It is difficult to pronounce any decisive judgement on a work in which there is so much rude ability displayed, yet in which there is so much matter for blame. The scenes of brutality are unnecessarily long and unnecessarily frequent; and as an imaginative writer the author has to learn the first principles of his art. But there is singular power in his portraiture of strong passion. He exhibits it as convulsing the whole frame of nature, distracting the intellect to madness, and snapping the heart-strings. The anguish of Heathcliff on the death of Catherine approaches to sublimity.

We do not know whether the author writes with any purpose; but we can speak of one effect of his production. It strongly shows the brutalizing influence of unchecked passion. His characters are a commentary on the truth that there is no tyranny in the world like that which thoughts of evil exercise in the daring and reckless breast.

Douglas Jerrold's Weekly Newspaper, 15 January 1848

Wuthering Heights is a strange sort of book, – baffling all regular criticism; yet, it is impossible to begin and not finish it; and quite as impossible to lay it aside, afterwards and say nothing about it. In the midst of the reader's perplexity the ideas predominant in his mind concerning this book are likely to be – brutal cruelty, and semi-savage love ... we have discovered none but mere glimpses of hidden morals or secondary meanings. There seems to us great power in this book but a purposeless power, which we feel a great desire to see turned to better account. We are quite confident that the writer of *Wuthering Heights* wants but the practised skill to make a great artist; perhaps, a great dramatic artist... In *Wuthering Heights* the reader is shocked, disgusted, almost sickened by details of cruelty, inhumanity, and the most diabolical hate and vengeance, and anon come passages of powerful testimony to the supreme power of love – even over demons in the human form...

We strongly recommend all our readers who love novelty to get this story, for we can promise them that they never have read anything like it before.

Atlas, 22 January 1848

Whether, as there is little reason to believe, the names which we have written are the genuine names of actual personages – whether they are, on the other hand, mere publishing names, as is our own private conviction – whether they represent three distinct individuals, or whether a single personage is the actual representative of the 'three gentlemen at once' of the title-pages – whether authorship of the poems and the novels is to be assigned to one gentleman or to one lady, to three gentlemen or three ladies, or to a mixed male and female triad of authors – are questions over which the curious may puzzle themselves, but are matters really of little account...

Wuthering Heights is a strange, inartistic story. There are evidences in every chapter of a sort of rugged power – an unconscious strength – which the possessor seems never to think of turning to the best advantage. The general effect is inexpressibly painful. We know nothing in the whole range of our fictitious literature which presents such shocking pictures of the worst forms of humanity... It casts a gloom over the mind not easily to be dispelled. It does not soften; it harasses, it extenterates... The reality of unreality has never been so aptly illustrated as in the scenes of almost savage life which Ellis Bell has brought so vividly before us.

... A few glimpses of sunshine would have increased the reality of the picture and given strength rather than weakness to the whole. There is not in the entire *dramatis personae* a single character which is not utterly hateful or thoroughly contemptible... Heathcliff himself, the presiding evil genius of the piece, the tyrant father of an imbecile son ... There is a selfishness – a ferocity in the love of Heathcliff, which scarcely suffer it, in spite of its rugged constancy, to relieve the darker parts of his nature.

New Monthly Magazine, January 1848

Wuthering Heights, by Ellis Bell, is a terrific story, associated with an equally fearful and repulsive spot. It should have been called *Withering* Heights, for any thing from which the mind and body would more instinctively shrink, than the mansion and its tenants, cannot be easily imagined.

G.W. Peck, *American Review*, June 1848

The book is original; it is powerful; full of suggestiveness. But still it is coarse. . . Setting aside the profanity, which if a writer introduces into a book, he offends against both politeness and good morals, there is such a general roughness and savageness in the soliloquies and dialogues here given as never should be found in a work of art. The whole tone of the style of the book smacks of lowness. . . A person may be unmannered from want of delicacy of perception, or cultivation, or ill-mannered intentionally. The author of *Wuthering Heights* is both. His rudeness is chiefly real but partly assumed . . . he is rude, because he prefers to be so. . .

Graham's Magazine, July 1848

This novel is said to be by the author of *Jane Eyre*, and was eagerly caught at by a famished public, on the strength of the report. It afforded, however, but little nutriment, and has universally disappointed expectation. There is an old saying that those who eat toasted cheese at night will dream of Lucifer. The author of *Wuthering Heights* has evidently eaten toasted cheese. How a human being could have attempted such a book as the present without committing suicide before he had finished a dozen chapters, is a mystery. It is a compound of vulgar depravity and unnatural horrors, such as we might suppose a person, inspired by a mixture of brandy and gunpowder, might write for the edification of fifth-rate blackguards.

E.P. Whipple, *North American Review*, October 1848

Acton★ . . . seems to take a morose satisfaction in developing a full and complete science of human brutality. In *Wuthering Heights* he has succeeded in reaching the summit of this laudable ambition. He [has] . . . made a compendium of the most striking qualities of tiger, wolf, cur, and wild-cat, in the hope of framing out of such elements a suitable brute-demon to serve as the hero of his novel. . . This coarseness . . . is

★Reviewer believes Acton (Anne) wrote both *Agnes Grey* and *Wuthering Heights*.

not the only characteristic of the writer . . . he aims further to exhibit the action of the sentiment of love on the nature of the being whom his morbid imagination has created. This is by far the ablest and most subtle portion of his labours, and indicates that strong hold upon the elements of character, and that decision of touch in the delineation of the most evanescent qualities of emotion, which distinguish the mind of the whole family.

Sidney Dobell, *Palladium*, September 1850

Not a subordinate place or person in this novel but bears more or less the stamp of high genius. Ellen Dean is the ideal of the pleasant playmate and servant of 'the family'. The substratum in which her mind moves is finely preserved. Joseph, as a specimen of the sixty years' servitor of 'the house', is worthy a museum case. We feel that if Catherine Earnshaw bore her husband a child, it must be that Cathy Linton, and no other. . .

. . . one looks back at the whole story as to a world of brilliant figures in an atmosphere of mist; shapes that come out upon the eye, and burn their colours into the brain, and depart into the enveloping fog. It is the unformed writing of a giant's hand: the 'large utterance' of a baby god. . .

Eclectic Review, 1 February 1851

That the work has considerable merit we admit. The scenery is laid in the North, the bleak, moorish, wild, character of which is admirably preserved. Ellis Bell was evidently attached to her native hills. She was at home amongst them; and there is, therefore, a vividness and graphic power in her sketches which present them actually before us . . . but the case is different with the dramatis personae. Such a company we never saw grouped before; and we hope never to meet with its like again. Heathcliff is a perfect monster. . . Hindley Earnshaw is a besotted fool . . . his son Hareton is at once ignorant and brutish, until, as by the wand of an enchanter, he takes polish in the last scene of the tale . . . the two Catherines, mother and daughter, are equally exaggerations . . . and absurdly unnatural in the leading incidents of their life. Isabella Linton is one of the silliest and most credulous girls that fancy ever painted. . .

As the characters of the tale are unattractive, so the chief incidents are sadly wanting in probability. They are devoid of truthfulness, are not in harmony with the actual world, and have, therefore, but little more power to move our sympathies than the romances of the middle ages, or the ghost stories which made our granddames tremble.

D.G. Rossetti, Letter to William Allingham, 19 September 1854

I've been greatly interested in *Wuthering Heights*, the first novel I've read for an age and the best (as regards power and sound style) for two ages ... But it is a fiend of a book – an incredible monster... The action is laid in hell, – only it seems places and people have English names there...

Agnes Grey by Acton Bell (1847)

New Monthly Magazine, January 1848

Agnes Grey, by Acton Bell, is a story of quite a different character. It is a simple tale of a governess's experiences and trials of love, borne with that meekness, and met by that fortitude, that ensure a final triumph. It has one advantage over its predecessor [*Wuthering Heights*], that while its language is less ambitious and less repulsive, it fills the mind with a lasting picture of love and happiness succeeding to scorn and affliction, and teaches us to put every trust in a supreme wisdom and goodness.

Atlas, 22 January 1848

Agnes Grey is a story of very different stamp. It is a tale of every day life, and though not wholly free from exaggeration (there are some detestable young ladies in it), does not offend by any startling improbabilities. It is more level and more sunny. Perhaps we shall best describe it as a somewhat coarse imitation of one of Miss Austin's [sic] charming stories ... the story, though lacking the power and originality of *Wuthering Heights*, is infinitely more agreeable. It leaves no painful impression on the mind – some may think it leaves no impression at all.

Douglas Jerrold's Weekly Newspaper, 15 January 1848

Of *Agnes Grey*, much need not be said, further than this, that it is the autobiography of a young lady during the time she was a governess in two different families; neither of which is a favourable specimen of the advantages of home education. We do not actually assert that the author must have been a governess himself, to describe as he does the minute torments and incessant tediums of her life, but he must have bribed some governess very largely, either with love or money, to reveal to him the secrets of her prison-house, or, he must have devoted extraordinary powers of observation and discovery to the elucidation of the subject.

The Tenant of Wildfell Hall by Acton Bell (1848)

E.P. Whipple, *North American Review*, October 1848

The Tenant of Wildfell Hall is altogether a less unpleasing story than its immediate predecessor [*Wuthering Heights*],★ though it resembles it in the excessive clumsiness with which the plot is arranged, and the prominence given to the brutal element of human nature. The work seems a convincing proof, that there is nothing kindly or genial in the author's powerful mind, and that, if he continues to write novels, he will introduce into the land of romance a larger number of hateful men and women than any other writer of the day... The reader of Acton Bell gains no enlarged view of mankind, giving a healthy action to his sympathies, but is confined to a narrow space of life, and held down, as it were, by main force, to witness the wolfish side of his nature literally and logically set forth. But the criminal courts are not the places in which to take a comprehensive view of humanity, and the novelist who confines his observation to them is not likely to produce any lasting impression, except of horror and disgust.

★Reviewer believes Acton wrote both *The Tenant of Wildfell Hall* and *Wuthering Heights*.

The 'Bells'

Spectator, 18 December 1847

[Here is] an attempt to give novelty and interest to fiction, by resorting to those singular 'characters' that used to exist everywhere, but especially in retired and remote country places ... [but] the incidents are too coarse and disagreeable to be attractive, the very best being improbable, with a moral taint about them, and the villainy not leading to results sufficient to justify the elaborate pains taken in depicting it...

... *Agnes Grey* ... is not of so varied or in its persons and incidents of so extreme a kind as [*Wuthering Heights*]; but what it gains in measure is possibly lost in power. We know not whether the names of Ellis Bell and Acton Bell, which appear on the title-pages of this publication, have any connexion with Currer Bell, the editor of *Jane Eyre*; but the works have some affinity. In each, there is the autobiographical form of writing; a choice of subjects that are peculiar without being either probable or pleasing, and considerable executive ability, but insufficient to overcome the injudicious selection of the theme and matter.

Athenaeum, 25 December 1847

Here are two tales so nearly related to *Jane Eyre* in cast of thought, incident and language as to excite some curiosity. All three might be the work of one hand – but the first issued remains the best. In spite of much power and cleverness; in spite of its truth to life in the remote nooks and corners of England *Wuthering Heights* is a disagreeable story. The Bells seem to affect painful and exceptional subjects: – the misdeeds and oppressions of tyranny – the eccentricities of 'woman's fantasy'. They do not turn away from dwelling on those physical acts of cruelty which we know to have their warrant in the real annals of crime and suffering, – but the contemplation of which taste rejects. . . Enough of what is mean and bitterly painful and degrading gathers round every one of us during the course of his pilgrimage through this vale of tears to absolve the Artist from choosing his incidents and characters out of such a dismal catalogue; and if the Bells, singly or collectively, are contemplating future or frequent utterances in Fiction, let us hope that they will spare us further interiors so gloomy as the one here elaborated with such dismal minuteness [i.e. in *Wuthering Heights*]. In this respect *Agnes Grey* is more acceptable to us, though less powerful. . . In both these tales there is so much feeling for character, and nice marking of scenery, that we cannot leave them without once again warning their authors against what is eccentric and unpleasant. Never was there a period in our history of Society when we English could so ill afford to dispense with sunshine.

James Lorrimer, *North American Review*, August 1849

But there are more latent objections to the tendency of this powerful book. . . In Jane herself there is a recklessness about right and wrong which is very alarming, and although in the great action of her life, that of leaving Rochester, she valiantly resists a very powerful temptation, and her general conduct is not very reprehensible, the motive by which she is actuated is seldom a higher one than worldly prudence; and there is often a kind of regretful looking-back, which makes us fear that the fate of Lot's wife may overtake her. In the other novels, *Wuthering Heights* and *The Tenant of Wildfellhall* [sic], these, like all the other faults of *Jane Eyre*, are magnified a thousand-fold, and the only consolation which we have in reflecting upon them, arises from the conviction that they will never be very generally read. With *Wuthering Heights* we found it totally impossible to get along. It commences by introducing the reader to a perfect pandemonium of low and brutal creatures, who wrangle with each other in language too disgusting for the eye or the ear to tolerate, and unredeemed, so far as we could see, by one single particle either of wit or humour, or even psychological truth, for the characters are as false as they are loathsome. . . *The Tenant of Wildfellhall* has a better beginning, and the conclusion is an unimpeachable instance of poetical justice; but in the body of the tale there are scenes in which the author seems to pride himself in bringing his reader into the closest possible proximity with naked vice, and there are conversations such as we had hoped never to see printed in English.

G.S. Lewes, *Leader*, 28 December 1850

And yet, although there is a want of air and light in the picture we cannot deny its truth; sombre, rude, brutal, yet true. The fierce ungoverned instincts of powerful organizations, bred up amidst violence, revolt, and moral apathy, are here seen in operation; such brutes we should all be, or the most of us, were our lives as insubordinate to law; were our affections and sympathies as little cultivated, our imaginations as undirected. And herein lies the moral of the book [*Wuthering Heights*], though most people will fail to draw the moral from very irritation at it.

Curious enough it is to read *Wuthering Heights* and *The Tenant of Wildfell Hall*, and remember that the writers were two retiring, solitary, consumptive girls! Books, coarse even for men, coarse in language and coarse in conception, the coarseness apparently of violence and uncultivated men – turn out to be the productions of two girls living almost alone, filling their loneliness with quiet studies, and writing these books from a sense of duty, hating the pictures they drew, yet drawing them with austere conscientiousness!

. . . we cannot doubt but that her [Charlotte's] two sisters, had they lived, would also have risen into greater strength and clearness, retaining the extraordinary power of vigorous delineation which makes their writings so remarkable.

The power, indeed, is wonderful. Heathcliff, devil though he be, is drawn with a sort of dusky splendour which fascinates, and we feel the truth of his burning and impassioned love for Catherine, and of her inextinguishable love for him. . . Edgar appeals to her love of refinement, and goodness, and culture; Heathcliff clutches her soul in his passionate embrace. Edgar is the husband she has chosen, the man who alone is fit to call her wife; but although she is ashamed of her early playmate she loves him with a passionate abandonment which sets culture, education, the world, at defiance. It is in the treatment of this subject that Ellis Bell shows real mastery, and it shows more genius, in the highest sense of the word, than you will find in a thousand novels. . .

... We cannot share Currer Bell's partiality for them [poems in 1850 edition of *Wuthering Heights and Agnes Grey*]; in no one quality distinguishing poetry and prose are they remarkable; but although their poetic interest is next to nought they have a biographical interest which justifies their publication. The volume is compact, and may be slipped into a coat pocket for the railway, so that the traveller may wile away with it the long hours of his journey in grim pleasure.

Charlotte on Her Sisters' Novels

Charlotte, Letter to W.S. Williams, 21 December 1847

You are not far wrong in your judgement respecting *Wuthering Heights* and *Agnes Grey*. Ellis has a strong, original mind, full of strange though sombre power. When he writes poetry that power speaks in language at once condensed, elaborated, and refined, but in prose it breaks forth in scenes which shock more than they attract. Ellis will improve, however, because he knows his defects. *Agnes Grey* is the mirror of the mind of the writer.

Charlotte, Letter to W.S. Williams, 14 August 1848

You say Mr Huntingdon [in *The Tenant of Wildfell Hall*] reminds you of Rochester. Does he? Yet there is no likeness between the two; the foundation of each character is entirely different. Huntingdon is a specimen of the naturally selfish, sensual, superficial man, whose one merit of a joyous temperament only avails him while he is young and healthy, whose best days are his earliest, who never profits by experience, who is sure to grow worse the older he grows. Mr Rochester has a thoughtful nature and a very feeling heart; he is neither selfish nor self-indulgent; he is ill-educated, misguided; errs, when he does err, through rashness and inexperience: he lives for a time as too many other men live, but being radically better than most men, he does not like that degraded life and is never happy in it. He is taught the severe lessons of experience and has sense to learn wisdom from them... His nature is like wine of a good vintage, time cannot sour, but only mellows him. Such at least was the character I meant to portray.

Heathcliff, again, of *Wuthering Heights* is quite another creation. He exemplifies the effects which a life of continued injustice and hard usage may produce on a naturally perverse, vindictive, and inexorable disposition. Carefully trained and kindly treated, the black gipsy-cub might possibly have been reared into a human being, but tyranny and ignorance made of him a mere demon. The worst of it is, some of his

386   *The Published Works*

spirit seems breathed through the whole narrative in which he figures: it haunts every moor and glen, and beckons in every fir-tree of the Heights.

IV The Places

Haworth

If you visit Haworth today you soon become very conscious of its being more than one place. The first effect is of a rather sprawling, untidy area which covers a topography consisting of a river valley and two quite steep hills. A closer look reveals that one of the hills is the location of the original Haworth – the one known to tourists, and by far the pleasanter one – with its little square bordered by shops near the church and the parsonage. The other Haworth at the valley's bottom and up the other rise has an air of depression. This is the younger part – most of the buildings seem late nineteenth- or early twentieth-century. It looks grey, unplanned and indeterminate as to its function – it seems neither completely mercantile nor residential. It has little character and it fills most of the four-mile distance between Haworth proper and Keighley – the larger town from which it was conspicuously separate in the time of the Brontës.

There can be no doubt that economic deprivation is as real as it is apparent both in Haworth and in other neighbouring parts of what used to be called the West Riding of Yorkshire. This area has suffered from what was originally a gradual, but is now a galloping decline of the textile industry. Mills and factories have disappeared or are in ruins and the consequences are only too plain in the localities that grew around them.

In 1810 Haworth ranked next to the now city of Bradford, and before Leeds and Halifax in the amount of wool used there in the worsted textile trade. The town was smaller then but very active and comparatively affluent. Despite industry the little river in the valley was clear and fast-flowing, not turgid and dirty as it is today. Keighley was the nearest town – the Brontës went there for library books and extras, for in Haworth itself few and only the most essential goods were sold.

Of its inhabitants, the millowners were perhaps the most influential, but most of them were of limited intellect and narrow interests. There were several old and venerated houses in the locality, but not one seems to have been inhabited by an educated and intellectually minded gentry.

The Heatons were the nearest approach to this in the time of the Brontës. In 1822 a Robert Heaton lived quietly in Haworth with his four brothers. He was the last of the direct line of the Heatons, dating from 1634. They owned a large library, but they were farming people and, it appears, seldom used it. Like many libraries of that time, it was for show rather than use. It is possible that the Brontës, especially Emily, who was at home more often than the others, did use it. The Heatons lived at Ponden Hall, which is about five miles from Haworth and, by tradition, the original of Thrushcross Grange in *Wuthering Heights*. The hall still stands but has a disquieting atmosphere of physical decay about it.

The millowners were the heirs of a craft which was introduced to the Haworth area in the days of Edward III, and for many decades the demands of woollen manufacture vied with the requirements of agriculture. From mediaeval times the citizens of Haworth either raised wool on the hoof or wove it in the mills – the village was an image of the West Riding itself.

Haworth, now, gives the impression of a growing dependence on the tourist trade and the older part of the town has something of the aspect of over-deliberate preservation and exploitation in many ways that (as is true of so many cultural shrines) have only a very peripheral connection with the only begetters of its fame. Haworth probably depends more on the Brontës than Stratford does on Shakespeare. The latter is near the centre of a flourishing agricultural area and is a busy market town, the former stands at the edge of a large and depressed industrial area.

Haworth was not mentioned in Doomsday book which, by English standards, debars it from receiving the full accolade of antiquity. The Romans were very active in the area, though there is no evidence that they had a settlement here. The Pennine Way passes near Haworth, and Colne (Roman Calunio) is just a few miles away, over the border in Lancashire. One topographer has claimed that at Crow Hill (1500 feet) near Haworth there was a cromlech – a druidical monument consisting of a six-ton flat stone, originally placed horizontally on two upright blocks, but now half-buried in the moss and heather.

The earliest settlement at Haworth is not known, but the first extant reference to it is a record known as Kirkby's Inquest in 1296, in Edward I's reign. It mentions a Godfrey de Haworth who, with two other people, had four oxgangs. They were heirs of John de Haworth. Oxenhope, the nearby village, was already settled, and owned by the family who gave their name to it. By 1316 both it and Haworth were owned by Nicholas de Audley who also held Bradford manor.

By 1380, in the reign of Richard II, Haworth had forty inhabitants, according to the Poll tax records – only one was exempt from tax, which amounted to fourpence a head.

In the fourteenth and fifteenth centuries there are several references to Haworth in the registers of the Archbishop of York. In 1317 the Vicar of Bradford and the freeholders of Haworth were told that they must pay the curate of Haworth Chapel the salary that was due to him in the proportions 'to which they had been liable from ancient times'. In 1338 the curate's income (which did not amount to much) was increased by the founding of a chantry in the chapel. This provided for a separate area where special masses for the souls of the dead could be celebrated. In some affluent churches and cathedrals the chantry was a small, separate structure within the main building, often noted for its architectural splendour – as in Prince Arthur's chantry chapel at Worcester cathedral – but the nature of Haworth's chantry is quite unknown. It is, however, known that it was endowed for the wife of Adam de Copley, Jane de Oxenhope. Adam died in 1337 and he left a 'messuage' – seven acres and twenty shillings rent to support a chaplain at Haworth who should 'celebrate divine service for the service of the said Adam and the souls of his ancestors, the souls of Thomas de Thornton [from which the name of Patrick Brontë's incumbency, where all his children were born, was derived] and Ellen, his wife'. Also it made provision for the souls of those deceased who had attended St Michael's, Haworth, to be prayed for every day in the chantry.

Chantry chapels were abolished in 1547 – in this year the Crown was granted, by statute, the revenues of all chantries that had survived the ministrations of Henry VIII – except Oxford, Cambridge, Eton and Winchester. During Edward VI's and Mary Tudor's reign the curate had no income from this endowment, but the people of Haworth, shortly after Elizabeth I's accession, provided a new endowment and they brought into being the so-called Elizabethan charter which was to play a large part in the subsequent ecclesiastical history of the little town. By subscription £36 was raised, and with it land was purchased at Stanbury which was vested in trustees. The first Trustees (who had to be freeholders of Haworth) were appointed in December 1599 and called the 'Trustees of the Church lands'. Out of the proceeds of this land a contribution was and still is made to the incumbent of Haworth, and the obligation to pay was accompanied by the privilege of the Trustees to accept or reject any clergy nominated by the Vicar of Bradford. The implications of what could happen when such checks and balances got out of synchronization is amply and amusingly evidenced in the events relative to Patrick Brontë's appointment to the church after his incumbency at Thornton. (*See* Family Portraits: Patrick Brontë.)

Haworth parish register's earliest entry dates from 1645, though some other entries are eighteenth-century copies of earlier originals. The incumbent was sympathetic to the Royalists during the Civil War, but he was ousted by Parliamentarians and succeeded by two Cromwellian sympathizers. After the Restoration, the Royalist was reinstated.

In 1638 a free grammar school for boys and girls was founded by the bequest of Christopher Scot(?) who provided a school house and an annuity of £18 towards the cost of a schoolmaster.

In the eighteenth century Haworth became important for the part it played in the Methodist revival, and the evangelical movement in general, a reputation enhanced by the arrival there, on 26 May 1752, of the new perpetual curate, William Grimshaw. (*See* Family Portraits: Patrick Brontë.) When Patrick Brontë came to Haworth, therefore, he was coming to a place with a rich and self-conscious history of virile activity in the religious life of Yorkshire. Haworth was no ecclesiastical backwater.

Twentieth-century transportation and twentieth-century rubbernecking curiosity about the famous dead have ensured that it is not a backwater of any kind now. It is second to Stratford upon Avon in the pecking order of British tourism, and as long as interest in the Brontë family continues to grow there seems no reason why Shakespeare should not have to continue to keep a watchful eye on his laurels.

And yet, for all the tourism and the pressures on a small community to cater for the lowest common denominator of interest, and taste, Haworth has contrived to maintain a good deal of historical and aesthetic integrity. The parsonage has been carefully and unfussily preserved; the additions to it, to provide for a museum and record office, have been tactfully done, and the museum is, indeed, in its quiet and unsensational way, a most attractive place. The contents of the record office need more space and more staff to handle them, but the existing personnel display outstanding skill, patience and that kind of helpful friendliness which gives the visiting research-worker pleasure as well as confidence.

Perhaps less sanguinity can be felt about some other properties connected, to one degree or another, with the Brontës which, it must be emphasized, are not the responsibility of the trustees of the Brontë Society who manage the parsonage property skilfully. Perhaps the creation of a more ambitious Trust, on the lines of the Shakespeare Birthplace Trust, might have prevented the disappearance of High Sunderland Hall and the depredations to the old bell tower at Thornton, and might, now, have taken action to stop further deterioration to Ponden Hall and – though it is less obvious – to the little church at Stanton, as well as warding off the environmental threat to Ellen Nussey's home, Rydings.

Oakwell Hall, the Red House at Gomersal and other places closely associated with the Brontës are as splendidly maintained as is Haworth parsonage. It would be a tragedy if the care expended on their abode either never extended to or reached too late all those many other homes from home and those places which kindled the sisters' imaginations which are scattered around the Haworth area.

[A number of guide books of Haworth and its immediate area are available. The Information Centre (open seasonally) situated in the little square near to the church has a comprehensive selection. For a detailed map of the immediate area see Ordinance Survey map no. 104. For a wider area of the Brontë country see Ordinance Survey map no. 103.]

Haworth Parsonage and Museum

The parsonage and its surroundings seem to have been chosen by some act of fate to conspire in completing the dark imagery of what we call the life of the Brontës. Their tragedies, vicissitudes, their intimate acquaintance with mortality, all seem to be aurally and visually echoed in the caws of rooks in the high trees, in the myriad-monumented churchyard, and in the implacable grey squareness of the parson's house and the house of God which stare stonily at one another across the graves.

Of such stuff is romance made, for there were no trees, and therefore no rooks in the Brontës' time, neither was the churchyard as extensive, and indeed the church they could see from any east-facing window of their house was not the one that now stands. The one the tourist sees is a Victorian replacement of the far less forbidding structure which was the Rev. Brontë's responsibility. Moreover, despite the admittedly severe outside aspect of the parsonage, the interior (even allowing for the careful twentieth century's almost therapeutic refurbishing) has enough left of the original to suggest a certain cosiness, and intimacy. The Brontës loved that house, and it has the feel of a house that has done good and pleasant service.

The house, the church, and other buildings nearby (the sexton's house and the Sunday school), owed their existence originally to the presence, in the fourteenth century, of the chantry chapel in the original church (whose revenues provided the wherewithal to help fund church property and, in particular, the income of the incumbent), and then to its successor, the trustee fund administered by the Trustees of the Church lands.

The first parsonage specially built by the Trustees was in 1778. Until this time incumbents found their own accommodation. Such as 'Sowdens', a house bought by the famous Rev. William Grimshaw in 1742. It became known as the parsonage in his time.

A certain John Richardson was the first to occupy the present building. He died in 1791. Whether the building replaced an earlier one on the site, or was the first, is not known.

It had a modest-sized garden and fronted to the east. The churchyard was at its eastern and southern side, and was enlarged in 1797 – possibly encroaching somewhat on the garden. In 1821, just before Patrick Brontë became incumbent, the churchyard was further extended. Certainly the churchyard and the garden were contiguous when the Brontës occupied the house, but it was not true, as Mrs Gaskell said, that their home was bordered on three sides by graves. To the south and west were open fields.

There was a gate leading from front garden to churchyard, providing access to the church for Mr Brontë's use. It is unlikely that the gate was in the same position as the existing one which is so commonly referred to as the gate of the dead. It seems improbable that Mr Brontë would have used as access to his church a gap which would have forced him to tread on graves.

Tall pine trees were planted in 1854 dominating the lawn with its bordering flowerbeds and fruit bushes. It is possible that a high wall existed at both back and front of the house, making it very resistant to prying eyes.

In all it was a house of quite neat, even dignified architectural symmetry, and well-windowed. It had two neatly designed chimney stacks. 'Late Georgian rectangular of modest pretensions' would possibly sum up its quality, but it was certainly a cut above the average for the time in this part of Haworth.

The front doorway was and is centrally placed with a room at each side both upstairs and downstairs and a small room immediately over the hallway (now described as Emily's bedroom, or sometimes as the children's room).

John Wade, who followed Patrick Brontë, was ambitious in his changes to the house. The Georgian windows, which had small panes, were replaced by large plate glass by 1866. The hallway, the storeroom, and kitchen floors had been stone covered with flags, regularly scrubbed with sandstone (or 'donkey stone') to provide a spotless off-white appearance – but Mr Wade raised the entire ground-floor level by five inches and added wooden flooring to the existing stone in the study and dining room (right and left of main front door). He had to reduce the height of the front door to accommodate the floor-raising, but the door the visitor now sees could well be the original of 1778. The interior was enlarged (Wade found the kitchen too small) and a gable added (for a new dining room) on the north side. He inserted marble mantelpieces, but the present interior doors may well be original.

So far as is known Patrick Brontë had effected no such large changes when he took occupancy. Perhaps to his mind the most significant addition was a lightning conductor he caused to be placed on the south chimney – Patrick was as magnetized by the products of scientific technology as he was sensitive to acts of God.

He was also highly conscious of the need for a healthy environment – and Haworth with its appalling record of disease arising from insanitary conditions was one of the best places in England to exercise his concern. In his notebook for September 1847 he records a payment of five shillings for cleaning of the well which supplied the parsonage with water, and whose source was on the hillside above. It had not been cleared for twenty years or more and had a yellow tinge from contamination by eight decomposing tins. The parsonage had two pump points for water.

Two years later Ellen Nussey sent Charlotte one of the latest devices – which may have fascinated Patrick Brontë without necessarily inducing him to use it. It was a shower bath supplied by Messrs Nelson of Leeds. William Wood is recorded as having been paid 2s.6d. for fitting it with knobs.

But if automation had reached the interior of the parsonage, it was probably absent from the outside privy – tucked away in the area behind the house. Mr Wade said there was no water-closet or bathroom when he took over the parsonage. One has to assume the privy was an earth closet and that the shower augmented the interior bathing arrangements common to most families of the time – the tin tub.

The references we have in letters, reminiscences and diary notes unerringly build up a picture of a lived-in home, not just an inhabited house. The small kitchen must have been in constant use for baking and boiling and braising and ironing and scrubbing and airing. The cellar was not just a hole under the house but was where the beer was brewed and stored. And everywhere there were animals and birds – dogs, cats, at one time a hawk, a canary, some geese.

Ellen Nussey completes the picture of a house significantly different from the Gothic romanticism of the image which most people would perhaps find more dramatic. She refers to the bright cheerfulness of fires that burned in the grates all over the house.

Present-day visitors to the parsonage would have to be remarkably insensitive not to 'feel' its atmosphere. It is, of course, very easy to endow a place with romantic haunting pictures invented by one's own imagination, and to falsify, by fancy, so to speak, the reality of any environment. But however many pinches of salt one employed either in the relentless pursuit of accuracy or the leering application of cynicism to the experience of Haworth parsonage, the truth seems to be that very few people are unmoved by the place's personality.

This is partly because the Trustees and administrators of the Brontë Parsonage and Museum have been careful to try and preserve the domesticity of the house and to assemble in it as many authentic relics of its most famous inhabitants as they have been able to find. The plain truth is that a very great deal of what can be seen there literally belonged to them – Patrick's spectacles, Charlotte's going-away dress, Anne's drawings, Branwell's portraits, and those little books to which they all contributed.

There is, perhaps paradoxically, perhaps even ironically, nothing like the existence of such palpabilities, to hasten the conjuring up of old ghosts. The remarkable fact is, however, that despite the miasma of gloom and doom which gossip and fable and, sometimes, over-zealous scholarship has cast around the Brontë family, the ghosts that haunt the parsonage do not seem unhappy. What indeed comes most easily to mind are the imagined aromas of Emily's cooking, the tramp of children's feet, the strident cries as the four great inhabitants of Angria and Gondal – Tallii, Brannii, Emmii and Annii – created the magic of their world, and the urgent scratching of pens and pencils as they recorded its affairs.

There is much pathos to be experienced, certainly, in the room where Emily tried to refuse to die, but there is much that is exhilarating in remembering how she and Charlotte and Anne (and Branwell before he learned to wander down the lane to the Black Bull) walked round and round that room in the excited throes of gossip, story and imaginative creation while the clock ticked on the stairs and Tabitha clucked her disapproval of late hours and the reverend gentleman sat in his own parlour writing poetry or blueprinting bombs.

[Summer and winter opening times of the parsonage and the museum differ. It is normally closed during the last three weeks of December for maintenance work. For information apply to The Curator, The Brontë Parsonage, Haworth, Keighley, West Yorkshire BD22 8DR; phone, (0535) Haworth 42323.]

Places Associated with the Brontës and Their Novels

[Distances given are approximate. Although many of them are short, the intending traveller is recommended to use private transport or special tours. Keighley and Bradford are the most convenient large centres in the area.]

Ambleside. On Lake Windermere, where C. visited the Kay Shuttleworths, at Briery Close, August 1880.

Banagher. Mr N.'s ancestral home in Ireland.

Birstall. Site of Rydings, family home of the Nusseys; 6 miles S. of Leeds. (Briarfield village, *SH*.)

Black Bull. Public house adjacent to Haworth church, much frequented by Branwell.

Blake Hall. At Mirfield, the home of the Inghams where Ae. governess, 1839.

Bradford. Large city 10 miles from Haworth; where B. set up as a portrait artist, May 1838.

Bridlington. East coast fishing town where C. and E.N. stayed, 1839.

Brookroyd. At Birstall; the Nussey family moved there from Rydings, 1836/7.

Broughton in Furness. 8 miles N.W. of Ulverston where B. was tutor to the Postlethwaites.

Brussels. Capital of Belgium where C. and E. pupils at the Pensionnat Heger 1842; C. returning there as teacher 1843. (The Villette of *V*.)

Chapel Royal. The centre for Anglican services in Brussels which C. attended.

Chapel-le-Breer 2 miles from Southowram where E. worshipped at St Anne's-in-the-Grove Church.

Chapter Coffee House. Near St Paul's where the Brontës stayed on visits to London.

Cluysenaar, Hôtel. In Brussels; later Hôtel Mengelle.

Cowan Bridge. 2 miles from Kirkby Lonsdale, between Leeds and Kendall; the School for Clergy Daughters there, attended by Maria, Elizabeth, C. and E., when small. (Lowood School, *J.E.*)

Crimsworth Dean. Steep wooded valley N. of Hebden Bridge.

Crow Hill. Dominant point on the moors flanking the Haworth/Colne road where a bog eruption occurred, September 1824; P. composed a sermon and verses about it.

Crystal Palace. Glass building, part of London's Great Exhibition, 1851; called by C. 'a mixture of a Genii Palace and a mighty Bazaar'.

Devonshire Arms. Hotel near Bolton Abbey where the Nusseys and the Brontës met, 1833.

Dewsbury. N.E. of Huddersfield, where Miss Wooler moved her school from Roe Head.

Easton House. 2 miles from Bridlington; home of the Hudsons, friends of C. and E.N. who stayed there.

Edinburgh. C. visited there briefly in 1850.

Filey. 8 miles S. of Scarborough where C. and E.N. went after Ae.'s death.

George Hotel. In York where C., Ae., and E.N. stayed on their way to Scarborough.

Gomersal. 6 miles S. of Leeds where the Taylors' home, The Red House, was. (Coloured windows from there now in the Parsonage Museum.)

Guiseley Church 14 miles from Haworth, 12 from Leeds, where P. and M.B. married, 1812.

Halifax. Industrial town, 10 miles from Haworth; where the Misses Patchett's Law Hill School was, where E. taught.

Hardcastle Crags. Above Hebden Bridge; favourite place of the Brontë children.

Harrogate. Spa town, W. Yorkshire.

Hartshead. 7 miles S. of Leeds; P. Minister here 1811.

Hathersage. In Derbyshire, near Sheffield, where Henry Nussey became Vicar.

Haworth. *See* sections on Haworth and the Parsonage.

Heaton Hall. 2 miles N. of Huddersfield on River Calder.

Heger, Pensionnat. In the Rue d'Isabelle, Brussels; school run by M. and Madame Heger, attended by C. and E. 1842/3.

High Sunderland Hall. Near Halifax, now demolished; known to E. when at Law Hill School. (Grotesque carvings at the front of Wuthering Heights possibly suggested by the external decoration of the Hall.)

Hollande, Hôtel de. Near the Pensionnat Heger; where P., C. and E. stayed the night before their arrival at the Pensionnat, 1842.

Huddersfield. Manufacturing town, 20 miles S. of Leeds.

Hunsworth Mills. Near Cleckheaton, 10 miles S.W. of Leeds.

Keighley. 3 miles W. of Haworth; where the Mechanics Institute, and its library, were, which P. joined, 1833.

Kilkee. S.W. Ireland; visited by C. and Mr N. on their honeymoon.

Kipping House. At Thornton; the home of the Firths.

Kirk Smeaton. Where Mr N. was temporarily a curate. Near Pontefract in Yorkshire.

Kirkby Lonsdale. Near Cowan Bridge in N.W. England, 20 miles N. of Lancaster.

Kirklees. Area of parkland and common near Hartshead.

Kirkstall Abbey. Between Leeds and Guiseley; visited by P. and M.B. before their marriage.

Knoll, The. At Ambleside; where Harriet Martineau lived; C. stayed there, December 1850.

Koekelberg. Pensionnat attended by Mary and Martha Taylor, 2 miles outside Brussels.

Law Hill. At Southowram, near Halifax; E. at school there.

Leeds. 10 miles E. of Bradford.

Liverpool. Merseyside sea port, visited by B.

Liversedge. One mile from Hartshead Church; P. and M.B. lived at Clough House, Hightown from March 1811. Maria and Elizabeth born there. (Rushedge, *SH*.)

Lothersdale. Near Skipton, where C. governess to the Sidgwicks, 1839.

Luddenden Foot. 12 miles from Haworth, 1 mile from Sowerby Bridge; B. employed there on the railway, 1841–2; frequented the Lord Nelson Inn; site of William Grimshaw's grave (*see* section on P.).

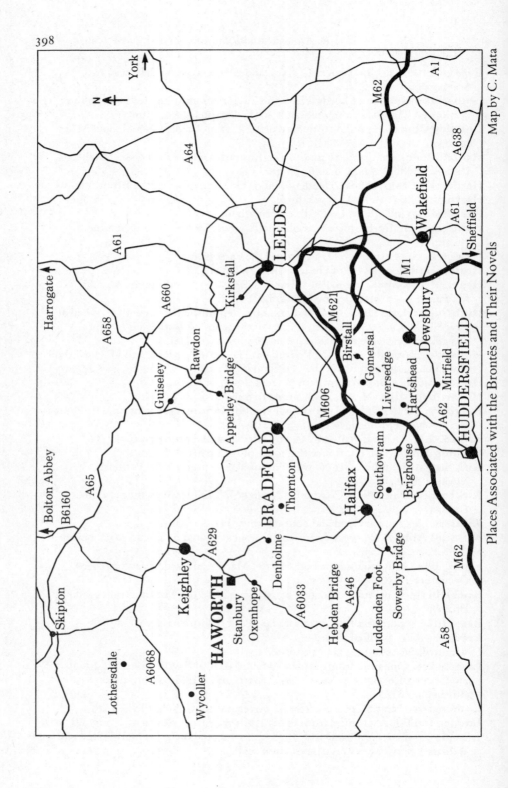

N

York

Harrogate

Bolton Abbey

Skipton

Lothersdale

Wycoller

A6068

A65

B6160

A658

A61

A64

A660

Guiseley

Rawdon

Apperley Bridge

Kirkstall

LEEDS

M621

M606

Birstall

Gomersal

Liversedge

Hartshead

Mirfield

A62

HUDDERSFIELD

Dewsbury

M1

Wakefield

A61

Sheffield

A638

A1

M62

Southowram

Brighouse

Halifax

Thornton

BRADFORD

Denholme

A6033

Hebden Bridge

A646

Luddenden Foot

Sowerby Bridge

A58

M62

HAWORTH

Stanbury

Oxenhope

Keighley

A629

Keighley

Places Associated with the Brontës and Their Novels

Map by C. Mata

Manchester. Northern manufacturing city; C. accompanied P. there for his cataract operation, 1846.

Mirfield. 3 miles from Dewsbury, 5 from Huddersfield; Roe Head pupils attended church there.

Moorseats. Near Hathersage. (House and environment resemble Moor House, *J.E.*)

Moscar Cross. 10 miles W. of Sheffield. (By tradition, Whitecross, *J.E.*)

Nora Lane. Thoroughfare which links Oakwell Hall with Birstall.

North Lees. Near Hathersage. (Improbable, but traditional source for Moor House, *J.E.*)

Norton Conyers. Near Ripon; visited by C. when staying at Swarlcliffe. (*J.E.* – second source for Thornfield Hall, where (interior) oak panelling, portraits, long gallery, bedroom with 18th century attribution of a madwoman, and (exterior) rookery, nearby church, are all strongly redolent of Thornfield Hall. *See also* Rydings.)

Oakwell Hall. Near Birstall; fine Elizabethan Hall (1583). (Fieldhead?, *SH*.)

Oxenhope. 2 miles from Haworth; church founded by Rev. Joseph Brett (q.v.).

Padiham. Near Gawthorpe; living there refused by Mr N.

Palais Royale. N. of Brussels.

Parsonage. *See* section on Haworth and Parsonage.

Pendle Hill. Flat-topped local Haworth landmark.

Peniston Quarry. On moors near Haworth; a tunnel there traditionally inhabited by fairies.

Ponden Hall. 3 miles from Haworth on Colne Road; home of the Heaton family.

Ponden Kirk. Rocky outcrop on Haworth moors near Stanbury.

Porte de Namur. Near former Place de Waterloo, Brussels.

Protestant Cemetery. In Brussels; C. visited Martha Taylor's grave there.

Rawdon. 6 miles from Bradford; C. governess to White family there.

Rawfolds Mill. Near Hartshead; where P. witnessed attack by militant millworkers, 11 April 1811.

Roe Head. 20 miles from Haworth, near Hartshead; C., E. and Ae. attended Miss Wooler's school there.

Rue d'Isabelle. *See* Heger, Pensionnat.

Rue Royale. In Brussels, where C. saw Queen Victoria 'flashing through', 1843.

Rydings. Birstall, near Leeds; home of the Nusseys. (*J.E.* – Thornfield Hall with its thorn bushes, a rookery, and an oak split by lightning. *See also* Norton Conyers.)

St George's Chapel. In Brussels; Anglican church attended by C.

Ste Gudule. Cathedral in Brussels, where in September 1843, C. 'actually did confess'.

Scarborough. East coast watering place, beloved by Ae. who died there, May 1849, at No. 2 The Cliff; buried in St Mary's churchyard.

Sheffield. Large S. Yorkshire manufacturing town. (*J.E., SH*.)

Shibden Hall. N. of Law Hill, near Halifax; known to E. (A contributing source for Wuthering Heights.)

Skipton. Mill town, 8 miles from Haworth.

Sowerby Bridge. Near Hebden Bridge, N. of Halifax; B. clerk on railway there, 1840.

Stanbury. 3 miles from Haworth on Colne Road; P. preached at its small church;

three-tiered pulpit, transferred there on demolition of the old Haworth church, still in use.

Stonegappe. Near Lothersdale, 4 miles from Skipton; C. governess to the Sidgwicks there April/May–July 1839.

Stubbing Lane. Haworth; where Tabby's sister lived.

Swarlcliffe. Near Harrogate; where the Sidgwicks spent the summer when C. governess.

Thornton. 3 miles from Bradford, 6 from Haworth; P. minister there 1815–20; C., E., B. and Ae., born at 74 Market Street.

Thorp Green. Hall at Little Ouseburn, 2 miles from York; home of the Robinsons, where Ae. governess, 1839–45. B. a tutor, 1843–5.

Tunstall, Church. 3 miles from Cowan Bridge; Rev. Carus Wilson preached there.

Ulverston. S.W. of Lake Windermere; B. tutor to the Postlethwaites there.

Wakefield. 6 miles E. of Dewsbury; site of Crofton Hall school.

Withins (Withens). 3 miles W. of Haworth; Top Withins, a (now derelict) farm there. (Traditionally claimed as source of Wuthering Heights.)

Woodhouse Grove. School at Rawdon, 6 miles from Bradford; P. taught and examined and first met M.B. there; school run by her uncle – Rev. J. Fennell.

Wycoller. Near Colne, off the Haworth/Colne road. (Ferndean Manor traditionally based on the ruined hall there, *J.E.*)

York. In N.E. Yorkshire. Visited by Brontë family.